Rethinking Peacekeeping, Gender Equality
and Collective Security

Thinking Gender in Transnational Times

Series Editors: **Clare Hemmings, Kimberley Hutchings, Hakan Seckinelgin** and **Sadie Wearing**

Titles include:

Gina Heathcote and Dianne Otto (*editors*)
RETHINKING PEACEKEEPING, GENDER EQUALITY AND COLLECTIVE SECURITY

Sumi Madhok, Anne Phillips and Kalpana Wilson (*editors*)
GENDER, AGENCY AND COERCION

Thinking Gender in Transnational Times
Series Standing Order ISBN 978-0-230-35843-0 hardback
(outside North America only)

You can receive future titles in this series as they are published by placing a standing order. Please contact your bookseller or, in case of difficulty, write to us at the address below with your name and address, the title of the series and the ISBN quoted above.

Customer Services Department, Macmillan Distribution Ltd, Houndmills, Basingstoke, Hampshire RG21 6XS, England

Rethinking Peacekeeping, Gender Equality and Collective Security

Edited by

Gina Heathcote
SOAS, University of London, UK

and

Dianne Otto
University of Melbourne, Australia

First published 2014 by
PALGRAVE MACMILLAN

Palgrave Macmillan in the UK is an imprint of Macmillan Publishers Limited, registered in England, company number 785998, of Houndmills, Basingstoke, Hampshire RG21 6XS.

Palgrave Macmillan in the US is a division of St Martin's Press LLC, 175 Fifth Avenue, New York, NY 10010.

Palgrave Macmillan is the global academic imprint of the above companies and has companies and representatives throughout the world.

Palgrave® and Macmillan® are registered trademarks in the United States, the United Kingdom, Europe and other countries.

ISBN 978–1–137–40020–8

This book is printed on paper suitable for recycling and made from fully managed and sustained forest sources. Logging, pulping and manufacturing processes are expected to conform to the environmental regulations of the country of origin.

A catalogue record for this book is available from the British Library.

A catalog record for this book is available from the Library of Congress.

Typeset by MPS Limited, Chennai, India.

Transferred to Digital Printing in 2014

Contents

v

Part III Danger

Part IV Silences

Part V Conclusions

List of Figures

Foreword

There is a system (there is always a system!), and it is always pretty much reflective of the power structures that it is there to maintain and regulate. The system dictates how things are done; and therein lies the problem as, once the system exists, those who were not included in the first place have to gate-crash and attempt to force change from within and, as all revolutionaries know, working behind the lines is replete with hidden dangers! Which is why this book is so important.

The United Nations (UN) is a peace organisation, or it was supposed to be. Its *raison d'être* is to prevent war and its Charter guarantees equality and dignity for all, but it needed the non-governmental organisation (NGO) gate-crashers of 2000 to force the Security Council to take women seriously in relation to international peace and security. Whatever we may think of the ultimate resolution adopted by the Council and those that have followed, the system's fortifications were breached and women are in! Optimists and many feminists use the word 'potential' a lot, but *Security Council Resolution 1325* (SCR 1325) gave, and gives, astonishing *potential* for change and the collection of chapters in this book reminds us of the vitality of thought and approach that is needed if that potential is to be realised.

Most potently, SCR 1325 needs to be applied to peacekeeping and peacebuilding. Despite the best of intentions (one hopes), incorporating a gender perspective is done badly or not at all because we are still grafting a 'new' concept onto existing modalities which were not created with gender equality in mind; quite the contrary. We have seen, from Bosnia to Haiti and from the Democratic Republic of the Congo to Kosovo, the ways in which cultures of masculinity undermine SCR 1325 in the most basic of ways. We know too that attempts to address this undercutting – through monitoring processes, applying gendered indicators, introducing results-based assessment and, inevitably, lots of bureaucracy – have impeded meaningful consultations and real participation, and resulted in a failure to secure human rights from a gender perspective. We know too that the age-old (non)solution of just counting women, and saying things are better if there are more, is still alive and well. So, in many peacekeeping scenarios, instead of providing a transition which creates the space for serious analysis of the gendered political economy of violence and its continuum of human rights violations, we have the reverse. From the initial negotiation of the peace agreement and the agenda for reform in-country, to the regulation of the conduct of peacekeepers, SCR 1325 is still not being implemented. The gendered hierarchy of the militarised system of international peace and security is still firmly in place, which enables some men to talk about 'hard' security issues, including the regulation and supply of guns and the negotiation of borders, and excludes all women. The promise of Article 26 of the UN Charter – that disarmament and the regulation of the arms trade are integral to peace – continues to be ignored. Peacekeeping mandates fail to mention social and economic rights, which are the locus for transformation, as women's material conditions will either enable participation or prevent it. Added to this is the continued dominance of concern about sexual violence, which has the effect of turning women into victims instead of agents, and we can see just how far away feminist change still is.

All of these problems have solutions, and the sort of analysis contained in this collection is exactly what we need: take each part of the problem, analyse it and then put it back into the mix knowing what needs to be done. The solutions involve making connections between the different parts of the problem and the solutions we craft. We need to continually examine our tool-box of options and see where our forums for advocacy and redress lie and understand how to use them.

And so we go on, making connections and finding allies, and being constantly vigilant. Women are behind the lines, in the heart of the biggest peace organisation ever created, and we must handle this location with care and show that security, real security, is the sum of all the UN's parts ... and that it is better than they thought!

Madeleine Rees
Secretary General, Women's International League for
Peace and Freedom (WILPF)

Acknowledgements

As editors we would like to thank each of the contributing authors for the part they have played in this project and especially for their patience in responding positively to our feedback and developing their chapters with care and thoughtfulness: learning from the differences in our thinking is precisely what the project of *Rethinking Peacekeeping, Gender Equality and Collective Security* is about, and we look forward to watching the conversations we have had extend into new projects, scholarship and activism. Thanks also to Secretary-General of the Women's International League for Peace and Freedom (WILPF), Madeleine Rees, for contributing the foreword to this book.

Heartfelt thanks are also due to Cathy Hutton, from the Asia Pacific Centre for Military Law at Melbourne Law School, for her invaluable assistance in the organisation of the international symposium 'Peacekeeping in the Asia-Pacific: Gender Equality, Law and Collective Security' held at Melbourne Law School in April 2012; Christine Chinkin, Judith Gardam and Gerry Simpson for supporting the original funding proposal and planning of the symposium from which the collection draws its inspiration; the British Academy, Asia Pacific Centre for Military Law, Melbourne Law School and the SOAS School of Law for funding the symposium and Philippa Grand at Palgrave for her enthusiasm and encouragement. Thank you also to the other speakers and participants who contributed to the symposium, especially Hilary Charlesworth, Penny Cumming, Helen Durham, Susan Hutchinson, Lesley Pruitt, Gabrielle Simm, Kathryn Spurling and Natasha Yacoub, whose voices and ideas are inflected in the pages of this book. Very special thanks to Mary Quinn for her diligent and proficient copy-editing and to Candice Parr who meticulously reviewed the final text.

Gina Heathcote would like to thank her Melbourne and London families for managing domestic spaces and providing happy homes for her to write in. She would also like to thank Dianne Otto for the commitment and intellectual leadership she has contributed to the project from the beginning to the end.

Dianne Otto would like to thank her partner, Joan Nestle for always believing in her work, Vesna Stefanovski for her indefatigable support, and Gina Heathcote who hatched the whole idea of this project.

Notes on Contributors

Sharon Bhagwan Rolls is Executive Director of FemLINKPACIFIC. Sharon has worked in the radio and television broadcast industry in Fiji since 1986. In April 2000, as the Secretary of the National Council of Women Fiji she coordinated the Blue Ribbon Peace Vigil and the Women's Action for Democracy and Peace (WAD'aP) when her country, Fiji, faced its second political coup. Sharon also launched Fiji and the Pacific's first women-led community radio network FemTALK 89.2 FM. Her work has appeared in a range of publications, including *ISIS Manila International Women in Action Magazine, Signs: Journal of Women in Culture and Society* and the *Women's Studies Centre Newsletter*. Since 2012 she has been a board member of the Global Partnership for the Prevention of Armed Conflict (GPPAC) and is a member of the Pacific Islands Forum Reference Group on Women, Peace and Security.

Róisín Burke is Government of Ireland Postdoctoral Research Fellow at the Irish Centre for Human Rights, National University of Ireland, Galway. Róisín completed her doctorate, titled 'Sexual Exploitation and Abuse by UN Military Contingents: Moving beyond the Current Status Quo and Responsibility under International Law', at the Asia Pacific Centre for Military Law, University of Melbourne Law School. She holds a Bachelor of Laws from the University of Limerick and a Master of Laws in International Human Rights Law from the Irish Centre for Human Rights. She has previously worked as a teaching fellow at Melbourne Law School; a research fellow at the Centre for Citizenship Development and Human Rights at Deakin University and as a legal intern at the United Nations Office of Legal Counsel, the International Criminal Tribunal for the Former Yugoslavia and the Special Court for Sierra Leone on the defence of Charles Taylor. She has published in the areas of international criminal law, peacekeeping and state and international organisation responsibility. Her work has appeared in the *Journal of Conflict and Security Law, Journal of International Peacekeeping* and *Thematic Prosecution of International Sex Crimes* (M. Bergsmo ed., 2012).

Stephanie Cousins holds a Bachelor of Arts, a Bachelor of Public Policy and Management (Hons) and is currently finalising a Master of Public and International Law at the University of Melbourne. Her research has focussed on gender and armed conflict, protection of civilians and climate change law. Stephanie is Humanitarian Advocacy Lead at Oxfam Australia, where she has worked since 2006. Her work at Oxfam focusses on promoting the rights of people affected by conflicts and disasters to a range of civil and military actors. Stephanie has supported humanitarian advocacy efforts in the Pacific, Sri Lanka and Indonesia, and has worked closely with former refugees and diaspora communities in Australia on a range of human rights issues.

Sharna de Lacy graduated from her Master of International and Community Development at Deakin University in 2010. Sharna is specialised in democratisation processes and security sector reform and, in particular, the reform of military institutions in transitional democracies. An interest in the role of the military and the militarisation of political systems led her to feminist critiques of these issues and in 2011 she joined WILPF and co-founded the Australian YWILPF section. Since this time, Sharna has worked on the Women, Peace and Security agenda in Australia, taking part in the non-governmental organisation consultations on Australia's National Action Plan and building a work programme with YWILPF that focusses on making young women more visible within the peace and security discourse.

Karen Engle is Minerva House Drysdale Regents Chair in Law, and Founder and Co-Director of the Bernard and Audre Rapoport Center for Human Rights and Justice at the University of Texas School of Law at Austin. She is also an affiliated faculty member of Latin American Studies and of Women's and Gender Studies. She was Professor of Law at the University of Utah prior to joining the University of Texas. Karen is the author of *The Elusive Promise of Indigenous Development: Rights, Culture, Strategy* (2010), which received the Best Book Award from the American Political Science Association Section on Human Rights. Other recent publications include 'The force of shame' (with A. Lottmann, in C. McGlynn and V. E. Munro (eds), *Rethinking Rape Law: International and Comparative Perspectives* 2010); 'Judging sex in war' (*Michigan Law Review*, 2008); 'Calling in the troops: The uneasy relationship among human rights, women's rights and humanitarian intervention' (*Harvard Human Rights Journal*, 2007); and 'Feminism and its (dis)contents: Criminalizing war-time rape in Bosnia and Herzegovina' (*The American Journal of International Law*, 2005).

Judith Gardam is Emerita Professor at the University of Adelaide Law School in South Australia and Fellow of the Academy of Social Sciences in Australia. Judith has published extensively in the areas of public international law, international humanitarian law and the use of armed force and feminist theory. She has worked on such issues as the treatment of civilians (in particular women) during times of armed conflict, the requirements of necessity and proportionality in the use of force and the human rights aspects of energy resources. She is the author of numerous books, including *Women, Armed Conflict and International Law* (with M. Jarvis, 2001) and *Necessity, Proportionality and the Use of Force by States* (2004).

Cara Gleeson has drawn on her passion for equality and social justice through her work with the Australian Government Office for Women, WIPLF International Geneva office and her academic background (Bachelor of Arts from La Trobe University and currently studying a Master of Social Research at Australian National University). She has worked on the women, peace and security agenda, enhancing participation of women in national and international institutions to promote equality, young women's leadership, gender machinery and mainstreaming and preventing violence against women. Cara is a founding member of YWILPF in Australia and is active within the YWCA movement. Cara is currently the senior project officer leading VicHealth on the Generating Equality and Respect Program, a world's first site-based intervention to prevent violence against women before it occurs in Victoria, Australia.

Gina Heathcote is Lecturer in Gender Studies and International Law at SOAS, University of London. In 2012 she published *The Law on the Use of Force: A Feminist Analysis*, the first book-length feminist study of the international legal regulation of the use of military force. Gina's research engages with the relationship between law, violence and gender while developing feminist method and thinking. Her recent publications have used feminist methods to analyse the war on terror and contemporary collective security structures. Gina is a member of the *Feminist Review* editorial collective.

Chloé Lewis is a doctoral candidate in International Development at the University of Oxford and is completing a Policy Research Fellowship with the NGO Working Group on Women, Peace and Security in New York. Her doctoral research examines men and masculinities within the context of conflict-related sexual violence. In particular, she focusses on the marginalisation of male-directed sexual violence within the international community, including in the women, peace and security framework. She also holds an MSc in Refugee and Forced Migration Studies from the University of Oxford, and a BA in Politics and International Studies from the University of Warwick, for which she attained First Class Honours. Chloé was also the former Co-Editor-in-Chief of the *Oxford Monitor of Forced Migration* (OxMo), a student-centred journal which critically engages with the policy, legal and field-based dimensions of forced displacement.

May Maloney's interest in women, peace and security was piqued while working on the *Age, Gender and Diversity Policy* of the United Nations High Commissioner for Refugees in Geneva. May has worked with the Centre for Refugee Research, University of New South Wales, in collaboration with refugee women in India, Jordan, Zambia and Uganda (and with women in situations of internal displacement in Colombia) to hold a global dialogue on refugee women's rights. May has supported refugee and asylum seeker women to attend and advocate on issues of sexual violence, women's participation in post-conflict reconstruction and other aspects of *Security Council Resolution 1325* at decision-making fora in Geneva. She is a humanitarian policy and advocacy advisor at Save the Children Australia and has worked with the International Women's Development Agency, Oxfam Australia, and the Victorian Foundation for Survivors of Torture. She holds a Bachelor of International Relations, a Diploma of Modern Languages and a Master of International and European Studies with a research focus on the prosecution of violence against women in regional human rights courts. She is a founding member of YWILPF Australia.

Fiona McAlpine has just returned from working with WILPF's PeaceWomen project at the United Nations Headquarters in New York, monitoring the Security Council and Commission on the Status of Women. Prior to this, her experience was largely in media capacity-building with newspapers in Cameroon and Nepal. Her undergraduate thesis was on the role of women in the media in West Africa, which she undertook by interviewing journalists in the field. She holds an undergraduate degree in International Studies and has also completed post-graduate studies in Communications. She now studies law at RMIT in Melbourne, Australia, and works as a paralegal at the Asylum Seeker Resource Centre.

Dianne Otto holds the Francine V. McNiff Chair in Human Rights Law and is Director of the Institute for International Law and the

Humanities at Melbourne Law School. She researches in the areas of public international law with a focus on gender and sexuality issues in the context of the UN Security Council, peacekeeping and international human rights law. Dianne's scholarship explores how international legal discourse reinforces hierarchies of nation, race, gender and sexuality, and aims to understand whether and how this can be resisted. She has recently edited three volumes on *Gender Issues and Human Rights* (2013) and prepared a bibliographic chapter, 'Feminist approaches', in *Oxford Bibliographies Online: International Law* (T. Carty ed., 2012). Dianne helped drafting a General Comment on women's equality for the Committee on Economic, Social and Cultural Rights and a General Recommendation on treaty obligations for the Committee on the Elimination of Discrimination against Women.

Felicity Ruby (formerly Felicity Hill) worked as Director of WILPF and of WILPF's UN Office in New York from 1998 to 2002, during which time she coordinated the NGO Working Group on Women, Peace and Security that lobbied the Security Council to adopt *Resolution 1325* on women, peace and security. She later worked for the United Nations Development Fund for Women (UNIFEM), where she developed the www.WomenWarPeace.org portal and provided research and writing support for the 2002 Independent Expert's report to the Security Council, focussing on the media, conflict prevention and peacekeeping chapters of the report. She is currently an advisor to Australian Greens Senator Scott Ludlam.

Laura J. Shepherd is Associate Professor of International Relations at the University of New South Wales, Australia. She works at the intersection of gendered global politics, critical approaches to security and international relations theory. Laura is the author/editor of five books, including *Gender Matters in Global Politics: A Feminist Introduction to International Relations* (2010) and *Gender, Violence and Security: Discourse as Practice* (2008). Laura has published many scholarly articles in journals such as *International Studies Quarterly*, *International Feminist Journal of Politics*, *Review of International Studies* and *Journal of Gender Studies*. She tweets from @drljshepherd and blogs at http://genderinglobalgovernancenet-work.net/comment and http://wpsac.wordpress.com/blogs/.

Olivera Simić is Lecturer at the Griffith Law School, Griffith University, Australia. Her research engages with transitional justice, international law and peacekeeping, gender and crime from an interdisciplinary perspective. She has published in journals such as *Law Text Culture*, the *Women' Studies International Forum*, the *Journal of International Women Studies* and *International Peacekeeping*, as well as books and book chapters. She is the author of *Regulation of Sexual Conduct in UN Peacekeeping Operations* (2012).

Dale Stephens spent over 20 years as a permanent legal officer in the Royal Australian Navy before transferring to the Navy Reserve in February 2013. He holds the rank of Captain in the Navy Reserve and is currently Associate Professor at Adelaide Law School. His previous appointments have included Director of Operations and International Law in the Australian Department of Defence, Fleet Legal Officer and Director of the Military Law Centre. He has served in senior legal positions on operations in East Timor and Iraq. He has considerable operational experience with the Australian Defence Force, the UN and with Coalition Forces. He holds an LL.M from Harvard Law School and is currently completing his SJD there. Dale is the recipient of the Conspicuous Service Medal and the (US) Bronze Star. He is the author of *The Use of Force in Peacekeeping Operations – The East Timor Experience* (2005), as well as numerous academic articles.

Jacqui True is Professor of Politics and International Relations and Associate Dean (Research) in the Faculty of Arts at Monash University, Melbourne, Australia. She is a specialist in gender and international relations, violence against women, international political economy and feminist research methodologies. Her research on gender mainstreaming and global/regional governance is among the most cited in the field. Since 2008 she has been researching the structural root causes and consequences of violence against women and girls and how globalisation processes are often exacerbating this violence, with the aim of contributing to its long-term prevention. Her book, *The Political Economy of Violence against Women* (2012), received the American Political Science Association's best book in human rights award, 2011–2013. Her new book, *Violence against Women: What Everyone Needs to Know*, will be published in 2015.

List of Abbreviations and Acronyms

AFP IDG	Australian Federal Police International Deployment Group
AusAID	Australian Agency for International Development
CAVR	Comissão de Acolhimento, Verdade e Reconciliação (Truth and Reconciliation Commission)
CEDAW	Convention on the Elimination of All Forms of Discrimination against Women
COIN	counterinsurgency
CRC	Convention on the Rights of the Child
CROP	Council of Regional Organisations in the Pacific
DCAF	Democratic Control of Armed Forces
DDR	disarmament, demobilisation and reintegration
DFS	Department of Field Support (UN)
DPKO	Department of Peacekeeping Operations (UN)
DRC	Democratic Republic of the Congo
ECHR	European Convention on Human Rights
FET	Female Engagement Team
ICCPR	International Covenant on Civil and Political Rights
NAP	national action plan
NATO	North Atlantic Treaty Organization
NGO	non-governmental organisation
OCHA	Office for the Coordination of Humanitarian Affairs (UN)
ODIHR	Office for Democratic Institutions and Human Rights (OSCE)
OMA	Office of Military Affairs (UN)
OSCE	Organization for Security and Co-Operation in Europe
PKO	peacekeeping operation
PPF	Participating Police Force (RAMSI)

PSVI	Preventing Sexual Violence Initiative
RAMSI	Regional Assistance Mission to Solomon Islands
RSIPF	Royal Solomon Islands Police Force
SCR	Security Council Resolution
SEA	sexual exploitation and abuse
SGBV	sexual and gender-based violence
SSR	security sector reform
UK	United Kingdom
UN	United Nations
UN-INSTRAW	United Nations International Research and Training Institute for the Advancement of Women
UNDP	United Nations Development Programme
UNFPA	United Nations Population Fund
UNHCR	United Nations High Commissioner for Refugees
UNIFEM	United Nations Development Fund for Women (now UN Women)
UNMIL	United Nations Mission in Liberia
US	United States
WILPF	Women's International League for Peace and Freedom
WPA	Women's Protection Adviser
WPS	women, peace and security
WRC	Women's Refugee Commission (formerly Women's Commission for Refugee Women and Children)
YWILPF	Young Women's International League for Peace and Freedom

Rethinking Peacekeeping, Gender Equality and Collective Security: An Introduction

Dianne Otto and Gina Heathcote

Collective security and peacekeeping, one of its progeny, have traditionally been thought to have little relevance to women, apart from providing a means to provide for their protection. Yet it takes only a moment's reflection to see the gendered shape of this thinking, which casts military men and diplomats as the primary actors, and women, often together with children, as the vulnerable potential victims whose defence and rescue help to motivate or even legitimate military intervention – whether forceful or with the consent of the state in question. This gendered schemata continues to pervade laws, policies and practices relating to the maintenance of international peace and security, as seen with the military interventions in Afghanistan and Iraq, which both relied heavily on the rationale of protecting women and advancing 'women's rights' to shore up waning public support in the west.[1] The same rationale is also frequently used to explain and justify peacekeeping and the engagement of the international community in post-conflict reconstruction. Through these means, the well-worn gender hierarchy, of masculine capability associated with strength and female vulnerability connected to lack, is constantly repeated and reconstituted, even in those places where the international community claims that it is helping to construct post-conflict societies that respect and promote women's equality.

Women's peace movements, human rights advocates and feminist activists and academics have struggled for at least the last century to challenge the gendered assumptions of militarism and the precarious security that military thinking offers.[2] Yet it is only relatively recently that feminist analysis has started to impact on mainstream developments in international law and international relations theory and practice. Whether these developments can be read hopefully, as providing footholds for challenging militarism and its gendered paradigm, or whether they mark the cooption of feminist ideas for militaristic purposes, is the subject of continuing feminist debate,[3] as also reflected in this collection. For present purposes, the watershed moment was the adoption of *Security Council Resolution 1325* (SCR 1325) on women, peace and security, in 2000.[4] Inspired by the leadership of the Women's International League for Peace and Freedom (WILPF), a coalition of feminist, human rights and humanitarian non-governmental organisations (NGOs) provided the Security Council with the draft of a resolution that they hoped would play a central role in disrupting the gendered assumptions of collective security discourse, principally by (re)presenting women as vital participants in conflict resolution and peacebuilding; as empowered rather than solely as victims.[5] The efforts of WILPF bore some early fruit with the statement of the then Security Council President, Bangladeshi Ambassador Anwarul Karim Chowdury, on International Women's Day in 2000, which linked peace 'inextricably' with gender equality.[6] It was a testament to the tenacity and creativity of the NGO coalition that, later that year, SCR 1325 was unanimously adopted (a substantially reworked version of the NGO draft) calling for, inter alia, the increased participation of women in decision-making related to the prevention, management and resolution of conflict.[7] Its adoption was especially noteworthy in light of the Security Council's longstanding reticence to engage with NGOs, as well as its institutional reluctance to accept that women might have a role to play in conflict resolution and peacebuilding.

Since 2000, the NGO coalition, formalised as the NGO Working Group on Women, Peace and Security,[8] and supportive states have worked tirelessly to hold the Security Council accountable for the commitments it made in SCR 1325. They have lobbied to promote dialogue between NGOs and Council members in New York; worked on the ground in peace support operations in partnership with local women's peace groups and human rights activists; and promoted the adoption of national action plans by states that contribute troops and other personnel to peace support operations. The WILPF's PeaceWomen project has also translated SCR 1325 into over 100 languages and produces a monthly e-newsletter to promote its utilisation by local groups.[9]

Following the adoption of SCR 1325, the Security Council has been persuaded to adopt several follow-up resolutions, which build upon and strengthen some of its components.[10] Yet these new resolutions suggest that the Council's nod towards women's empowerment in SCR 1325 was very precarious. Four of the six follow-up resolutions focus solely on women as victims of sexual violence, and the increasingly concrete measures of accountability that they establish are all directed towards addressing sexual violence during armed conflict.[11] Seeing women returned so quickly to the singular designation of victimhood has caused many to despair, showing yet again that the Security Council and, more broadly, the institutional framework of international peace and security are highly resistant to efforts to challenge their gendered underpinnings. Yet hope has recently been revived, with the adoption of *Security Council Resolution 2122* (SCR 2122), in which the Security Council recognises its own responsibility to ensure the implementation of SCR 1325's agenda of women's empowerment, acknowledges that a 'significant implementation shift' is required and commits itself to organising a high-level review of implementation in 2015.[12] Feminist engagement with international law and institutions is perhaps condemned to such cycles of hopefulness and despair.

While not wanting to discount the urgency of the need to condemn the widespread occurrence of sexual and gender-based violence, during armed conflict and in its aftermath, or to impugn the establishment of measures to end the impunity that perpetrators have enjoyed, this collection seeks to promote a wider view of issues relating to women, peace and security, beyond even what was achieved in SCR 1325. In fact, it is our view that the development of effective responses to sexual violence in armed conflict is itself reliant on a broader understanding of the relationship between women, peace and security, one that extends to fundamentally rethinking the deeply gendered paradigms of peacekeeping and collective security. By bringing together the perspectives of activists, international law and international relations scholars, military lawyers and peacebuilding practitioners, *Rethinking Peacekeeping, Gender Equality and Collective Security* aims to push security thinking and feminist analysis beyond the prevailing preoccupation with sexual violence to promote action on other aspects of the spectrum of gender issues that must be confronted in both theory and practice, if the militarised framework of international peace and security is to be radically transformed.

The collection emerged from a symposium, jointly convened by its editors, entitled *Peacekeeping in the Asia-Pacific: Gender Equality, Law and Collective Security*, held at Melbourne Law School in April 2012.[13] A wide range of activists, policymakers, practitioners, military actors and academics were invited to participate, in order to encourage debates and connections across disciplinary and professional boundaries. During the symposium participants examined the mutually constitutive role that theory and practice play in the development of feminist thinking, fostering a forward-looking analysis of the praxis required to better understand and realise the nexus between women's equality, peace and security.

The starting point for the symposium was to critically examine what the Security Council's 'willingness to incorporate a gender perspective into peacekeeping operations', expressed in SCR 1325,[14] has meant in practice. Against the backdrop of acknowledging the dangers that can flow from institutional embrace of the term 'gender', the hope was to build on the lessons learned so far from feminist engagement with the Security Council's work, in order to identify better ways to realise the transformative outcomes that were hoped for by the original drafters of SCR 1325. Amongst the dangers of institutionalisation is the likelihood that incorporation of a gender perspective is reduced to a technocratic tool in the hands of United Nations (UN) policymakers and peacekeeping personnel, seriously diluting SCR 1325's critical political potential.[15] Symposium participants were encouraged to interpret gender as a social construct, rather than merely as a synonym for women, and to draw on their own experiences, and/or the experiences of those living in peacekeeping contexts, of trying to work politically and transformatively with issues of gender. All of the contributors to this collection were participants in the symposium; however, the final text considerably enlarges on the discussions and debates that took place and broadens the view from the Asia-Pacific to focus globally.

Engagement with the central terms in the title of the collection – peacekeeping, gender equality and collective security – also binds the diverse contributions together. However, these terms are intensely contested and their meanings continually shift. We have encouraged our contributors to engage with them in a range of ways, both in the substance of their interpretation and the contours of their critique. Old debates are revisited with fresh insights; new debates are fostered; and the underlying paradox of calling for increased women's participation in militarised peace support operations haunts the entire collection. Several of these debates provide the themes around which we have structured the collection: the politics of shame, the continuing hope that motivates grassroots and transnational women's movements, the dangers of institutional cooption, and the damaging silences and blind spots in feminist thinking. Together, the contributors provide a compelling picture of the dynamism and diversity of feminist thinking. While the common focus is on the way that gender structures the institutions and practices of international peace and security, there is also acute awareness that gender intersects with other axes of inequality and marginalisation and that adopting a gender perspective cannot, alone, provide the basis for the radical change that feminist peace advocates have imagined, and tried to live, for so long.

Ultimately, this is a book about the complexities of the people, laws, policies, practices and events that have so far given meaning to the idea of incorporating a gender perspective into peacekeeping operations. This book is also about the diversity of gender perspectives borne of SCR 1325, and about both the feminist and institutional actors that have fostered them. Finally, as a set of critical reflections on post-SCR 1325 efforts to reshape our understanding of collective security, the book offers some thought-provoking inducements to rethink these efforts, emphasising again and again the importance of grassroots leadership and participation. Before elaborating on the structure of the book, organised around the four themes of shame, hope, danger and silences, we briefly introduce the three terms that constitute our title: peacekeeping, gender equality and collective security.

Peacekeeping

At the heart of this book sits the idea of peacekeeping: established during the Cold War as a strategy which enabled the otherwise deadlocked Security Council to authorise the patrol of buffer zones between disputing states and the monitoring of ceasefires by third-party troops.[16] The ambitions of peacekeeping remained limited until the end of the Cold War, when it emerged as one of the new sites for possible cooperation between Security Council members. Significantly, this new-found cooperation enabled the Council to identify many internal armed conflicts as a threat to international peace and security, which gave it the power to act in a considerably expanded range of situations.

The more expansive conception of international peace and security had dramatic repercussions for peacekeeping activities, prompting then UN Secretary-General Boutros Boutros-Ghali to identify, in 1992, four types of activity: preventative diplomacy and peacemaking; expanding the possibilities for the prevention of conflict and the making of peace; the implementation and verification of negotiated peace settlements; and assisting post-conflict micro-disarmament.[17] This list soon lengthened to include the extremely ambitious projects of peace enforcement and peacebuilding.

Peace enforcement, euphemistically described as 'robust' peacekeeping, refers to the Security Council's authorisation of the use of force within a peacekeeping mandate, which was strictly prohibited during the Cold War. The incorporation of authorised force as a component of peacekeeping blurs the traditional distinction between peacekeeping and the use of force, which raises pressing questions about the increasing militarisation of peacekeeping. In this collection the problematic nexus between military and peacekeeping goals is examined by various authors, in particular Stephanie Cousins and Olivera Simić. To date, however, Security Council resolutions on women, peace and security have sought to incorporate a gender perspective into peacekeeping while ignoring feminist critiques of militarisation, a limitation that is discussed in Felicity Ruby's chapter.

Peacebuilding refers to the expansion of peacekeeping operations to provide assistance in the implementation of negotiated peace settlements, which often means the assumption of a longer term role over a number of years to assist with the establishment of legal institutions, monitor elections, train local police and military personnel and build democratic governmental structures and capacities, although the lack of integration with economic rebuilding is highly problematic, as Jacqui True argues in this collection. Contemporary practices of transitional justice may also involve the international community in establishing truth and reconciliation commissions and international or hybrid criminal tribunals to prosecute high-ranking officials responsible for international crimes committed during the conflict. Feminists continue to identify the gaps between SCR 1325's call for women's participation at all stages in the transition to peace, and the realities on the ground.[18] Yet, as many of our authors identify, not only does the Security Council's agenda fail to expand options for women's participation, but the woefully inadequate implementation of its women, peace and security framework has often failed to recognise women's existing participation in the promotion and building of peace, let alone expand it. Laura Shepherd's discussion of 'recovery' as a politics of hope demonstrates the need for integrating strategies into peace negotiations and peacebuilding that pay attention to gender at the conceptual and empirical levels, as well as in everyday practice.

For the purposes of this collection, the term peacekeeping encompasses the spectrum of peacekeeping techniques and practices, including peace negotiations, peace monitoring, peace enforcement, peacebuilding and mechanisms that provide for transitional justice. The chapters range across this spectrum identifying emergent best practices, as well as some disturbing limitations, including the neo-colonial and neoliberal allegiances that underpin these interventions. Undeniably, peacekeeping in its many forms occupies a prominent position in the Security Council's array of collective security strategies and practices, shaping the everyday lives and future prospects of war-torn communities, promising new hope for security and a life of dignity. Viewed in this light, peacekeeping offers an opportunity to establish sustainable peace, with the assistance of the international and/or regional community, and is thus of intense interest to feminist activists and scholars alike because of the emancipatory potential it presents for women and other marginalised and disadvantaged groups. However, as will quickly become apparent from the contributions to this collection, the transformative promise of peacekeeping is a very long way from realisation. In many respects, peacekeeping demands thorough rethinking if ever it is to challenge the gendered architecture of collective security.

Gender equality

Also at the heart of this book is the idea of incorporating gender perspectives into peacekeeping, as called for by SCR 1325,[19] which we understand as a call for gender equality. This call has been interpreted in many different ways to serve many different agendas, often to the dismay of feminists.[20] As already alluded to, SCR 1325 is commonly interpreted narrowly to require prioritisation of measures aimed at identifying perpetrators of sexual violence and, to a lesser extent, addressing the needs of their victims. While some of our contributors identify measures to enhance current efforts to address conflict-related sexual violence, like Róisín Burke who argues that the human rights obligations of troop-contributing states may be engaged by victims of sexual offences perpetrated by military peacekeepers, most contributors reflect critically on the manner in which sexual violence has been (over) emphasised, especially Karen Engle.

In the limited instances that women's participation has been operationalised within the SCR 1325 framework, it has usually been interpreted to require 'gender balance', achieved by merely increasing the numbers of women deployed in peace support operations. Gender balance strategies have often been derided by feminists as merely 'adding women and stirring', rather than accomplishing substantive structural change. In its most robust form, in theory at least, incorporating a gender perspective means 'gender mainstreaming' which, in the UN definition, requires taking account of the concerns of both women and men in all policies and programmes, and addressing them in a way that has the achievement of substantive gender equality as its goal.[21] The collection challenges the move from gender mainstreaming to gender balancing, while also showing how both approaches can, in practice, be tokenistic and piecemeal. The limited impact of incorporating a gender perspective centred on counting the number of women 'participating' is repeatedly highlighted.

In contrast, gender perspectives are engaged by our authors as providing a set of tools that reach beyond gender as a synonym for women or merely a descriptive term. Gender is understood as a critical interrogative device where the practices and discourses of international laws and policies are analysed in terms of the analytically embedded gendered assumptions they contain. The goal of gender equality necessitates exposing and destabilising these underlying semiotic structures, which also reinforce other hierarchies of power associated with race, nation, ethnicity, religion, sexuality, disability and so on. Contributors also highlight the importance of working with local expressions of gender and alongside local movements for change, rather than imposing 'universal' gender norms that may be deeply implicated in colonial histories, as well as the inequitable global order of the present. This is an aspect taken up in Gina Heathcote's chapter that analyses women's participation in the post-conflict community of Bougainville and highlights the tensions between international and local gender norms.

It is evident from the contributions to this collection that, no matter which approach to incorporating a gender perspective into peacekeeping is adopted, much depends on the commitment, vision, goals and capacity of those directly involved in its framing and implementation. Every possible method of incorporation runs the risk of cooption to the service of institutional agendas, conversion to bureaucratic targets and performance indicators, being condensed to a synonym for women or, conversely, requiring an end to all women-specific policies and programmes. The project of gender integration will always be subject to forces intent on removing any commitment to the political goals of feminism. In this collection, the possibilities for resisting the dangers of institutional take-up of feminist knowledge are explored by Dianne Otto. She and other contributors reiterate the need to keep the transformative redistributive and disarmament goals of feminist peace activism in mind, as one way to maintain a critical distance from the institutional project of the Security Council and ensure that structural change in gender relations and global hierarchies of power remain the focus.

The Security Council's willingness to incorporate gender perspectives into peacekeeping also presents new opportunities to promote substantive change in gender relations in post-conflict societies, as well as to destabilise the gendered assumptions of the larger framework of international peace and security. The challenge is how to invigorate this potential and resist the depoliticising effects of institutionalisation. Every contributor offers a thoughtful perspective on how this conundrum might be approached, from rethinking basic assumptions to building feminist modes of participation and service delivery. Chloé Lewis, for example, challenges the feminist and institutional myopia about male experiences of sexual violence during armed conflict. The concluding chapter, by Judith Gardam and Dale Stephens, attempts a 'conversation' between feminist and military perspectives by taking a closer look at recent military innovations that have been, in part, a response to SCR 1325.

Throughout, the collection demonstrates that it matters that there is political will at the highest levels, as well as local engagement and support, if the essentialised gendered assumptions embedded in collective security and peacekeeping are to be challenged. The importance of involving grassroots women's groups – which ensures that strategies to incorporate a gender perspective have local cultural resonance and backing, and a future beyond the peacekeeping period – is emphasised again and again. For example, Sharon Bhagwan Rolls' account of the use of SCR 1325 to build a successful women's media network in the Pacific demonstrates the potential of these resolutions to provide a lever to realise new projects that build local capacities and foster self-determination. The young WILPF women (YWILPF) identify the need for gender strategies to encourage the participation and perspectives of young people in peacekeeping decision-making and activism, particularly those of young women. The issues of endemic poverty and sexual violence, and the tiny numbers of women involved in peacekeeping, arise repeatedly, but from different perspectives and with fresh insights. Despite the many limitations identified, none of the contributors conclude that engaging with the Security Council to promote the incorporation of a gender perspective in peacekeeping operations is doomed to failure, although they all emphasise the project's dangers and the importance of continuing critical feminist analysis and vigilance.

Collective security

Peacekeeping is located within the larger discourse of collective security. Under the *Charter of the United Nations* (UN Charter), the maintenance of international peace and security is the primary responsibility of the

Security Council and its role is to achieve this by engaging states in collective dispute resolution.[22] The UN Charter envisages the use of a very wide range of actions, including voluntary measures aimed at the peaceful settlement of disputes, under Chapter VI of the UN Charter, and binding forceful measures, including the imposition of sanctions and the authorisation of the use of military force, under Chapter VII. To date, collective security has been interpreted by the Security Council as primarily a military endeavour. The UN Charter makes no reference to peacekeeping as we know it today, yet it has become an immensely important component of collective security, using militaries to assist the establishment of the essential elements of sustainable peace in post-conflict societies.

The Security Council's women, peace and security agenda sits largely within its peacekeeping endeavours and the resolutions that set out this agenda have been adopted under Chapter VI. Nevertheless, aspects of the agenda also relate to the Security Council's Chapter VII obligations, including its undertaking to take gender issues into account when it imposes sanctions under Article 41;[23] its condemnation of sexual violence as a tactic of war;[24] and its indication that widespread and systematic sexual violence may potentially be a trigger for authorisation of forceful intervention.[25] The reach of the Security Council's women, peace and security resolutions into matters regarding the use of force is a double-edged sword for feminists, as it opens the way for women's rights to be instrumentalised to justify the use of force – which is an irony indeed.[26] On the other hand, it creates a broader canvas for feminists to use SCR 1325, and the other resolutions that have followed in its wake, to work against militarism, promote disarmament and foster methods of peaceful resolution, daunting as this prospect may seem.

In general, though, the hope is that introducing gender perspectives into peacekeeping provides a niche for feminist efforts to reshape the broader collective security framework by disrupting militarist assumptions and stereotypes of gender that reinforce inequality and serve to legitimate military ways of thinking, providing a continuing rationale for masculine modes of political and economic governance. In addition, engagement with collective security through the Security Council has created a pivotal location for feminist activism, including many opportunities to refocus collective security towards the realisation of human rights; enhancing local empowerment and participation; and promoting the radical redistribution of wealth, power and resources. Throughout the collection, the tensions between feminist notions of security as guaranteed through peaceful dispute resolution, gender equality and economic justice, and the Council's militaristic approach, are palpable. Thus, the collection sits firmly in the tradition of feminist anti-militarism, redistributive justice and gender-inclusive peace that commenced long before the Security Council's adoption of SCR 1325.

The structure of this collection

As previously mentioned, the affective themes around which this collection is organised – shame, hope, danger and silences – emerged from the symposium discussions, helping to foster interdisciplinary thinking and provide bridges between different panels and topics. Following the symposium, we decided that these four themes, together, best captured the mixture of enthusiasm, ambivalence, despair and solidarity that the symposium engendered. The use of affective imagery to locate and connect the contributions to this collection is also an effort to resist the separation of deeply felt conviction, which is so much a part of feminist activism and scholarship, from dispassionate intellectual discussion of peacekeeping, gender equality and collective security. The personal is, after all, political. It is hoped that our approach may encourage more serious engagement with feelings and passions, as part of incorporating gender perspectives into re-imagining collective security and its peace-keeping endeavours.

Shame

An international system that has no universally applicable means of law enforcement relies heavily on shaming to persuade governments to act according to their international legal obligations. In this sense, shame is understood as productive, as having a political and moral influence on state behaviour. However, in the context of the current hyper-attention to sexual violence in the framework of international peace and security, shame also serves more problematic purposes, which is the subject of Karen Engle's contribution to the collection. Engle is not only critical of the relentless focus on sexual violence as the quintessential harm of war, with the consequent silencing of other concerns that may have greater priority for women (and men) whose lives have been thrown into chaos by armed conflict. She is also critical of the popularisation of the issue by celebrity calls for solidarity with victims of sexual violence. Engle demonstrates this point by examining a UN inter-agency initiative, UN Action against Sexual Violence, arguing that shame plays a central role in the depiction of sexual violence victims, and their communities, as forever damaged and in need, therefore, of (non-damaged) first world global citizens 'taking action', by following the lead of celebrities like Charlize Theron and adding their photographs to the campaign's Stop Rape Now website.[27] She extends her analysis to include the Council's other thematic resolutions on protecting children and civilians and challenges feminists to rethink both the categories of women that are recognised by SCR 1325 and its follow-up resolutions – as victims and as agents of peace.

The second chapter, written by Gina Heathcote, questions the peacekeeping 'success' story of the Papua New Guinean autonomous province of Bougainville. Through an analysis of the approaches taken to advancing women's participation by the Security Council's women, peace and security resolutions, Heathcote argues that gender essentialism is entrenched and that there is an urgent need to learn from the failures of past practices in the next stage of the life of the resolutions. Focussing on the post-conflict processes in the matrilineal communities of Bougainville, where it might be expected that the participation components of the women, peace and security agenda would be fully implemented, Heathcote demonstrates the shameful fact that women's already substantial contributions to peace are insufficiently recognised in formal post-conflict political and economic developments. Despite this, she suggests that the recent SCR 2122, adopted in 2013, opens some transformative possibilities. Heathcote argues that the current focus on women's participation needs to shift to addressing the problem of the over-representation of men in post-conflict institutions, to resisting gender essentialism by responding to the diversity of women's lives and to acknowledging the gendered normative assumptions of the Security Council itself.

Taking a more familiar approach to shame as a means of persuading states to comply with their international legal obligations, in the third chapter Róisín Burke proposes what is in this context an innovative strategy: to shame states into taking responsibility for sexual exploitation and abuse perpetrated by military personnel engaged in peacekeeping. Burke argues that the current emphasis on requiring troop-contributing countries to undertake disciplinary action or criminal prosecution of alleged offenders does not go far enough. Burke proposes, in addition, that the human rights obligations of troop-contributing countries towards victims be engaged. She argues that a state's failure to take reasonable measures to prevent sexual exploitation and abuse by its military personnel, and the failure to effectively investigate and prosecute soldiers accused of sexual offences in peacekeeping operations may trigger the extra-territorial responsibility of troop-contributing countries for the human rights violations that occur as a result. Burke draws on the jurisprudence of international and regional human rights bodies to support her argument, providing a useful guide to those who may wish to pursue such a strategy.

Hope

Hope is, of course, what has always inspired feminist engagement with international law and politics. Understanding hope as a process interwoven in feminist ethics, and as a springboard for transforming international relations scholarship on peace and security, is the focus of Laura Shepherd's contribution to the book. Shepherd challenges international relations scholars to pay attention to emotion and curiosity as they have been theorised by feminists, to leave aside disciplinary preoccupations with fear and move to embrace multiple strategies for transforming the discipline. She weaves together insights from feminist poststructuralism, postcolonialism and the study of emotionality, ethics and contemporary mental health strategies, to emphasise empathy, compassion and critique in rethinking 'recovery' as a guiding principle for peacebuilding. Shepherd demonstrates the need for a shift away from a case management model – where peacekeeping interventions are top-down processes – which remains dominant in peacekeeping practice, despite Security Council initiatives in the post-millennium period directed towards understanding recovery as a 'process' involving encouragement of bottom-up agency, opportunity and hope.

The second chapter in the section on hope is written by Sharon Bhagwan Rolls, the Director of FemLINKPACIFIC, a regional transnational network that uses media as a platform to empower and incorporate women's participation in peacemaking and peacebuilding processes.[28] Bhagwan Rolls explains how activists in the Pacific used SCR 1325's call for the effective participation of women in conflict prevention, conflict resolution and peacekeeping as a lever to establish the media network. Her contribution reminds us that the media, in situations of unrest and violence, can make both positive and negative contributions. Access to media production is therefore a vital aspect of any strategy for lasting peace. Her contribution shows how the innovative thinking of women's networks can propel their participation into traditionally male public spaces. Grassroots communication through women's community radio has enabled women in the Pacific to rise to the challenge presented by SCR 1325 and embrace their role as local agents of critical change, raising hope across the region about what women's participation can achieve, within and between post-conflict communities.

Stephanie Cousins' critical examination of the implementation of gender mainstreaming by the Regional Assistance Mission to Solomon Islands (RAMSI), in its police reform initiatives, concludes the section on hope. Utilising the findings of the RAMSI People's Survey, undertaken annually to obtain a sense of local perceptions of the gender sensitivity of policing practices, Cousins examines the impact of RAMSI's gender policies. On the one hand, she finds that SCR 1325 has prompted RAMSI's leadership on gender mainstreaming. On the other hand, despite the numerous policy commitments, she finds that beyond recruitment initiatives to attract more women into local forces, many other policing reforms remained gender-blind. In addition, many of Cousins' informants, who worked in various capacities for RAMSI, indicated that people simply did not know what to do to incorporate a gender perspective into their work. Cousins' research highlights an important connection between local perceptions of transitional processes and peacekeeping successes. Echoing Shepherd's call for recovery centred on local agency, Cousins affirms that gender policies must resonate with local cultural norms and foster recovery through active consultative processes. She warns of the continuing danger of misreading gender as merely a quantitative indicator, which betrays all hope for women's emancipation.

Danger

While the feminist strategy of engagement with the Security Council is hopeful, it also presents many dangers for feminist ideas and goals. Dianne Otto argues that the competing narratives of victory and danger in feminist analyses of efforts to engage with the Security Council have turned much of the debate inwards and promoted unhelpful tensions between feminist activism and (academic) critique. Hoping to promote a more productive approach, Otto examines three of the assumptions that are common to the two narratives: first, the selection of the Security Council as a fruitful site for feminist engagement; second, the use of gender as a synonym for women; and, third, the idea that the resolutions empower local women's movements. Her examination teases out the larger politics that have been occluded by the focus on weighing the positives and negatives of the strategy. What emerges is a shared narrative of 'progress' which is highly amenable to supporting the Security Council's politics of securitised militarism, made more palatable by gesturing towards the inclusion of women as a marker of progress. Otto urges feminists to abandon the 'progress' thread to their stories of the resolutions, in order to advance more resistive analyses that promote a deeper understanding of how transformative change might be fostered.

Activist Felicity Ruby, former Director of WILPF's New York office, reflects on what has been achieved since the adoption of SCR 1325. She expresses her frustration that the activism associated with SCR 1325 has become fixated on the Security Council, forgetting that its adoption and implementation is not an end in itself, but rather a means, or a multifaceted 'tool' as she prefers, to achieve the larger feminist goal of conflict prevention, which includes disarmament, an equitable international economic order and transformed gender relations. While acknowledging that SCR 1325 has opened some doors for women to be involved in policy development, and raised awareness of the gendered underpinnings of collective security measures, she argues that the focus of SCR 1325 activism must be turned towards eliminating the everyday socio-economic causes of armed conflict. Ruby calls for a broader vision of what can be achieved by utilising SCR 1325, and the courage to pursue it. In her view, a thorough rethinking of SCR 1325 activism is necessary to avert the danger of its instrumentalisation by the Security Council and to stay focussed on the long-standing radical goals of feminist peace campaigners.

Olivera Simić is concerned with the dangers arising from the conflicting expectations placed on women who are increasingly deployed in peacekeeping operations as police and military personnel, pursuant to SCR 1325, in the name of achieving 'gender balance'. Simić argues that the UN Department of Peacekeeping Operations' primary rationale for promoting gender balance is to develop responsiveness to the needs of local women and, in particular, to diminish the incidence of sexual abuse and exploitation of host country women and girls by (male) peacekeepers. Yet studies have shown that women involved in peacekeeping aspire simply to be good at their jobs of soldiering and policing. Simić argues that female peacekeepers often do not think of themselves as having any special empathy for local women. Nor do they wish to assume responsibility for the prevention of sexual violence perpetrated by their male colleagues. Consequently, achieving a numerical increase in the number of women in peacekeeping operations does not, by itself, translate into gender-inclusive missions capable of taking full account of the complex needs and experiences of women, men, girls and boys. To claim otherwise places those women deployed in the name of gender balance in an impossible situation.

Silences

'Searching for the silences' is a feminist methodology that is often used in international law and politics because it can be revealing about where women, and the issues considered 'feminine' or 'other' to the mainstream, are positioned. This final section of the book looks to the future of feminist engagement with peacekeeping and collective security by identifying some of the 'others' present yet silenced by policies and practices, so as to demonstrate the need to include them. The method, when applied by Chloé Lewis to feminist responses to sexual violence in armed conflict and its aftermath, finds a reverse silencing of the experience of male victims. Lewis argues that to focus only on women is to ignore the relational character of gender and reduce its transformative potential. Critically exploring representations of men and masculinities in international sexual violence discourse, Lewis traces three recurring masculine figures: the 'Male Perpetrator', the 'Strategic Ally' and the elusive 'Male Victim Subject'. She demonstrates how these restrictive tropes limit the conceptual, legal and programmatic spaces available to males within conflict and peacekeeping contexts. Against this backdrop, the author explores three possible avenues to build on the traces of the 'Male Victim Subject' in sexual violence policies and practices, and considers some of the implications of each particular pathway.

The authors of the second chapter in this section, Sharna de Lacy, Cara Gleeson, May Maloney and Fiona McAlpine, are all active members of YWILPF, an international network of young women promoting awareness of SCR 1325. They argue that the relative invisibility of young women within established women, peace and security policies and strategies needs to change. Compounding the situation, most demographic studies of young people in conflict centre on masculine experiences and cast young women in passive victim and/or reproductive roles. Emphasising the importance of intergenerational solidarity amongst women peace activists, the authors challenge the view that young women cannot be agents of change, arguing for acknowledgement of their particular and varied experiences during and after conflict; and urging that their contributions to building sustainable peace be welcomed and facilitated. The chapter draws on a small empirical study, which documents the experiences of young women peace activists from six countries. The YWILPF contribution to the collection challenges assumptions that young people are disruptive or disinterested, emphasising the importance of actively engaging them in peacebuilding initiatives, especially as they often constitute a majority in post-conflict populations.

Finally, Jacqui True highlights the lack of connection between the international security and socio-economic reconstruction agendas in peacebuilding. True is critical of the priority that is given to security concerns, which silences the social and economic dimensions of building a sustainable peace that is capable of delivering women's equality and rights. True argues that the present paradigm perpetuates the marginalised economic status of women relative to men, which greatly hampers nation-building and reconstruction efforts. The consequence is further exclusion of women from economic and social decision-making. Taking a feminist political economy approach, she calls for a re-conceptualisation of peacebuilding so that the underlying gendered structures of socio-economic inequality, which fuel insecurity and violence, are addressed. She urges the Security Council and international economic institutions to link security with economic development in peacebuilding, promoting women's economic empowerment as well as women's political participation. Implementing this reconceived framework, including gender-inclusive reparations, employment and training opportunities, would go a long way toward realising the substance, not just the text, of SCR 1325.

Conclusions

Provocatively, the collection concludes with a conversation between a feminist academic lawyer, Professor Judith Gardam, and a naval legal officer on academic secondment, Captain Dale Stephens. Functioning as a postscript, the final chapter is a reminder of the complex and challenging conversations required to rethink peacekeeping, gender equality and collective security, which must necessarily involve militaries and feminists finding ways to talk to each other. Yet military institutions, and the people who inhabit them, are usually hostile to feminist goals. While acknowledging the potential hazards of opening a conversation between these two long-standing antagonists, Gardam and Stephens argue that a better understanding of each other's perspectives may prove fruitful. They begin their conversation by identifying some of the crosscutting themes of the symposium, from which this collection has emerged, revealing some surprising commonalities, as well as the entrenched differences that might be expected. The discussion then turns to a more strenuous testing of the potential for a productive exchange of ideas by focussing on two recent military initiatives: first, the new approach to balancing civilian casualties and force protection in counterinsurgency warfare, as exemplified in the United States Army Marine Corps Counterinsurgency Handbook; and second, the possible advantages of the use of Female Engagement Teams in Afghanistan. Their dialogue highlights the challenges of such exchanges, where the stakes can be literally a matter of life and death, and thus demonstrates the utter importance of learning to speak to each other, despite our differences.

As its editors, we hope that this collection, in its parts and as a whole, speaks to many different constituencies who have a stake in rethinking the incorporation of gender perspectives into peacekeeping and, more broadly, into the theories and practices of international collective security.

Notes

1. Laura Bush launched President George W. Bush's 'women's rights' campaign in Afghanistan on the President's weekly radio address, on 17 November 2001: see D. Stout, 'A nation challenged: The First Lady; Mrs Bush cites women's plight under the Taliban', *The New York Times* (18 November 2001), p. 4. Starting just before the invasion of Iraq in 2003, Iraqi women were heralded by the US Administration as promoters of freedom and democracy: see N. Al-Ali, 'Embedded feminism – Women's rights as justification for war', *Gunda Werner Institute*, http://www.gwi-boell.de/web/un-resolutions-embedded-feminism-nadje-al-ali-2811.html (last accessed October 2013). Contrast with P. J. Dobriansky, M. Alattar, Z. Al-Suwaij, T. Gilly and E. Naama, 'Human rights and women in Iraq: Voices of Iraqi women', *US Department of State Archive* (6 March 2003), http://2001-2009.state.gov/g/rls/rm/2003/18477.htm (last accessed October 2013).
2. L. B. Costin, 'Feminism, pacifism, internationalism and the 1915 International Congress of Women', *Women's Studies International Forum*, Vol. 5, No. 3–4 (1982), p. 301; A. Wiltsher, *Most Dangerous Women: Feminist Peace Campaigners of the Great War* (London: Pandora Press, 1985); L. Rupp, *Worlds of Women: The Making of an International Women's Movement* (Princeton: Princeton University Press, 1997); J. A. Tickner, *Gender in International Relations: Feminist Perspectives on Achieving Global Security* (New York: Columbia University Press, 1992); and C. Enloe, *Maneuvers: The International Politics of Militarizing Women's Lives* (Berkeley: University of California Press, 2000).
3. See, for example, D. Otto, 'Power and danger: Feminist engagement with international law through the UN Security Council', *Australian Feminist Law Journal*, Vol. 32 (2010), p. 97.
4. *Security Council Resolution 1325*, UN Doc. S/RES/1325 (31 October 2000) (SCR 1325).
5. C. Cohn, H. Kinsella and S. Gibbings, 'Women, peace and security: Resolution 1325', *International Feminist Journal of Politics*, Vol. 6, No. 1 (2004), p. 130; D. Otto, 'A sign of "weakness"? Disrupting gender certainties in the implementation of Security Council Resolution 1325', *Michigan Journal of Gender and Law*, Vol. 13, No. 1 (2006), p. 113.
6. United Nations Department of Public Information, 'Peace Inextricably Linked with Equality between Women and Men Says Security Council, in International Women's Day Statement' (Press Release No. SC/6816, United Nations, 8 March 2000): '[T]he Security Council recognize[s] that peace is

inextricably linked with equality between women and men ... [and] that the equal access and full participation of women in power structures and their full involvement in all efforts for the prevention and resolution of conflicts are essential for the maintenance and promotion of peace and security'.

7. SCR 1325, paras 1–4.

8. Five organisations were initially involved in the NGO Working Group on Women, Peace and Security: the Women's International League for Peace and Freedom; International Alert; Amnesty International; the Women's Commission for Refugee Women and Children; and the Hague Appeal for Peace. They have since been joined by: Femmes Africa Solidarité; International Women's Tribune Centre; Women's Action for New Directions; Women's Division of the General Board of Global Ministries of the United Methodist Church; and the Women's Environment and Development Organization. The Women's Caucus for Gender Justice in the International Criminal Court was also a member for a period of time. See further *NGO Working Group on Women, Peace and Security* (2013), http://www.womenpeacesecurity.org (last accessed October 2013).

9. *PeaceWomen*, http://www.peacewomen.org, a project of WILPF. The e-newsletter can be found at http://www.peacewomen.org/publications_enews.php (last accessed October 2013).

10. *Security Council Resolution 1820*, UN Doc. S/RES/1820 (19 June 2008) (SCR 1820); *Security Council Resolution 1888*, UN Doc. S/RES/1888 (30 September 2009) (SCR 1888); *Security Council Resolution 1889*, UN Doc. S/RES/1889 (5 October 2009) (SCR 1889); *Security Council Resolution 1960*, UN Doc. S/RES/1960 (16 December 2010) (SCR 1960); *Security Council Resolution 2106*, UN Doc. S/RES//2106 (24 June 2013) (SCR 2106); and *Security Council Resolution 2122*, UN Doc. S/RES/2122 (18 October 2013) (SCR 2122).

11. The first of these resolutions, SCR 1820, does not establish any accountability mechanisms as such. The second, SCR 1888, para. 4, requests the UN Secretary-General to appoint a Special Representative to provide leadership in order to ensure that sexual violence during armed conflict is addressed; and para. 8, calls on the Secretary-General to establish a Team of Experts who can be deployed rapidly to situations of specific concern. The third, SCR 1960, paras 3, 4, 6 and 7, establishes listing, monitoring and sanctions procedures to enable the Security Council to hold parties to armed conflict, who are credibly suspected of perpetrating sexual violence, to account. The fourth, SCR 2106, para. 6, calls for more timely and reliable information to enable more effective prevention and response.

12. SCR 2122, paras 1 and 15.

13. *Peacekeeping in the Asia-Pacific: Gender Equality, Law and Collective Security*, Melbourne Law School, 19–20 April 2012, an international symposium hosted by the Asia Pacific Centre for Military Law (APCML), in conjunction with the Centre for Gender Studies, SOAS, University of London. Funding was generously provided by the British Academy, APCML, the United Nations Population Fund and Melbourne Law School.

14. SCR 1325, para. 5.

15. S. Whitworth, *Men, Militarism and UN Peacekeeping: A Gendered Analysis* (Boulder: Lynne Rienner, 2004), p. 120.

16. The first operation of this kind was the UN Emergency Force, established by the UN General Assembly to secure an end to the 1956 Suez Crisis with

Resolution 1001 (ES-I) on 7 November 1956. The UN Emergency Force was deployed on both sides of the armistice line.

17. B. Boutros-Ghali, *An Agenda for Peace: Preventative Diplomacy, Peacemaking and Peace-Keeping* (New York: United Nations, 1992), para. 20.

18. C. Bell and C. O'Rourke, 'Peace agreements or pieces of paper? The impact of UNSC Resolution 1325 on peace processes and their agreements', *International and Comparative Law Quarterly*, Vol. 59, No. 4 (2010), p. 941; F. Ní Aoláin, 'Women, security, and the patriarchy of internationalized transitional justice', *Human Rights Quarterly*, Vol. 31, No. 4 (2009), p. 1055.

19. SCR 1325, para. 5.

20. D. Otto, 'The Security Council's alliance of "gender legitimacy": The symbolic capital of Resolution 1325', in H. Charlesworth and J. Coicaud (eds), *Fault Lines of International Legitimacy* (New York: Cambridge University Press, 2010), p. 239.

21. Office of the Special Adviser on Gender Issues and Advancement of Women, *Gender Mainstreaming: An Overview* (New York: United Nations, 2002), p. 1.

22. *Charter of the United Nations*, opened for signature on 26 June 1945, 1 UNTS XVI (entered into force on 24 October 1945) (UN Charter).

23. SCR 1325, para. 14; SCR 1960, para. 7; and SCR 2106, para. 13.

24. SCR 1820, para. 1; SCR 1888, para. 1; SCR 1960, para. 1; and SCR 2106, para. 1.

25. SCR 1820, para. 1; SCR 1888, para. 1; SCR 1960, para. 1; and SCR 2106, para. 1.

26. For elaboration, see G. Heathcote, *The Law on the Use of Force: A Feminist Analysis* (Abingdon: Routledge, 2011).

27. *Stop Rape Now*, http://www.stoprapenow.org (last accessed October 2013). See also UN Action against Sexual Violence in Conflict, 'UN Action public service announcement – Stop rape now', *YouTube* (10 May 2010), http://www.youtube.com/watch?v=J9fg2oHHBaM (last accessed October 2013).

28. *FemLINKPACIFIC* (2007), http://www.femlinkpacific.org.fj (last accessed October 2013).

Part I
Shame

1
The Grip of Sexual Violence: Reading UN Security Council Resolutions on Human Security

Karen Engle

Introduction

The issue I would like to pose in this chapter is about the grip of sexual violence on human security discourse. I do not want to address the violence itself, but to consider why many feminist – and even non-feminist – discussions about human rights and security have become inextricably connected to concerns about sexual violence, primarily but not exclusively against women. I consider here the United Nations (UN) Security Council resolutions on what is termed 'human security', and debates and media around them. I do so because I believe they are representative of an escalating emphasis on the horrors of sexual violence more generally within international human rights and humanitarian law, discourse and advocacy.

Although the seeming relentless attention to sexual violence in at least some of the Security Council resolutions that I consider is partly a result of the success of a particular feminist strategy, a number of feminists have been critical of it. Women's peace activists, for example, have expressed concern that the resolutions that emphasise women's victimisation detract from the goal of seeing women as agents of change during peacemaking.[1] Some have sought or supported a number of other resolutions that call for increased participation of women in peacebuilding. Indeed, two types of resolutions about women – those that concentrate on women as victims of conflict and others that see women as central to the peace process – tend to leapfrog over each other in terms of passage at the Security Council.

Yet, the understanding of the harm of sexual violence as one of the worst injuries that can occur during armed conflict, I contend, can be found in nearly all the resolutions and among those who express competing perspectives on the extent to which the resolutions should focus on sexual violence. My chapter is therefore aimed largely at those who have expressed the criticism I just described. I hope to encourage them to rethink their own assumptions about the harm of sexual violence, rather than simply consider where the attention should be concentrated.

In this chapter, I situate the Security Council resolutions on human security and the discourse around them within three trends that I see in human rights and humanitarian law and advocacy more generally. First, the past few years have seen increased attention to *sexual* violence, even as against gender-based violence against women. Sometimes the two are elided, while other times women are no longer the specific concern. Either way, the prevailing view of sexual violence continues to be that it is a 'fate worse than death'. Second, human rights law, advocacy and discourse have, over the past 20 years, increasingly turned to criminal law for enforcement, with the fight against impunity as central to that turn. Consequently, those who oppose sexual violence often do so by focussing on ending impunity for perpetrators.[2] Third, celebrity calls for first-world solidarity with mostly third-world victims of human rights violations have become increasingly popular in recent years. Some of the work of the UN to end sexual violence in conflict deploys such calls.

These three trends partly come together in the work of UN Action against Sexual Violence (UN Action), a multi-agency initiative begun in 2007 to bring attention and response to sexual violence in war. Its Stop Rape Now Campaign is a multimedia and largely web-based effort designed to provoke indignation at sexual violence, with at least the partial hope that it will result in individuals pressuring Security Council member states to pass resolutions on sexual violence. I will consider here two YouTube videos produced and disseminated by UN Action, and will argue that, in their attempt to appeal to first-world outrage, they oversimplify both sexual violence and conflict in ways that display and reinforce an assumption that victims are forever destroyed, in part due to shame and stigmatisation that they see as accompanying sexual violence in conflict. Similar oversimplifications can be seen in the resolutions, as well as in the international criminal responses to sexual violence that the Security Council resolutions call for.

I share with many women's peace activists the concern that calls for an analysis of the gendered nature and production of war (and peace) have often been responded to by an emphasis on the harm of sexual violence for women. I show, however, how over time the scope has been extended to sexual violence against men and children (both boys and girls) as well. And I explore, perhaps a bit more than many of the critics, what that attention to sexual violence means. I do so at the risk of perpetuating the very hyper-attention to sex I criticise. I attribute much of this hyper-attention to something akin to what queer theorists call 'sex panic'.[3] Seen through this lens, the Security Council resolutions, including those promoted by the women's peace movement, aid in the production or at least reinforcement of particular types of 'proper' sexuality (heterosexual, of a certain age, monogamous, within the same ethnic group and so on).[4] They also, perhaps inadvertently for some, reinforce the shame of rape.

This chapter proceeds as follows. The first section provides some of the context of the resolutions, and then demonstrates how they have become increasingly concerned with sexual violence – against both males and females. It also considers the various understandings of the harm of sexual violence that the resolutions convey. The next section discusses UN Action's multimedia campaign to show how some of the same assumptions and trends I identify in the resolutions can be found there, as well as to shed light on how human rights law and discourse circulate in that public space.

United Nations Security Council resolutions and sexual violence

Initially prompted by a group of states that banded together in 1999 to form the 'human security network', the UN Security Council had, by mid-2013, passed 20 thematic resolutions that attend specifically to the treatment in armed conflict of civilians, children and women (three distinct, if overlapping, categories for the resolutions).[5] All passed unanimously. They largely embody international humanitarian law, and increasingly seek to apply the rules not only to states and non-state actors, but to the UN as well in its peacekeeping operations. As is the pattern with Security Council resolutions in general, there is much repetition and self-reference in the resolutions, with each one becoming more specific than the one that preceded it about the harm to be attended to and the various enforcement mechanisms that should be used to address it. In 2009, the Security Council passed four such resolutions that are reflective of the group focus they have taken – one on civilians, one on children, one primarily on women as victims of war and one considering the need to ensure women's participation in the peacebuilding process.[6] In 2010, however, *Security Council Resolution 1960* (SCR 1960) broke the mould by turning to sexual violence as a theme. As I discuss below, SCR 1960 explicitly addresses sexual violence against women and children but, because its operative paragraphs are gender-neutral, some have read it as applying to sexual violence against men as well. A later resolution, *Security Council Resolution 2106* (SCR 2106), specifically references men and boys as victims of sexual violence.

A number of other chapters in this collection consider *Security Council Resolution 1325* (SCR 1325), passed in 2000.[7] It constitutes the first of the Security Council resolutions on women that feminists and women's peace activists generally consider. It is often discussed, along with *Security Council Resolution 1889* (SCR 1889) – one of the 2009 resolutions mentioned above – as somewhat exceptional because the two specifically focus on the role of women in peacebuilding, rather than on women's victimisation in war as civilians. These two resolutions can be contrasted with *Security Council Resolution 1820* (SCR 1820) and *Security Council Resolution 1888* (SCR 1888), as well as with SCR 1960 and SCR 2106, which are seen by a number of women's peace activists to place too much emphasis on women's victimisation.[8]

While most feminists who have considered the treatment of sexual violence in the resolutions have concentrated on these resolutions that are specific to women or sexual violence, I believe that we gain important insight into the Security Council's understanding of both gender-based and sexual violence when looking at these resolutions in tandem with those more broadly on civilians and those that pertain primarily to children. In doing so, we can identify a general trend from an emphasis on gender-based violence against women and girls; to a specific concern about sexual violence against 'women and girls' and sometimes 'women and children'; and finally to an explicit attention to sexual violence, regardless of those against whom it is aimed. In this section, I demonstrate that trend before turning to the way in which sexual violence, in nearly all the resolutions and the discussion around them, has come to be treated as the quintessential harm of war – for males and females as well as children and adults.

From gender-based violence to sexual violence against women and children

The treatment of civilians constitutes the primary concern of most of the resolutions, regardless of the group of civilians on which they concentrate. The two early resolutions aimed broadly at the protection of civilians in armed conflict refer to both women and children as particularly vulnerable groups that require special attention.[9] The first mention of sexual violence can be found in *Security Council Resolution 1261* (SCR 1261), passed in 1999. That resolution, which is also the first specifically on children, condemns as grave breaches the 'targeting of children' through sexual violence as well as 'killing and maiming', 'abduction and forced displacement', 'recruitment and use of children in armed conflict in violation of international law' and 'attacks on ... schools and hospitals'.[10] The same resolution is the first to mention 'gender-based violence', urging parties of armed conflict to 'protect children, in particular girls, from rape and other forms of sexual and gender-based violence'.[11] It thus sees rape as one form of both sexual and gender-based violence.

In many ways, the three early resolutions set the stage for some of the concerns that SCR 1325 addresses. Perhaps because SCR 1325 is specifically about females, however, its operative paragraphs refer to 'women and girls', rather than 'women and children', thus becoming the first resolution to suggest a strong distinction between the treatment of girl children and boy children. It calls on actors in armed conflict to protect women and girls from 'gender-based violence, particularly rape and other forms of sexual abuse, and all other forms of violence'.[12] SCR 1325 is the final resolution in the human security series of resolutions to consider sexual violence as a subset of gender-based violence.[13] Yet, all but one resolution since 1325, whether generally about civilians, or specifically about children or women, mention the need to protect that group from sexual violence.[14]

From SCR 1325 in 2000 through SCR 1820 in 2008, most of the attention on sexual violence singlled out women and girls as particularly vulnerable to it. Thus, while those resolutions no longer discuss 'gender-based violence', which would presumably include the gendered effects or motives of other types of violence, they see sexual violence as gendered in that they consider women and girls as most in need of protection against it. In the resolutions on children, certain girls are noted to be particularly at risk, with those who are 'sexually exploited' offered as an example of a vulnerable group alongside those 'heading households, orphaned' and 'used as combatants'.[15] Two resolutions on children also list women as a subject of concern, grouped alongside children, 'especially girls', as most likely to suffer sexual exploitation in armed conflict.[16] A 2004 resolution on children contains much the same list of harms against children as is contained in the first children's resolution, discussed above. It adds to 'rape and other sexual violence', however, that it is 'mostly committed against girls'.[17]

Although a 2005 and a 2006 resolutions (one on children and one on civilians) fail to distinguish between boy and girl children for the purposes of sexual violence,[18] SCR 1820, the 2008 resolution that was the second specifically on women and the first to look nearly exclusively at sexual violence against women, again identifies girls as particularly vulnerable.

Unlike SCR 1325, SCR 1820 does not see sexual violence as an example or subset of gender-based violence. In fact, the term 'gender' is used only once in the resolution.[19] Rather, the predominant concern of the resolution, as I discuss further below, is sexual violence against civilians, particularly against women and girls. Although most of the references are to women and girls, the resolution does sometimes refer to 'women and children'. As with other resolutions that use such a reference, SCR 1820 arguably expresses a gendered understanding of sexual exploitation and violence that equates what happens to children with what happens to women.

Since SCR 1820, however, the resolutions have become increasingly gender-neutral, with regard both to children and adults. As we see further below, sexual violence has also become increasingly and explicitly divorced from gender-based violence.

From sexual violence against women and girls to sexual violence against everyone

Almost immediately after it was passed, SCR 1820 came under attack for a number of reasons. In addition to those who complained that its focus is on women as victims rather than as agents of change,[20] some critics contended that the resolution's treatment of women and girls as the primary victims of sexual violence fails to take into account the ways that men might be victims of sexual violence. Even though the resolution at times references sexual violence against civilians, one commentator has maintained that the resolution's 'focus provides no space to think about the rape of men, nor to think about how forcing a man to rape a woman can be understood as a form of gender based violence'.[21]

Subsequent resolutions, beginning with the four passed in 2009, retreat from at least this reading of SCR 1820, by explicitly expanding concerns about sexual violence to all children (not just girls) and arguably to all civilians (men as well as women).[22] Because the resolutions no longer refer to gender-based violence, they concentrate on the sexual aspect of the violence rather than its gendered implications – for males or females.[23]

The beginning of this shift can be seen in the 2009 resolutions. With the exception of SCR 1889, which continues SCR 1325's emphasis on women and peacebuilding and references women and girls throughout the text,[24] the resolutions are mostly gender-neutral, at least with regard to children. SCR 1888, for example, primarily concerned like SCR 1820 with sexual violence, generally replaces the 'women and girls' language found in SCR 1325 and SCR 1820 with 'women and children' (to read more like the resolutions on children and civilians).[25] The resolution also refers to the sexual violence committed more broadly against civilians,[26] although noting at times that civilians include 'women and children',[27] who are often in 'particular' need of protection.[28]

SCR 1888's failure to distinguish between boy and girl children is also seen in *Security Council Resolution 1882* (SCR 1882), the 2009 resolution on children that is largely about sexual violence. SCR 1882, however, does not group children with women, as does SCR 1888 or as had earlier children's resolutions. Moreover, the language in SCR 1882 is gender-neutral. Boy children are apparently included as subjects of the resolution's 'concern about the high incidence and appalling levels of rape and other forms of sexual violence'.[29] Subsequent resolutions on children – *Security Council Resolution 1998* in 2011 and *Security Council Resolution 2068* in 2012 – continue the gender-neutral language and leave out references to women as in the same category as children.[30]

This move toward gender neutrality with regard to children was extended to adults in 2010, in SCR 1960. That resolution has sexual violence as its theme, and it sets up what the UN itself has called a 'naming and shaming' mechanism, by which 'parties credibly suspected of patterns of sexual violence' are to be listed, along with detailed information on such parties, in annual reports required to be submitted by the Secretary-General under SCR 1820 and SCR 1888.[31] Although one preambular paragraph mentions women and children as particular targets of sexual violence and another notes that the UN Security Council has repeatedly condemned such violence,[32] most of the preambular paragraphs and all of the operative paragraphs are gender-neutral.

The resolution uses the term 'conflict-related sexual violence',[33] and reflects an intentional move away from previous terminology. According to Margot Wallström, who was at the time the Secretary-General's Special Representative on Sexual Violence in Conflict, the new explicit concentration on sexual violence was needed because

[s]exual violence as a tactic or consequence of war could not be captured under existing categories. Cases against men and boys did

not fall under 'violence against women'; 'harmful traditional practices' mischaracterised sexual violence as cultural or traditional; and 'gender-based violence' did not reflect sexual violence as a method of ethnic cleansing or a tactic of terror.[34]

Similarly, UN Action's summary of its 'Analytical & Conceptual Framing of Conflict-Related Sexual Violence', put together to determine the criteria by which parties would be listed under the resolution, considers SCR 1960 as a recognition by the Security Council that conflict-related sexual violence is a 'self-standing issue of concern'.[35] 'To foster greater specificity and disaggregation of incidents', UN Action contends that 'conflict-related sexual violence should no longer be treated as synonymous or interchangeable with' a number of terms, including 'gender-based violence' and 'violence against women'.[36] For the listing purpose of SCR 1960, UN Action defines conflict-related sexual violence as 'rape, sexual slavery, forced prostitution, forced pregnancy, enforced sterilization, or any other form of sexual violence of comparable gravity, *against women, men, girls or boys*'.[37]

The Security Council's gender neutrality in SCR 1960 has been lauded by many, including Harvard University's Program on Humanitarian Policy and Conflict, which notes that the resolution is distinct from 'previous resolutions in the Women, Peace, and Security thematic agenda topic', asserting that it is important that 'the resolution's operative paragraphs implicitly recognize that adult men may also be victims of sexual violence in armed conflict'.[38] For others, however, the separation of sexual violence from gender is problematic. As the Women's International League for Peace and Freedom states in the report on a 2011 conference it sponsored:

> sexual violence in conflict and post-conflict settings should ... be understood as a component of a broader category of gender based violence. ... [I]f SGVB [sexual and gender-based violence] is approached too narrowly, donor agents run the risk of attacking the symptom while failing to thoroughly address discriminating gender relations as one of the underlying problems.[39]

In June 2013, the Security Council passed a follow-up resolution on sexual violence in conflict. Expressing deep concern with 'the slow implementation' of SCR 1960, SCR 2106 offers greater operational detail than SCR 1960, and also focuses more intensely on ending impunity for sexual violence. Moreover, it explicitly recognises men and boys as victims of sexual violence, thereby confirming the trend toward gender neutrality that some have read into SCR 1960 and that I date back to even earlier resolutions.[40]

Without commenting directly on the debate about whether sexual violence against men and women should be treated similarly or receive equal amounts of attention, I hope to have documented here the way in which the focus on violence against women in conflict has, over the years, been transformed into a more generalised concern with to sexual violence – against everyone. My aim is to draw attention to and question the assumption that the sexual component of the violence is what makes it particularly harmful.

The harm of sexual violence

The Security Council resolutions might have, over the years, suggested varying views on who are the principal victims of sexual violence, but they have all been in agreement that the harm suffered is significant. In line with the second broad trend in human rights that I identified in the introduction to this chapter, the resolutions increasingly refer to sexual violence as an international criminal matter, indicating that it can constitute a war crime, a crime against humanity or an act of genocide, as well as a violation of other prohibitions listed under the *Rome Statute of the International Criminal Court*.[41] They also increasingly refer to the need to end impunity for sexual violence, such that the UN titled the Security Council debate that preceded passage of SCR 2106 'Addressing Impunity: Effective Justice for Crimes of Sexual Violence in Conflict'.[42] SCRs 1325 and 1820 specifically consider the exclusion of sexual violence from amnesty provisions. While in SCR 1325, such exclusion should be made 'where feasible', no such qualifying language appears in SCR 1820.[43]

To the extent that the resolutions further delineate the harm of sexual violence as an international crime, they often describe it as a tactic of war distinguished from a group of isolated events. At least in some articulations, the harm of shame constitutes a principal motive for the use of sexual violence as a war tactic. This view can be found, for example, in SCR 1820, which notes 'that civilians account for the vast majority of those adversely affected by armed conflict; that women and girls are particularly targeted by the use of sexual violence, including as a tactic of war to humiliate, dominate, instil fear in, disperse and/or forcibly relocate civilian members of a community or ethnic group'.[44] As we will see in the next section, UN Action uses similar language in its public campaign against sexual violence in conflict. This description of the harm also follows the reasoning of the International Criminal Tribunal for Rwanda in its conviction of Jean-Paul Akayesu of responsibility for acts of rape that were found to be constitutive of genocide, in part because of the public humiliation brought by the rapes and the resulting 'physical and psychological destruction of Tutsi women, their families and their communities'.[45] In this understanding, sexual violence humiliates not only women and girls, but also their communities. It instils fear and shame in the entire community so that the community disperses or relocates.

SCRs 1888, 1960 and 2106 also refer to sexual violence as a tactic of war, though without articulating the motives behind its use.[46] That said, the discourse surrounding the resolutions repeats some of the assumptions of shame, which, as the victim class expands, are now often extended to men. In a speech congratulating the Security Council for its passage of SCR 1960, for example, Secretary-General Ban Ki-moon stated: 'Victims are shamed and marginalised. Their husbands reject them. Men and boys who are sexually attacked often suffer isolation and discrimination. Just when these individuals need support from their communities, it falls away'.[47] And there is more: 'Sexual violence shatters lives, devastates countries and destroys hope'. It is almost impossible to recover from, which means that '[v]ictims who might have contributed to development are shunned. Girls who might have grown into great leaders cannot even attend school'.[48] Rape victims are thus seen as different from most women and girls outside the west who, as Inderpal Grewal has noted, are 'represented as objects of charity and care by the West but could become subjects who could participate in the global economy and become global citizens'.[49] To do that – or for 'women' to be recognised as 'human' – as she puts it, they must become autonomous individuals who could recognise their oppressions and struggle to become citizens of a global society.[50]

The Security Council resolutions and attendant discourse treat victims of sexual violence, and perhaps the communities from which they hail, as beyond even the type of subjectivity that Grewal describes. Others must step in to prevent, protect and – now the increasingly proposed solution – prosecute so as to end impunity with the hope that doing so will stop sexual violence before it is allowed to cause its inevitable harm. SCR 1960 proposes the shaming of perpetrators as the response to the harm of shame experienced by victims. The resolution's mandate to create a 'list of shame', as the UN has referred to it,[51] aims to transfer the shame from the victims to the perpetrators of the violence.

This general understanding of the harm of sexual violence seen in the Security Council is reflective of international humanitarian law more generally and is in need of contestation. Yet, it is often accepted, even by its critics. The Global Network of Women Peacebuilders, for example, in a critical open letter to members of the Security Council complaining that SCR 1960 'speaks only of women as victims of sexual abuse during conflict and does not mention that if women were recognized as participants in decision making they would be less vulnerable to attack', includes language about the effects of rape that largely agrees with 1960 and similar previous resolutions. According to the letter, '[r]ape is the worst crime that women or men can endure and survive. The trauma lasts a lifetime and has ripple consequences of ostracism from family and community as well as physical damage'.[52]

This approach perpetuates the understanding of rape as a 'fate worse than death', projecting a Victorian idea of the effects of loss of honour – which, as Hilary Charlesworth told us long ago, feminists had hoped to distance themselves from[53] – onto women (and all children and perhaps men) in war-torn countries. Only now, as I have argued elsewhere, their communities (even those that have been victims of forced displacement, ethnic cleansing or genocide) are often blamed for the effects.[54] Moreover, as we saw in the Secretary-General's statement, the resolutions, as well as the discourse that produces and supports them, reinforce the idea that women and girls (and now men and boys) who have experienced sexual violence can never be full citizens or even subjects of development in their own communities or elsewhere.

Human rights, social media and celebrity diplomacy

The Security Council resolutions and their understanding of the harm of sexual violence are mirrored in the work of UN Action, which was created in 2007 to '[unite] efforts across the UN system with the goal of ending sexual violence during and in the aftermath of armed conflict'.[55] It combines the forces of 13 different UN entities and is supported by a coordinating Secretariat that reports to the Special Representative to the Secretary-General on Sexual Violence in Conflict. It lobbied for SCR 1820 and consulted on the reporting provision of that resolution. It has also been tasked with designing the monitoring and analysis required under resolutions 1888 and 1960.[56]

Much of its effort has been put into its Stop Rape Now Campaign, which is organised around a web-based advocacy strategy based on the theme 'Get cross: No security without women's security'.[57] Through its engagement in a media campaign, UN Action demonstrates the third trend I mentioned in the introduction – the popularisation of human rights and the uses of celebrity voices to champion various social justice and philanthropic initiatives. I turn to the campaign here both to highlight this trend and to continue to study representations of the harm of sexual violence. I should note that, although UN Action has also begun to consider sexual violence against men and boys in its monitoring design, that consideration is not yet reflected in its media campaign, which only discusses women and girls.

The aims of UN Action's campaign can perhaps best be understood by a question raised by 'The Vagina Monologues' creator, Eve Ensler, who in recent years has taken her own project transnational. At the UN Action launch event at UN Headquarters, Ensler asked: 'What is it about women getting raped that isn't grabbing people's imagination, isn't seizing people's conscience or isn't getting people to stand up?'[58] I would contend that, far from being immune to rape, Ensler's imagined audience – much as the Security Council in its unanimous passage of the resolutions – was more than ready to be seized by it. Still, she and UN Action aimed to get people from around the world to 'stand up' in opposition to sexual violence in conflict. They therefore ended their launch event by having audience members stand with their arms crossed over their chests to show support for the effort. That became the campaign's symbol.

While crossed arms could be seen as a 'don't touch me' or a 'handcuffs' gesture,[59] it was used here to call on people around the world to 'get cross'. One notice read: '200,000 Women Raped during the War in Congo – 200,000 People Say Never Again. *Will you be one of them?'* Asking readers to join the 'Never Again' crowd, the notice continued: 'Add your crossed-arm photo to a growing global coalition calling for action to end sexual violence as a tactic of war and impediment to peace'.[60]

The campaign also produced a YouTube video for its website that resonates with, and indeed was meant to raise support for, SCR 1820. An anonymous narrator lists the numbers of women raped in Rwanda, Sierra Leone, the Democratic Republic of the Congo, Bosnia and Herzegovina and Darfur, and then continues as the video displays a series of images that show women and girls covering their faces with their hands or in the shadows: 'These are not the random acts of individual soldiers. They are military tactics used to shame and demoralize women, tear communities apart, and control populations'.[61]

Later, the campaign enlisted the help of Charlize Theron and Nicole Kidman in the production of a second video. Theron had recently been named a UN Ambassador for Peace 'for her work focusing attention and mobilising efforts on social issues, particularly in her native South Africa'.[62] Kidman had, since early 2006, been a Goodwill Ambassador for the UN Development Fund for Women (now UN Women).

Such bringing together of celebrities with the aim of creating, primarily in the global north, a sense of outrage about what is happening in the global south has become big business.[63] As John Colapinto explains in a March 2012 *New Yorker* article on what he calls 'the new boom in celebrity philanthropy', celebrities sometimes hire companies to help them determine what causes to support.[64] For a not insubstantial fee (US$25,000 per month), for example, the Global Philanthropy Group will work with celebrities to determine where the stars should put their attention and money. As a part of the process, the Global Philanthropy Group asks them 100 quick-fire questions, including: 'What fills you with outrage when you watch the news?'; 'What awakens your empathy?'; and 'What did your family talk about around the dinner table?'[65]

Some critics have pointed out, with regard to both celebrity charity and celebrity diplomacy, that 'celebrit[ies'] passions, rather than expert judgment', guide the allocation of funds and also affect foreign policy priorities.[66] Others have suggested that simply taxing stars at a realistic rate would make more sense than having celebrities benefit from their charitable whims,[67] particularly given that celebrities tend to avoid complex issues. As Colapinto points out, 'a complex issue like health-care-policy reform may seem less appropriate to a starlet's brand than taking a stand against puppy mills'.[68]

UN Action works within this framework of both deploying the passions of celebrities and presenting the issues in a way that eschews their complexity. For its video with its chosen movie stars, it also enlisted 'high-profile personalities representing the spectrum of actors needed to address sexual violence'.[69] Theron and Kidman thus joined three human rights celebrities (another new category resulting from the popularisation of human rights): former peacekeeper and retired Dutch Major General Patrick Cammaert, Liberian peace activist Leymah Gbowee (who has since been awarded a Nobel Peace Prize) and Congolese gynaecologist Dr Denis Mukwege. Each has been recognised internationally for work involving sexual violence against women. In a display of celebrity diplomacy in which the legitimacy of the professional humanitarians and stars is mutually reinforcing, the five made an appeal.

The roughly one-minute video begins in silence, with the camera moving through thick vegetation. Eerie music begins to play as the following segments flash on the screen:

> After killing my son ...
> they raped me.
> They called other soldiers
> dragged me into the bush
> and one after another ...
> they raped me.

Perhaps because it is assumed that it would be too shameful for a woman who has been raped in conflict to speak or to show herself – even more so than in the first video where the faces were partially obscured but attached to bodies – viewers never see or hear the imagined woman; they can only read the words attributed to her on the screen. The lack of an image of any particular person also permits Theron to appeal to viewers to identify with the victim as though she were their female relative. As the eerie music fades out, Theron emerges, standing in front of the Stop Rape Now logo and speaking to the camera slowly: 'She could be your mother, your sister, your daughter'. Of course, she assumes that the viewer would feel compassion toward the victim, not shun her as the first video suggests would her 'real' family and community.

Theron dissolves and the other speakers appear sequentially and make short statements about the dangers and harm of sexual violence: 'It is perhaps more dangerous to be a woman than a soldier in armed conflict' (Cammaert); 'Those responsible for sexual violence must be held accountable' (Kidman); 'Wars are being fought on the bodies of women and children' (Gbowee); 'Sexual violence is the monstrosity of our century' (Mukwege). Theron reappears with the final spoken message: 'Go to stoprapenow.org to learn more and to take action'. The music turns upbeat, as she moves her arms into the 'get cross' gesture. She is joined by the other speakers who also make the sign. The video ends with a shot of a larger group 'get[ting] cross', followed by a screenshot of the website's address.

The video depicts rape as harmful, but it does so much more abstractly than the first one. We are meant to understand that sexual violence is a monstrosity and that it occurs during wartime. Women and children are its unwitting victims. (Again, the video was made before the passage of SCR 1960. My guess is that any subsequent video would be gender-neutral, or at least be inclusive of men and boys.) Perpetrators should be stopped. Like the first video, this second video does not imagine a future for the victims. Rather, the aim is the production of ideal, benevolent global citizens – who do not shun raped women and who might respond to the call to stop rape now.

In this particular incarnation, the appeal depends upon 'ordinary' people's fantasies about becoming celebrities. The website to which obedient viewers are taken offers them the chance to 'take action'. The banner at the top of the main page includes an image of the five celebrities crossing their arms and a deliberately unidentifiable woman inside an orange text box that reads: 'GET CROSS! Add your image now'. Below this banner is a map of the world, with an 'x' to indicate all the countries from which people have uploaded photographs. A click on any given 'x' allows users to view all of the photographs from that country, so that all who have uploaded a photo can have their picture viewed on the same screen as the celebrities. Adding one's picture, the website makes clear, is a way to 'Take Action'; it is offered as one of the things that viewers can do 'to stop the use of rape as a weapon of war'.

To whom are these appeals made? To take action in this way requires not only that one be sympathetic. He or she must also speak English and have access to the internet, a camera and equipment for uploading photographs. Women who have been victims of rape in war play no role in the appeal, either as living, knowable victims or as agents of change to support. As we saw in the Secretary-General's statement in the previous section, they are largely seen as forever destroyed – in part due to humiliation and shame.

Conclusion

Dianne Otto has argued that the Security Council's resolutions on human security represent

> an attempt to arrest its flagging legitimacy at the end of the twentieth century by ... show[ing] its commitment to the collective good, especially to those who are more likely to be adversely affected by contemporary armed conflict and the Security Council's own interventions – namely civilians, children and, with SCR 1325, women.[70]

In its attempt to reflect, if not promote, the collective good, however, the Security Council has created a site for struggle, particularly among feminists. Even though each resolution passed unanimously, I have aimed in this chapter to demonstrate various tensions among the advocates and drafters of the resolutions, as well as ongoing debates about their meaning.

At the same time, I have sought to show how, despite those disagreements, discernible trajectories can be traced with regard to the understanding of the nature and harm of sexual violence; the groups and individuals considered to be most affected by it; and the ways in which it should be addressed. These trajectories, I contend, can be seen and even best understood by looking at all the human security resolutions, not only those on women, despite a lack of coherent advocacy regarding the various sets of resolutions. They also track trends that I identify more broadly in human rights and humanitarian law and advocacy, especially but not exclusively with regard to women's rights.

One constant in the resolutions, and in the discussion and media advocacy around them, is the sense that sexual violence is one of the greatest harms – if not the greatest harm – that one can experience during war. Increasingly, the description of the harm has been tied to the shame and stigmatisation that are seen to adhere to all victims of sexual violence – male and female – as well as to the communities and families to which they belong. The UN's appeals suggest that this shame is a given, and yet that it is limited to the communities engaged in armed conflict. UN Action therefore anticipates a different audience for its multimedia campaign, one whose members can and will sympathise with the victims as though they were their own daughters, sisters and mothers – whom of course they would never shun.

In conclusion, I want to consider the move to expand the victim class to include civilian boys and men. (Note that the perpetrator class – noncivilian men – remains unquestionably the same.) What is to be gained by creating new identity categories of raped and/or sexually assaulted civilians, particularly when shame and stigmatisation are seen invariably to attach to such violence?

Could we imagine categories beyond violated or peacemaking women and violated and violating men? Could we open ourselves to the multiple desires of women and men – economic, social, sexual and political – without reinforcing assumptions about shame and even about peace? Women's and men's lives, including their security issues, do not (need to) revolve around such dichotomies.

Notes

I am grateful to Dianne Otto and Gina Heathcote for the invitation to participate in this collection and in the exciting symposium on which it is based. I benefitted greatly from their feedback, as well as from that provided by audiences at the University of Wisconsin, Madison; Yale University, Yale Law School; and the Institute for Global Law and Policy at Harvard Law School. Many thanks to Maddy Dwertman and Sherin Varghese for their outstanding research assistance.

1. In this volume, see G. Heathcote, 'Participation, Gender And Security'; D. Otto, 'Beyond Stories of Victory and Danger: Resisting Feminism's Amenability to Serving Security Council Politics'; and F. Ruby, '*Security Council Resolution 1325*: A Tool for Conflict Prevention?'. See also S. Cook, 'Security Council Resolution 1820: On militarism, flashlights, raincoats, and rooms with doors – A political perspective on where it came from and what it adds', *Emory International Law Review*, Vol. 23, No. 1 (2009) 125, p. 127; G. Heathcote, 'Feminist politics and the use of force: Theorising feminist action and Security Council Resolution 1325', *Socio-Legal Review*, Vol. 7 (2011) 23, p. 38; G. Heathcote, 'Naming and shaming: Human rights accountability in Security Council Resolution 1960 (2010) on women, peace and security', *Journal of Human Rights Practice*, Vol. 4, No. 1 (2012) 82, pp. 85–7, 99–100; and D. Otto, 'The exile of inclusion: Reflections on gender issues in international law over the last decade', *Melbourne Journal of International Law*, Vol. 10, No. 1 (2009) 11, p. 24.

2. Although I will only touch upon this trend at a couple of points in this chapter, it deserves more thorough treatment than I am able to offer here. I have discussed this trend elsewhere, although not in the context of sexual violence. See K. Engle, 'Self-critique, (anti) politics and criminalization: Reflections on the history and trajectory of the human rights movement', in J. M. Beneyto and D. Kennedy (eds), *New Approaches to International Law: The European and American Experiences* (The Haag: TMC Asser Press, 2012) 41. Janet Halley specifically places her analysis of the treatment of rape in the *Rome Statute of the International Criminal Court*, opened for signature on 17 July 1998, 2187 UNTS 3 (entered into force on 1 July 2002) within a broader frame of criminalisation favoured by those whom she calls 'governance feminists'. See J. Halley, 'Rape at Rome: Feminist interventions in the criminalization of sex-related violence in positive international criminal law', *Michigan Journal of International Law*, Vol. 30, No. 1 (2008) 1, p. 5 (emphasis original): '[Governance feminists] seek to wield the sovereign's scepter and especially his sword. Criminal law is their preferred vehicle for reform and enforcement; and their idea of what to do with criminal law is not to manage populations, not to warn and deter, but to *end impunity* and *abolish*'.

3. As Dianne Otto posits in her critique of the overly broad zero tolerance policy for UN peacekeeping personnel, which I discuss further below: 'Sex itself becomes the harm, the total harm, divorced from the material conditions under which it takes place. Such over-determined sexual and gender stereotypes provide ready fodder for "sex panics" which can serve to displace other fears and anxieties onto sexual activity. Sexual panics not only divert attention from underlying problems, but also make it relatively easy for the state, or the international community of states, to enact new "protective" laws that extend its power to regulate erotic behavior'. D. Otto, 'Making sense of zero tolerance policies in peacekeeping sexual economies', in V.E. Munro and C.F. Stychin (eds) *Sexuality and the Law: Feminist Engagements*

(Abingdon: Routledge-Cavendish, 2007) 259, p. 262, citing A.M. Miller, 'Sexuality, violence against women, and human rights', *Health and Human Rights*, Vol. 7 (2004) 17, p. 19. Otto's analysis of sex panics draws in part upon the work of theorists Gayle S. Rubin and Carole S. Vance. See G.S. Rubin, 'Thinking sex: Notes for a radical theory of the politics of sexuality', in C.S. Vance (ed.), *Pleasure and Danger: Exploring Female Sexuality* (Boston: Routledge & Kegan Paul, 1984) 267, p. 297; C.S. Vance, 'Epilogue', in C.S. Vance (ed.), *Pleasure and Danger: Exploring Female Sexuality* (Boston: Routledge & Kegan Paul, 1984) 431, p. 434. For a discussion of how tendencies within legal feminism to account for sexuality in terms of either dependency or 'danger' combine with a focus on the harm of sexual violence to obscure those positive domains of sexuality that are often considered by queer theorists, see K. Franke, 'Theorizing yes: An essay on feminism, law, and desire', *Columbia Law Review*, Vol. 101, No. 1 (2001) 181. For a recent, provocative discussion of sex panic in the United States, including in its global interactions, see R.N. Lancaster, *Sex Panic and the Punitive State* (Berkeley: University of California Press, 2011).

4. One of the few places in which this concern is specifically mentioned with regard to the treatment of wartime sexual violence is in reference to an international gathering on gender and transitional justice in the mid-2000s. Reflecting on some of the debates that emerged at the event, Vasuki Nesiah notes that 'there were questions about whether the focus on sexual violence feeds into a regressive sex panic that is then used to regulate and further criminalize women's sexuality – with particular consequences for women who were involved in sex work in conflict contexts. Did the preoccupation with sexual violence to the exclusion of other issues accompany, and even engender, a preoccupation with "legitimate" and "illegitimate" sex, policing the borders of the "decent" and the "deviant," only to then reinscribe heteronormative models and approaches?': V. Nesiah, 'Discussion lines on gender and transitional justice: An introductory essay reflecting on the ICTJ Bellagio Workshop on Gender and Transitional Justice', *Columbia Journal of Gender and Law*, Vol. 15, No. 3 (2006) 799, p. 806.

5. On civilians generally, the resolutions are: *Security Council Resolution 1265*, UN Doc. S/RES/1265 (17 September 1999) (SCR 1265); *Security Council Resolution 1296*, UN Doc. S/RES/1296 (19 April 2000) (SCR 1296); *Security Council Resolution 1674*, UN Doc. S/RES/1674 (28 April 2006) (SCR 1674); *Security Council Resolution 1738*, UN Doc. S/RES/1738 (23 December 2006) (SCR 1738) (regarding the protection of journalists); and *Security Council Resolution 1894*, UN Doc. S/RES/1894 (11 November 2009) (SCR 1894). Those specifically on children are: *Security Council Resolution 1261*, UN Doc. S/RES/1261 (25 August 1999) (SCR 1261); *Security Council Resolution 1314*, UN Doc. S/RES/1314 (11 August 2000) (SCR 1314); *Security Council Resolution 1379*, UN Doc. S/RES/1379 (20 November 2001) (SCR 1379); *Security Council Resolution 1460*, UN Doc. S/RES/1460 (30 January 2003) (SCR 1460); *Security Council Resolution 1539*, UN Doc. S/RES1539 (22 April 2004) (SCR 1539); *Security Council Resolution 1612*, UN Doc. S/RES/1612 (26 July 2005) (SCR 1612); *Security Council Resolution 1882*, UN Doc. S/RES/1882 (4 August 2009) (SCR 1882); *Security Council Resolution 1998*, UN Doc. S/RES/1998 (12 July 2011) (SCR 1998); and *Security Council Resolution 2068*, UN Doc. S/RES/2068

(19 September 2012) (SCR 2068). Those on women are: *Security Council Resolution 1325*, UN Doc. S/RES/1325 (31 October 2000) (SCR 1325); *Security Council Resolution 1820*, UN Doc. S/RES/1820 (19 June 2008) (SCR 1820); *Security Council Resolution 1888*, UN Doc. S/RES/1888 (30 September 2009) (SCR 1888); and *Security Council Resolution 1889*, UN Doc. S/RES/1889 (5 October 2009) (SCR 1889). SCR 1325 and SCR 1889 are generally seen as applying to women as peacemakers, while the other two are primarily concerned with women as victims of sexual violence. *Security Council Resolution 1960*, UN Doc. S/RES/1960 (16 December 2010) (SCR 1960) and *Security Council Resolution 2106*, UN Doc. S/RES/2106 (24 June 2013) (SCR 2106) contain a thematic focus on sexual violence, and apply to all of the categories above. As this book was going to press, the Security Council passed its 21st such resolution, *Security Council Resolution 2122*, UN Doc. S/RES/2122 (18 October 2013) (SCR 2122). It follows SCR 1325 and SCR 1889 in its focus on women as peacemakers, thereby leapfrogging over SCR 1960 and SCR 2106.

6. See SCR 1894 (civilians generally); SCR 1882 (children); SCR 1888 (women as victims); and SCR 1889 (women as peacemakers).

7. In this volume, see Heathcote, 'Participation, Gender And Security'; L.J. Shepherd, 'The Road to (and from) "Recovery": A Multidisciplinary Feminist Approach to Peacekeeping and Peacebuilding'; S. Bhagwan Rolls, 'Thinking Globally and Acting Locally: Linking Women, Peace and Security in the Pacific'; Otto, 'Beyond Stories of Victory and Danger'; Ruby, 'Security Council Resolution 1325'; and O. Simić, 'Increasing Women's Presence in Peacekeeping Operations: The Rationales and Realities of "Gender Balance"'. For a thorough discussion of SCR 1325, its situation in the women's peace movement and its gender representations both in the language of the resolution and in its implementation, see D. Otto, 'A sign of "weakness"? Disrupting gender certainties in the implementation of Security Council Resolution 1325', *Michigan Journal of Gender and Law*, Vol. 13, No. 1 (2006) 113.

8. An article on the October 2013 passage of SCR 2122, for example, notes that the 'focus on peace processes in the new resolution is seen by some as a way of rebalancing the emphasis on violence in conflict [seen in SCR 2106] to the important role women can play in conflict resolution'. L. Ford, 'UN passes new resolution on women's role in peace processes', *The Guardian* (21 October 2013), http://www.theguardian.com/global-development/2013/oct/21/un-resolution-2122-women-peace-processes (last accessed October 2013).

9. See, for example, SCR 1265, preamble para. 4 ('gravely concerned by the hardships borne by civilians during armed conflict … especially women, children, and other vulnerable groups'); SCR 1296, para. 9 ('*Reaffirms* its grave concern at the harmful and widespread impact that armed conflict has on women, children and other vulnerable groups' (emphasis original). For discussion of the ways in which the category 'women and children' has long been a stand-in for the category 'civilian', see generally H.M. Kinsella, *Image before the Weapon: A Critical History of the Distinction between Combatant and Civilian* (Ithaca: Cornell University Press, 2011).

10. SCR 1261, para. 2. SCR 1539, SCR 1882, SCR 1998 and SCR 2068 also list sexual violence in the context of these other grave breaches against children,

but add 'denial of humanitarian access' as a violation of primary concern. SCR 1539 also lists 'trafficking, forced labour and all forms of slavery'.

11. SCR 1261, para. 10.
12. SCR 1325, para. 10.
13. Only one resolution passed prior to SCR 1960 uses the term 'gender-based violence' and it lists it alongside, but potentially separates from, sexual violence. SCR 1674, para. 5. The term similarly appears on occasion in SCR 1960 and SCR 2106 (SCR 1960, para. 15; SCR 2106, preamble para. 10, paras. 9, 14, 16(c)). These few mentions of gender-based violence in the latter two resolutions, however, should be contrasted with the nearly 50 references to sexual violence in each of them.
14. The only exception to this inclusion of sexual violence is SCR 1738, which is primarily about protecting journalists during times of conflict.
15. SCR 1314, para. 13; and SCR 1379, para. 11.
16. SCR 1460, para. 10; and SCR 1539, para. 10.
17. SCR 1539, para. 1. SCR 1612, in 2005, does not include such language.
18. See SCR 1612 on children; and SCR 1674, para. 5.
19. SCR 1820, para. 11.
20. See Note 1. Otto also complains that the resolution perpetuates several myths, including 'that sexual violence is "the worst" harm, even worse than death, that can happen to women', often placing them in a privileged position vis-à-vis other women and men affected by war: Otto, 'The exile of inclusion', p. 24.
21. P. Scully, 'Vulnerable women: A critical reflection on human rights discourse and sexual violence', *Emory International Law Review*, Vol. 23, No. 1 (2009) 113, p. 117. Sandesh Sivakumaran has made a similar critique, though she acknowledges that the resolution is not limited to females in its description of the 'problem of sexual violence'. Still, the exclusory language of 'women and girls' is used when 'specifying concrete, detailed measures of implementation or enforcement'. S. Sivakumaran, 'Lost in translation: UN responses to sexual violence against men and boys in situations of armed conflict', *International Review of the Red Cross*, Vol. 92, No. 877 (2010) 259, pp. 266–8.
22. Sivakumaran discusses how, by 2009, the Secretary-General had begun to interpret SCR 1820 in gender-neutral terms. Its report on SCR 1820 from that year, for example, notes that '[w]hile women and girls are particular targets and are the majority of the victims of sexual violence, the case-law of the International Criminal Tribunal for the Former Yugoslavia (ICTY) and the Special Court for Sierra Leone (SCSL) also bears testimony to the use of sexual violence against men'. Sivakumaran, 'Lost in translation', p. 273, quoting *Report of the Secretary-General pursuant to Security Council Resolution 1820*, UN Doc. S/2009/362 (15 July 2009).
23. This is not to say that there are no gendered assumptions about the meaning of rape for males and females, but only that there is no explicit discussion of it nor even any further reference to 'gender-based violence' in the 2009 resolutions.
24. Even though it explicitly expresses concern that women in conflict situations 'continue to be often considered as victims and not as actors in addressing and resolving situations of armed conflict', as with SCR 1325, it

contains operative paragraphs on violence. Both such paragraphs reference 'all forms of violence', a term that includes 'rape and sexual violence' against women and girls. See SCR 1889, paras 3, 12. The latter paragraph calls for the protection of all civilians from all forms of violence, but adds 'in particular women and girls'. The same language appears earlier in SCR 1820, though without the 'in particular' language. See SCR 1820, para. 2.

25. The one exception is in the preamble, when it mentions the lack of progress in eradicating sexual violence 'in particular against women and children, notably against girls'. See SCR 1888, preamble para. 2.

26. See SCR 1888, para. 2 (emphasis original): '*Reiterates* its demand for the complete cessation by all parties to armed conflict of all acts of sexual violence with immediate effect'.

27. See SCR 1888, para. 3.

28. See SCR 1888, paras 3, 25.

29. SCR 1882, preamble para. 12. See also paras 1, 3, 16.

30. See SCR 1998, paras 1, 6(a), 6(b); SCR 2068, para. 2.

31. SCR 1960, para. 3. For extensive discussion and critique of this resolution, see Heathcote, 'Naming and shaming'. SCR 1379 (2001) on children and armed conflict was the first of the resolutions on human security to implement a requirement that the Secretary-General list violating parties, in that case those who 'recruit or use children in violation of ... international obligations': SCR 1379, para. 16. SCR 1882 (2009) added a listing requirement for those who commit sexual violence against anyone under 18. SCR 1882, para. 3.

32. See SCR 1960, preamble paras 2, 3.

33. SCR 1960, para. 8.

34. United Nations Department of Public Information, 'Security Council Adopts Text Requesting Detailed Information on Suspected Perpetrators of Sexual Violence during Armed Conflict' (Press Release No. SC/10122, United Nations, 16 December 2010).

35. UN Action against Sexual Violence in Conflict, 'Analytical & conceptual framing of conflict-related sexual violence: Summary' (UN Action, June 2011), p. 3. The complete document is not publicly available.

36. UN Action, 'Analytical & conceptual framing of conflict-related sexual violence', p. 3. The summary further explains that '[g]ender-based violence (GBV), which includes acts that are not sexual in nature, such as physical assault or the denial of economic resources, ... is an overly-broad category for 1960 reporting purposes'. It also distinguishes sexual violence from 'harmful traditional practices' (without 'specific justification' for equating them), 'sexual exploitation and abuse' (which it claims is dealt with elsewhere) and 'survival sex' ('unless the circumstances are coercive and vitiate consent'). It appears that the document might have been responding to criticisms from a number of different perspectives, including those regarding the zero tolerance policy on sexual exploitation and abuse. For criticisms of the zero tolerance policy from feminist perspectives, see, for example, Otto, 'Making sense of zero tolerance policies'; D. Otto, 'The sexual tensions of UN peacekeeping operations: A plea for "sexual positivity"', *Finnish Yearbook of International Law*, Vol. 18 (2007) 33; O. Simić, *Regulation of Sexual Conduct in UN Peacekeeping Operations* (New York: Springer, 2012).

37. UN Action, 'Analytical & conceptual framing of conflict-related sexual violence', p. 3 (emphasis added). The Secretary-General's 2012 report submitted pursuant to SCR 1960 also makes clear the need to attend to male victims. See *Conflict-Related Sexual Violence: Report of the Secretary-General*, UN Doc. A/66/657–S/2012/33 (13 January 2013), para. 3: 'Sexual violence, and the long shadow of terror and trauma it casts, disproportionately affects women and girls. However, recent information underscores that the situation of male victims and the plight of children born as a result of wartime rape require deeper examination'.

38. D. Lewis, 'New UN "listing" mechanism aimed at combating sexual violence in armed conflict', *Program on Humanitarian Policy and Conflict Research, Harvard University* (20 December 2010), http://www.hpcrresearch.org/blog/dustinlewis/2010-12-20/new-un-listing-mechanism-aimed-combating-sexual-violence-armed-conflict (last accessed October 2013). This response is part of a growing literature on sexual violence against men in conflict. See, for example, C. Lewis, 'Systemic Silencing: Addressing Sexual Violence against Men and Boys in Armed Conflict and its Aftermath', in this volume; M.E. Baaz and M. Stern, 'The complexity of violence: A critical analysis of sexual violence in the Democratic Republic of Congo (DRC)' (Working Paper on Gender Based Violence, Swedish International Development Cooperation Agency, May 2010), pp. 43–7; S. Sivakumaran, 'Sexual violence against men in armed conflict', *European Journal of International Law*, Vol. 18, No. 2 (2007) 253; Sivakumaran, 'Lost in translation', pp. 259–277; S. Solangon and P. Patel, 'Sexual violence against men in countries affected by armed conflict', *Conflict, Security & Development*, Vol. 12, No. 4 (2012) 417; United Nations High Commissioner for Refugees, 'Working with men and boy survivors of sexual and gender-based violence in forced displacement' (Need to Know Guidance No. 4, United Nations High Commissioner for Refugees, 2012).

39. Women's International League for Peace and Freedom, 'From impunity to accountability: Ending impunity for sexual and gender based violence in conflict and post-conflict settings' (Women's International League for Peace and Freedom, June 2011), p. 4.

40. That said, the resolution emphasises that women and girls experience disproportionate victimisation. See SCR 2106, preamble para. 6 ('Noting with concern that sexual violence in armed conflict and post-conflict situations disproportionately affects women and girls, as well as groups that are particularly vulnerable or may be specifically targeted, while also affecting men and boys and those secondarily traumatized as forced witnesses of sexual violence against family members').

41. The first resolution specifically calling for a criminal justice response to sexual violence is SCR 1325 (2000), which '*[e]mphasizes* the responsibility of all States to put an end to impunity and to prosecute those responsible for genocide, crimes against humanity, and war crimes including those relating to sexual and other violence against women and girls, and in this regard *stresses* the need to exclude these crimes, where feasible from amnesty provisions'. SCR 1325, para. 11 (emphasis original). But calls for ending impunity appear with greater frequency in subsequent resolutions, particularly those regarding women and children and in SCR 1960 and SCR 2106 on sexual violence. In the resolutions on children, ending sexual violence was

generally framed as a goal of humanitarian intervention/peacekeeping until SCR 1882 in 2009, which explicitly '*[c]alls upon* concerned Member States to ... bring to justice those responsible for such violations that are prohibited under applicable international law ... through national justice systems, and where applicable, international justice mechanisms and mixed criminal courts and tribunals, with a view to ending impunity for those committing crimes against children'. SCR 1882, para. 16 (emphasis original).

42. See United Nations Department of Public Information, 'Understanding Extent of Sexual Violence in Conflict Essential for Effectively Protecting Women, Girls, Secretary-General Tells Security Council Debate' (Press Release No. SC/11044, United Nations, 24 June 2013), which includes the title of the debate in its publication of the Secretary-General's remarks. For the debate itself, in which nearly every speaker discusses the need to end impunity, see United Nations Security Council, *Agenda: Women, Peace and Security – Sexual Violence in Conflict*, UN Doc. S/PV.6984 (24 June 2013). For an example of the resolution's focus on ending impunity, see para. 2 ('*calls upon* Member States to comply with their relevant obligations to continue to fight impunity by investigating and prosecuting those subject to their jurisdiction who are responsible for such crimes; *encourages* Member States to include the full range of crimes of sexual violence in national penal legislation to enable prosecutions for such acts; *recognizes* that effective investigation and documentation of sexual violence in armed conflict is instrumental both in bringing perpetrators to justice and ensuring access to justice for survivors' (emphasis original)).

43. See SCR 1325, para. 11; SCR 1820, para. 4. Identical language to that found in SCR 1325 can also be found with regard to amnesty for crimes against children more broadly in SCR 1314, para. 2 and SCR 1379, para. 9(a). Although the amnesty language is absent from the 2009 resolutions, it reappears in SCR 2106. See SCR 2106, para. 12.

44. SCR 1820, preamble para. 6.

45. *Prosecutor v. Akayesu (Judgement)* (International Criminal Tribunal for Rwanda, Trial Chamber I, Case No. ICTR 96-4, 2 September 1998), para. 731. I have critiqued this reasoning elsewhere. See K. Engle and A. Lottman, 'The force of shame', in C. McGlynn and V.E. Munro (eds), *Rethinking Rape Law: International and Comparative Perspectives* (New York: Routledge, 2010) 76.

46. All three resolutions do refer to some effects of its use as a tactic of war, stating that it 'can significantly exacerbate ... situations of armed conflict and may impede the restoration of international peace and security'. SCR 1888, para. 1; SCR 1960, para. 1; and SCR 2106, para. 1.

47. Ban Ki-moon, 'Statement to Security Council open debate on sexual violence in conflict', *UN News Centre* (16 December 2010), http://www.un.org/apps/news/infocus/sgspeeches/search_full.asp?statID=1038 (last accessed October 2013).

48. Ban Ki-moon, 'Statement to Security Council open debate on sexual violence in conflict'.

49. I. Grewal, *Transnational America: Feminisms, Diasporas, Neoliberalisms* (Durham: Duke University Press, 2005), p. 130.

50. Grewal, *Transnational America*.

51 For this use of the term in the context of the children's resolutions, see United Nations Department of Public Information, 'Security Council

Reaffirms Commitment to Address Widespread Impact of Armed Conflict on Children, after Hearing over 60 Speakers in Day-Long Debate' (Press Release No. SC/9646, United Nations, 29 April 2009): 'Secretary-General Ban Ki-moon urged the 15-nation body to "strike a blow against [...] impunity", by, at a minimum, expanding its criteria to include on the so-called "list of shame", parties committing rape and other serious sexual violence against children in armed conflict'.

52. 'UNSCR 1960 and the need for focus on full implementation of UNSCR 1325: Open letter to member states of the Security Council re: Res 1960', *The Global Network of Women Peacebuilders* (7 January 2011), http://www.gnwp.org/unscr-1960-and-the-need-for-focus-on-full-implementation-of-unscr-1325 (last accessed October 2013). I learned about this letter from Gina Heathcote's work. See Heathcote, 'Naming and shaming', p. 11.

53. See H. Charlesworth, 'Not waving but drowning: Gender mainstreaming and human rights in the United Nations', *Harvard Human Rights Journal*, Vol. 18 (2005) 1.

54. See, for example, Engle and Lottman, 'The force of shame'; K. Engle, 'Feminism and its (dis)contents: Criminalizing wartime rape in Bosnia and Herzegovina', *American Journal of International Law*, Vol. 99, No. 4 (2005) 778. Many thanks to Frédéric Mégret for helping me articulate this implication of some of my early work.

55. UN Action, 'Strategic framework 2011–2012' (UN Action, January 2011), p. 3.

56. UN Action, 'Strategic framework 2011–2012', p. 3.

57. UN Action, 'Strategic framework 2011–2012', p. 7.

58. R.B. Carter, '"Stop rape now": UN agencies against sexual violence as a tactic of war', *UNICEF* (5 March 2007), http://www.unicef.org/protection/57929_38552.html (last accessed October 2013).

59. I have learned that the 'handcuffs gesture' has become quite controversial during sports matches. See, for example, Soccernet Staff, 'Mourinho handed three-match ban for handcuffs gesture', *ESPN FC* (22 February 2010), http://soccernet.espn.go.com/news/story?id=745726&sec=europe&cc=5901 (last accessed October 2013); J. Ley, 'Chelsea's Salomon Kalou denies "handcuff" goal celebrations gesture', *The Telegraph* (29 January 2009), http://www.telegraph.co.uk/sport/football/teams/chelsea/4383376/Chelseas-Salomon-Kalou-denies-handcuff-goal-celebrations-gesture.html (last accessed October 2013).

60. UN Action, 'Get cross! Join the Stop Rape Now Campaign', *Say No: Unite to End Violence against Women* (1 February 2010), http://saynotoviolence.org/join-say-no/get-cross-join-stop-rape-now-campaign (last accessed October 2013).

61. The video, *Stop Rape Now*, is available at *Stop Rape Now: UN Action against Sexual Violence in Conflict*, http://www.stoprapenow.org (last accessed October 2013).

62. 'Actor and advocate Charlize Theron named UN messenger of peace', *UN News Centre* (14 November 2008), http://www.un.org/apps/news/story.asp?NewsID=28951 (last accessed October 2013).

63. The roles that celebrities play in raising money and affecting foreign policy have also become a significant focus of the relatively new field of celebrity studies. See, for example, the special issue of *Celebrity Studies*,

entitled 'Celebrity and the transnational', at Vol. 2, No. 1 (2011) 1, as well as its forum on 'The legacies of Oprah Winfrey', at Vol. 3, No. 1 (2012) 104 (Various Authors).

64. J. Colapinto, 'Looking good: The new boom in celebrity philanthropy', *The New Yorker* (26 March 2012) 56.
65. Colapinto, 'Looking good', p. 60.
66. Colapinto, 'Looking good', p. 61, citing an interview with Ken Berger. See also K. Lofton and B.R. Weber, 'The legacies of Oprah Winfrey: Celebrity, activism and reform in the twenty-first century', *Celebrity Studies*, Vol. 3, No. 1 (2012) 104; and M.K. Goodman and C. Barnes, 'Star/poverty space: The making of the "development celebrity"', *Celebrity Studies*, Vol. 2, No. 1 (2011) 69.
67. See, for example, J. Peck, 'Looking a gift horse in the mouth: Oprah Winfrey and the politics of philanthropy', *Celebrity Studies*, Vol. 3, No. 1 (2012) 106.
68. Colapinto, 'Looking good', p. 61, citing an interview with Ken Berger.
69. UN Action, 'Second consolidated annual progress report on activities implemented through the UN Action against Sexual Violence in Conflict multi donor trust fund' (United Nations Development Programme, 31 May 2011), p. 11. The 'Stop rape now PSA' is available at *Stop Rape Now: UN Action against Sexual Violence in Conflict*, http://stoprapenow.org/ (last accessed October 2013).
70. Otto, 'The exile of inclusion', p. 21.

2
Participation, Gender and Security

Gina Heathcote

The conflict and post-conflict period in the Papua New Guinea (PNG) province of Bougainville provides a useful case study for the examination of the participation components of the women, peace and security framework. The matrilineal community structures,[1] as well as women's roles in negotiating peace in Bougainville,[2] reveal the complexity and variation of gender norms that require attention in strategies to enhance women's participation in conflict resolution and post-conflict decision-making structures. The conflict in Bougainville extended from 1988 through to 2001. On 31 August 2001, the *Bougainville Peace Agreement* was signed and the demilitarisation processes, as well as the withdrawal of PNG forces, commenced.[3] The Bougainville shift toward peace straddles the period in which the Security Council's women, peace and security framework mushroomed from a single resolution, adopted in 2000,[4] to a sequence of seven resolutions on women, peace and security by the end of 2013.[5] The combination of the emergent international understanding of the nexus between women, peace and security and the central role of Bougainville women in local decision-making structures, as well as the general sense of collective security achieved,[6] suggests that Bougainville might also be expected to be a story of success in relation to gender-balanced participation.

Yet women's representation in the central post-conflict institution, the Autonomous Bougainville Government (ABG), is low because it is effectively capped by a quota of three seats for women in the 39-seat government. This low quota was adopted despite the prevalence of matrilineal power structures in Bougainville, despite women playing a crucial role during the conflict in the shift toward peace and despite women in the post-conflict period continuing to play a significant role in community decision-making away from the formal decision-making forums. Addressing the unequal participation of women in the formal structures of the Bougainville government becomes increasingly urgent as the independence referendum, scheduled for between 2015 and 2020, looms.[7]

This chapter examines the components of the women, peace and security framework that are centred on women's participation and how these contain a narrow understanding of women's subjectivity that risks gender and cultural essentialism.[8] I build on Ratna Kapur's argument that a multidimensional understanding of subjectivity is required to foreground the multilayered experience of women.[9] While Kapur's analysis is applied to the international human rights framework and the development of strategies within that framework to challenge violence against women, I take Kapur's claims about the need for recognition of women's diverse roles,[10] as well as the need to challenge the normative assumptions in international institutions,[11] and consider them in the context of the Security Council's women, peace and security resolutions. Kapur connects gender essentialism with cultural essentialism,[12] demonstrating how international instruments geared towards protecting women in the third world often rely on cultural essentialism to diminish the importance of local knowledge and understanding. Kapur also argues in favour of feminist legal projects that take peripheral subjects as a starting point to disrupt 'the normative assumptions about gender, sexuality and culture' within existing power structures.[13]

The autonomous province of Bougainville exists on the periphery of mainstream international attention for a range of reasons. Bougainville is not a state and thus is often invisible within the international legal system that prioritises the interests of states. Further, as a matrilineal community, Bougainville disrupts western assumptions about how gender relations function within a community, including assumptions about non-western communities and traditional practices that are often assumed to contain negative gender stereotypes. In this sense, Bougainville, and in particular Bougainville women, provide a view of international law from the peripheries. With little capacity to contribute directly to the Security Council's agenda, yet the subjects of post-conflict processes, the peripheral subjects of peacebuilding are also the recipients of the Security Council's women, peace and security agenda. Following Kapur, to transform peacebuilding requires seeing the experiences and knowledge of peripheral subjects as relevant to the normative contours of the Security Council's work on women, peace and security.

The people of Bougainville are postcolonial subjects that have twice been subjected to forms of colonisation: first, through the region's colonial history, including the international community's mandate and trusteeship systems and, second, through the incorporation, at the end of the trusteeship period, of Bougainville into the larger state of PNG. In addition to both of these processes, the role of economic interests, particularly with respect to the operation of the Panguna copper mine,[14] led to further economic subjugation and external interventions into Bougainville from western mining multinationals.[15] Current debates about the return of multinational mining corporations to Bougainville indicate the precarious relationship between the province and western economic actors.[16] As postcolonial subjects, women in Bougainville exist on the peripheries of international debates and international decision-making structures;[17] yet, as Bougainville landowners, women are central to local dispute resolution, as well business and economic decision-making.

It is important to acknowledge that the Security Council's provisions for participation in the women, peace and security framework retain some resonance with feminist goals and represent hard-won feminist achievements.[18] However, without consideration of alternative feminist practices articulated by peripheral subjects and without appreciation of the lessons to be learnt from past peacebuilding operations, the gendered assumptions within international instruments continue to draw from primarily white, western and economically privileged women's experiences. As a result, the women, peace and security resolutions reinforce negative stereotypes of the non-western victim subject, to whom restricted agency and seemingly perpetual vulnerability are attributed and who are dislocated from formal global and local decision-making processes.

In the following section of the chapter I examine how the women, peace and security framework addresses participation. While considerable attention has been focussed on the Security Council's sexual violence resolutions, I provide an analysis of the participation directives in *Security Council Resolution 1325* (SCR 1325) and *Security Council Resolution 1889* (SCR 1889), as well as a short description of the narrower participation components in the sexual violence resolutions.[19] I then turn to *Security Council Resolution 2122* (SCR 2122) and examine its potential to transform future Security Council participation strategies. At the same time I acknowledge the persistence of three specific assumptions about gender across the seven resolutions: the persistence of gender as a term that can be collapsed to refer to women (and girls); the continued adoption of strategies for counting women rather than transforming gender relations; and the limited application of the resolutions to the decision-making structures of the Security Council.

After considering the participation components of the various resolutions I turn to the Bougainville case study and illustrate the limited model of participation developed in the post-conflict period in Bougainville. I argue that the excluded voices of Bougainville women, together with other peripheral subjects, need to be heard and used to reshape the Security Council's women, peace and security participation framework. Listening to peripheral subjects requires a turn toward complex understandings of subjectivity and requires consideration of gender as implicated in power relations rather than as an isolated site of discrimination and harm. The process of making visible multidimensional subjectivity also requires an understanding of how gender intersects with additional factors that limit (or facilitate) access to participation.

Throughout I argue for the need for the Security Council to examine its own participation practices, which must be changed to include women from the social and economic peripheries. There may exist, in SCR 2122, productive spaces for challenging the status quo of gender relations in the Security Council's work and in peacebuilding processes. I conclude that SCR 2122 must be a springboard from the past successes and acknowledged limitations of the participation components of the earlier resolutions. This type of shift in the approach to women, peace and security requires listening to, hearing and speaking with the recipients of past women, peace and security practice, especially those that remain on the peripheries of our attention.

Participation in the Security Council resolutions on women, peace and security

In this section I analyse how participation is articulated in the resolutions on women, peace and security. I emphasise SCR 1325 and SCR 1889 and only briefly discuss the four sexual violence resolutions. Drawing on Kapur's understanding of gender essentialism, I consider the construction of subjectivity in the resolutions as well as the gendered normative assumptions that are evident in the resolutions. I then turn to SCR 2122 to consider the potential of the Security Council to develop a new participation framework that responds to lessons from past peacekeeping practice and that may work towards challenging gender essentialism.

In SCR 1325, the Security Council begins by urging all member states 'to ensure increased representation of women at all decision-making levels in national, regional and international institutions and mechanisms for the prevention, management, and resolution of conflict'.[20] SCR 1325 also addresses women's participation in peace negotiations and calls for the adoption of gender perspectives, drawing attention to repatriation, reintegration and post-conflict reconstruction, local women's initiatives and women's human rights in the creation of new governmental processes and foundational documents.[21] These commitments remain a vital starting point for participation strategies. The adoption of SCR 1325 was an important breakthrough for the Security Council, recognising the need to enhance women's participation in decision-making structures during conflict, its resolution and the post-conflict period. The recognition in SCR 1325 of the need for increased representation of women across national, regional and international institutions remains crucial to securing and maintaining peace. In addition, the range of processes identified in SCR 1325 for incorporating women's participation into prevention, management and resolution of conflict remains necessary.

Post-SCR 1325 practice, however, has centred on the pursuit of increased representation of women in national decision-making structures, albeit with limited success, and paid little attention to international and regional decision-making processes. The consequences include little or no engagement with the question of which women gain access to decision-making forums and only incremental increases in the number of women in national decision-making structures have been achieved. At the same time, men's over-representation in formal decision-making structures has not been identified as a significant barrier to increasing women's representation, while international and regional organisations have not received the same level of scrutiny with respect to women's representation as national institutions in post-conflict states.

Furthermore, SCR 1325 does not address the intersection of gender with other vectors of privilege and marginalisation. The complex intersections of gender with race, ethnicity, sexuality, physical ability and religious privilege, and how this manifests in specific post-conflict communities, require attention. The deployment in SCR 1325, then, of the term 'women' is limited in its emancipatory value as women, across communities, are represented as a uniform group with uniform needs. The failure of the Security Council resolutions on women, peace and security to address women's diversity and difference is then reinforced by the invisibility of men as diverse and differently privileged actors. The assumption that all men already have access to decision-making structures constructs masculinity as uni-dimensional and masculine diversity as invisible. It is through understanding, rather than assuming, how male access to decision-making structures is maintained that additional power relationships can be understood and that gender privilege might begin to be dismantled. While Kapur's analysis of gender essentialism centres on the postcolonial victim subject constructed in strategies to combat violence against women, the Security Council's resolutions (leaving aside the victim subject identified in the sexual violence resolutions)[22] essentialise the category of women by assuming all women are missing from decision-making structures and that all men have access to decision-making structures. At no point in SCR 1325 are men identified as a gendered group and the implicit assumption that communities comprise of men and women fulfilling stereotyped gender roles is consequently unchallenged.

Looking further at the participation components of SCR 1325, not only do strategies need to be informed by reflection on how gender norms are understood within specific post-conflict communities, there is the need for critical awareness of the assumptions about gender that are implicit in the SCRs and the peacebuilding practices of the international community. SCR 1325 alone provides an insufficient framework for achieving this type of transformation as, despite the recognition of the need for cross-level strategies – national, regional and international – to increase women's representation, gender perspectives have not been incorporated into the Security Council's own decision-making bodies and structures. SCR 1325 provides a starting point for addressing women's participation yet provides a limited structure for transformation of international or regional institutions. There is no attention to the need for post-conflict states to ensure gender privilege is eradicated from choices around who participates in regional and international forums. At the same time there is no recognition that international and regional institutions, including the Security Council and its subsidiary organs, also function through a series of gendered normative assumptions. The imposition of gender perspectives on the post-conflict state without attention to the need to apply these to the Security Council's own work perpetuates a form of cultural essentialism that fails to reflect sufficiently on the assumptions of those with existing access to decision-making forums.

Despite the limited scope of the participation components of SCR 1325, the subsequent Security Council resolutions on sexual violence in armed conflict serve to narrow further the approach of SCR 1325. The sexual violence resolutions trade the general requirement of attending to women's participation at all levels with a specific call for women to participate as peacekeepers and negotiators to facilitate combating sexual violence. That is, in the sexual violence resolutions the rationale for increased women's representation is that 'their presence may encourage women from local communities to report acts of sexual violence'[23] and 'that the presence of women peacekeepers may encourage local women to participate in the national armed and security forces'.[24] These resolutions introduce a form of 'protective' participation where the rationale for increasing women's participation is premised on the need to protect women from the excesses of armed conflict, rather than on a commitment to women's right to equal participation in all levels of decision-making.[25] This approach compounds the gender essentialism of SCR 1325 by representing women beneficiaries of peacekeeping missions as not only needing protection, but as primarily experiencing conflict as victims. Third-world female vulnerability then becomes the justification for increased first-world women's participation, for example, as gender advisors in peacebuilding missions. This model correlates with Kapur's study of victim essentialism in international human rights law, whereby the detrimental gendered normative structures in non-conflict states are ignored at the same time that post-conflict states have their culture particularised as harmful and in need of change to meet a global standard.[26]

In contrast, in SCR 1889, drafted and agreed during Viet Nam's presidency of the Council in 2009, a more robust understanding of women's participation is developed and, to a degree, structural factors that hinder women's participation are identified. Some of the structural deficits of SCR 1325 are attended to by SCR 1889, in particular the need to shift from a focus on formal participation toward addressing substantive issues. At the same time, the cultural and gender essentialism of the earlier resolutions is not significantly challenged and, notably, the gendered normative assumptions within the Security Council's own work remain unaddressed.

SCR 1889 begins with stronger language regarding the issue of women's participation, as the Security Council expresses 'deep concern at the under-representation of women at all stages of peace processes'[27] and highlights that social, cultural, economic and legal structures can function as persistent obstacles to women's full involvement in the spectrum of peace processes.[28] The preamble also links the low levels of women's participation in post-conflict communities to inadequate funding[29] and notes the need to focus on empowerment of women, not only on their protection, in post-conflict spaces.[30] The language of empowerment marks a shift away from the protective participation articulated in the sexual violence resolutions; and is also a modification of the focus on representation in SCR 1325. In addition, SCR 1889 reiterates the general focus of SCR 1325 on women's participation across the spectrum of institutions and post-conflict processes[31] and articulates mechanisms that will assist the Security Council, the Secretary-General, member states and civil society to build women's empowerment, participation and involvement in post-conflict processes and peacebuilding, including the mobilisation of resources;[32] training geared toward women having the skills to be appointed to high-level mediation and negotiation posts;[33] and proposals to enhance women's capacity to 'engage in public decision-making at all levels'.[34] It is in SCR 1889 that women's low levels of participation are directly connected to other (state-level) policy and institutional decisions, including funding decisions, limited strategies to combat violence against women and/or gender-based violence and the limited provision of training opportunities for women. The language of participation, empowerment and inclusion also points to strategies to address gender imbalances in institutions and decision-making structures via a range of additional social, policing and economic reforms, signalling a move towards addressing substantive factors that hinder women's participation. This is a significant extension from the original focus on participation characterised by a focus on formal representation in SCR 1325.

Unfortunately, despite the stronger commitments to enhancing women's empowerment and participation in SCR 1889, the key paragraphs that have created action have been those that require the identification of indicators and collation of data on women's participation in United Nations (UN) missions[35] and the submission of a report, by the Secretary-General, on women's participation and inclusion in peacebuilding and planning in the aftermath of conflict.[36] While clearly important, these processes focus on 'counting the women' and do not question the gender essentialism implicit in the assumption that women can be represented as a uniform group within communities. These developments also fail to acknowledge men as gendered actors; do not question which women gain access to decision-making forums; nor address the gendered assumptions that inform the work of the Security Council itself. At the same time, since 2010, the Secretary-General's annual reports on women, peace and security have provided detailed recommendations on enhancing women's participation across the Security Council's work.[37]

Analysing SCR1325 and SCR 1889 indicates that, while the former contains structural limitations through the focus on formal representation, the latter has addressed some of these limitations by drawing attention to substantive factors that prevent women's participation in formal decision-making structures. Yet the implementation of SCR 1889 has been neglected, as the sexual violence resolutions have been given more energy and time from the Security Council and its subsidiary organs. In addition, the post-SCR 1889 use of indicators has formulated an implementation model that reverts to the representation model of SCR 1325, where gender perspectives are assumed to involve counting women's involvement and presence. Embedded in both the structural and implementation deficits are the two forms of gender essentialism that Kapur counsels against. First, the failure to address the range of different ways women experience gendered harm through the failure to see women's diversity within a community. Second, international institutions remain subject to their own gendered normative assumptions that fail to see women's diversity across communities. While the text of SCR 1889 shifts away from a sense of women's participation as best addressed through a singular focus on formal representation and indentifies social and economic factors that limit women's access to participation, there is insufficient recognition of women's existing participation within communities or of the diversity and multilayered experiences of women.

In fact, SCR 1889 retains the language of 'women' and 'women and girls' rather than a deployment of gender as a reference to social practices and their socially constructed meanings. Consequently, like SCR 1325 before it, SCR 1889 gives the impression that women represent a uniform group with the same set of needs and participation aspirations and that gender perspectives do not directly address men or the construction of masculinitiy. This writes out women's diversity both across and within communities. Furthermore, the limited implementation model, centred on indicators that count the number of women in decision-making positions, insufficiently captures the intersection of gender with other power relations. As a result, while SCR 1889 indicates a shift toward recognition of substantive inequalities, the implementation returns to a model of gender essentialism because of the reliance on the term 'women' to indicate a unitary group, the invisibility of men as a gendered group, the lack of capacity for local understanding of local gender norms to inform practices and the lack of analysis of the gendered assumptions that are being imposed by the international community.

More recently, the adoption of SCR 2122 in October 2013 marks a new consolidation of the previous participation components of the women, peace and security agenda. SCR 2122 not only substantially increases the type of participation required, drawing on the work of the Secretary-General's reports since the adoption of SCR 1889, but also represents a small but significant shift away from the gender essentialism of the prior resolutions. Importantly, SCR 2122 projects the participation and implementation directives inward and indicates that the Security Council is a site where gendered assumptions need to be challenged, while also identifying, albeit briefly, women's diversity within post-conflict communities as an important consideration.[38] Consequently, SCR 2122 can be described as providing a small move towards the recognition of women's multi-subjectivity and away from cultural essentialism.

At the same time, the terminology of SCR 2122 largely references women and girls. While use of the terms 'gender equality' and 'gender bias',[39] as well as the 'gender dimensions of peace processes'[40] and the 'consideration of gender-related issues',[41] are all present in the resolution, there is no reference to men as a gendered group or the role of harmful masculinities in the perpetuation of gender-based violence and discrimination. Women's diversity is, consequently, only briefly articulated through recognition of the need to consult representatives of socially and economically excluded groups of women.[42] This provision only applies to the work of the Secretary-General and Special Representatives, rather than marking an overall shift towards inclusion of peripheral subjects, resulting in a limited recognition of women's diverse requirements. This is, nevertheless, an important signal from the Security Council that a uniform approach to women's needs within a community overlooks the complex interaction of power relationships that inhibit women's participation.

In addition, specific paragraphs in SCR 2122 acknowledge the need for the Security Council to commit itself to 'a significant implementation shift';[43] to increase its attention to the components of the women, peace and security agenda in all of its thematic areas of work;[44] and to engage in regular meetings with local women's groups during field visits.[45] These aspects of SCR 1889 appear to demonstrate that Security Council has begun to recognise the problem of cultural essentialism in the past women, peace and security resolutions and that it needs to adapt its work accordingly.

Despite the emergence of some mechanisms to challenge to gender essentialism in SCR 2122, this is articulated without a significant disruption of previous approaches, in particular the silence on male privilege and masculinity as a gendered practice is maintained; the use of 'women and girls' language which reasserts a limited engagement with diversity is continued; and the earlier limited models of participation are reiterated – representative participation (SCR 1325),[46] protective participation (SCRs 1820, 1888, 1960 and 2106)[47] and substantive participation (SCR 1889).[48] It remains open to question whether the reiteration of the past structure will threaten the important move towards discarding gender essentialism in SCR 2122. Recalling SCR 1889, questions regarding the implementation of SCR 2122 are also crucial.

It is clear that SCR 2122 responds to some of the limitations of the earlier participation components of the women, peace and security framework. Central to the argument in this chapter, however, is the need to review past practices with respect to women's participation in post-conflict structures, in order to draw attention to what can be learnt from them. Through observing women's experiences of past practice it is apparent that a shift away from gender essentialism also requires greater understanding of women's existing participation within communities and a need for Security Council work to accommodate existing gender arrangements that are positive for women, as well as challenge arrangements that exclude them. The following section, in examining women's participation in Bougainville peacebuilding, takes up this issue and proposes a further need to engage peripheral subjects to avoid the repetition of past participation failures.

Participation, peace and security in Bougainville

As Bougainville shifted towards peace in 2001, not only was SCR 1325 in its infancy, the role of the UN in peacebuilding in Bougainville remained minimal. The UN had, in 1996, established the UN Political Mission in Bougainville. This body remained until 2003 when it was replaced by the UN Observer Mission in Bougainville, which was tasked with completing residual tasks in the transition to the newly autonomous province. Over the same period Pacific states contributed troops to the Australian-led Truce Monitoring Group (renamed Peace Monitoring Group in 1998), which remained in Bougainville after the withdrawal of PNG and the establishment of the ABG in 2003. These international and regional missions were conscious of gender relations within Bougainville, not only because of SCR 1325 and powerful local and regional women's groups,[49] but also because of Bougainville women's participation as landowners, as actors during the conflict and as orchestrators of the first peace conference in 1996. Nevertheless, the imposition of a gender quota to ensure women's participation in the ABG imported a limited formal equality model that has, in practice, been unable to respect the existing gender relations in Bougainville.[50] The forthcoming independence referendum, scheduled for between 2015 and 2020, is likely to require international support for building a local democracy model that is representative of the local constituencies. The risk is that the existing post-conflict model, the ABG, will be considered satisfactory for the newly independent state of Bougainville.

The three reserved women's seats in the transitional ABG create the perception that women are already represented through the quota system. During elections, each voter is able to cast votes for three candidates; one vote is for a candidate in the local constituency, one vote to elect an ex-combatant (three seats are also reserved for ex-combatants) and one vote to elect candidates for the women's seats. This gives the sense of all voters casting support for women candidates, even though this has not shifted the number of women represented in the ABG, with three women being elected in the post-conflict elections.[51] The three seats reserved for women, and the capacity for everyone to cast a vote for these candidates, creates the impression of representation of women in the national decision-making structure, as championed by SCR 1325. This marginal participation is further compounded by the situation in the national PNG Parliament, where the 2012 election resulted in the election of three women into the 111-seat PNG parliament.[52] The PNG government remains the overarching governing structure in Bougainville, despite the devolved powers of the ABG, and Bougainville women remain citizens of PNG at least until after the referendum.

Substantive and structural inequalities in Bougainville and in PNG also diminish women's capacity to participate in either the ABG or the PNG parliament.[53] These include inequalities in health laws,[54] education standards[55] and family law rights.[56] Yet the diversity of women's lives across the various Bougainville islands indicates the need for effective representation of women in formal decision-making structures beyond the quota structure. Substantive strategies that encourage women to contest local seats would facilitate the representation of women's diverse needs in the formal decision-making processes, in particular with respect to the environmental and health issues faced by the landowners closest to the (now closed) Panguna mine;[57] the insecurity experienced by women on more remote islands as sea levels rise and their status as local landowners come to be at risk;[58] and the need for participation in the revived consultations with multinational mining companies about the resumption of mining.[59]

Importantly, Bougainville women's absence from formal peace processes and their limited formal recognition as decision-makers within Bougainville communities begins not with the post-conflict period, but rather during its colonial, mandate and trusteeship history.[60] After World War I Bougainville, previously part of German Guinea, became a mandate territory controlled by Australia. Following World War II, as part of New Guinea, Bougainville was included in the UN trusteeship system, again under Australian control, until PNG gained independence in 1975. Although geographically part of the nearby Solomon Islands, Bougainville remained part of PNG and, since the peace agreement in 2003, has functioned as a self-governing autonomous province of PNG.[61] German colonial governance and successive Australian administrations failed to recognise the Bougainville system of matrilineal gender relations as something that mattered and thus facilitated a system of 'Big Man' politics that later become one of the factors that fuelled the conflict in Bougainville.[62] 'Big Man' politics centres on key (male) figures, endowed with local, village-level privilege in the aftermath of colonialism and continues to impact on Bougainville today. This system had consequences for agreements on the use of land by those with mining interests in Bougainville, particularly after the independence of PNG in 1975.[63] For example, an in-country study by the UN Development Fund for Women found the mining companies had negotiated with local male leaders when building the Panguna mine, leaving out consultations with women, who are the primary landowners in most Bougainville communities.[64] The decisions over land use and revenue made in the period after decolonisation resulted in the exploitative labour practices and environmental impact of the Panguna mine, which helped trigger the outbreak of the conflict in 1988.[65] Constructions of masculinity that perpetuate, and those that end, conflicts thus become an aspect of gender perspectives that remain under-examined in contemporary women, peace and security dialogues: to focus only on counting women or adding a few seats for women fails to sufficiently undo embedded gender privilege in formal decision-making structures. Recognition of the international community, and its projects and processes, as a site of gendered assumptions (and privileges) needs to be a component of strategies that embrace gender perspectives.

Top-down assumptions, imposed by the Security Council and the rest of the international community, regarding what constitutes 'normal' gender relationships, have perpetuated the colonial heritage of male privilege in Bougainville. This renders invisible the specific needs of the diverse groups of women in Bougainville. A top-down approach to gender perspectives cannot capture the varied local conditions and gender practices. In SCR 2122, the shift toward understanding women's diversity is articulated as a need for,

> the Secretary-General's Special Envoys and Special Representatives to United Nations missions, from early on in their deployment, to regularly consult with women's organizations and women leaders, including socially and/or economically excluded groups of women.[66]

Unfortunately this is the only moment of recognition in SCR 2122 of the need to see women experiencing gender discrimination in conjunction with other forms of social and economic exclusion. The text falls short of recognising that gender inequality intersects with other vectors of power within communities. In Bougainville, women are in some ways economically powerful due to their traditional ownership of land, yet they remain excluded by the existing system of representation in government that perpetuates the gender privileges of the colonial period. The complexity of gender relations in Bougainville remain insufficiently addressed in women, peace and security initiatives.

The post-conflict outcome of a small quota for women in the ABG stands in contrast to the evidence of women's roles during conflict, which included women crossing between fighting factions;[67] women negotiating for peace;[68] and women maintaining informal networks and community structures: for example, the supply of essential goods and medicines, safe water and networks to counter the impact of hardship caused by the blockade of Bougainville during the conflict.[69] Prior to the creation of the ABG, the *Bougainville Peace Agreement* was signed in Arawa, Bougainville, in 2001.[70] Despite women's earlier efforts, and its post-SCR 1325 timing, this agreement was negotiated and signed without the participation of women's groups and without substantive provisions addressing SCR 1325 participation issues.[71] At the official signing, peace activist and wartime blockade runner, Ruby Miringka addressed participants, outlining a central role for women in Bougainville in the future. Her speech echoed the 50 women who were previously present in Lincoln, New Zealand, for the signing of the 1998 ceasefire agreement and who had collectively drawn up an adjoining statement on peace, which stated:

> We, the women, hold custodial rights of our land by clan inheritance. We insist that women leaders must be party to all stages of the political process in determining the future of Bougainville.[72]

Yet these events remained an adjunct to the official process; women were present but not participants. The formal processes and outcomes in Bougainville have not only been unable to capture the subtle gendered cultural practices that permit men to speak only on the advice of women as landholders, they have not acknowledged women's existing roles in conflict and peacetime in post-conflict structures. For the communities of Bougainville with matrilineal kinship and landownership, this further cements the colonial model of seeing men and not hearing women.

It is important to recognise that the matrilineal structures in Bougainville also entrench certain gender privileges that have contributed to this outcome. For example, in most Bougainville communities, while women remain the primary decision-makers, they rarely command public space and women's decisions tend to be communicated through men.[73] This underscores the importance of international structures and processes that are responsive to local conditions and that are, in particular, able to develop processes for addressing both visible and invisible gender privileges. Seeing women as decision-makers who also have limited access to public decision-making forums, even within matrilineal communities, requires appreciation of the manner in which gender relations function within communities and how gender relations are not uniform across states or even within states. Ultimately, the deployment of Security Council structures without listening to local actors, women and men, to inform how gendered processes operate at the local level does risk alienating the same actors the women, peace and security agenda is envisaged to assist.

The final act of the peacebuilding process in Bougainville will be the referendum on independence. In Braithwaite et al.'s study of the Bougainville post-conflict transition, the Bougainville peace process is described as

> shaped by bottom-up traditional and Christian reconciliation practices and a carefully crafted top-down political settlement ... for the student of peacebuilding, there is much to learn from the symbiosis

between top-down architecture of credible commitment and bottom-up reconciliation.[74]

While the authors analyse the limitations and dangers of both top-down and bottom-up strategies, they do, ultimately, celebrate Bougainville as a peacekeeping and peacebuilding 'success' story.[75] The women, peace and security framework, however, gives us additional tools to assess and understand peacebuilding successes, and women's groups in Bougainville continue to challenge the gap between their (unrecognised) contributions to achieving peace and the gender imbalances in the transitional institutions.[76] If the key outcome in relation to the SCR 1325 framework is a quota of three seats for women in the 39-seat ABG, then there is a need to re-examine both the implementation of the resolutions on women, peace and security and the resolutions themselves. Constructing quotas and setting numerical targets for women's participation maintains the intersectional gender privileges entrenched in international and local communities while depending on the term 'women' in a manner that fails to respond to women's diversity. The adoption of numerical targets ignores women's existing roles in the prevention, management and resolution of conflict, permitting these to continue to be undervalued and fails to address substantive inequalities that limit, to varying degrees, all women's access to representation in formal decision-making forums.

Women's networks in Bougainville, such as the Leitana Nehan Women's Development Agency and the Bougainville Council of Women, continue to identify SCR 1325 as relevant to challenging the loss of status, lack of employment opportunities and low participation of women in the post-conflict governing structures.[77] The adoption of SCR 2122 gives renewed opportunity to consider how gender interacts with formal decision-making power in specific post-conflict contexts and to take account of the variations in social and economic circumstances amongst women. In addition, SCR 2122 commits the Security Council to further consultation and inclusion of women in the processes which lead to situation-specific resolutions, as an adjunct to the seven thematic resolutions on women, peace and security.

Lessons can be learnt from the women, and men, who have lived through the post-SCR 1325 period of peacebuilding, to further understand how gender-based violence (not just sexual violence), access to education and cultural and social stereotypes, combined with low economic power, keep women out of leadership and decision-making roles. Facilitating the opportunity for individual women to participate in conflict-related and peacebuilding decision-making is only one component of promoting women's inclusion and empowerment: recognition of women's existing roles, as local leaders and in organising informal community activities and services, is at least as important.

Conclusion

In her study of gender and cultural essentialism, Kapur distinguishes between the third-world victim subject of international human rights law, which is 'an exclusionary category built on racist perceptions and stereotypes of third world women', and the need to recognise 'different subjectivities and peripheral subjects'.[78] In this chapter, I have examined how the Security Council's resolutions on women, peace and security create a similar racialised subject through the participation components that assume, on the one hand, a global sisterhood that can be encompassed through references to women as a unitary group and, on the other hand, women in third-world peacebuilding communities who need western assistance to be recognised by formal decision-making structures. The resolutions do not take seriously the knowledge of peripheral subjects, their existing forms of participation and the capacity of the peripheral subject to contribute meaningfully to international policies and practices so that women's diversity within peacebuilding communities is acknowledged.

The recognition of socially and economically disadvantaged women and of the need for the Council to examine the gendered assumptions in its own practices, in SCR 2122, creates new spaces for challenging the status quo of gender relations in the Security Council and in post-conflict structures. The implementation of SCR 2122, however, must be a springboard from past experiences of success and acknowledged limitations of the participation components of the previous resolutions on women, peace and security.

While the Security Council's women, peace and security framework does identify the importance of promoting women's representation in decision-making structures, in practice this approach has proved to be insufficient to change the gender imbalances in decision-making structures or to fully accommodate the nuanced gendered realities of peripheral subjects. In SCR 1325 the focus is on getting more women into decision-making roles, rather than on changing the gendered structures themselves or challenging the gendered norms that operate to disadvantage women. Gender structures outside of the peripheries remain untouched by these processes and are assumed to offer beneficial models for change.

While a few more women may be included, women's structural inequality, compounded for many by other intersecting forms of discrimination, remain unaddressed. In contrast, SCR 1889 expands the participation components of the women, peace and security resolutions beyond representation to consider women's empowerment and promotes a form of substantive participation. The adoption of SCR 2122 provides a further shift forward, as it capitalises on the strengths of SCR 1325 and SCR 1889 while addressing some of the previously acknowledged structural and implementation issues. Questions remain as to whether SCR 2122 achieves the complexity required to fully challenge the repetition of the dominance of male actors in post-conflict practices and whether it can successfully address the gendered privilege entrenched in the Security Council's own structures. Importantly, a move towards the recognition of multilayered subjectivity is signalled with the acknowledgement in SCR 2122 of the need to consult with 'socially and/or economically excluded groups of women'[79] and the Security Council is identified as a significant site where the women, peace and security framework needs to be implemented.[80]

In this chapter, the case study of Bougainville challenges the perception that women's participation in local decision-making is missing. Bougainville men and women have a history of working in partnership with respect to decision-making and women are documented as assuming active leadership roles in negotiating peace during the Bougainville conflict. However, the outcome was not only women's absence as participants at the signing of the peace agreement, but an extremely limited role for women in the key negotiations over disarmament and the creation of the ABG, continuing rather than eliminating gender privileges with respect to formal representation.

To address the perpetuation of gender privilege in decision-making structures in peacebuilding processes may require renewed feminist attention to situations on the Security Council's agenda, as opposed to further thematic resolutions on women, peace and security. Enhancing women's participation also requires feminist attentiveness to the diversity and relevance of local women's perspectives and understandings. For feminist actors, challenging gender privileges requires further feminist debate – that includes the participation of peripheral subjects – about what the existing Security Council resolutions and Secretary-General reports on women, peace and security make possible.

With a high-level review of SCR 1325 scheduled for 2015,[81] and the move toward secession scheduled for Bougainville between 2015 and 2020, as well as the renewed focus on interconnections between women's under-representation, women's human rights and empowerment in SCR 2122, it is time for intense debates on SCR 1325 and its framework. Strengthening the participation components of the women, peace and security framework must include efforts to dismantle gender essentialism. This requires learning from the experience of women who have already been recipients of SCR 1325 strategies, including women in the Pacific region, such as Bougainville, where the women, peace and security framework may have unwittingly contributed to the failure to see women's participation as already occurring.

Notes

1. K. Hakena, 'Peace in Bougainville and the work of the Leitana Nehan Women's Development Agency', *War Resisters' International* (1 January 2001), http://wri-irg.org/nonviolence/nvse08-en.htm (last accessed October 2013). Hakena describes all but two of Bougainville's districts as matrilineal.
2. J.T. Sirivi and M.T. Havini (eds), *As Mothers of the Land: The Birth of the Bougainville Women for Peace and Freedom* (Canberra: Pandanus Books, 2004). See also J. Braithwaite, H. Charlesworth, L. Dunn and P. Reddy, *Reconciliation and Architectures of Commitment: Sequencing Peace in Bougainville* (Canberra: ANU E Press, 2010), pp. 93–94.
3. Braithwaite et al., *Sequencing Peace in Bougainville*, p. 56.
4. *Security Council Resolution 1325*, UN Doc. S/RES/1325 (31 October 2000) (SCR 1325).
5. *Security Council Resolution 1820*, UN Doc. S/RES/1820 (19 June 2008) (SCR 1820); *Security Council Resolution 1888*, UN Doc. S/RES/1888 (30 September 2009) (SCR 1888); *Security Council Resolution 1889*, UN Doc. S/RES/1889 (5 October 2009) (SCR 1889); *Security Council Resolution 1960*, UN Doc. S/RES/1960 (16 December 2010) (SCR 1960); *Security Council Resolution 2106*, UN Doc. S/RES/2106 (24 June 2013) (SCR 2106); *Security Council Resolution 2122*, UN Doc. S/RES/2122 (18 October 2013) (SCR 2122).
6. Braithwaite et al., *Sequencing Peace in Bougainville*, p. 2.
7. The independence referendum is guaranteed in Part 17 of the Autonomous Bougainville constitution. On Bougainville independence, see I. Nicholas, 'PNG: Momis warns of independence "clock ticking" for Bougainville', *Pacific Media Centre: Te Amokura* (10 February 2011), http://www.pmc.aut. ac.nz/pacific-media-watch/2011-02-10/png-momis-warns-independence-clock-ticking-bougainville (last accessed October 2013).
8. See R. Kapur, *Erotic Justice: Law and the New Politics of Postcolonialism* (London: Glasshouse Press, 2005), ch. 4.
9. Ibid., p. 99.
10. Ibid., p. 104.
11. Ibid., p. 127.
12. Ibid., p. 107.
13. Ibid., p. 131.
14. Braithwaite et al., *Sequencing Peace in Bougainville*, pp. 12–20.

15. K. Lasslett, 'State terror and the Bougainville conflict', *International State Crime Initiative*, multimedia installation available at: http://www.statecrime. org/testimonyproject/bougainville (last accessed October 2013), ch. 2.
16. M. Santhebennur, 'UN to assist in Bougainville mine remediation', *Australian Mining* (5 September 2013), http://www.miningaustralia.com.au/news/ unitednationstoassistinbougainvillemineremediation (last accessed October 2013).
17. However, note S. Bhagwan Rolls, 'Thinking Globally and Acting Locally: Linking Women, Peace and Security in the Pacific', in this volume, for an understanding of the ways in which women in the Pacific continue to subvert this assumption.
18. See F. Ruby, '*Security Council Resolution 1325*: A Tool for Conflict Prevention?', in this volume.
19. SCR 1820, SCR 1888, SCR 1960 and SCR 2106.
20. SCR 1325, para. 1.
21. Ibid., para. 8.
22. See G. Heathcote, 'Feminist politics and the use of force: Theorising feminist action and Security Council Resolution 1325', *Socio-Legal Review*, Vol. 7 (2011) 23.
23. SCR 1960, preamble.
24. SCR 1888, preamble.
25. See further O. Simić, 'Increasing Women's Presence in Peacekeeping Operations: The Rationales and Realities of "Gender Balance"', in this volume.
26. Kapur, *Erotic Justice*, p. 100.
27. SCR 1889, preamble para. 7.
28. Ibid., preamble paras 8, 10.
29. Ibid., preamble para. 10.
30. Ibid., preamble para. 11.
31. Ibid., para. 1.
32. Ibid., para. 14.
33. Ibid., para. 4.
34. Ibid., para. 10.
35. Ibid., para. 18.
36. Ibid., para. 19.
37. *Report of the Secretary-General on Women's Participation in Peacebuilding*, UN Doc. A/65/354–S/2010/466 (7 September 2010); *Report of the Secretary-General on Women, Peace and Security*, UN Doc. S/2011/598* (29 September 2011); and *Report of the Secretary-General on Women, Peace and Security*, UN Doc. S/2012/732 (2 October 2012).
38. SCR 2122, para. 7(a).
39. Ibid., preamble.
40. Ibid., para. 1.
41. Ibid., para. 7
42. Ibid., para. 7(a).
43. Ibid., para. 15.
44. Ibid., para. 3.
45. Ibid., para. 6.
46. Ibid.

47. Ibid., preamble; para. 5, although the focus is on gender-based violence rather than sexual violence in armed conflict.
48. Ibid., para. 10; although, as indicated above, a key limitation of SCR 1889 has concerned implementation.
49. See Bhagwan Rolls, 'Thinking Globally and Acting Locally'.
50. For discussion, see L. Fung, 'Engendering the peace processes: Women's role in peacebuilding', in H. Durham and T. Gurd (eds), *Listening to the Silences: Women and War* (Leiden: Brill, 2005) 225, p. 237.
51. Changes to this are recorded here: http://www.cpahq.org/cpahq/core/parliamentInfo.aspx?Committee=BOUGAINVILLE (last accessed October 2013).
52. For further discussion of gendered participation in PNG, see J. Chandler, 'Taim bilong ol Meri?: A new agenda in PNG', *Griffith Review*, Vol. 40 (2013) 66, available at: http://griffithreview.com/images/stories/edition_articles/ed40_pdfs/jo%20chandler%20-%20taim%20bilong%20ol%20meri.pdf (last accessed October 2013).
53. PNG National Council of Women, 'The CEDAW shadow report on the status of women in Papua New Guinea and the autonomous region of Bougainville' (PNG National Council of Women, 2010) 1–46, available at: http://www.iwraw-ap.org/resources/pdf/46_shadow_reports/G2L/Papua_New_Guinea/CEDAW_SHADOW_REPORT.pdf (last accessed October 2013).
54. Ibid., 'The CEDAW shadow report', p. 46.
55. Ibid., p. 44.
56. Ibid., p. 49.
57. J. Garrett, 'UNEP to help Bougainville manage clean up of Rio Tinto mine', *Radio Australia* (23 September 2013), http://www.radioaustralia.net.au/pacific/2013-09-04/unep-to-help-bougainville-manage-cleanup-of-rio-tinto-mine/1185677 (last accessed October 2013).
58. PNG National Council of Women, 'The CEDAW shadow report', p. 39.
59. K. Lasslett, 'AusAID fuels Bougainville mining tension', *New Matilda* (23 April 2013), https://newmatilda.com/2013/04/23/ausaid-fuels-bougainville-mining-tensions (last accessed October 2013).
60. On the history of interventions in Bougainville, including those of mining companies, see R. Ewins, 'The Bougainville conflict', *Rory Ewin's Pacific Island Politics* (9 December 2003), http://speedysnail.com/pacific/bougainville.html (last accessed October 2013); and Amnesty International, 'Bougainville: The forgotten human rights tragedy' (AI Doc. ASA/34/01/97, 26 February 1997).
61. On the trusteeship system in New Guinea and thus Bougainville, see M. Leifer, 'Australia, trusteeship and New Guinea', *Pacific Affairs*, Vol. 36, No. 3 (1963) 250. See also the history of Bougainville as recorded by Solidarity South Pacific: http://www.eco-action.org/ssp/bougainville.html (last accessed October 2013).
62. Braithwaite et al., *Sequencing Peace in Bougainville*, pp. 11–12, 97.
63. However, additional factors – including the geographic inclusion of Bougainville in Papua New Guinea's decolonisation despite the physical and cultural links to the Solomon Islands, the environmental degradation wrought by the mine and the small amount of profits from the mine that came back to the Bougainville people – also contributed to the tensions around the mine.

64. S. Douglas, V. Farr, F. Hill and W. Kasuma, 'Case study: Bougainville – Papua New Guinea', in S. Douglas and F. Hill (eds), *Getting It Right, Doing It Right: Gender and Disarmament, Demobilization and Reintegration* (New York: United Nations Development Fund for Women, 2004) 20, p. 23.
65. Braithwaite et al., *Sequencing Peace in Bougainville*, pp. 15–18; and Douglas et al., 'Case study: Bougainville – Papua New Guinea', p. 22.
66. SCR 2122, para. 7(a).
67. See Braithwaite et al., *Sequencing Peace in Bougainville*, pp. 41–42, ch. 8.
68. See L. Garasu, 'The role of women in promoting peace and reconciliation', in A. Carl and L. Garasu (eds), *Weaving Consensus: The Papua New Guinea – Bougainville Peace Process* (London: Conciliation Resources in collaboration with BICWF, 2002) 28.
69. Hakena, 'Peace in Bougainville'.
70. For discussion and description, see E.P. Wolfers, '"Joint creation": The *Bougainville Peace Agreement* – And beyond', in A. Carl and L. Garasu (eds), *Weaving Consensus: The Papua New Guinea – Bougainville Peace Process* (London: Conciliation Resources in collaboration with BICWF, 2002) 44.
71. Douglas et al., 'Case study: Bougainville – Papua New Guinea'.
72. Quoted in Douglas et al., 'Case study: Bougainville – Papua New Guinea', pp. 24–25.
73. Above Note 71, at 28.
74. Braithwaite et al., *Sequencing Peace in Bougainville*, p. 1.
75. See also D. Hegarty and A. Regan, 'Peacebuilding in the Pacific Islands: Lessons from Bougainville, Solomon Islands and Fiji', in Centre for Humanitarian Dialogue, *Handbook on Conflict and Mediation in Asia* (Geneva: Centre for Humanitarian Dialogue, 2006) 57.
76. See, for example, Pacific Cooperation Foundation, 'Stories from Bougainville Participants' (Bougainville – New Zealand Track II Dialogue: 'Women and Land', 28–29 June 2010), available at: http://www.pcf.org.nz/documents/Stories%20from%20Bougainville%20Participants.pdf (last accessed October 2013).
77. See C. Wilson, 'Women leaders key to post-conflict development on Bougainville', *London Progressive Journal* (12 November 2011), http://london progressivejournal.com/article/view/894 (last accessed October 2013).
78. Kapur, *Erotic Justice*, p. 135.
79. SCR 2122, para. 7(a).
80. Ibid., paras 1, 15.
81. See *Report of the Secretary-General on Women and Peace and Security*, UN Doc. S/2011/598* (29 September 2011), para. 74(f). See also SCR 2122, para. 15.

3
Shaming the State: Sexual Offences by UN Military Peacekeepers and the Rhetoric of Zero Tolerance

Róisín Burke

Introduction

As of 31 August 2013 there were 15 United Nations (UN) peacekeeping operations deployed across the world, consisting of 115,582 personnel.[1] UN peacekeepers have done much to contribute to peace and security in many conflict-affected states. These peacekeeping operations are increasingly multidimensional, requiring UN military contingents to engage in activities that necessitate interaction with and close proximity to civilian populations of UN mission host states, including women and children.[2] Since the 1990s, the contributions made by UN peacekeepers have been marred by numerous allegations of sexual exploitation and abuse (SEA) by UN peacekeepers, including allegations of serious crimes, such as rape, forced prostitution, 'rape disguised as prostitution',[3] sexual abuse of children, trafficking and other forms of sexual violence.[4] SEA by UN peacekeepers is not only morally reprehensible, it violates the relationship of trust between peacekeepers and the civilian populations they have been sent to protect. Moreover, the continued incidence of SEA by UN peacekeepers,[5] and impunity for such, discredits UN operations and undermines the values the organisation seeks to promote.

There are several categories of personnel deployed on UN operations, including experts on mission (this includes military observers), UN volunteers, contractors, consultants and police units. Allegations of SEA have been made against all categories of UN peacekeepers. These different categories of personnel each have distinct legal status, giving rise to separate legal and practical considerations when examining the issue of SEA.[6] This chapter will focus solely on UN military contingent personnel, specifically the ordinary rank and file soldiers.[7] Military contingents are the largest component of UN operations.[8] These personnel remain in the employ of their troop-contributing state and are subject to its exclusive criminal and disciplinary jurisdiction while deployed on UN operations. This is generally provided for under a 'status of forces agreement' negotiated between the UN and the mission host state,[9] and the memorandums of understanding or troop-contribution agreements negotiated between the UN and troop-contributing states.[10] Yet, states rarely prosecute military contingent personnel alleged to have committed sexual offences while deployed on UN operations, despite obligations to do so and to inform the UN of the outcome.[11]

State reluctance to investigate and prosecute soldiers alleged to have committed sexual offences while deployed on UN operations could be for a range of reasons, including perhaps fear of being named and shamed; the inconvenience of and resources required to undertake an investigation and prosecution for crimes committed in UN mission host states; or such offences not being considered sufficiently grave. Where states fail to effectively investigate and prosecute soldiers perpetrating sexual offences, this contributes to the continuing problem of SEA on UN operations and impunity for such. Soldiers committing criminal offences, including sexual offences, in UN mission host states cannot be prosecuted by host state authorities given that they have been granted immunity from host state criminal jurisdiction. This is despite the fact that these peacekeepers are required to respect host state laws.[12] The implementation of the UN's zero tolerance of almost all sex between peacekeeping personnel and the local beneficiaries of peace support operations rests to a large extent with troop-contributing states.[13] The UN also has no power to take criminal or disciplinary action against members of military contingents committing crimes in UN mission host states. The only measure that can be taken by the UN is repatriation of individuals to the troop-contributing states.

Failure to take effective action against soldiers perpetrating sexual offences in UN mission host states sends a message that such conduct is tolerated. In 2000, the UN Security Council adopted *Security Council Resolution 1325*, in which it calls for an end to gender-based violence in situations of armed conflict. Emphasis is placed on the responsibility of states to prosecute perpetrators of violence against women and girls, including sexual offences.[14] A series of related resolutions have since been adopted by the Security Council, which have emphasised the need for an end to sexual violence against women in armed conflict; the prosecution of perpetrators of such violence; affirmation of the UN's zero tolerance of SEA by peacekeepers; and the need for better training of peacekeepers in relation to SEA and gender issues.[15] *Security Council Resolution 1820*, passed in 2008, highlights the important part peacekeeping personnel should play in tackling sexual violence against women and girls.[16] Indeed, part of their role is to assist with establishing more secure environments in post-conflict and conflict states.[17] Impunity for SEA by UN peacekeepers contributes to the broader lack of security of women and children in conflict-affected areas and it undercuts international efforts aimed at ending violence against women. Moreover, it undermines UN efforts to re-establish the rule of law, the fulfilment of mission mandates and the ability of peacekeepers to build trust among the local population.

In dealing with the problem of SEA by UN military peacekeepers, much of the focus to date has been on criminal or disciplinary responsibility of individuals.[18] This chapter will consider whether troop-contributing states may also have a level of responsibility towards victims of SEA due to the extraterritorial conduct of their troops. More specifically, it will question whether these states may be in breach of their obligations under human rights treaties they have ratified, when they fail to effectively investigate and, where appropriate, prosecute soldiers alleged to have perpetrated SEA.

Part I will address, in brief, the UN's definitions of SEA and the array of conduct covered. The focus of this chapter, however, is on serious sexual offences perpetrated by soldiers deployed on UN operations. The central concern is with the conditions under which the human rights obligations of a UN troop-contributing state might be triggered in relation to victims of SEA. This raises two central considerations, which will be addressed in turn in Part II. First, whether SEA by UN military contingent personnel can ever be considered attributable or imputable to a troop-contributing state and, second, whether the troop-contributing state can be said to exercise extraterritorial jurisdiction for the purpose of the relevant human rights treaty, so that its obligations under the treaty might be triggered towards victims of SEA. If an act or omission is not attributable to a state, or if its human rights obligations do not apply outside its territory, then SEA victims will have no claim against the troop-contributing state. This chapter will focus primarily on the issue of extraterritorial jurisdiction. It will be argued that a troop-contributing state's human rights treaty obligations could potentially be triggered towards victims of sexual offences by soldiers it deploys on a UN operation, in particular instances.

Part III will consider, in brief, possible human rights obligations owed by states towards victims of SEA perpetrated by their soldiers and what this might mean for states failing to take effective action against soldiers perpetrating SEA in mission. It will be argued that troop-contributing states should at very least be held to a standard of due diligence, and are required to do what is reasonable in the circumstances to prevent SEA by their soldiers and to hold perpetrators to account. Human rights treaty monitoring bodies and courts may afford victims of SEA with an alternative route to some measure of redress, alongside present efforts to invoke individual criminal or disciplinary responsibility. Significantly, human rights mechanisms could be used to name and shame states, and to pressure them into taking more effective action against soldiers violating the rights of civilians they have been deployed to protect.

Defining sexual exploitation and abuse

Amongst a range of measures aimed at responding to allegations of SEA by UN peacekeepers, in 2003 the UN Secretary-General promulgated a *Bulletin on Special Measures for Protection from Sexual Exploitation and Sexual Abuse* (Bulletin).[19] The Bulletin defines 'sexual abuse' as 'any actual or threatened physical intrusion of a sexual nature, whether by force or under unequal or coercive conditions'.[20] Sexual exploitation is defined as 'any actual or attempted abuse of a position of vulnerability, differential power, or trust, for sexual purposes, including, but not limited to, profiting monetarily, socially or politically from the sexual exploitation of another'.[21] These definitions potentially cover a broad array of sexual conduct, some of which may not necessarily be illegal. The definitions adopted in the Bulletin find no equivalent in international or domestic criminal laws.[22] This has given rise to significant debate about the appropriateness of these definitions.

The UN's zero tolerance policy has been criticised for being overtly patriarchal, portraying women solely as victims and men as protectors,[23] for conflating women with children and for failing to adequately take into account the agency of women and young girls engaging in consensual prostitution.[24] Yet, consideration has to be given to the types of environments in which such encounters all too often take place. Armed conflict often results in political and social instability, poverty, institutional collapse, erosion of the rule of law, insufficient control of international borders, lack of economic opportunity and widespread human rights and international humanitarian law violations, all of which contribute to environments where rape, trafficking, prostitution (forced or otherwise) and other forms of SEA are more likely to be prevalent.[25] Desperation, poverty, separation of children from families, amongst other factors, may force vulnerable women and children to engage in 'survival sex', in exchange for money, goods, food or services.[26] The difficulty with sexual encounters between UN peacekeepers and 'prostitutes' in conflict and post-conflict environments is that it is questionable whether women and girls are exercising a real choice.

Nevertheless, prostitution is not illegal in all states, nor is it illegal under international law, and there are concerns that the UN's zero tolerance policy on SEA may interfere with relationships that appear 'ordinary' and consensual.[27] Not all sexual encounters between UN peacekeepers and local civilians can be considered crimes. The Bulletin prohibits sexual interactions with anyone under the age of 18, irrespective of the local age of consent, which differs across UN mission host states, and indeed in the laws of troop-contributing states. Dianne Otto opines that the UN's SEA zero tolerance policy subverts attention from the need to address underlying factors such as gender inequality and poverty.[28] On another note, the Bulletin's failure to distinguish between commercial prostitution and otherwise clearly legal consensual sex, and serious criminal offences of a sexual nature, such as rape, forced prostitution,[29] sexual exploitation and abuse of children, trafficking and other forms of sexual violence,[30] also risks trivialising the latter forms of abuse. This chapter is particularly concerned with serious sexual offences committed by UN military contingent personnel.

State human rights obligations and Sexual Exploitation and Abuse by UN soldiers

Numerous international human rights treaties and soft law instruments provide for the protection of women and children from SEA either directly or indirectly. Rape, for instance, is specifically prohibited under several human rights instruments,[31] as is trafficking in women and children and the exploitation of the prostitution of others.[32]

Where not explicitly prohibited, rape is understood as a violation of other human rights, including the prohibition of torture and other cruel, inhuman or degrading treatment, in particular circumstances.[33] Where women are repeatedly raped or are subject to enforced prostitution,[34] this may amount to sexual slavery.[35]

Article 6 of the widely ratified *Convention on the Elimination of all forms of Discrimination against Women* (CEDAW) requires state parties to 'suppress all forms of traffic in women and exploitation of prostitution of women'.[36] In General Recommendation 19, the CEDAW Committee states that '[g]ender-based violence is a form of discrimination that seriously inhibits women's ability to enjoy rights and freedoms on a basis of equality with men'.[37] It further stated that the prohibition of such violence is provided for under Article 1 of CEDAW, and includes 'acts that inflict physical, mental or sexual harm or suffering, threats of such acts, coercion and other deprivations of liberty'. Possible human rights that may be violated by gender-based violence and state failure to act with due diligence in this regard include, for instance, 'the right to life', 'the right not to be subject to torture or to cruel, inhuman or degrading treatment or punishment', 'the right to equal protection according to humanitarian norms in time of international or internal armed conflict', 'the right to liberty and security of person', 'the right to equal protection under the law' and 'the right to the highest standard attainable of physical and mental health'.[38]

The *Convention on the Rights of the Child* (CRC), which has been almost universally ratified,[39] specifically prohibits sexual abuse, sexual exploitation and trafficking, requiring states to take 'all appropriate national, bilateral and multilateral measures' to protect children from such crimes.[40] Article 39 of the CRC obliges states to establish support systems for child victims of abuse by their nationals. A child is defined under the CRC as anybody under the age of 18 unless the age of majority is earlier in the relevant state.[41] Although not yet widely ratified, the CRC *Optional Protocol on the Sale of Children, Child Prostitution and Child Pornography* explicitly requires states to prohibit child prostitution, child pornography and sex tourism involving children, whether committed 'domestically or transnationally'.[42]

Clearly, many incidents of SEA by armed forces deployed on UN operations may amount to human rights violations. Where troop-contributing states have ratified human rights instruments, they may open avenues for victims of SEA to seek some form of redress, and could be used as a means to 'name and shame' states failing to take action against soldiers perpetrating SEA. The question, however, is when might the human rights treaty obligations of troop-contributing states towards SEA victims be triggered?

Attribution of responsibility

UN military contingent personnel remain part of an organ of their troop-contributing state and under its employment. At the same time, they operate as part of a UN operation, as a subsidiary organ of the Security Council and under a UN mandate. Therefore, both the troop-contributing state and the UN exercise varying degrees of control over these military personnel while deployed on UN operations. Whether the state or UN can be held responsible for a wrongful act or omission, perpetrated by a member of a military contingent deployed on a UN operation, will depend on the level of control they exercise over the perpetrator. According to the International Law Commission, the conduct of an organ of a state, or an organ or agent of an international organisation that is placed at the disposal of another international organisation, shall be considered under international law an act of the latter organisation if the organisation exercises *effective control* over that conduct.[43] Of essence in the context of SEA by UN military contingent personnel is that the sending state retains full criminal and disciplinary jurisdiction over troops. Given the level of control exercised by troop-contributing states over their soldiers and commanders, in particular disciplinary control, states' responsibility might arise for their acts or omissions in relation to SEA by troops deployed on UN operations. Troop-contributing state responsibility is most likely to arise through omission, namely the failure to exercise due diligence to prevent SEA in the first instance and to hold perpetrators to account, rather than for the original act of SEA.[44]

Troop-contributing human rights obligations abroad

It is generally recognised that state's obligations under human rights treaties are primarily limited to those within their territory, yet they may be triggered extraterritorially, under certain circumstances. For a state's human rights treaty obligations to be triggered towards a victim of SEA by troops deployed on UN operations, what is key is the level of de facto control, authority or power exercised by that state or its agents over the victim.[45] Legal opinion on the level of control required varies and may depend on the jurisdictional clause of the relevant human rights treaty.[46] What is clear is that a sufficient link must be established between the victim and the troop-contributing state. Such a link might be established where a state's agent exercises state authority over individuals abroad ('state agent authority'); where an injurious act is the effect of and caused by a state's extraterritorial acts ('cause and effect'); or where a state exercises control over an area in which a human rights violation occurs.

Extraterritorial jurisdiction and the International Covenant on Civil and Political Rights

By way of example, many states deploying troops to UN operations are party to the *International Covenant on Civil and Political Rights* (ICCPR). Article 2(1) of the ICCPR provides that 'each State Party to the present

Covenant undertakes to respect and to ensure to all individuals *within its territory and subject to its jurisdiction* the rights recognised in the present Covenant' (emphasis added). There is significant disagreement around whether, in order for a state's obligations under the ICCPR to be triggered towards an individual, this provision requires that the victim must be 'within' a state's territory *and* 'subject to its jurisdiction' when the violation occurs,[47] or whether these terms can be read disjunctively.[48] However, in relation to the ICCPR, it has generally been recognised by the International Court of Justice, the Human Rights Committee (which monitors the implementation of the ICCPR) and in much of the literature that, 'while the jurisdiction of States is primarily territorial, it may sometimes be exercised outside the national territory'.[49]

The *Optional Protocol to the ICCPR* allows the Human Rights Committee to examine individual complaints of violations of the ICCPR where states are party to the Protocol.[50] Article 1(1) of the Protocol simply refers to state obligations to those 'subject to its jurisdiction'. The Human Rights Committee has stated that reference to 'subject to its jurisdiction' in Article 1(1) relates 'not to the place where the violation occurred, but rather to the relationship between the individual [the victim] and the State in relation to a violation of any of the rights set forth in the Covenant, wherever they occurred'.[51] Elaborating on state obligations under the ICCPR, the Human Rights Committee has also stipulated that states must ensure the rights of individuals:

within the *power or effective control* of that State Party, even if not situated within the territory of the State Party ... regardless of the circumstances in which such *power or effective control* was obtained, *such as forces constituting a national contingent of a State Party assigned to a national peacekeeping* or peace-enforcement operation.[52]

The Human Rights Committee clearly contends that state obligations under the ICCPR may arise extraterritorially where states deploy troops to UN operations and exercise power or effective control over persons through their military personnel. Following the Human Rights Committee's approach, troop-contributing states may also owe extraterritorial obligations under the ICCPR where 'power or effective control' is exercised over an SEA victim. In the case of sexual offences, physical power over a victim may be clearly evident.

The International Court of Justice has also recognised the extraterritorial application of the ICCPR and the CRC, amongst other human rights treaties, in particular with respect to those within territories occupied by a state and those who are under its effective control.[53] Effective control over territory evidences control over persons. This is relevant to contemporary UN peacekeeping operations where substantial control over territory is exercised, through the exercise of public powers such as in the case of transitional administrations.[54]

In the ICCPR case of *Gueye v. France*, France paid Senegalese retired soldiers a lower pension than it paid French soldiers, which was not due to place of residence or lower living costs. The Human Rights Committee found France to be in violation of the ICCPR, stipulating that the soldiers were 'not generally subject to French jurisdiction, expect that they rely on French legislation in relation to the amount of their pension rights'.[55] It was this reliance on French legislation that brought them within the control or under the authority of France and, thus, its jurisdiction. The situation of victims of SEA by UN military personnel might be compared insofar as access to justice or redress is tied to the troop-contributing country's exclusive criminal jurisdiction over its military personnel. As the host state's courts cannot exercise criminal jurisdiction over UN military contingent personnel, SEA victims must rely on the troop-contributing state effectively investigating and prosecuting UN soldiers accused of perpetrating sexual offences in the host state. This could be considered a form of power over SEA victims.

The Human Rights Committee has specifically recognised that human rights violations by UN military contingent personnel can give rise to extraterritorial obligations owed by the troop-contributing state under the ICCPR. Belgian peacekeepers deployed as part of the UN Operation in Somalia II, during the 1990s, were accused of a series of human rights violations including the sexual abuse of a Somali girl.[56] On the basis of 'effective control over persons' exercised by Belgium, the Human Rights Committee, in its Concluding Observations on Belgium, criticised the state for failing to meet its obligations under the ICCPR. It elaborated:

> The State party should respect the safeguards established by the Covenant, not only in its territory but also when it exercises its jurisdiction abroad, as for example in the case of peacekeeping missions or NATO military missions, and should train the members of such missions appropriately.[57]

The Human Rights Committee contended that Belgium was under an obligation to 'prohibit, and punish effectively, any conduct by military personnel ... that is contrary to human rights'.[58] It seems logical that

UN troop-contributing states may also have such obligations in relation to victims of SEA in UN mission host states, and failures to meet these obligations could result in a violation of the ICCPR.

Extraterritorial jurisdiction and the inter-American human rights system

The inter-American human rights monitoring bodies have also taken a relatively broad approach to when a state's obligations under the inter-American human rights treaties might be triggered due to the conduct of its agents abroad. For example, in the case of *Coard v. United States of America*, 17 applicants alleged that the United States (US), during military action in Grenada, violated a number of their rights under the *American Declaration on the Rights and Duties of Man* (American Declaration).[59] Amongst their claims, they alleged that US forces had illegally detained them and that during that period they had been mistreated. The Inter-American Commission on Human Rights held that the US had contravened its *American Declaration* obligations in relation to the arrest and detention,[60] despite the acts being carried out extraterritorially. It stated that responsibility of the US was dependent, not necessarily on the presence of an individual in the territory of the state, but rather on whether 'the State observed the rights of a person subject to its authority and control'.[61] The act of arresting and detaining brought the individuals under US 'authority and control'.

Following this approach, it is plausible that victims of SEA could be brought within a troop-contributing state's jurisdiction if the state's soldiers or agents exercise some form of authority or power extraterritorially over victims of SEA. The level of authority or power required over a victim is unclear; however, it seems that if sexual offences occur at the hands of soldiers while an individual is detained this, at the very least, would trigger a state's human rights obligations.

The European human rights system and extraterritorial jurisdiction

Article 1 of the *European Convention on Human Rights* (ECHR) provides that 'the High Contracting Parties shall secure to everyone *within their jurisdiction* the rights and freedoms defined in Section 1 of this Convention' (emphasis added). The jurisprudence of the European Commission on Human Rights and the European Court of Human Rights on the interpretation of this provision has been considerably varied. There is little coherence in the case law on the appropriate test to be applied in order to ascertain whether extraterritorial jurisdiction has been triggered.[62] The jurisprudence of the Commission and the Court has alternated between a narrow territorial approach to jurisdiction and a broader recognition that the extraterritorial exercise of authority, unrelated to control over territory, by state agents abroad ('state agent authority' test) may bring a person within the jurisdiction of a state. State extraterritorial acts producing effects outside its territory have also been held to trigger state ECHR obligations ('cause and effect' test).[63]

The European Commission of Human Rights which, for many years, was required in essence to consider and filter cases before they were submitted to the European Court of Human Rights, generally took the position that states have obligations under the ECHR towards 'all persons under their actual authority and responsibility whether that authority is exercised within their own territory or abroad'.[64] It further recognised that the acts or omissions of state agents, including their armed forces, 'bring any other persons or property "within the jurisdiction" of that State, to the extent that they exercise authority over such persons or property'.[65] Taking this 'state agent authority' approach, which is like the 'authority and control' approach of the Inter-American Commission, a troop-contributing state could be held to have obligations towards a victim of SEA where it exercises authority or responsibility over the victim.

In the early case law of the European Court of Human Rights there was a gradual shift, from the control over victims approach of 'state agent authority' and the 'cause and effect' approach, to a control over territory approach for establishing extraterritorial jurisdiction, yet the Court does not explicitly reject either approach to jurisdiction[66] until the *Banković* case, in 2001. For victims of SEA, a narrow, territorial approach to jurisdiction would restrict the circumstances in which troop-contributing state obligations could arguably be triggered towards them, by confining the application of the ECHR to individuals within territory controlled by a state. This would mean that if insufficient control is exercised over territory by a state its human rights obligations would not be triggered for extraterritorial acts of state agents, including soldiers.

The *Banković* case involved the North Atlantic Treaty Organization (NATO) bombing of a radio and television building in the former Yugoslavia. The relatives of the victims and survivors alleged that their rights under the ECHR had been violated. They argued that the act of bombing had brought them within the jurisdiction of the 17 NATO states parties to the ECHR.[67] The Court stated that in order for jurisdiction to apply extraterritorially it would need to be demonstrated that 'exceptional circumstances exist'.[68] Exceptional circumstances, it deemed, include where a state through 'military occupation or through the consent, invitation or acquiescence of the Government of that territory exercises all or some of the public powers normally to be exercised by that Government'.[69] The Court also stated that state responsibility may be engaged where 'effective control' is exercised over territory abroad through 'military action – whether lawful or unlawful ... whether it be exercised directly, through its armed forces, or through a subordinate local administration'.[70] The *Banković* Court expressly rejected the 'cause and effect' approach to jurisdiction,[71] making it harder to establish extraterritorial jurisdiction of the ECHR.[72] The Court stated that the ECHR was not intended to apply everywhere in the world and to any person who might claim to be a victim,[73] but that it was intended to apply with the legal space of the Council of Europe.[74] This position has been much criticised.[75]

The *Banković* case is highly controversial.[76] Certainly, if the Court's approach to extraterritorial jurisdiction in this case were taken, this would not be positive for victims of human rights abuses by European military personnel deployed on UN operations. Most incidents of SEA by UN peacekeepers have occurred outside Council of Europe states, in places such as Sudan, Haiti and the Democratic Republic of the Congo. It would therefore be extremely difficult to demonstrate that a European troop-contributing state's ECHR obligations had been triggered towards an SEA victim.

However, a recent series of cases issued in 2008, relating to Turkey and Northern Cyprus, indicate an alteration in approach by the European Court of Human Rights, and a return to a 'state agent authority' and 'cause and effect' approaches to jurisdiction.[77] One such case is *Andreou v. Turkey*,[78] involving allegations against Turkey for acts occurring during a demonstration in or near the UN buffer zone. The applicant was shot by Turkish troops by a bullet coming from, what the Court deemed, a Turkish-controlled area in Northern Cyprus, but the result actually occurred outside that area on the Southern Cyprus side of the buffer zone. If an 'effective control' over territory approach was taken at the material time, the applicant would not have been 'within the jurisdiction' of Turkey. The applicant argued that this would be an 'unduly formalistic interpretation' of *Banković*.[79] The Court agreed and reaffirmed the 'state agent authority' approach to jurisdiction. In deciding that Turkey did in fact exercise extraterritorial jurisdiction, however, it relied on a 'cause and effect' analysis. The Court held that:

> even though the applicant sustained her injuries in territory over which Turkey exercised no control, the opening of fire on the crowd

from *close range*, which was the direct and immediate cause of those injuries, was such that the applicant must be regarded as 'within [the] jurisdiction' of Turkey[80]

In *Solomou v. Turkey*, the European Court of Human Rights also stipulated that Article 1 of the ECHR 'cannot be interpreted so as to allow a State party to perpetrate violations of the Convention on the territory of another State which it could not perpetrate on its own territory'.[81]

The recent *Al Skeini* case before the Grand Chamber of the European Court of Human Rights seems to consolidate this move away from *Banković*.[82] The case involved the deaths of six Iraqi citizens, five in isolated incidents occurring in houses or streets in Iraq at the hands of British soldiers, and the other in a British prison in Iraq.[83] At the time the United Kingdom (UK) was an occupying power in Iraq. It was alleged that the UK had violated the ECHR by failing to conduct an adequate inquiry into the incidents. The European Court of Human Rights held that where a state exercises some public powers of another state this may give rise to extraterritorial jurisdiction.[84] It further stipulated that 'in certain circumstances, the use of force by a State's agents operating outside its territory may bring the individual thereby brought under the control of the State's authorities into the State's Article 1 jurisdiction'.[85] The Court rejected the idea that extraterritorial jurisdiction is tied to 'the control exercised by the Contracting State over the buildings, aircraft or ship in which the individuals were held'. It qualified that '[w]hat is decisive in such cases is the exercise of physical power and control over the person in question'.[86] The Court noted the UK was exercising certain public powers. It stated that the acts of British soldiers in the area of operation were sufficient to establish that the UK exercised 'authority and control' over the individuals killed to establish a jurisdictional link.[87] This again reflects the 'state agent authority' approach. The Court also notes that the ECHR can apply outside the territory of Council of Europe member states.[88]

So what might this all mean for victims of SEA by UN military contingent personnel? Applying a 'state agent authority' over victim approach, it seems plausible that a troop-contributing state's human rights treaty obligations could be triggered in relation to a SEA victim. Physical power over the victim by the state agent perpetrating the act might well be demonstrated in cases of non-consensual sex. Decisions of a contingent commander or a state, whether or not to take effective action against a soldier perpetrating SEA, also affect the victim's rights and constitute an exercise of authority. Jurisdiction might be more difficult to establish using an 'effective control' over territory approach, unless SEA is perpetrated against a victim within an area controlled by the troop-contributing state, such as inside a military base. Where a contingent is exercising considerable control over, and public powers in, an area outside the base, this might also be taken into account, as it demonstrates greater control over those with an area of operation.

Conclusion: extraterritorial jurisdiction

As illustrated, tests for extraterritorial application of human rights treaties revolve around state authority or control over persons and/or control over the territory where the human rights abuse takes place.[89] In the context of UN peacekeeping operations, state military contingents may exercise varying degrees of territorial control and public powers, in particular in the context of transitional administrations, even if under a UN mandate.[90] To confine the test for establishing jurisdiction to 'effective control' over territory (or an area) is not widely accepted.[91] A 'state agent authority' approach has also been applied in the case law, which requires that the alleged victim be placed under the 'control', 'power', 'authority' or 'responsibility' of the state through the extraterritorial acts of its agents. An additional approach to extraterritorial jurisdiction taken in the case law is that of 'cause and effect', wherein state obligations may be triggered by acts of the state or its agent's acts which produce effects extraterritorially, causing an injury.

Actual physical control is more likely to give rise to state obligations. Physical control or power over a victim of SEA will be more evident in cases such as rape or forced prostitution. It is also generally accepted that if a state detains an individual he/she will come within the state's jurisdiction.[92] If SEA occurs, for instance, on a military base controlled by a particular contingent, or if a soldier detains a victim, this could also evidence extraterritorial jurisdiction and trigger a state's human rights obligations. However, the view that a victim needs to actually be detained by a state's agents in order to come 'within its jurisdiction' is uncertain. To maintain that no human rights obligations arise for the state where a state's agent purposefully kills, rapes or otherwise violates an individual's fundamental human rights, but that obligations arise where a state agent detains the individual and the same act is perpetrated, is indefensible. Troop-contributing states have exclusive criminal jurisdiction over UN military contingent personnel and this arguably could be considered sufficient power, responsibility or authority over the victim, to bring the victim within their jurisdiction.[93] Where a troop-contributing state does not effectively investigate and, where appropriate, prosecute those alleged to have perpetrated SEA, under 'cause and effect' notions of jurisdiction this could also arguably bring the victim within its jurisdiction. The failure of states to hold perpetrators of SEA to account is in itself a human rights violation.

State obligations

If state extraterritorial jurisdiction is established, the troop-contributing state should, at the very least, adhere to a standard of due diligence when it comes to sexual offences by members of their military contingents.[94] This means that states should do what is reasonable in the circumstances to protect the rights of victims of SEA by their troops. A state's failure to effectively investigate and, where appropriate, prosecute human rights violations by its military personnel, involving serious incidents of SEA, is best conceived of as a distinct state omission, giving rise to state responsibility independently of the original act.

Due diligence entails state responsibility, not only for its own acts or those of its agents, but also for its omissions where it fails to meet positive obligations under human rights instruments it has ratified towards persons falling within its jurisdiction.[95] Due diligence revolves around a standard of 'reasonableness'.[96] The Inter-American Court of Human Rights has held that a state is required 'to take *reasonable* steps to prevent human rights violations committed within its jurisdiction, to identify those responsible, to impose the appropriate punishment and to ensure the victim adequate compensation'.[97]

According to the Human Rights Committee, states may be in violation of the ICCPR for 'permitting or failing to take appropriate measures or to exercise due diligence to prevent, punish, investigate or redress the harm caused by such acts of private persons or entities'.[98] The General Assembly's *Declaration on the Elimination of Violence against Women*, although non-binding, requires states to '[e]xercise due diligence to prevent, investigate and ... punish acts of violence against women, whether those acts are perpetrated by State or private persons'.[99]

The UN Special Rapporteur on Violence against Women has stipulated that due diligence is a useful 'yardstick' against which to weigh state actions in relation to ending violence against women, with respect to the conduct of both state and private actors,[100] including in the context of peacekeeping operations.[101] The due diligence standard has also been applied by UN bodies to the context of human trafficking[102] and other sexual offences.[103]

Troop-contributing states should at very least exercise due diligence in dealing with SEA by their troops. They should take all measures within their capacity to deal with alleged perpetrators and afford victims some form of remedy. The right of access to justice is increasingly recognised as a right of victims of human rights violations, and may well form part of a remedy.[104] States have a duty under international law to prosecute or extradite those allegedly responsible for certain egregious international crimes such as torture.[105] Rape may constitute torture under certain circumstances. With respect to other forms of human rights violations, it is increasingly recognised that states may also have obligations to prosecute perpetrators[106] and to effectively investigate violations, even where this is not explicitly provided for in a human rights treaty.[107]

In the context of SEA by UN military contingent personnel, prosecution alone is not enough. In redressing harm caused to victims of SEA, other measures might include the provision of effective remedies, including the provision of physical, economic and emotional support to victims. Troop-contributing states should take preventative measures, such as ensuring adequate training of their military personnel on SEA, women's rights, children's rights and UN standards of conduct. States may need to draft additional legislation, applicable to military contingents abroad, covering sexual offences against women and children in host states, in order to fulfil their obligations. There may also be a need to provide both ongoing physical and psychological support to SEA victims. Financial support, either provided by the perpetrator or the troop-contributing state, should clearly be made available in cases of babies born from SEA by UN peacekeepers, where paternity is established.[108]

State failure to meet their human rights treaty obligations may open avenues for some form of redress for victims of SEA to be pursued. Complaints by individuals, groups of individuals, states and non-governmental organisations to treaty monitoring bodies are permitted under certain international human rights instruments. Subject to the prior exhaustion of local remedies,[109] human rights bodies provide for a range of preventative and reparative measures for SEA victims.[110] For instance, the ECHR allows contracting states, individuals, non-governmental organisations and groups of individuals allegedly victims of state violations of the ECHR to submit complaints to the European Court of Human Rights.[111] The Court may award 'just satisfaction' to victims,[112] which for SEA victims might include some form of compensation.[113] The Inter-American Commission for Human Rights and the Inter-American Court for Human Rights have in the past also ordered reparative measures for victims of human rights abuses, such as compensatory damages and requiring states to investigate and, where appropriate, prosecute perpetrators of human rights violations.[114]

These are but a limited sample. Other non-judicial mechanisms may be used to shame and pressurise states to take effective action with respect to soldiers perpetrating sexual offences while deployed on UN operations. These might include, for example, the Universal Periodic Review under the Human Rights Council, UN Special Rapporteur reports and the Concluding Observations of human rights monitoring bodies. While non-binding, these mechanisms may issue politically influential recommendations; generally states do not want to be named and shamed. As previously noted, the Human Rights Committee, in its Concluding Observations, has specifically criticised troop-contributing states for failure to investigate and prosecute UN military contingent personnel for human rights violations while deployed on UN operations.

Conclusion

It is essential to the promotion of human rights and the rule of law in UN mission host states that those who seek to promote these standards do not themselves violate them. The failure of some UN troop-contributing states to take their obligations seriously, to effectively investigate and prosecute soldiers perpetrating sexual offences while deployed on UN operations, in effect leaves SEA victims without an effective remedy. If a narrow perspective is taken on extraterritorial jurisdiction for the purpose of international human rights law, one is left to question why human rights are normatively universal and yet the obligations that arise under them are not.[115] A broader, and now widely accepted, interpretation of extraterritorial jurisdiction which focuses not only on state control over territory, but also on state control or authority over victims, better reflects the reality that states can and do affect the rights of persons beyond their borders.

SEA by soldiers deployed on UN operations might give rise to troop-contributing state human rights obligations where there is a failure to take reasonable measures to prevent such abuse and to take action against perpetrators. This may open up avenues for victims of SEA to seek some form of reparation or redress using human rights treaty monitoring mechanisms. Moreover, these mechanisms could be used as a means to tackle state complacency and pressure states into taking effective action against soldiers perpetrating SEA while deployed on UN operations.

Notes

1. UN Department of Peacekeeping Operations (DPKO), 'Peacekeeping factsheet', *United Nations Peacekeeping* (31 August 2013), http://www.un.org/en/peacekeeping/resources/statistics/factsheet.shtml (last accessed October 2013).

2. For details on various UN missions and their mandates, see *United Nations Peacekeeping*, http://www.un.org/en/peacekeeping (last accessed October 2013).

3. *A Comprehensive Strategy to Eliminate Future Sexual Exploitation and Abuse in United Nations Peacekeeping Operations*, UN Doc. A/59/710 (24 March 2005), para. 6 (*Zeid Report*).

4. F. Elliott and R. Elkins, 'UN shame over sex scandal', *The Independent* (UK) (7 January 2007), available at http://www.humanrightsvoices.org/site/articles/?a=4009&view=print (last accessed October 2013); O. Simić, 'Accountability of UN civilian police involved in trafficking of women in Bosnia and Herzegovina', *Peace & Conflict Monitor* (November 2004), http://www.monitor.upeace.org/archive.cfm?id_article=219 (last accessed October 2013); M.E. Vandenberg and K. Peratis, 'Hopes betrayed: Trafficking of women and girls to post-conflict Bosnia and Herzegovina for forced prostitution', *Human Rights Watch* (November 2002), p. 14, http://www.hrw.org/reports/2002/bosnia (last accessed October 2013).

5. For the most recent SEA statistics, see 'Overview of statistics', *United Nations Conduct and Discipline Unit* (2010), http://cdu.unlb.org/Statistics/OverviewofStatistics.aspx (last accessed October 2013): 56 allegations were made against military personnel in 2007; 49 in 2008; 55 in 2009; 41 in 2010; and 41 in 2011.

6. See further M. Kanetake, 'Whose zero tolerance counts? Reassessing a zero tolerance policy against sexual exploitation and abuse by UN peacekeepers', *International Peacekeeping*, Vol. 17, No. 2 (2010) 200.

7. This category of personnel does not include military observers.

8. DPKO, 'Peacekeeping factsheet'. The largest troop-contributing states include Pakistan, Bangladesh, Ethiopia, Egypt, Ghana, India, Jordan, Nepal, Nigeria and Rwanda. Western states deploy comparatively few military contingent personnel to UN operations. This is not to suggest that troops from western countries have not been implicated in SEA to an equal extent *per capita*. For current figures on troop deployments, see DPKO, 'Troop and police contributors', *United Nations Peacekeeping*, http://www.un.org/en/peacekeeping/resources/statistics/contributors.shtml (last accessed October 2013).

9. *Draft Model Status-of-Forces Agreement between the United Nations and Host Countries*, UN Doc. A/45/594 (9 October 1990) annex, paras 4, 5.8 (*Draft Model Status-of-Forces Agreement*). For discussion of these jurisdictional immunities, see R. Burke, 'Status of forces deployed on UN peacekeeping operations: Jurisdictional immunity', *Journal of Conflict & Security Law*, Vol. 16, No. 1 (2011) 63.

10. *Manual on Policies and Procedures concerning the Reimbursement and Control of Contingent-Owned Equipment of Troop/Police Contributors Participating in Peacekeeping Missions*, UN Doc. A/C.5/63/18 (29 January 2009), ch. 9 (*Contingent-Owned Equipment Manual*).

11. *Implementation of the Recommendations of the Special Committee on Peacekeeping Operations: Report of the Secretary-General*, UN Doc. A/64/573 (22 December 2009), para. 84; and *Report of the Special Committee on Peacekeeping Operations*, UN Doc. A/64/19 (22 February–19 March 2010), para. 53. States have only responded to 99 of 350 UN requests for information on action taken against alleged perpetrators of SEA, since 2007. There is little to no information on the content of these responses. See 'UN follow-up with member states (sexual exploitation and abuse)', *United Nations Conduct and Discipline Unit* (27 September 2013), http://cdu.unlb.org/Statistics/UNFollowupwithMemberStatesSexualExploitationandAbuse.aspx (last accessed October 2013).

12. *Draft Model Status-of-Forces Agreement*, UN Doc. A/45/594 (9 October 1990) annex, para. 6; and *Contingent-Owned Equipment Manual*, UN Doc. A/C.5/63/18 (29 January 2009).

13. *Secretary-General's Bulletin: Special Measures for the Protection from Sexual Exploitation and Sexual Abuse*, UN Doc. ST/SGB/2003/13 (9 October 2003) (Bulletin).

14. *Security Council Resolution 1325*, UN Doc. S/RES/1325 (31 October 2000), paras 1, 3.

15. *Security Council Resolution 1820*, UN Doc. S/RES/1820 (19 June 2008) (SCR 1820); *Security Council Resolution 1888*, UN Doc. S/RES/1888 (30 September 2009); *Security Council Resolution 1889*, UN Doc. S/RES/1889 (5 October 2009); *Security Council Resolution 1960*, UN Doc. S/RES/1960 (16 December 2010); *Security Council Resolution 2106*, UN Doc. S/RES/2106 (24 June 2013); and *Security Council Resolution 2122*, UN Doc. S/RES/2122 (18 October 2013).

16. SCR 1820, paras 6, 8.

17. DPKO and UN Department of Field Support (DFS), 'DPKO/DFS guidelines: Integrating a gender perspective into the work of the United Nations military in peacekeeping operations' (DPKO and DFS, March 2010), p. 8.

18. *Report of the Group of Legal Experts on Making the Standards Contained in the Secretary-General's Bulletin Binding on Contingent Members and Standardizing the Norms of Conduct So That They Are Applicable to All Categories of Peacekeeping Personnel*, UN Doc. A/61/645 (18 December 2006); and *Zeid Report*, UN Doc. A/59/710 (24 March 2005).

19. Bulletin, UN Doc. ST/SGB/2003/13 (9 October 2003).

20. Ibid., section 1.

21. Ibid.

22. N. Quénivet, 'The role of the International Criminal Court in the prosecution of peacekeepers for sexual offences', in R. Arnold (ed.), *Law Enforcement within the Framework of Peace Support Operations* (Leiden: Martinus Nijhoff, 2008) 399, pp. 411–412.

23. For discussion, see N. Puechguirbal, 'Discourse on gender, patriarchy and Resolution 1325: A textual analysis of UN Documents', *International Peacekeeping*, Vol. 17, No. 2 (2010) 172.

24. D. Otto, 'Making sense of zero tolerance policies in peacekeeping sexual economies', in V.E. Monro and C.F. Stychin (eds), *Sexuality and the Law: Feminist Engagements* (Abingdon: Routledge-Cavendish, 2007) 259, p. 260; and O. Simić, 'Rethinking "sexual exploitation" in UN peacekeeping operations', *Women's Studies International Forum*, Vol. 32, No. 4 (2009) 288.

25. See, for example, P. Higate, *Gender and Peacekeeping Case Studies: The Democratic Republic of the Congo and Sierra Leone* (Pretoria: Institute for Security Studies, 2003), pp. 61–63.

26. See, for example, UN High Commissioner for Refugees (UNHCR) and Save the Children UK, 'Sexual violence and exploitation: The experience of refugee children in Guinea, Liberia and Sierra Leone' (UNHCR and Save the Children UK, February 2002). See also C. Csáky, 'No one to turn to: The under-reporting of child sexual exploitation and abuse by aid workers and peacekeepers' (Save the Children UK, 2008), p. 7.

27. For a discussion of the complexity of issues that arise in relation to sexual relationships between peacekeepers and local civilians and the degree of agency that may, or may not, be genuinely exercised by women or girls in peacekeeping mission areas, see further Higate, *Gender and Peacekeeping Case Studies*, pp. 22–23, 43–44. See also Otto, 'Making sense of zero tolerance', p. 260; Simić, 'Rethinking "sexual exploitation"', pp. 288–95.

28. Otto, 'Making sense of zero tolerance', pp. 267–270.

29. *Zeid Report*, UN Doc. A/59/710 (24 March 2005), para. 6.

30. See, for example, sources listed at above Note 4.

31. See, for example, *Inter-American Convention on the Prevention, Punishment and Eradication of Violence against Women*, opened for signature on 9 June 1994, 33 ILM 1534 (entered into force on 5 March 1995); *Council of Europe Convention on Preventing and Combating Violence against Women and Domestic Violence*, opened for signature on 11 May 2011, CETS No. 210 (not yet in force); and *Protocol to the African Charter on Human and Peoples' Rights on the Rights of Women in Africa*, opened for signature on 13 September 2000, OAU Doc. CAB/LEG/66.6 (entered into force on 25 November 2005), art. 11.

32. *Convention on the Elimination of All Forms of Discrimination against Women*, opened for signature on 1 March 1980, 1249 UNTS 13 (entered into force on 3 September 1981), art. 6 (CEDAW); *Convention on the Rights of the Child*, opened for signature on 20 November 1989, 1577 UNTS 3 (entered into force on 2 September 1990), art. 34 (CRC); and *Optional Protocol to the Convention on the Rights of the Child on the Sale of Children, Child Prostitution and Child Pornography*, opened for signature on 25 May 2000, 2171 UNTS 227 (entered into force on 18 January 2002) (*Optional Protocol to the CRC*).

33. *Convention against Torture and Other Cruel, Inhuman or Degrading Treatment or Punishment*, opened for signature on 10 December 1984, 1465 UNTS 85 (entered into force on 26 June 1987) (CAT); *International Covenant on Civil and Political Rights*, opened for signature on 16 December 1966, 999 UNTS 171 (entered into force on 23 March 1976), art. 7 (ICCPR); *European Convention for the Protection of Human Rights and Fundamental Freedoms*, opened for signature on 4 November 1950, 213 UNTS 221 (entered into force on 3 September 1953), art. 3 (ECHR); *African Charter on Human and Peoples' Rights*, opened for signature on 27 June 1981, 1520 UNTS 217 (entered into force on 21 November 1986), art. 5 (*African Charter*); and *Inter-American Convention on Human Rights*, opened for signature on 22 November 1969, 1144 UNTS 123 (entered into force on 18 July 1978).

34. See further UN Commission on Human Rights, *Contemporary Forms of Slavery: Systematic Rape, Sexual Slavery and Slave-Like Practices during Armed*

Conflict: Update on the Final Report Submitted by Ms Gay J. McDougall, UN Doc. E/CN.4/Sub.2/2000/21 (6 June 2000), p. 51.

35. *Convention to Suppress the Slave Trade and Slavery*, opened for signature on 25 September 1926, 60 LNTS 253 (entered into force on 9 March 1923), as amended by *Protocol amending the Slavery Convention*, opened for signature on 23 October 1953, 182 UNTS 51 (entered into force on 7 December 1953), art. 1; and ICCPR, art. 8(1).
36. CEDAW, art. 6.
37. Committee on the Elimination of Discrimination against Women, *General Recommendation No. 19: Violence against Women*, UN Doc. A/47/38 (29 January 1992) (*General Recommendation No. 19*).
38. *General Recommendation No. 19*, UN Doc. A/47/38 (29 January 1992).
39. For ratification status, see '*Convention on the Rights of the Child*', United Nations Treaty Collection, http://treaties.un.org/pages/viewdetails. aspx?src=treaty&mtdsg_no=iv-11&chapter=4&lang=en (last accessed October 2013).
40. CRC, arts 34, 35. See also Committee on the Rights of the Child, *Concluding Observations: Lebanon*, UN Doc. CRC/C/LBN/CO/3 (8 June 2006), para. 82(e).
41. CRC, art. 1.
42. *Optional Protocol to the CRC*, art. 3(1).
43. International Law Commission, *Draft Articles on the Responsibility of International Organizations*, UN Doc. A/CN.4/L.778 (30 May 2011), art. 7. On the issue of attribution of responsibility in the context of UN peacekeeping operation and SEA, see further R. Burke, 'Attribution of responsibility: Sexual abuse and exploitation, and effective control of blue helmets', *Journal of International Peacekeeping*, Vol. 16, No. 1–2 (2012) 1.
44. This is because the original act is likely to be private in nature, beyond the scope of official duties. Unless international humanitarian law applies, this means that it will not be attributable directly to a state. A *lex specialis* rule operates in the context of international humanitarian law, generally making all acts of a state's armed forces attributable to it. Burke, 'Attribution of responsibility', pp. 38–43.
45. M. Scheinin, 'Extraterritorial effect of the *International Covenant on Civil and Political Rights*', in F. Coomans and M. Kamminga (eds), *Extraterritorial Application of Human Rights Treaties* (Antwerp: Intersentia, 2004) 73, p. 79.
46. Article 2(1) of the ICCPR, for instance, provides that a state party assumes responsibilities with respect to everyone 'within its territory and subject to its jurisdiction'. Conversely, there is no mention of 'territory' in the jurisdictional limitation clause of the *Inter-American Convention on Human Rights*. Some international human rights law treaties, such as the *International Covenant on Economic, Social and Cultural Rights* and the *African Charter*, do not have a jurisdictional limitation clause. See *International Covenant on Economic, Social and Cultural Rights*, opened for signature on 16 December 1966, 993 UNTS 3 (entered into force on 3 January 1976) (ICESCR). Other treaties specifically require the exercise of extraterritorial jurisdiction: see, for example, CAT, art. 2(1).
47. See, for example, M. Dennis, 'Application of human rights treaties extraterritorially to detention of combatants and security internees: Fuzzy thinking all around?', *ILSA Journal of International & Comparative Law*, Vol. 12, No. 2

(2006) 459; and D. McGoldrick, 'Extraterritorial application of the Covenant on Civil and Political Rights', in F. Coomans and M. Kamminga (eds), *Extraterritorial Application of Human Rights Treaties* (Antwerp: Intersentia, 2004) 41, pp. 47–55.

48. Human Rights Committee, *General Comment No. 31: Nature of the General Legal Obligation Imposed on States Parties to the Covenant*, UN Doc. CCPR/C/21/Rev.1/Add.13 (26 May 2004), para. 12; and T. Meron, 'Extraterritoriality of human rights treaties', *The American Journal of International Law*, Vol. 89, No. 1 (1995) 78, p. 79.

49. *Legal Consequences of the Construction of a Wall in the Occupied Palestinian Territory (Advisory Opinion)* [2004] ICJ Rep. 136, [109] (*Wall Case*). See, for example, Human Rights Committee, *Concluding Observations: United States of America*, UN Doc. CCPR/C/79/Add.50 (3 October 1995), para. 284; Meron, 'The extraterritoriality of human rights treaties', p. 79; and T. Buergenthal, 'To respect and ensure: State obligations and permissible derogations', in L. Henkin (ed.), *The International Bill of Rights: The Covenant on Civil and Political Rights* (New York: Columbia University Press, 1981) 72, p. 74.

50. *Optional Protocol to the International Covenant on Civil and Political Rights* (Optional Protocol to the ICCPR), opened for signature on 16 December 1966, 999 UNTS 302 (entered into force on 23 March 1976).

51. Human Rights Committee, *Views: Communication No. 52/1979*, UN Doc. CCPR/C/13/D/52/1979 (29 July 1981), para. 12.2 (*Saldías de López v. Uruguay*).

52. Human Rights Committee, *General Comment No. 31*, UN Doc. CCPR/C/21/Rev.1/Add.13 (26 May 2004), para. 10 (emphasis added); Human Rights Committee, *Views: Communication No. 56/1979*, UN Doc. CCPR/C/13/D/56/1979 (29 July 1981) (*Celiberti de Casariego v. Uruguay*).

53. *Wall Case* [2004] ICJ Rep. 136, [109]–[111]. See also Human Rights Committee, *Concluding Observations: Israel*, UN Doc. CCPR/CO/78/ISR (21 August 2003), para. 11; Human Rights Committee, *Concluding Observations: Israel*, UN Doc. CCPR/C/79/Add.93 (18 August 1998), para. 10; and *Armed Activities on the Territory of the Congo (Democratic Republic of the Congo v. Uganda) (Judgment)* [2005] ICJ Rep. 168, [216]–[221]. See also *Legal Consequences for States of the Continued Presence of South Africa in Namibia (South West Africa) notwithstanding Security Council Resolution 276 (1970) (Advisory Opinion)* [1971] ICJ Rep. 16, [118].

54. Although this context will be further complicated by the issue of attribution, given that UN military contingent personnel will be operating under a UN mandate.

55. Human Rights Committee, *Views: Communication No. 196/1985*, UN Doc. CCPR/C/35/D/196/1985 (6 April 1989), para. 9.4 (*Gueye v. France*).

56. Human Rights Committee, *Concluding Observations: Belgium*, UN Doc. CCPR/C/79/Add.99 (19 November 1998), para. 14. See also T. McCormack, '*Their* atrocities and *our* misdemeanours: The reticence of states to try their "own nationals" for international crimes', in M. Lattimer and P. Sands (eds), *Justice for Crimes against Humanity* (Oxford: Hart, 2003) 107, pp. 127, 138–139.

57. Human Rights Committee, *Concluding Observations: Belgium*, UN Doc. CCPR/CO/81/BEL (12 August 2004), para. 6 (*Concluding Observations: Belgium*).

58. *Concluding Observations: Belgium*, UN Doc. CCPR/CO/81/BEL (12 August 2004), para. 9.

59. *Coard v. United States* (Inter-American Commission on Human Rights, Report No. 109/99, Case No. 10.951, 29 September 1999), [1], [6] (*Coard*).
60. *Coard* (Inter-American Commission on Human Rights, Report No. 109/99, Case No. 10.951, 29 September 1999), [6].
61. *Coard* (Inter-American Commission on Human Rights, Report No. 109/99, Case No. 10.951, 29 September 1999), [37].
62. M. Milanovic, *Extraterritorial Application of Human Rights Treaties: Principles and Policy* (Oxford: Oxford University Press, 2011), p. 4.
63. See, for example, *Loizidou v. Turkey (Merits)* (1997) 23 EHRR 513, [52]. In *W.M. v. Denmark* the European Commission on Human Rights employed a test of 'authority' over the victim and a 'cause and effect' test (that is, that the state was the cause of an act or omission resulting in a human rights violation): *W.M. v. Denmark* (1992) 73 Eur. Comm. HR 193, [1], [73]. The cause and effect approach was reaffirmed in *Loizidou v. Turkey (Preliminary Objections)* (1995) 310 Eur. Court HR (ser. A), [62].
64. *Cyprus v. Turkey (Admissibility)* (1975) 2 Eur. Comm. HR 125, [8].
65. *Cyprus v. Turkey (Admissibility)* (1975) 2 Eur. Comm. HR 125, [8]. See also *Cyprus v. Turkey* (1976) 4 EHRR 482.
66. See, for example, *Loizidou v. Turkey (Preliminary Objections)* (1995) 310 Eur. Court HR (ser. A), [62].
67. *Banković v. Belgium (Admissibility)* [2001] XII Eur. Court HR 333, [46], [52]–[53] (*Banković*).
68. Ibid., [74].
69. Ibid., [71]. See also *Ilaşcu v. Moldova* (2004) 40 EHRR 46.
70. *Loizidou v. Turkey (Preliminary Objections)* (1995) 310 Eur. Court HR (ser. A), [62].
71. *Banković* [2001] XII Eur. Court HR 333, [75]. As noted previously, state acts producing effects outside its territory have been held to trigger state ECHR obligations. This has been termed a 'cause and effect' approach to extraterritorial jurisdiction. It is not linked to control over territory.
72. See, for example, E. Roxstrom, M. Gibney and T. Einarsen, 'The NATO bombing case (*Banković et al. v. Belgium et al.*) and the limits of western human rights protection', *Boston University International Law Journal*, Vol. 23, No. 1 (2003) 55, pp. 87–8; and L. Loucaides, 'Determining the extra-territorial effect of the *European Convention*: Facts, jurisprudence and the *Banković* case', *European Human Rights Law Review*, No. 4 (2006) 391, p. 401.
73. *Banković* [2001] XII Eur. Court HR 333, [75].
74. Ibid., [80].
75. See generally Roxstrom et al., 'The NATO bombing case'.
76. See, for example, O. De Schutter, 'Globalization and jurisdiction: Lessons from the *European Convention on Human Rights*', *Baltic Yearbook of International Law*, Vol. 6 (2006) 185, pp. 194–196; and R. Lawson, 'Life after *Bankovic*: On the extraterritorial application of the *European Convention on Human Rights*', in F. Coomans and M. Kamminga (eds), *Extraterritorial Application of Human Rights Treaties* (Antwerp: Intersentia, 2004) 83.
77. As noted previously, the exercise of authority by state agents abroad may bring a person within the jurisdiction of a state; this has been referred to as a 'state agent authority' approach to extraterritorial jurisdiction. State acts producing effects outside its territory have also been held to trigger state

ECHR obligations; this is referred to as a 'cause and effect' approach to extra-territorial jurisdiction.

78. *Andreou v. Turkey* (European Court of Human Rights, Chamber, Application No. 45653/99, 3 June 2008) (*Andreou*).
79. *Andreou* (European Court of Human Rights, Chamber, Application No. 45653/99, 3 June 2008).
80. *Andreou* (European Court of Human Rights, Chamber, Application No. 45653/99, 3 June 2008), [51] (emphasis added). A 'state agent authority' approach was applied in *Solomou*, a case involving the shooting of a man in the UN buffer zone between Northern and Southern Cyprus: *Solomou v. Turkey* (European Court of Human Rights, Chamber, Application No. 36832/97, 24 June 2008), [48]–[50]. Similarly, a 'state agent authority' approach was again adopted by the European Court of Human Rights in the case of *Isaak*, which involved the brutal beating to death of a man in the UN buffer zone: *Isaak v. Turkey* (European Court of Human Rights, Chamber, Application No. 44587/98, 24 June 2008), 1. See also *Issa v. Turkey (Merits)* (2005) 41 EHRR 27, [71]–[82].
81. *Solomou v. Turkey* (European Court of Human Rights, Chamber, Application No. 36832/97, 24 June 2008), [45].
82. *Al-Skeini v. United Kingdom* (European Court of Human Rights, Grand Chamber, Application No. 55721/07, 7 July 2011) (*Al-Skeini*).
83. *Al-Skeini* (European Court of Human Rights, Grand Chamber, Application No. 55721/07, 7 July 2011), [6].
84. Ibid., [135].
85. Ibid., [136].
86. *Al-Skeini* (European Court of Human Rights, Grand Chamber, Application No. 55721/07, 7 July 2011). Some previous cases have linked jurisdiction to control over premises such as detention centres, embassies and so on. See, for example, *Al-Saadoon v. United Kingdom (Admissibility)* (2009) 49 EHRR SE11, [88].
87. *Al-Skeini* (European Court of Human Rights, Grand Chamber, Application No. 55721/07, 7 July 2011), [149].
88. Ibid., [142].
89. See, for example, *Hess v. United Kingdom* (1975) 2 Eur. Comm. HR 72; and *Al-Saadoon v. United Kingdom (Admissibility)* (2009) 49 EHRR SE11, [88].
90. *Banković* [2001] XII Eur. Court HR 333, [71].
91. See, for example, F.J. Hampson, 'The relationship between international humanitarian law and human rights law from the perspective of a human rights treaty body', *International Review of the Red Cross*, Vol. 90, No. 871 (2008) 549, p. 570; Meron, 'The extraterritoriality of human rights treaties', p. 82.
92. S. Wills, *Protecting Civilians: The Obligations of Peacekeepers* (Oxford: Oxford University Press, 2009), p. 477.
93. *Contingent-Owned Equipment Manual*, UN Doc. A/C.5/63/18 (29 January 2009), art. 7 *quinquiens*.
94. *Rodríguez v. Honduras* (Inter-American Court of Human Rights (ser. C) No. 4, 29 July 1988), [172]; J.H. Knox, 'Horizontal human rights law', *The American Journal of International Law*, Vol. 102, No. 1 (2008) 1, p. 23.

95. See, for example, *General Recommendation No. 19*, UN Doc. A/47/38 (29 January 1992), para. 9; and *X and Y v. The Netherlands* (1985) 91 Eur. Court HR (ser. A), [11].

96. R.P. Barnidge, 'The due diligence principle under international law', *International Community Law Review*, Vol. 8, No. 1 (2006) 81, p. 120.

97. *Rodríguez v. Honduras* (Inter-American Court of Human Rights (ser. C) No. 4, 29 July 1988), [174] (emphasis added).

98. Human Rights Committee, *General Comment No. 31*, UN Doc. CCPR/C/21/ Rev.1/Add.13 (26 May 2004), para. 8. See also R. Coomaraswamy, *Report of the Special Rapporteur on Violence against Women, Its Causes and Consequences*, UN Doc. E/CN.4/1997/47 (12 February 1997).

99. *Declaration on the Elimination of Violence against Women*, UN Doc. A/RES/ 48/104 (20 February 1993), art. 4(c).

100. Y. Ertürk, *The Due Diligence Standard as a Tool for the Elimination of Violence against Women: Report of the Special Rapporteur on Violence against Women*, UN Doc. E/CN.4/2006/61 (20 January 2006) (*Ertürk Report*).

101. *Ertürk Report*, UN Doc. E/CN.4/2006/61 (20 January 2006).

102. *Recommended Principles and Guidelines on Human Rights and Human Trafficking: Report of the United Nations High Commissioner for Human Rights*, UN Doc. E/2002/68/Add.1 (20 May 2002) (*UNHCR Report*).

103. *UNHCR Report*, UN Doc. E/2002/68/Add.1 (20 May 2002).

104. M.C. Bassiouni, 'International recognition of victims' rights', *Human Rights Law Review*, Vol. 6, No. 2 (2006) 203, pp. 212, 263–266; R. Manjoo, *Report of the Special Rapporteur on Violence against Women, Its Causes and Consequences*, UN Doc. A/HRC/14/22 (19 April 2010), p. 2 (*Manjoo Report*).

105. See, for example, *Convention on the Prevention and Punishment of the Crime of Genocide*, opened for signature on 9 December 1948, 78 UNTS 277 (entered into force on 12 January 1951), arts 4–6; *Convention against Torture*, arts 7, 8, 12, 13.

106. S.K. Miller, 'Accountability for the conduct of UN-mandated forces under international human rights law: A case study concerning sexual abuse of the UN Mission in the Democratic Republic of the Congo (MONUC)', in R. Arnold and G.-J.A. Knoops (eds), *Practice and Policies of Modern Peace Support Operations under International Law* (Ardsley: Martinus Nijhoff, 2006) 261.

107. J. Murray, 'Who will police the peacebuilders? The failure to establish accountability for the participation of United Nations civilian police in the trafficking of women in post-conflict Bosnia and Herzegovina', *Columbia Human Rights Law Review*, Vol. 34, No. 2 (2003) 475, p. 515; and Human Rights Committee, *General Comment No. 31*, UN Doc. CCPR/C/21/Rev.1/ Add.13 (26 May 2004), para. 15.

108. *Zeid Report*, UN Doc. A/59/710 (24 March 2005).

109. P. Rowe, *The Impact of Human Rights Law on Armed Forces* (Cambridge: Cambridge University Press, 2006), p. 129.

110. *Manjoo Report*, UN Doc. A/HRC/14/22 (19 April 2010), para. 14.

111. ECHR, arts 33, 34.

112. Ibid., art. 41.

113. See, for example, *Lordos v. Turkey (Just Satisfaction)* (European Court of Human Rights, Chamber, Application No. 15973/90, 10 January 2012); and *Aksoy v. Turkey* [1996] VI Eur. Court HR 2260.

114. P. Leach, 'Beyond the Bug River: New approaches to redress by the ECHR', *European Human Rights Law Review*, Vol. 10 (2005) 148, pp. 209–214. See, for example, *Jiménez v. Ecuador* (Inter-American Commission on Human Rights, Report No. 107/01, Case No. 11.542, 11 October 2001).
115. See generally S.I. Skogly, 'Extraterritoriality: Universal human rights without universal obligations?', in S. Joseph and A. McBeth (eds), *Research Handbook on International Human Rights Law* (Cheltenham: Edward Elgar, 2010) 71.

Part II
Hope

4
The Road to (and from) 'Recovery': A Multidisciplinary Feminist Approach to Peacekeeping and Peacebuilding

Laura J. Shepherd

Introduction

Feminist interventions in the practices and politics of peace and security at the international level have represented enactments of *hope*, of belief in the possibility of positive change resulting from specific actions in this arena. In this chapter, I draw together insights from disparate academic disciplines, including peace studies, international relations, social psychology, mental health care literature and conflict studies, to construct a framework through which to approach peacekeeping and peacebuilding – a framework that is organised around hope. This kaleidoscope of knowledge does not result in prescriptions for outcomes. Instead, I offer an exploration of work from which we might (*hope*-fully) begin to formulate a new, different approach to some old, familiar issues. I undertake such a project for two reasons: first, I hope that the discipline within which I locate my work (international relations) can be made to think differently about its priorities, agendas and exclusions by bringing insights from other disciplines into play as I seek to better understand the contemporary global politics of peace. Second, I hope that, through such critical interventions drawn from feminist ethics, the works that we produce can be made meaningful to those currently marginalised by the priorities, agendas and exclusions of international relations as a discipline and the world of/to which it speaks. Neta Crawford suggests that perhaps the only emotion with which conventional international relations is entirely comfortable is fear;[1] I choose to hope rather than fear, and I conceive of practising hope as a profoundly political activity.

I refer to 'practising hope' instead of the more usual 'hoping' in order to capture both the concrete commitment (*hope* as a chronologically transcendent noun rather than mere present participle) and the recognition that hope represents a mode of engagement with the world that is neither intuitive nor easy to maintain in international relations – and thus needs practice. Practising hope is political because significant amounts of disciplinary labour power have been invested in keeping hope out of the study of global politics. It is political because a commitment to practising hope may thus enable different insights, the production of different knowledges, and the constitution of different realities through our engagement with both local and global politics. I explore the implications of practising *hope* in the study of peacekeeping and peacebuilding in an approach that blends feminist ethics and an orientation towards peacekeeping and peacebuilding inspired by models of practice in social psychology and mental health care. I conclude with reflections on how approaching peace activities as an ongoing process of recovery grounds such activities in the lived and thus emotional experiences of affective communities, which can reinforce and is reinforced by the practicing of hope.

The political and analytical context

As discussed elsewhere in this volume, there have been quite extensive reform initiatives in the United Nations (UN) system related to peacekeeping and peacebuilding in recent years. In a programme first made publicly visible with the publication in 2000 of the *Report of the Panel on United Nations Peace Operations*,[2] the UN Department of Peacekeeping Operations (DPKO) has engaged in ongoing review and reform of peacekeeping practices; the most recent iteration of the review and reform process is the 'New Horizon' initiative which was first proposed in a discussion paper circulated in 2009. This document, written by the DPKO and the Department of Field Support (DFS), proposes a 'partnership' model, which 'rests on a shared understanding *among all stakeholders* of the objectives of UN peacekeeping and the role that each plays in their realization'.[3] The DFS now provides support in the areas of finance, logistics, information communications technology, human resources and general administration to help missions promote peace and security, while the DPKO continues to undertake increasingly complex and challenging missions in volatile political contexts. The recognition of peacekeeping 'stakeholders' represents a significant departure from 'first generation' peacekeeping management, which operated within a logic of top-down status quo oriented governance, albeit with the consent of 'host' nations, to 'fix' peace in a conflict society in a relatively disengaged fashion.[4]

In its reorientation to a tripartite 'partnership' model ('partnership in purpose', 'partnership in action' and 'partnership for the future'),[5] the DPKO echoes the foundational commitments of the UN Peacebuilding Commission, the organisation created in 2005 to oversee peacebuilding activities that are carried out under the auspices of various UN bodies. The Commission was inaugurated as an intergovernmental advisory body following the adoption of resolutions by both the UN Security Council and the UN General Assembly (1645 and 60/180 respectively). In *Security Council Resolution 1645* (SCR 1645),[6] the Security Council tasked the Commission with developing outlines of best practice in post-conflict reconstruction and securing political and material resources to assist states in transition from conflict to peacetime. As explained in an addendum to the 2005 report *In Larger Freedom: Towards Development, Security and Human Rights for All*, then Secretary-General Kofi Annan suggested that the Commission should

> provide a central node for helping to create and promote comprehensive strategies for peacebuilding both in general terms and in country situations. It should encourage coherent decision-making on peacebuilding by Member States and by the United Nations Secretariat, agencies and programmes. ... It must also provide a forum in which representatives of the United Nations system, major bilateral donors, troop contributors, relevant regional actors and organizations, the international financial institutions and the national or transitional authorities of the country concerned can share information about their respective post-conflict recovery activities, particularly as pertains to achieving coherence between the security/political and development/economic issues, in the interests of greater effectiveness.[7]

Organisationally, the Peacebuilding Commission defers to the UN Security Council, as it is the Council that mediates requests for assistance from governing authorities. Under normal circumstances, 'client' countries, or countries who seek to include their peacebuilding activities on the agenda of the Commission, must submit a request first to the Security Council and the General Assembly, the former of which then refers the case to the Commission. Client countries are therefore responsible for bringing their cases to the Commission, in order to allow the Commission management of their cases. I will return to a discussion of this model of intervention below.

As with the DPKO, which lists 'consent of the parties' affected first in its presentation of the three core principles of peacekeeping,[8] the Peacebuilding Commission notes that it 'is likely to deal only with countries emerging from conflict ... Countries would be expected to express an interest in appearing before the [Commission]. A referral against the wish of the Government is unlikely to take place'.[9] The Commission is also required to encourage consultation 'with civil society, non-governmental organizations, including women's organizations, and the private sector engaged in peacebuilding activities, as appropriate',[10] according to the terms laid out in the founding resolutions. Again, this echoes the desire of the DPKO to pursue the integration and representation of all stakeholders in strategic and operational discussions. The Commission works in conjunction with both the UN Peacebuilding Support Office and the UN Peacebuilding Fund to discharge all UN peacebuilding field operations, capacity building programmes and both long- and short-term responses to requests for assistance.

Taken as a whole, the UN peace enterprise is a complicated and multi-dimensional set of priorities, activities and interests, which has begun to take seriously the inclusion of 'stakeholders' or 'partners' – those whose daily lives are constituted or affected by conflict. The organisational and discursive logics of peace activities, however, still tend towards the hierarchical, valuing some knowledges (those issuing from the UN itself) over others (those issuing from stakeholders of partners). I have referred to this in related work as a manifestation of a 'trickle-down theory of expertise',[11] where the institutional privilege of the UN is implicit but nonetheless evident and is reproduced through the UN's management of peace. This is in part because peace activities comprise a series of micro- and macro-level political processes that are also inherently social practices: protecting individuals or communities from specific or structural violences; distributing resources; policing temporary settlements or more permanent housing arrangements; building physical structures and socio-political or legal institutions; and negotiating peace and reconstruction. Recognising the social – and therefore relational – aspect of peacekeeping and peacebuilding in contemporary global politics requires that we think beyond technocratic 'solutions' to the 'problem' of peace and instead ask what we might learn from studies of human society rather than science. Such a recognition demands a corollary admission that peacekeeping and peacebuilding are activities practised by people: people alone or in groups; organised formally or informally; supported with international financing or other resources or developing out of locally motivated actions.

Placing people at the centre of an exploration of peace politics prompts the question, following the inspiration of Marysia Zalewski,[12] of what work gender was (and is) doing in these sites, given that all social practices operate in and through logics of gender. I am interested not only – indeed, perhaps not even primarily – about the work that gender is doing *empirically* in peacekeeping and peacebuilding operations (that is, how resources are distributed according to gendered logics, how access to peace negotiations and political discussion is or is not explicitly related to gender identity and so on, although these are, of course, important questions), but also about the work that gender is doing *conceptually* to organise the way we think about peacekeeping and peacebuilding. My contribution, then, is a theoretical contribution, a contribution aimed at thinking through and theorising peacekeeping practice and management structures. The contribution lies not so much in the provision of answers to questions but in formulating the questions themselves (though, as I explain below, I see this form of contribution as a type of practice, in as far as a distinction between theory and practice is meaningful). This is the task I undertake in this chapter: to draw together different theoretical insights that may enable a critically aware approach to peace.

Feminist ethics and recovery: a framework in/of two parts

International relations scholars have offered a range of insights attuned to the relational aspects of power inherent in peacekeeping and peacebuilding as social – and therefore political – practices. David Chandler, for example, has sought to 'engage the terminology of race and culture'[13] to highlight links between liberal peacebuilding and previous interventionist exercises of imperial power; in doing so he contributes to so-called 'fourth generation' interpretations of peacekeeping and peacebuilding that have begun to gain purchase in scholarly literature on the subject.[14] As Oliver Richmond explains, these approaches to ending conflict 'should aim at a just distribution of political, social and economic resources, operate in a non-exclusionary manner, and export institutions, structures and norms that are welcomed and required by recipients'.[15] The necessity for dialogue with 'recipients', then, in order to establish their requirements, is of paramount importance, as is a critical awareness of the need to mitigate exclusions as far as possible in pursuit of economic and political justice in a post-conflict or transitional setting. International relations, clearly, can engage – and has engaged – successfully with the politics of peace. And yet none of these scholarly works mentioned is attuned to gender in even the most basic of ways, as an identity category that might have an impact on the peacekeeping and peacebuilding experience.

The lack of attention paid to gender within international relations scholarship on peacekeeping, however, troubles me and is one of two reasons for my multidisciplinary approach. Despite the recognition among peacebuilding agencies, notably the UN Security Council, of the need 'to integrate a gender perspective' into their operations,[16] some scholars in the field of peace research and research on peacebuilding still tend to assume that peacebuilding activities are experienced similarly irrespective of gender identity/performance. Mary Moran notes, for example, that '[Roland] Paris's influential book *At War's End: Building Peace After Conflict* (2004) ... contains no index entries for "women", "men", or "gender"';[17] an online survey of the contents of *International Peacekeeping*, the premier journal that 'reflects debates about peacebuilding and monitoring of agreements', reveals that only four per cent of articles published in the journal since its inception in 1994 contain 'gender' in the title or abstract. As I conceive of gender as a foundational construct that affects and is affected by all other relations of power,[18] gender is implicated in every social process and, as outlined above, peacekeeping and peacebuilding are fundamentally social processes. International relations has not, historically, been attentive to gender, power or social processes, which justifies looking beyond the boundaries of its disciplinary knowledge.

The second reason I espouse a multidisciplinary approach relates to how I conceive of theory. I envision theories as packages of ideas about how the world has worked (and does and indeed could work). If we build our theories – or, as I prefer to think of it, if we 'theorise'[19] – relying solely on ideas that we have already had then our theorising will be limited by experience and engagement with existing worlds. As Stuart Hall notes, '[w]e mainly tell stories like we've told them before, or we borrow from the whole inventory of telling stories'.[20] I suggest that in order to provide new packages of ideas, to draw new connections between existing ideas and perhaps put them together in different ways, and to re-figure *hope* in our analysis, we need to be creative. I propose the inclusion of Anna Agathangelou and L.H.M. Ling's '*poisies*' as a guiding rationale for multidisciplinarity,[21] which has no literal English translation but can be understood as the creative and necessarily social activity of making meaning. As Agathangelou and Ling argue, story-telling, however undertaken, creates 'a space to critique *and* reconstruct our worlds by voicing, seeing understanding, and bridging the differential locations and subjectivities of selves and others [and] ... helps us politicize social relations *critically*, thereby unleashing creative possibilities for change'.[22] It is these 'creative possibilities for change' that I am most interested in investigating, and so I begin by drawing out insights from feminist scholars – in international relations and elsewhere – to constitute the first aspect of the multidisciplinary approach I am offering as I seek to tell different stories about peace. I then turn to the 'recovery' model of long-term mental health care, which informs the second aspect of my approach.

Feminist curiosity and the ethics of peace encounters

I draw inspiration from Cynthia Enloe, who reminds us of the need for a 'feminist curiosity'.[23] We must be curious about the work gender is doing in any given situation, and we must be curious about the ideas that people hold about gender, bodies and behaviours and remain curious about how these ideas manifest in the material realm. 'Ideas matter', Enloe concludes, ideas about modernity, security, violence, threat and trust. 'Each of these ideas is fraught with blatant and subtle presumptions about masculinity and femininity. Ideas about both masculinity and femininity matter. This makes a feminist curiosity a necessity'.[24] It is a necessity, for without feminist curiosity our understanding of peacekeeping and peacebuilding can only ever be partial, but a 'simple' curiosity about gender is insufficient. That is, it is important to ask that attention is paid to which bodies are doing what in peacekeeping and peacebuilding activities, but it is also important to ask how logics of gender, ideas about gender, inform those behaviours. It is crucial to be curious about '*which* women are included [in peace discussions and operations] and are we expecting more from women (superheroines) than we expect of men?'[25] Taking seriously Carol Cohn, Sheri Gibbings and Helen Kinsella's reminder to ask 'which women are included' also requires us to be curious about how gender intersects with class, race, sexuality, able-bodiedness and other axes of exclusion to form hierarchies of privilege.

Without understanding that gender is at once a noun, a verb and a logic, it is near impossible to understand that gender is a relational and dynamic construct that operates in and through other power relations. Without actively exercising a feminist curiosity, which I take to mean a curiosity about how gender is working in any given situation (not only to constitute identity but also to organise what, and how, we think), I think it is difficult to understand relationships between subjects, given that human subjects are inescapably gendered entities. International relations is, after all, about relationships between international subjects; without attending to differences within categories of identity (such as 'women' and 'men', for example), we can neither apprehend nor comprehend exclusion and/or privilege. If we cannot apprehend these structures we cannot *hope* to change them. As Shirin Rai has asked, 'what structural inequalities are proving to be most resistant to change, and why might this be the case? Why are certain accommodations regarding gender relations more feasible than others?'[26] Only a feminist curiosity, which understands that the 'concept, nature and practice of gender are key' to social practices and human interactions,[27] can enable us to understand *how* gender matters in peacekeeping and peacebuilding.

One of the core ways in which gender works in relation to peacekeeping and peacebuilding, in international relations at least, is to discourage the explicit theorisation of the role of emotions. This works through the fetishisation of rationality in international relations, as discussed above. My disciplinary training – my disciplining, in the Foucauldian sense of the term – encouraged me *not* to face encounters with discomfort and certainly *not* to explore these encounters as the foundations of an approach to research. But, as noted in a recent discussion, 'emotions do not corrupt research, but involve a process of owning up to being human'.[28] 'Owning up to being human', in this context, means that I own my privilege (as a secure, middle-class, white female academic) and proceed not only with a reflexive awareness of the contingency of my theoretical contribution but also, and more importantly, with empathy towards the practices, processes and subjects I encounter. Empathy is necessary, because emotional attachment demands that efforts are made to feel not only on our own behalves but also on the behalf of others. Christine Sylvester explored the potential of empathy in international relations over a decade ago, and her formulation remains useful, as she determined that 'empathetic cooperation' enables scholars to research, learn and teach more inclusively by attending to 'the concerns, fears and agendas one is unaccustomed to heeding'.[29] Further, and more recently, Sylvester has argued that we must also be empathetic in our appreciation of our own multiple subjectivities and learn from our own 'skill in going back and forth between daily experiences of being in different parts of one's identity repertoire in different situations'[30] to cooperate with others whose desires, will and wishes we do not immediately comprehend.

Borrowing from feminist philosophy, then, I add to a feminist curiosity a concern for ethics. The work of Kimberly Hutchings is particularly insightful on this topic:

Ethics is political not only because ethical values and principles emerge out of political contestation and contexts, but also because the patterns and hierarchies of inclusion and exclusion required by ethics produce distinctions between right or wrong, good or bad, and have concomitant implications for what it may therefore be permissible to do to whom and how.[31]

In the context of theorising an approach to peacekeeping and peace-building, I would add to Hutchings' deliberation of what it may be permissible to do *to* whom a discussion of what it may be permissible – or desirable; or frowned upon – to do *for* and *with* whom and how. I do not conceive of ethics as intangible guidelines meant to influence how we as human beings behave towards other human beings, but as the necessarily social practices of that engagement, from the level of policy formulation right down to the distribution of food within a household. Ethics, what it means to *be* good, must include what it means to *do* good, and nowhere is this more relevant a part of discussion than in the realm of peacekeeping and peacebuilding.

I see the consideration of ethical practice as particularly pertinent because of the discursive power of 'peace': peace is inherently A Good Thing, and no one can be 'against' peace. A feminist curiosity reminds us to resist the closure implied in any discourse of peace, remembering that it is always important to ask on whose behalf peace is being sought or claimed and with what effects. Meanwhile, an approach that also draws on feminist ethics asks that we are humble about our contributions and willing to encounter multiple others (and, potentially, our multiple selves) from a position of empathy and compassion. Compassion is also indicated by ethics, if we understand compassion to be concern for suffering. According to K.M. Fierke, who also draws on Nussbaum's theory of grief and compassion, the latter 'requires the experience of pain at the thought of a separate person's suffering'.[32] Compassion can usefully coincide with tolerance as an organising ethico-political principle, which might in turn be politically preferable to perpetuating discourses of tolerance uncritically given that 'tolerance operates as a coin of liberal imperialism ... and at times abets in legitimizing the very violence it claims to abhor or deter'.[33] Compassion is active where tolerance is passive; compassion seeks empathetic attachment where tolerance seeks only to 'live and let live'.[34]

Compassionate practice, in this conceptualisation, draws heavily on Fiona Robinson's articulation of a 'feminist relational moral ontology specific to feminist care ethics'.[35] This is not an ethic of care that presupposes a biologically sexed feminine subject, but rather the ethico-politics of a subject 'always in process, never fully formed as a gendered or cultural being' but that is necessarily relationally constituted.[36] Robinson recognises that there are always inequalities (produced by and productive of varying levels of autonomy/dependence) in human interactions but, first, that such inequalities cannot be resolved by fiat (by stating 'this is a meeting of equals' in the hope that it will be so)[37] and, second, that such inequalities require that we are attentive to the needs of those 'with whom we exist in relations of interdependence and responsibility'.[38] Attentiveness in conjunction with empathy seems to constitute compassion. Robinson specifically mentions peacebuilding as an activity that is linked to other fields of practice through the potential contribution of caring values:

> Care ethics emphasises the existence of dependency and vulnerability as normal ways of 'being human'. Learning how to listen effectively to others, especially those who – at that particular moment in time and space – may be more vulnerable to the outcomes of dialogue than you are, requires the cultivation of moral attitudes of patience, attentiveness and trust.[39]

Feminist ethics, then, provides a simple and fundamental insight that can be built in to the framework I sketch out here: to be human is to be relationally involved with other humans and to be relationally involved is to be vulnerable.[40] Some people will be more vulnerable than others at a 'particular moment in time and space' but we should not presume *a priori* that we know or understand the needs of others. Rather, we need to ensure that we listen to those others and prioritise listening – rather than 'giving voice' – as part of an ethical peacebuilding strategy.

The road to (and from) 'recovery'

International relations as a discipline has long insisted on conceiving of states as men writ large,[41] and realist political philosophy, the legacy of which dominated the development of international relations as a discipline, consistently conceptualises the domestic populations of states as bodies politic, with the implication of biological system and logic that such a metaphor entails. It was perhaps, therefore, inevitable that international relations theories would come to extend that metaphor and begin to investigate the ways in which a state in conflict can be conceived of as akin to an individual mood disorder or disorder of the mind. In this section, I explore the possibilities of drawing on long-term mental health care for inspiration in developing an approach to peace-building. One of the most persuasive explorations into this sphere was conducted by Vanessa Pupevac, who argues that 'a therapeutic under-standing has been assimilated into international policy. ... Essentially, the international model views trauma as causing dysfunctionalism and necessitating psychosocial intervention to break vicious cycles of trauma and violence'.[42] Pupevac is highly critical of this model of peacebuilding intervention, suggesting that such an approach inevita-bly implies the need for external expertise to be brought in to remediate local conflicts and for the top-down management of 'pathologies' that manifest in cycles of violence.

Along with Pupevac, I do not hold that it is at all useful – at worst, in fact, it may be singularly *unhelpful* – to subscribe to a medicalised model of peacekeeping and peacebuilding that diagnoses trauma and treats the traumatised as peace inhibitors by virtue of the likelihood that they will visit violence upon future generations as violence was visited upon them. What Pupevac describes as a 'new therapeutic security paradigm'[43] is singularly unhelpful in its approach to conflict manage-ment and post-conflict reconstruction, as it 'pathologizes the recipient population by locating the source of conflict in the personality of the population, *thereby questioning its capacity for self-government*'.[44] It is this latter aspect of the therapeutic paradigm when applied to peacekeeping and peacebuilding that is so profoundly problematic: the medicalisa-tion of the peace enterprise *requires* the application of (assumed: white, western, scientific) rationality to the 'problem' of (assumed: non-white, non-western, natural) emotional 'imbalance'.

This is entirely at odds with the commitments I have outlined above, in that it perpetuates the kind of dichotomous logics that feminism has taught me to be curious about, and it suggests that the activities of peace practitioners should be to 'fix' conflict societies rather than to listen to them and engage in such encounters with respect. And yet, I wonder whether there may be critical purchase to the discursive shift toward the 'new therapeutic security paradigm' that could be apprehended. There have been excellent analyses of the emotional aspects of conflict and traumatised affect in global politics,[45] which can act as a foundation for such an intellectual intervention; and there have also been recent developments in social psychology, to which I now turn, that can inform a more nuanced and less exclusionary approach. Such an approach derives its core elements from what has become known in mental health services as a 'recovery' model of long-term care.

Traditionally, the dominant model of care for long-term mental health problems has been a 'case management' model. 'Case management' requires a foundational distinction between the patient and the health care professional; the latter assesses the former and develops a care plan, which is then implemented by various actors through and on behalf of various agencies (this is of course a necessarily much-simplified overview). This is remarkably similar in outline to 'first generation' peacekeeping and peacebuilding practice; as outlined by Tamara Duffey, traditional peacekeeping forces were politically impartial, disengaged and militarily-neutral and in place only to 'stabilise conflict zones'[46] in the same way that mental health care professionals, according to the 'case management' model, seek to stabilise the patient. The expertise of the professional is assumed and the experiential knowledge of the patient generally disregarded. This model also represents the type of therapeutic intervention that Pupevac seeks to critique, in that 'the therapeutic conception of the subject as a vulnerable damaged victim requires third-party enablers for self-empowerment'.[47] This collates with peacekeeping and peacebuilding practice where the vulnerability and frailty of post-conflict communities have in international relations, and associated disciplines, become characterised as a damaged space requiring third-party intervenors and enablers for self-empowerment.

A 'recovery' model is markedly different, however: recovery is a *process* rather than a goal and the concept of recovery in mental health care echoes the reorientation of peacekeeping and peacebuilding under the auspices of the UN toward 'partnership' engagement with multiple stakeholders, in that all actors are seen as contributors to the recovery process. William Anthony is generally credited with the first exposition of the concept in a mental health setting[48] and he describes it thus:

> [R]ecovery from a catastrophe does not change the fact that the experience has occurred, that the effects are still present, and that one's life has changed forever. Successful recovery does mean that the person has changed, and that the meaning of these facts to the person has therefore changed. They are no longer the primary focus of one's life.[49]

Recovery therefore entails different mechanisms, methods and modalities of interaction than a 'case management' approach, as practitioners and service professionals seek to understand the experience, to listen attentively to the person and her/his account of the effects, to validate the knowledge that she/he brings regarding her/his mental illness and to develop in conjunction with all stakeholders ways to move forward toward a life in recovery.

The parallels between this model and the approach to peacebuilding I have begun to describe above are obvious. Both require the reorientation of a professional care-giving enterprise away from a dichotomous model that situates the (peacebuilding/psychiatric) expert in a position of authority and power over a client or patient. Both require recognising the validity of different forms of knowledge and capacity, and recognising first-hand accounts of lived experience *as* knowledge. Both require different methods of engagement: qualitative rather than quantitative; human- rather than metric-focussed; and facilitative, empathetic and attentive rather than prescriptive, professionalised and detached. What this insight offers in practice are a number of core concepts that can be brought in to a multidisciplinary approach to peace, as they have as much purchase at the collective level of peace politics as they do at the individual level of long-term mental health care. Central to these concepts is hope, consistently identified within the literature as a foundational element of recovery-oriented practice. Hope, according to scholars and practitioners in this field,[50] is the condition of possibility of recovery; without hope to sustain motivation and the belief that targeted actions will result in positive change, the process of recovery is unlikely to succeed.

I am not proposing we *apply* the recovery model to peace encounters. Although Pupavac's critique is levelled at psychosocial intervention that owes more to case management than recovery, any approach to peacekeeping and peacebuilding that treats the society as a homogenous whole or the individuals within it as in need of psychosocial intervention *a priori* would be subject to a similar critique. That is, just because the recovery model of mental health care provision is preferable to a case management model, it does not mean that either are suitable models of practice in the field of peace politics. What I propose instead is that we might borrow from the recovery model its insistence that we practise hope. In Anthony's original formulation, '[r]ecovery is a way of living a satisfying, *hopeful*, and contributing life';[51] in peace encounters we and the people with whom we interact deserve lives full of hope as well.

Recovery and the value of critique

Although I am not suggesting that we can conceptualise post-conflict reconstruction as 'recovery', the terms are sometimes used interchangeably by development institutions and other international organisations, which implies an affinity.[52] The United States Institute for Peace defines post-conflict recovery as:

> the long-term rebuilding of a society in the aftermath of violent conflict. It includes political, socioeconomic, and physical aspects such as disarming and reintegrating combatants, resettling internally displaced persons, reforming governmental institutions, promoting trauma work and reconciliation, delivering justice, restarting the economy, and rebuilding damaged infrastructure.[53]

Recovery at the collective level is every bit as complex and nuanced as recovery at the individual level, but its complexity should not mean that its potential utility as a guiding principle should be discounted.

Using insights drawn from mental health service provision regarding the implementation of recovery as a process, guided by feminist curiosity and care ethics in a multidisciplinary approach to peacekeeping and peacebuilding, may allow for alternative engagements with peace activities than those traditionally undertaken. As discussed above, both peacekeeping and peacebuilding have entered a phase (or 'wave' or 'generation', depending on your terminological preference) where collective action replaces top-down instruction; where equality replaces hierarchy; and where local voices are brought into the dialogical process. As also noted above, however, these so-called 'fourth generation' scholarly approaches to peacebuilding (and, by extension, peacekeeping) that are 'concerned with emancipation and social justice beyond the state'[54] do not generally attend to gender, nor do they conceptualise peace activities as care activities that prioritise recovery through the nurturing and practicing of hope. While such new approaches propose 'a more realistic recognition of the possibilities of, and dynamics of, contextual and local peacebuilding agencies within international peacebuilding, development and institutional architecture and policies',[55] I borrow from the recovery model and propose instead a re-cognition, a phase of knowing again and knowing differently the possibilities of hope as a guiding principle of peace enterprise. For scholars, this could entail reorienting research towards the affective and relational dimensions of peace activities, requiring different modes of engagement and different research methodologies. For practitioners, practising hope could entail finding – and funding – activities that sustain positive emotional connections within communities and nurture belief in positive outcomes.

This is an everyday politics, a necessarily postcolonial politics of peace as it engages with structures of power and institutions of governance other than those traditionally located in the inter/national sphere. Crucially, however, the approach I outline here envisions plural forms of agency and opportunity manifesting in the micro-politics of peacekeeping and peacebuilding, which Richmond refers to as 'the everyday': 'The everyday captures these dynamics and spaces *where a new politics may emerge beyond the liberal peace*'.[56] The everyday *hopes* for new configurations of power and possibility 'beyond the liberal peace', which has had demonstrably ill effects in contemporary global politics. Steps towards building peace in ways that centralise recovery and practice hope are in fact already evident. The RAISE Hope for Congo campaign is an example of a project that is explicit (in its naming) both about practising hope and about committing to the recovery of Congolese societies from ongoing conflict through a variety of interventions, which include a 'conflict-free campus initiative' and an initiative aimed at reforming United States policy governing the trade of extracted minerals from the area. The project connects macro-level national and international policy with the micro-politics of everyday life; RAISE Hope has worked with survivors of sexualised violence to raise awareness of such violence and demand its punishment. Margot Wallström, then UN Special Representative of the Secretary-General on Sexual Violence in Conflict, described the courage shown by the survivors of violence as '[p]erhaps the brightest glimmer of hope shining a light in the face of darkness'.[57] In emphasising hope in these encounters we can consider more fully the performative function of such activities and how they produce and are productive of belief in positive change.

The recent shifts in organisational discourse within the UN towards a partnership model of peace activities have resulted in less problematic peacekeeping and peacebuilding practices than the earliest incarnations of such endeavours; contemporary practices are more inclusive than the previous top-down and interventionist approaches that uncritically perpetuated the dichotomy of the 'development expert' advising the 'local government' on strategies of stabilisation and then modernisation. As the above exploration has illustrated, however, even 'inclusive' peace activities engaging with civil society organisations and other stakeholders tend to operate according to implicit logics of space and gender that privilege the international over the local and the (assumed: male) technocrat (perhaps rebranded as a 'facilitator') over the (assumed: female) civil society organiser. The approach I offer may achieve something different, given that

[c]alls to describe an alternative paradigm of 'peace', or to enable its operationalisation, miss the point completely. This is not to essentialise and categorise the everyday, or to offer a new international model for IR or peace. Contextually reconstructing IR and its related peacebuilding or statebuilding enterprise cannot be achieved in general theory.[58]

The production of a 'grand theory' of peacekeeping and/or peacebuilding is not necessarily a worthwhile endeavour, for what is important is contextualisation, attention to specificity and emphasis on the value of listening rather than telling. I *hope* that the approach I sketch out here may result in new methodologies, new practices and new ways of thinking about how we engage in the pursuit of peace in contemporary global politics; there is so much at stake that we cannot afford not to try.

Notes

1. N.C. Crawford, 'The passion of world politics: Propositions on emotion and emotional relationships', *International Security*, Vol. 24, No. 4 (2000) 116, pp.116–117.
2. *Report of the Panel on United Nations Peace Operations*, UN Doc. A/55/305–S/2000/809 (21 August 2000) (also known as the *Brahimi Report*).
3. DPKO and DFS, *A New Partnership Agenda: Charting a New Horizon for UN Peacekeeping* (DPKO and DFS, July 2009) (emphasis added).
4. T. Duffey, 'United Nations peacekeeping in the post-Cold War world', *Civil Wars*, Vol. 1, No. 3 (1998) 1, pp. 5–6.
5. DPKO, 'The "new horizon" process', *United Nations Peacekeeping*, http://www.un.org/en/peacekeeping/operations/newhorizon.shtml (last accessed October 2013).
6. *Security Council Resolution 1645*, UN Doc. S/RES/1645 (20 December 2005) (SCR 1645).
7. *In Larger Freedom: Towards Development, Security and Human Rights for All*, UN Doc. A/59/2005/Add.2 (23 May 2005).
8. DPKO, 'Principles of UN peacekeeping', *United Nations Peacekeeping*, http://www.un.org/en/peacekeeping/operations/principles.shtml (last accessed October 2013).
9. 'Country-specific configurations', *United Nations Peacebuilding Commission*, http://www.un.org/en/peacebuilding/countryconfig.shtml (last accessed October 2013).
10. SCR 1645, para. 21.
11. L.J. Shepherd, *Gender, Violence and Security: Discourse as Practice* (London: Zed Books, 2008), p. 97.
12. M. Zalewski, 'Well, what is the feminist perspective on Bosnia?', *International Affairs*, Vol. 71, No. 2 (1995) 399.

13. D. Chandler, 'Race, culture and civil society: Peacebuilding discourse and the understanding of difference', *Security Dialogue*, Vol. 41, No. 4 (2010) 369, p. 370.
14. O.P. Richmond, *Maintaining Order, Making Peace* (Basingstoke: Palgrave Macmillan, 2002), p. 191. See also P. Darby, 'Rolling back the frontiers of empire: Practising the postcolonial', *International Peacekeeping*, Vol. 16, No. 5 (2009) 699; O.P. Richmond, 'Resistance and the post-liberal peace', *Millennium: Journal of International Studies*, Vol. 38, No. 3 (2010) 665; and M. Pugh, 'Local agency and political economies of peacebuilding', *Ethnicities and Nationalism*, Vol. 11, No. 2 (2011) 308.
15. Richmond, *Maintaining Order*, p. 191.
16. *Security Council Resolution 1325*, UN Doc. S/RES/1325 (31 October 2000), para. 5; and SCR 1645, para. 20.
17. M.H. Moran, 'Gender, militarism and peace-building: Projects of the post-conflict moment', *Annual Review of Anthropology*, Vol. 39 (2010) 261, p. 262.
18. For a full explanation of this conceptual framework, see Shepherd, *Gender, Violence and Security*, pp. 49–54.
19. M. Zalewski, '"All these theories yet the bodies keep piling up": Theories, theorists, theorising', in S. Smith, K. Booth and M. Zalewski (eds), *International Theory: Positivism and Beyond* (Cambridge: Cambridge University Press, 1996) 340, p. 346.
20. S. Hall and J. O'Hara, 'The narrative construction of reality: An interview with Stuart Hall', *Southern Review*, Vol. 17, No. 1 (1984) 3.
21. A.M. Aganthangelou and L.H.M. Ling, *Transforming World Politics: From Empire to Multiple Worlds* (London: Routledge, 2009), p. 91.
22. Aganthangelou and Ling, *Transforming World Politics*, p. 7.
23. C. Enloe, *The Curious Feminist: Searching for Women in a New Age of Empire* (Berkeley: University of California Press, 2004); C. Enloe, *Globalization and Militarism: Feminists Make the Link* (Lanham: Rowman & Littlefield, 2007).
24. Enloe, *Globalization and Militarism*, p. 161.
25. C. Cohn, H. Kinsella and S. Gibbings, 'Women, peace and security: Resolution 1325', *International Feminist Journal of Politics*, Vol. 6, No. 1 (2004) 130, p. 136 (emphasis original).
26. S.M. Rai, *The Gender Politics of Development: Essays in Hope and Despair* (London: Zed Books, 2008), p. 2.
27. Zalewski, 'Well, what is the feminist perspective on Bosnia?', p. 341.
28. S. Parashar, 'Embodied "otherness" and negotiations of difference', *International Studies Review*, Vol. 13, No. 4 (2011) 696, p. 698.
29. C. Sylvester, *Feminist Theory and International Relations in a Postmodern Era* (Cambridge: Cambridge University Press, 1994), p. 317.
30. C. Sylvester in interview with the University of Gothenburg, *University of Gothenburg: School of Global Studies* (2010), http://www.globalstudies.gu.se/english/research/guest-researcher-programme/christine-sylvester (last accessed October 2013).
31. K. Hutchings, 'Feminist ethics and political violence', *International Politics*, Vol. 44, No. 1 (2007) 90, 99.
32. K.M. Fierke, 'Whereof we can speak, thereof we must not be silent: Trauma, political solipsism and war', *Review of International Studies*, Vol. 30, No. 4 (2004) 471, p. 474.

33. W. Brown, *Regulating Aversion: Tolerance in the Age of Identity and Empire* (Princeton: Princeton University Press, 2006), p. 204.
34. Brown, *Regulating Aversion*, p. 38.
35. F. Robinson, 'Stop talking and listen: Discourse ethics and feminist care ethics in international political theory', *Millennium: Journal of International Studies*, Vol. 39, No. 3 (2011) 845, p. 847.
36. V. Jabri, 'Feminist ethics and hegemonic global politics', *Alternatives*, Vol. 29, No. 3 (2004) 265, pp. 278–9.
37. Robinson, 'Stop talking and listen', p. 851.
38. Ibid., p. 856.
39. Ibid., pp. 859–60.
40. See further L.J. Shepherd, *Gender, Violence and Popular Culture: Telling Stories* (London: Routledge, 2013), p. 121.
41. Kimberly Hutchings refers to this as a 'cognitive short-cut' common to conventional theories of global politics: K. Hutchings, 'Cognitive short cuts', in J.L. Parpart and M. Zalewski (eds), *Rethinking the Man Question: Sex, Gender and Violence in International Relations* (London: Zed Books, 2008) 23.
42. V. Pupavac, 'War on the couch: The emotionology of the new international security paradigm', *European Journal of Social Theory*, Vol. 7, No. 2 (2004) 149, p. 150.
43. Ibid., p. 152.
44. ibid., p. 163 (emphasis added).
45. See, for example, Fierke, 'Whereof we can speak'; K.M. Fierke, 'Bewitched by the past: Social memory, trauma and international relations', in D. Bell (ed.), *Memory, Trauma and World Politics: Reflections on the Relationship between Past and Present* (Basingstoke: Palgrave Macmillan, 2006) 116; E. Hutchison, 'Trauma and the politics of emotions: Constituting identity, security and community after the Bali Bombing', *International Relations*, Vol. 24, No. 1 (2010) 65; E. Hutchison and R. Bleiker, 'Emotional reconciliation: Reconstituting identity and community after trauma', *European Journal of Social Theory*, Vol. 11, No. 3 (2008) 385; M. Zembylas, 'The politics of trauma: Empathy, reconciliation and peace education', *Journal of Peace Education*, Vol. 4, No. 2 (2007) 207; and M. Zembylas, 'The politics of shame in intercultural education', *Education, Citizenship and Social Justice*, Vol. 3, No. 3 (2008) 263.
46. Duffey, 'United Nations peacekeeping', p. 6.
47. Pupavac, 'War on the couch', p. 161.
48. See S. Ramon, B. Healy and N. Renouf, 'Recovery from mental illness as an emergent concept and practice in Australia and the UK', *International Journal of Social Psychiatry*, Vol. 53, No. 2 (2007) 108, p. 111.
49. W. Anthony, 'Recovery from mental illness: The guiding vision of the mental health service system in the 1990s', *Psychosocial Rehabilitation Journal*, Vol. 16, No. 4 (1993) 11, p. 14.
50. See, for example, G. Roberts and P. Wolfson, 'The rediscovery of recovery: Open to all', *Advances in Psychiatric Treatment*, Vol. 10, No. 1 (2004) 37; L. Davidson, 'Recovery, self management and the expert patient: Changing the culture of mental health from a UK
perspective', *Journal of Mental Health*, Vol. 14, No. 1 (2005) 25; H. Lester and L. Gask, 'Delivering medical care for patients with serious mental illness or promoting a collaborative model of recovery?', *British Journal of Psychiatry*,

Vol. 188, No. 5 (2006) 401; and Ramon et al.,,, 'Recovery from mental illness as an emergent concept and practice'.

51. Anthony, 'Recovery from mental illness', p. 15 (emphasis added).
52. See, for example, 'Post-conflict and post-disaster responses: Mission – About us', *United Nations Educational, Scientific and Cultural Organization*, http://www.unesco.org/new/en/unesco/themes/pcpd/mission (last accessed October 2013); 'Post-conflict development', *International Rescue Committee* (2013), http://www.rescue.org/our-work/post-conflict-development (last accessed October 2013); and 'Post-conflict recovery & fragile states', *Innovations for Poverty Action* (2011), http://poverty-action.org/postconflict (last accessed October 2013).
53. United States Institute for Peace, 'Post-conflict recovery', *Glossary of Terms for Conflict Management and Peacebuilding* (2011), http://glossary.usip.org/ resource/post-conflict-recovery (last accessed October 2013).
54. Richmond, 'Resistance and the post-liberal peace', p. 666.
55. Ibid., p. 668.
56. Ibid., p. 691 (emphasis added).
57. M. Wallström, 'A glimmer of hope for the women in Congo', *Huffington Post Blog* (30 May 2012), http://www.huffingtonpost.com/margot-wallstrom/a-glimmer-of-hope-for-the_b_1555962.html (last accessed October 2013).
58. Richmond, 'Resistance and the post-liberal peace', p. 682.

5
Thinking Globally and Acting Locally: Linking Women, Peace and Security in the Pacific

Sharon Bhagwan Rolls

Introduction

In the Pacific Island region, women have been greatly marginalised from formal decision-making structures as a result of the predominantly patriarchal governance structures from the time of colonial administrations and continuing after independence. Yet, despite such obstacles, in Bougainville and the Solomon Islands, as well as Fiji, women were instrumental in brokering peace during the height of crises and continue to play a vital role in building and sustaining peace in their communities. This has reflected our hope for peace, security and political stability in our region.

When it comes to notions of 'traditional' security, women remain invisible. This practice continues despite the fact that women around the world, including the Pacific Island region, have been instrumental and often the group trusted most by both sides of a conflict. As such, women have often been the first negotiators for a ceasefire.[1] Women have often paved the way for United Nations (UN) and regional peacekeeping and peace support operations, for the signing of peace agreements and the introduction of transitional processes. Yet even as women participate in these processes, peacekeeping and post-conflict processes continue to subsequently exclude women.

Women are often combatants during conflict and, if they are not, they are certainly the wives, partners or daughters of combatants and therefore have an acute stake in the processes of disarmament, demobilisation and reintegration (DDR) programmes. Women have also been caught in the crossfire of war and armed conflicts through sexual exploitation including the use of rape as a 'weapon of war'. Women have also borne the brunt of sexual exploitation by those assigned the task of upholding peace and human rights.

As discussed throughout this collection, on 31 October 2000, the UN Security Council unanimously passed *Resolution 1325* (SCR 1325).[2] It is the first resolution ever passed by the Security Council that specifically addresses the impact of war on women and women's contributions to conflict prevention and sustainable peace. SCR 1325 remains a watershed for collective security, because it demonstrated what is possible when the UN, member states and women's civil society collaborate.

The resolution signalled a shift in the role of women from victimhood to critical change agents in conflict prevention, management and peacebuilding. This happened because SCR 1325 not only focussed on the protection of women in crisis situations, but also called for the effective participation of women in conflict prevention, resolution and peacebuilding; the mainstreaming of gender equality in peacekeeping missions; and the UN to appoint women to strategic positions related to peace and security.

The focus of the resolution is on three pillars. The first pillar is *participation*, identifying the important role of women in the prevention and resolution of conflict and in peacebuilding and post-conflict recovery, and the need to increase their role in decision-making. The second pillar is *peacekeeping* and recognises the urgent need to mainstream a gender perspective into peacekeeping operations (PKOs) and provide specialised training to military, police and civilians as part of PKOs on the protection and human rights needs of women and children in conflict situations. The third pillar is *protection*, acknowledging that women and children account for the vast majority of those adversely affected by armed conflict, including high levels of sexual violence. This has a consequent impact on durable peace and reconciliation.

In the Pacific, as well as globally, unequal power relations; intolerance; lack of respect and valuing; and lack of access to and control over resources characterise the position of women relative to men. This fuels the pervasive nature of violence and the exclusion, marginalisation and invisibility of women at all levels of decision-making, which is detrimental to the human security of the entire Pacific region.

This chapter is informed by the efforts of Pacific activists who belong to the Pacific Women's Media and Policy Network on UN Security Council Resolution 1325, which is coordinated by FemLINKPACIFIC,[3] and which includes the Leitana Nehan Women's Development Agency of the Autonomous Region of Bougainville of Papua New Guinea,[4] Vois Blong Mere Solomon of Solomon Islands[5] and Ma'afafine moe Famili of

Tonga.[6] Our network uses community media as a platform to communicate and integrate SCR 1325 into the regional and national peace and security architecture in Bougainville, Fiji, Solomon Islands and Tonga. As well as the support and knowledge that FemLINKPACIFIC provides, the network uses media as a mechanism for mobilising women. This chapter also links to the recent work by the Pacific Regional Working Group on Women, Peace and Security, and the opportunity to integrate SCR 1325 and *Security Council Resolution 1820*[7] in the future of peacekeeping and peace support operations involving Pacific troop-contributing countries.

Within our '1325' network in the Pacific we have experienced the presence of peacekeepers in our communities following the war in Bougainville and the 2006 riots in Nukualofa (Tonga); and as a result of the Regional Assistance Mission to Solomon Islands (RAMSI) which was mobilised in response to the armed conflict in Solomon Islands in 2000. Yet in each situation, women were not consulted on the nature of the tour of duty, the deployment of the peacekeeping mission or the peace process.

As for the Fiji Islands, even though women have paved the way in the peace movement, we have been marginalised from many of the initial official interventions since the military coup on 6 December 2006. Fiji has also been a troop- and police-contributing country to UN peacekeeping missions since the mid-1970s, providing personnel to UN assistance missions to the Middle East and more recently in Iraq. Peacekeepers are the fathers, sons and brothers of women who remain at home taking on the responsibilities of the family and community and, increasingly, Fijian peacekeepers are women.

Since the formation of our network in 2007, we have reaffirmed that the application of SCR 1325 in the context of peacekeeping is not about recruiting and arming women. In fact, from our perspective, SCR 1325 is about the support for the disbandment of military structures and enabling and supporting armed combatants to return to civilian life. FemLINKPACIFIC's work connects women to policy and political commitments through community media, and our approach helps women make the linkages between faith values and human rights standards, and assists them in articulating their peace and human security priorities.

FemLINKPACIFIC emerged from the Blue Ribbon Peace Vigil Initiative, a response by women who mobilised in Suva, the capital of the Fiji Islands, following the civilian coup on 19 May 2000. We emerged recognising that while we had created a space for women and their families to gather and act together, there was much more to be done to transform a society through the full and active participation of women in leadership positions. This, as in many conflict situations experienced in our region, required us to work across the traditional ethnic and political barriers, while also considering the need for the transformation of our own broader women's movement. The founding collective of FemLINKPACIFIC recognised that while we received media coverage of our peace efforts, and had a series of formal dialogues and engagements with traditional leaders and the military council, there remained a stereotypical and patriarchal approach to the 'rules of engagement' when it came to dialogue for peace – including by the international community. Challenging this approach required maintaining a visibility of women's peace efforts not only in the available media spaces, but also by creating our own media to provide women with the spaces to discuss our issues and provide our own recommendations – we were grounding our work in Section J of the *Beijing Platform for Action*[8] until we received a message from Anne Walker, then at the International Women's Tribune Centre in New York, regarding the adoption of SCR 1325 ... *use this, she said, and we did!*

Community media for us has become an enabling and participatory process to empower and inform the transformation of our own political spaces and processes, including within our own movements and organisations. We believe that Pacific women must be assisted in being innovative, not simply accepting the status quo but demanding a transformation so that governments, the broader civil society and faith organisations are held accountable in relation to their commitments to women's human rights, gender equality, development and peace. However, assistance can never be a top-down imposition, and the FemLINKPACIFIC media strategy centres on creating space for women to communicate and hear other women, enlarging women's political voice and consciousness at the same time. Local women's civil society representatives must be involved in helping to redefine and ensure implementation of the new human security agenda, including representation on local and national councils and on committees addressing a broad range of security issues.

Our work has brought voices of the marginalised and unrepresented, particularly from grassroots communities, into the political arena, and linked them with Pacific PeaceWomen's[9] notion of peace, to advocate for a peace and security framework defined not just in military security and political terms, but also in terms of human security rooted in a combination of political, economic, personal, community and environmental factors. FemLINKPACIFIC has worked to translate SCR 1325, not only in the literal sense but to also operationalise the resolution, to demonstrate the opportunities for advocacy and input that exist at a policy level and a community level, as well as within our own women's networks, with the benefit of transnational links and support.

For FemLINKPACIFIC, women's security is all-encompassing. It is not just related to armed conflict – or even to domestic violence – but affects every area of women's lives. The question of women's security is one of the welfare and status of women, human security and the impact of decisions related to the military, the police and the broader security sector on women. While concerns include the elimination of violence against women and children, there is also a broader concern that includes the need to advocate for gender mainstreaming and relevant training for peacekeeping operations; the importance of gender-sensitive demobilisation programmes for security and military personnel; and for women to be engaged in the planning of humanitarian assistance.

As we have heard from the stories we have documented in each of these four locations of our work, more guns do not mean more security. Through women's eyes, there is a broader notion of security – one that is defined in human, rather than in military, terms. Women most affected by guns often have the best ideas about how to remove them from the community. However, successive peace support operations in our region have failed to formally engage with women, the peacemakers, and as a result numerous incentives have been provided to ex-combatants – yet the guns remain.

However, we persist, continuing to promote our notions of peace and security. During April 2012, history was made when the first Fiji Women's Forum was held, bringing a diversity of women together to promote Fijian women's participation in government.[10] The Forum adopted an important parallel process to monitor and hold the state accountable to human rights resolutions and treaties, including SCR 1325 and the *Convention on the Elimination of All Forms of Discrimination against Women*[11] (CEDAW), while also enhancing collaboration between key women's organisations and networks. As a result, women will be supported to increase their participation in national political processes, especially from within their local communities. Women leaders have reaffirmed that the return to civilian-led parliamentary democracy must include security sector reforms as a critical issue that must engage women. In addition to enhancing the protection of women within their homes and communities, through improved delivery of police services as well as strategies to prevent domestic violence, it is necessary to conduct a review of defence and national security policy, their postures and budgeting processes, in order to meet human security needs. There is also a need to ensure gender sensitivity training of security sector personnel, in full compliance with SCR 1325, in order to support the implementation of existing commitments and utilise tools such as gender-based early-warning indicators.

Also in April 2012, in Bougainville, over 1,000 women and girls from various churches and community-based organisations in the 14th constituency of North Bougainville marched to Bel Isi Park (Peace Park) with placards and banners calling for the total disposal of arms and appealing to the Autonomous Bougainville Government to provide active leadership in dealing with gun issues and other law and order problems facing the region. The forum was organised by the Leitana Nehan Women's Development Agency, in response to the escalation of gun violence, and called for their rightful place in weapons disposal programmes. Women have called for a clear framework and timeline to collect and dispose of guns, as well as for rehabilitation programmes for ex-combatants.

These are just two examples of the spectrum of activities that FemLINKPACIFIC facilitates through the creation of both the network and the communications spaces for women, women's groups and community organisations. In the following two sections I take a closer look at the role of women's media in the Pacific, in the context of Fiji and with respect to promoting the *Regional Action Plan on Women, Peace and Security*. I then conclude the chapter by outlining some thoughts on the way forward, drawing from the Pacific experiences of implementing SCR 1325.

Community radio: a tool for peace in FIJI

So why does women's community radio matter? Shouldn't we be mainstreaming and making news, shaking things up in the mainstream media? I only wish it were that easy. After departing from a career in corporate media more than a decade ago, where I was constantly trying to find ways to take the messages from our women's movement beyond the confines of annual International Women's Day and 16 Days of Activism against Gender Violence Campaign (16 Days Campaign) events, I connected my work with the vision of Virginia Woolf for women to have the resources to define our spaces, including to be able to challenge war and violence. The main objective of FemLINKPACIFIC is to bring the stories of our women and their communities to the forefront, to help promote peace and reconciliation in multi-ethnic Fiji.

Since 2009, FemLINKPACIFIC has linked the 16 Days Campaign to our rural women's community media '1325' network, building on the monthly meetings where rural women leaders share and articulate their women, peace and human security priorities using a SCR 1325 lens. In 2011, 139 rural women and 24 young women shared their personal stories, and the stories of their families, their community groups and clubs, during our 16 Days Campaign across Fiji. SCR 1325 reaffirms that women are crucial partners in shoring up the three pillars of lasting peace: economic recovery, social cohesion and a stable political system. But our political reality is that we still have a long way to go to be able to claim spaces in a legitimate political system, even to simply challenge the state's spending priorities. By using women's media, local women are empowered through the dissemination and control of information, while listening women are connected to the same information.

The 2012 theme of the UN Security Council Open Debate on SCR 1325[12] reiterated the need to support women's civil society roles in peacebuilding and conflict prevention, which means that local and national action plans to implement SCR 1325 must be inclusive of women's definitions of peace and human security. It also requires a transformation of structures to ensure the full and equal participation of women in decision-making. The 16 Days Campaign in 2012 was based around an interactive learning programme for our current young women producers and broadcasters, and a group of potential volunteers from Suva and from the '1325' network in Nausori, not far from Suva, to work with two outstanding feminist communicators – Vanessa Griffen and Shirley Tagi. They worked together to enhance their collective knowledge of the 16 Days Campaign as well as to develop a series of messages that aired during the campaign. These are the media spaces we have created to enable women, including young women, to talk about issues closest to them: to connect formal and informal processes of participation and define where transformation is needed, especially here in Fiji during an often tense period of constitutional transition.

This is thinking globally and acting locally.

Enhancing accountability: the role of a regional action plan on women, peace and security

Since the unanimous adoption of SCR 1325 in 2000, there has been increasing recognition in the Pacific of women's role in conflict prevention and peacebuilding and awareness that sexual- and gender-based violence is a security threat in the region. There have also been significant consultations on these issues, and priorities for action have been identified. In December 2010, as part of the 10th anniversary commemoration of SCR 1325, a Pacific Regional Working Group on Women, Peace and Security (Working Group) was established with members from the UN, Council of Regional Organisations in the Pacific (CROP)[13] agencies, Pacific Island Forum Members and civil society. In June 2011, the Working Group was given the task of developing a *Regional Action Plan on Women, Peace and Security* (Regional Action Plan) by the Pacific Islands Forum Regional Security Committee. This was subsequently supported by Pacific Women's Ministers in August of the same year and was formally adopted in 2012.

The Regional Action Plan provides a framework for Pacific Island countries to enhance women's leadership in conflict prevention and peacebuilding, mainstream gender in security policymaking and ensure that the human rights of women and girls are protected in humanitarian crises, transitional contexts and post-conflict situations. The Regional Action Plan also establishes a regional mechanism that will support regional and national implementation efforts. The purposes of the Regional Action Plan include providing an enabling environment at the regional level to improve women's leadership in conflict prevention and management, peacekeeping and security policy decisionmaking; ensure the human rights of women and girls are protected; and strengthen the engagement of civil society, women's groups and gender equality advocates with regional security and conflict prevention policy and decision-making.

The Regional Action Plan is broad-based to the extent that it focuses on conflict/post-conflict, transitional contexts and humanitarian settings. This is based on our experience that humanitarian, peacebuilding and conflict prevention scenarios and responses must be inter-linked. The Regional Action Plan also focuses efforts on preventing conflict, not just on responding once violence erupts and governance systems are disrupted. There are significant parallel efforts underway in the region to ensure women are protected from gender- and sexual-based violence and that the relief needs of women and girls are met following natural disasters and other humanitarian crises. As a result, the focus on gendered violence in the Regional Action Plan is limited to where added value is discernible from a women, peace and security perspective.

The primary focus area of the Regional Action Plan is on gender mainstreaming and promoting women's leadership in conflict prevention and management; political decision-making; and peacebuilding and peacekeeping. This seeks to address the reality that, since 1992, women have represented fewer than three per cent of mediators and eight per cent of negotiators to major peace processes in the Pacific. These numbers have not markedly improved since the passage of SCR 1325 in 2000. The Regional Action Plan provides a political mechanism to improve on this poor record.

The development of the Regional Action Plan also recognises that women continue to play an important role in brokering peace by helping to foster confidence and trust in the community, and are more likely to address issues of concern to women and marginalised groups. Women also often have critical advance knowledge of impending instability and violence and have frequently actively reported their concerns, despite at times facing threats to their personal security. Women have a long history of peace activism at the local level, in terms of conflict prevention and management, mediation and dialogue, but this is not sufficiently recognised and, as a result, women do not receive enough support to participate in formal efforts at the regional or national level. These problems of exclusion are compounded by the low level of women's political representation at all levels of political decision-making in the region. In this context, the Regional Action Plan aims to achieve the following:

- Strengthened capacity and networking of women leaders from government, civil society and the private sector in mediation, dialogue, peace negotiations and constitutional reforms;
- Enhanced capacity of governments to adopt measures to increase women's representation at all levels of leadership and decision-making; and
- More effective participation of women leaders in the context of the *Biketawa Declaration*, (which outlines guiding principles for good governance and courses of action for a regional response to crises in the region)[14] and the Good Office role of the Secretary-General of the Pacific Islands Forum Secretariat.

Given the widespread involvement of Pacific Island countries in RAMSI,[15] and an increasing number of police, military and civilian personnel from the region participating in UN peacekeeping and peace support operations, the Regional Action Plan also aims to ensure women, peace and security commitments are reflected in participating country peacekeeping policies.

The way forward

Women are 'waging peace' across the Pacific, but there is a critical need to shift from commitments to operationalisation of SCR 1325 and CEDAW to ensure an effective response to the complex and multifaceted threats and challenges to human security. An effective response requires the participation, recognition and valuing of the experiences, knowledge and role of women. The women who have crossed conflict lines to promote non-violence, peace and human rights, despite the personal risks associated with such actions, remain outside of the formal peace process.

The reality for many women, in the Pacific Island region and around the world, is that we are excluded from the structures that make the decisions to sustain peace or to engage in conflict. Yet it is imperative that women's civil society be inextricably linked to any peace plan, particularly as there are few women in political and civil service leadership positions across Pacific Island countries. Despite the important role played by women's groups in prevention and recovery efforts, their representation in decision-making bodies remains marginal, whether these relate to recovery planning or formal peace processes, including peacekeeping or peace support operations. Women's hopes and expectations of peacekeeping and peace support operations are much more than the recruitment and training of troops. Yes it is critical that all troop- and police-contributing countries engage gender experts and expertise in all aspects of peace operations and ensure that pre- and post-deployment training complies with SCR 1325, international human rights standards, UN policies regarding violence against women and 'zero tolerance' of sexual offences.[16] However, FemLINKPACIFIC also believes that peacekeeping and peace support operations are part of broader conflict transformation and conflict prevention processes. Therefore these operations must also include sustainable DDR programmes to mend the divisions in a conflict- or war-torn society; ensure that the time frame for the mission is holistic; and go beyond supporting only those who carried guns in the conflicts.

FemLINKPACIFIC's conceptions of women, peace and human security require UN member states to ensure gender analysis is incorporated into all aspects of small arms and light weapons disposal programmes by including women civil society experts in working groups, including those concerned with border security and control, to stop gun running. DDR programmes should equitably benefit ex-combatants and those taking up, or forced into, support roles in armed groups. Reintegration and pension packages should include reasonable compensation for years of service, injury, illness, including mental illness, as well as stress counselling and retraining. Peacekeeping and peace support efforts should also ensure resources and safe women's spaces are available for peace- and trust-building activities as a precursor to women's full involvement in the peace process. Women must be supported to have equal participation in all processes and programmes that relate to their personal security and recovery, including in the planning and management of camps and services for internally displaced persons.

Finally, community media, particularly radio, must be integrated into any peacebuilding strategy: as a local measure developed globally. Peace support operations must support women, both as producers of media information and as subjects of it that go beyond their being victims. This is vital. Otherwise, women's role in peacebuilding will continue to be ignored, and the primary images we get from conflict zones will continue to be of despair, rather than hope.

In the Pacific the realities of the impact of climate change and natural disasters also require an application of women's human rights measures, including SCR 1325, to ensure that humanitarian assistance and operations ensure proactive engagement with women in preparing disaster risk reduction and management strategies, especially as women are at the real centre of planning and disaster management, from the household to community level. This includes ensuring women are proactively engaged in planning and managing evacuation centres, and that all disaster risk reduction and management strategies are inclusive, not only of women, but also of persons with disabilities, children and the elderly, and are safe for all members of the community. Additionally, Pacific communities need access to technical and weather information in language that they can decipher, on a regular basis, especially through radio and television.

One of the next steps is to review existing regional commitments, such as the *Biketawa Declaration*, to ensure that the commitments in the Regional Action Plan are integrated into all the regional peace and security architecture. This could certainly be one of the key responsibilities of the Pacific Islands Forum Regional Security Committee's oversight role.

Conclusion

Peace processes do more than end conflict. If done skilfully, peace processes can build a foundation for nation-building and restoring community life. It is therefore critical that women are included as active agents of transformation. Realising women's formal political participation in decision-making is more than involving women as observers and having a few women candidates standing in elections. Women should be included in all discussions about security and about resource allocation. Too often, women's approaches to these issues are not heard because they are excluded from the process or their contributions and opinions are devalued. To overcome these obstacles to effective inclusion and just nation-building, women's civil society representation must be deliberately and systematically built into every peacebuilding process, including peacekeeping and peace support operations.

Real hope for peace will come from women and men working together for conflict resolution and peacebuilding, which make it easier to foster dialogue rather than taking up arms. In the Pacific, the development and formal adoption of the Regional Action Plan have demonstrated that there are ways in which women's innovations and initiatives can be recognised and integrated into existing political processes. Global initiatives like SCR 1325 can be utilised as a transformation tool at the local level by, for example, using community radio to build on women's history of negotiating and bringing about peace in the Pacific. It is critical that women's peace activism and civil society collaboration is strengthened and sustained to assist Pacific Governments to develop relevant national programmes and strategies on women, peace and security and ways to accelerate implementation of SCR 1325 and CEDAW. Achieving sustainable peace in the Pacific relies on developing gender-inclusive peacemaking and peacebuilding processes, and involving young women and young men in imagining and creating more hopeful futures.

Notes

1. S.N. Anderlini, 'What the women say: Participation and UNSCR 1325 – A case study assessment' (International Civil Society Action Network and Center for International Studies, Massachusetts Institute of Technology, October 2010).
2. *Security Council Resolution 1325*, UN Doc. S/RES/1325 (31 October 2000).
3. *FemLINKPACIFIC* (2007), http://www.femlinkpacific.org.fj (last accessed October 2013).
4. H. Hakana, P. Ninnes and B. Jenkins (eds), *NGOs and Post-Conflict Recovery: The Leitana Nehan Women's Development Agency Bougainville* (Canberra: ANU E Press, 2006).
5. 'Vois Blong Mere', *Peace Portal* (2013), http://www.peaceportal.org/web/vois-blong-mere/home (last accessed October 2013).

6. For discussion, see 'Tonga: First women-led community radio consultation', *Pacific Media Centre: Te Amokura* (6 April 2011), http://www.pmc.aut.ac.nz/pacific-media-watch/2011-04-06/tonga-first-women-led-community-radio-consultation (last accessed October 2013).

7. *Security Council Resolution 1820*, UN Doc. S/RES/1820 (19 June 2008).

8. *Report of the Fourth World Conference on Women*, UN Doc. A/Conf. 177/20 (17 October 1995), p. 4, setting out the *Beijing Declaration and Platform for Action*.

9. See *PeaceWomen*, www.peacewomen.org (last accessed February 2013).

10. See 'Fiji Women's Forum: Amplifying the voices of 49% of the population', *International Women's Development Agency* (31 May 2012), http://www.iwda.org.au/2012/05/31/fiji-womens-forum-amplifying-the-voices-of-49-percent (last accessed October 2013).

11. *Convention on the Elimination of All Forms of Discrimination against Women*, opened for signature on 1 March 1980, 1249 UNTS 13 (entered into force on 3 September 1981).

12. See 'Women and peace and security: Side events and activities linked to the 2012 open debate of the Security Council', *PeaceWomen*, http://www.peacewomen.org/news_article.php?id=345&type=event (last accessed October 2013).

13. See 'CROP', *Pacific Islands Forum Secretariat*, http://www.forumsec.org/pages.cfm/about-us/crop/ (last accessed October 2013).

14. See *Biketawa Declaration* (31st Summit of Pacific Islands Forum Leaders, Kiribati, October 2000), http://www.forumsec.org/pages.cfm/political-governance-security/biketawa-declaration/ (last accessed October 2013).

15. See further S. Cousins, 'Gender and Transnational Police Reform: Lessons from the Regional Assistance Mission to Solomon Islands', in this volume.

16. See R. Burke, 'Shaming the State: Sexual Offences by UN Military Peacekeepers and the Rhetoric of Zero Tolerance', in this volume.

6
Gender and Transnational Police Reform: Lessons from the Regional Assistance Mission to Solomon Islands

Stephanie Cousins

Introduction

Gender equality and the advancement of women's rights are now finally on the agenda of international peace and stabilisation operations, thanks to the sustained activism of women's groups from the grassroots to the United Nations (UN) Security Council. Spurred on by the landmark *Security Council Resolution 1325* (SCR 1325) and subsequent resolutions on women, peace and security, peacekeeping missions are now expected to 'incorporate a gender perspective' into their operations.[1] They are furthermore expected to expand the role and contribution of women in field-based operations and, increasingly, to design specific strategies to protect women in conflict and address gender-based violence. The gender agenda has permeated not only UN peacekeeping but also, gradually, regional and other non-UN-led missions, including those focussed on broader stabilisation and security sector reform (SSR).

Gender equality considerations are now generally well reflected in UN peacekeeping mission mandates and there has been some progress in advancing the role of women in peacekeeping, employing gender advisors and in the provision of gender training to peacekeeping personnel.[2] Nevertheless, progress has varied between missions and end results for women on the ground have been inadequate. For example, women are still over-represented in casualty and conflict displacement statistics and grossly under-represented in peace negotiations and institutions relating to the management of conflict (including within the UN itself).[3] There is still much work to do to transform peacekeeping missions into champions for gender equality, and maintaining the hope that this is possible requires continuing persistence.

While there is a growing body of literature focussing on this challenge in relation to UN peacekeeping, there has been less attention on non-UN-led missions, which make up a growing proportion of peace and stabilisation operations worldwide. This chapter contributes to filling this gap by examining the gender mainstreaming practice of the Regional Assistance Mission to Solomon Islands (RAMSI), a police-led regional mission mandated by the Pacific Islands Forum and deployed in 2003, at the invitation of the Solomon Islands Prime Minister, and under authorisation of the Solomon Islands National Parliament. The deployment of RAMSI marked the end of five years of ethnic tensions in Solomon Islands, and a coup in 2000, which had a devastating impact on the law and order situation in the country and resulted in widespread violence. Australia and New Zealand lead and fund RAMSI and provide most of its police personnel, although all 15 Forum countries contribute in some way to the mission.

A core pillar of RAMSI's work in Solomon Islands has been supporting the reform of the law and justice sectors – in particular the Royal Solomon Islands Police Force (RSIPF). In this sense RAMSI is a prime example of a mission engaged in transnational police reform – a component of SSR practice that focuses on reforming police institutions to enable, as specified in policy guidelines, a 'professional and accountable police service practicing a style of policing that is responsive to the needs of local communities'.[4] Transnational police reform initiatives make up an increasing component of international peacekeeping and stabilisation missions.[5] Reform activities typically involve supporting local police capacity development through training and mentoring; providing advice and assistance regarding structural and process reforms; monitoring progress and assistance with accountability mechanisms; and providing executive policing functions where necessary to fill gaps in local capabilities.[6] RAMSI has engaged in each of these police reform activities.

In this case study I consider the extent to which gender equality has been considered in the design and monitoring of RAMSI police reform interventions through its various stages of deployment. This is a critical issue, as much of the research on gender sensitive police reform demonstrates that for missions to be genuinely gender sensitive, gender equality must be treated as a core rather than additional or peripheral consideration.

I start by briefly canvassing the literature relating to strategies for gender sensitive police reform and define 'gender balancing' and 'gender mainstreaming' as the two core approaches used. I then analyse

RAMSI's gender mainstreaming practices over four phases of the mission: 2003–2004; 2004–2005; 2006–2009; and post-2009. This analysis points to some positive and innovative gender mainstreaming practices within RAMSI, such as the collection of sex-disaggregated data in the annual RAMSI People's Survey. Nevertheless, on the whole the police component of the mission has not made gender equality a core consideration, although this has started to change, since 2009, due mainly to the strong influence of the Australian Agency for International Development (AusAID) and gender champions within the Solomon Islands Government. The case study enables me to offer a number of reflections on how RAMSI's approach to gender sensitive police reform can be strengthened. Recommendations include ensuring that local women's groups and civilian agencies with gender expertise have greater involvement in mission design and planning from the outset; adjusting the methodology and purpose of public perception surveys so they provide useful insights for gender analysis; and establishing women's rights objectives for the mission to report against.

The findings outlined in this chapter are based on a review of literature relating to RAMSI and gender sensitive police reform in general, as well as on interviews with a small but diverse range of key informants (see Appendix 1). Interview participants were selected on the basis of their direct experience with RAMSI – from within the mission, within the Solomon Islands Government, as a member of civil society and as a researcher. Participants were selected to enable a mix of local and regional informants.

Gender sensitive police reform

Gender sensitive police reform has developed as a field of practice in earnest since 2007 and now boasts a range of toolkits, manuals and policies to guide practitioners.[7] On one hand, gender sensitive police reform is about avoiding the reinforcement of gender discrimination – by building an enabling environment for inclusive, socially responsive, non-discriminatory and representative security institutions and functions.[8] On the other hand, it is about utilising the opportunities present in post-conflict societies to open up space for women's leadership and positively contribute to the transformation of gender relations. Related to these two dimensions, strategies and approaches for gender sensitive police reform can be grouped under two interrelated and complementary strategies: gender balancing and gender mainstreaming.[9]

Gender balancing is about promoting the equal participation of women and men in all aspects of the policing system – both as a way of upholding men's and women's right to participate equally in decision-making relating to security,[10] and of ensuring the security system is representative of society as a whole.[11] Given men are highly over-represented within policing and broader security sector institutions throughout the world, gender balance initiatives usually focus on recruiting, retaining and advancing women as well as providing opportunities for civil society organisations, including women's organisations, to participate in reforms.[12] Gender balancing is also based on the premise there are practical benefits that flow from women's participation, 'by virtue of the fact that women can play roles which men cannot'.[13] This is particularly relevant with regard to providing policing services to women victims of crime in discriminatory or repressive societies, for example relating to sexual and gender-based violence (SGBV), although feminist scholarship has rightly questioned the gender essentialism that underlies these claims.

Gender mainstreaming places emphasis on the ways that the security sector can work to address gender-based discrimination and power inequalities, in order to meet the needs of women, girls, men and boys in society and achieve gender equality. It is defined in SSR literature as:

> the process of assessing the implications for women and men of any planned action, including legislation, policies or programmes, in all areas and at all levels. It is a strategy for making women's as well as men's concerns and experiences an integral dimension of the design, implementation, monitoring and evaluation of policies and programmes in all spheres so that women and men benefit equally and inequality is not perpetuated.[14]

Practical gender mainstreaming strategies highlighted in policy manuals and guidelines include: *gender sensitive assessment*,[15] including the collection and analysis of sex- and age-disaggregated data[16] and consideration of gender in SSR impact assessments and consultation processes; *recognising the need for gender expertise*, including the involvement of gender experts in planning SSR policies and programmes;[17] *gendered planning and accountability mechanisms*, including incorporating gender objectives and indicators into action plans,[18] performance frameworks and monitoring, evaluation and learning processes for particular programmes;[19] and *establishing targeted programmes* to address specific gender equality and women's rights goals where appropriate, such as establishing specialised SGBV units within police in order to investigate such crimes sensitively and refer victims to appropriate support providers.[20]

The strategies espoused for gender sensitive police reform tend to focus on 'technical and bureaucratic processes' to enhance equal opportunity,[21] which obscures the inherently political and cultural roles that transnational police play when intervening to help 'reform' post-conflict states and divided societies. As Otwin Marenin points out, the nature of policing means it is inevitable that transnational police will be 'forced to take sides in societal disputes' within the environment of a mission.[22] Just as transnational police cannot be neutral bystanders to social tensions along cultural or ethnic lines in the communities they are helping to police, neither can they be neutral to the gender politics. By their actions and omissions, transnational police may replicate existing gender inequalities or promote their transformation.

As such, it is important to understand gender sensitive police reform as a 'transformative process' that not only involves technical changes to institutions and structures,[23] but also makes an important contribution to changing cultural norms that sustain unequal gender relations. For this transformative process to have any chance of success, it is critical that gender equality is a core aim and consideration in assessing, planning and evaluating police reform initiatives – rather than an 'add on' consideration.

RAMSI police reform and gender practice

With this challenge in mind, I now turn to the Solomon Islands to examine the extent to which gender equality has been considered as a core aim and consideration in the design of RAMSI police reform interventions in the four phases of the mission. I focus on the gender mainstreaming aspects of the mission, as RAMSI's gender balancing practice has been examined elsewhere and found to have some positive aspects, while further effort is needed to ensure it is adequately integrated into all policies and practices.[24] This analysis is structured chronologically according to the key phases of the RAMSI mission. First, the early stages of deployment from 2003, when the mission involved a large military contingent and was engaged proactively in direct provision of security for Solomon Islanders. Second, the shift towards police reform from late 2004 and the introduction of the RAMSI Performance Framework in 2005 to monitor implementation. Third, from 2006, a period of growing influence and involvement of AusAID and the introduction of the RAMSI People's Survey. And fourth, the adoption of the RAMSI *Partnership Framework* in 2009, which incorporated gender as a cross-cutting theme.

Early stages of RAMSI – strong military presence

RAMSI was initially deployed in July 2003 under Operation Helpem Fren ('helping friends' in Solomon Islands Pidgin).[25] RAMSI is a police-led mission with a Participating Police Force (PPF) initially comprised of around 300 transnational police personnel from five Pacific Island Forum countries, two thirds of whom came from Australia.[26] Around 1,800 military personnel were also deployed in the early stages of the mission, the vast majority being from the Australian Defence Force.[27]

It is clear that in the early stages of RAMSI's deployment gender equality was not a key consideration in planning and programme design, and gender issues were almost entirely absent from early documentation about the mission. The mission's mandate, as agreed by Pacific Islands Forum members in the *RAMSI Treaty*, was to:

> assist in the provision of security and safety to persons and property; maintain supplies and services essential to the life of the Solomon Islands community; prevent and suppress violence, intimidation and crime; support and develop Solomon Islands institutions; and generally to assist in the maintenance of law and order in Solomon Islands.[28]

The preamble of the Treaty notes that the 'deteriorating law and order and security in Solomon Islands poses a threat to good governance and economic prosperity of Solomon Islands',[29] but makes no reference to the gendered dimensions of the crisis or indeed any reference to women, girls, men or boys at all.

The decision to deploy RAMSI marked a dramatic shift in Australia's foreign policy at the time, reflective of the changed post-9/11 global security environment and Australia's participation in the United States-led global 'war on terror'.[30] That is, Australia's decision to take a leadership role in RAMSI was officially justified by perceived threats that instability in Solomon Islands presented to Australia's national security – despite wide recognition that such regional threats were exaggerated.[31]

Against this atmosphere of 'crisis', John Roughan, an influential civil society actor and commentator in Solomon Islands, argues that from the outset there was a disconnect between the posture of RAMSI's military and police personnel and the tasks they had before them:

RAMSI troops landed in Henderson Airfield and these young fellows had thought the Solomon Islands was a dangerous place, killings on the Weather Coast [of Guadalcanal] etc. They thought, if it's not a battle zone, it's close to it. When they got out of the plane they were to secure the perimeters – but what they saw was not in the military manual. They met women and children along the chain link fence who were very happy and singing to them! These soldiers were prepared for the worst – but not for singing women and children.[32]

Consequently, during this phase of RAMSI's deployment, the PPF and military contingents were essentially in a peacekeeping role, providing a 'security pause' within which to (re)establish law and order.[33] Thankfully, by 2004 the military component had been significantly reduced, and the PPF shifted to concentrating on the 'consolidation of law and order, institutional reform and reviving the economy'.[34] Still, security was understood by RAMSI in a very narrow sense as directly addressing the threat of armed groups, rather than encompassing the broader human security concerns of Solomon Islanders – relating to highly gendered social, economic and environmental threats and vulnerabilities.[35]

Shift to police reform and the 2005 Performance Framework

By early 2005 the PPF was concentrating on police reform in earnest, with a focus on capacity development of the local police by working within the RSIPF and training and mentoring local officers.[36] In mid-2005 RAMSI developed the Performance Framework to assist in monitoring the implementation of its programmes against three overarching objectives: contributing to a safer and more secure Solomon Islands ('law and justice' pillar); helping Government to better serve the Solomon Islands people ('machinery of government' pillar); and contributing to a more prosperous Solomon Islands ('economic governance' pillar).[37] The Performance Framework was entirely gender-blind, with no objectives or performance indicators relating to gender equality or gender balance in RAMSI programmes.

A Gender Situational Analysis, conducted in 2006 by AusAID, found that gender considerations were 'largely invisible' in RAMSI policy and planning documents, despite the formal commitments to gender sensitive policing.[38] As noted by retired veteran Solomon Islands Government public servant Ruth Liloqula:

People were trying to do gender mainstreaming on an ad hoc basis with ad hoc information. No one had done a gender audit properly to really focus on which areas we really needed to concentrate on. People would have a particular belief and that was it – it wasn't a holistic or systematic approach. It really turned off those [local people] with the power to allow gender mainstreaming to happen.[39]

The absence of gender equality as a core aim, and consequent lack of gender analysis underpinning RAMSI planning and implementation, resulted in poorly coordinated efforts and compounded resistance to gender mainstreaming on the ground.

While there were a growing number of examples of positive gender practice within the PPF – including gender sensitive human resource reforms in the RSIPF, the promotion of women leaders and initiatives focussed on addressing SGBV – an Australian Federal Police researcher conceded that, overall, these initiatives were 'not strategically brought together within a framework for mainstreaming gender through the mission'.[40] Within the Australian-dominated PPF, there was a sense that promoting gender equality and a gendered approach was peripheral, and not integral to or embedded in, either the PPF's executive policing or capacity building role.[41]

Introduction of the RAMSI People's Survey and influence of AusAID

While RAMSI remained a police-led mission, the involvement of civilian aid agencies, most notably AusAID, increased progressively as the mission shifted to focus more on capacity building functions. In 2006 AusAID began to play an influential role in addressing the gender blindness of RAMSI's police reform approach, producing a 'Transitional Country Strategy', which provided a framework for AusAID assistance to Solomon Islands delivered through RAMSI and Australia's bilateral aid programme. The strategy committed to investing in poverty and vulnerability analysis, including analysis of gender issues in Solomon Islands 'in recognition of current information gaps and in preparation for the development of a longer term framework for Australia's assistance'.[42] AusAID also committed to funding a survey of public opinion, undertaken by Australian National University researchers, within key areas of reform targeted by RAMSI.

Called the RAMSI People's Survey, and following a pilot in 2006, the survey was expanded in 2007 to cover a fully representative sample of the population with over 5,000 respondents.[43] It has been conducted annually since then and the findings are reported publicly. The survey is unique to RAMSI, as other international assistance missions do not survey public opinion in such a thorough manner. It contains sex-, age- and geographically-disaggregated data on a range of issues including perceptions about women as leaders; community trust and confidence in the police and government officials; perceptions about the law and order situation; and experiences of safety at the national, community and, more recently, household levels. The data therefore has the potential to shed light on the gender-differentiated impacts of the mission's reform initiatives on women, men, boys and girls and therefore inform gender mainstreaming planning and implementation. Indeed, the PPF has used the findings of the People's Survey to track its own performance and the RSIPF now also uses the survey to report against their key performance indicators regarding building community trust and confidence in the police.[44]

While the People's Survey is an example of strong practice in the collection of sex-disaggregated data, it does not appear to be well utilised for gender analysis, gender sensitive planning or accountability purposes. Given the survey is RAMSI's primary vehicle for demonstrating and communicating impact, there is also a perception locally that it is designed to be 'self-praising' rather than a critical assessment, planning and monitoring tool.[45] Little attention is given to analysis of the sex-disaggregated data, nor is there any meaningful analysis of gendered trends from previous years.[46] While the survey each year includes some focus group methodology, the published survey material is predominantly quantitative. As such, its ability to shed light on the *reasons* for differential impacts and trends over time is also limited. Several of the survey questions have been altered over the years, or removed altogether, undermining the potential of the survey for understanding trends. Without analysis of trend data it is difficult to imagine how RAMSI could use the survey meaningfully to monitor its impact over time.

In spite of these limitations, there is untapped potential to use the eight years of survey data for gender analysis, programme design and monitoring. Yet to date there has been no comprehensive gender analysis of the survey or causal trends. While a comprehensive analysis would require further qualitative research, a range of interesting gender differential trends are evident from the existing published data. I will briefly illustrate some of these trends in order to indicate how the People's Survey could be more effectively utilised in the future for gender sensitive planning purposes.

Unpacking gender-differentiated trends from multi-year RAMSI People's Survey Data

Responses to a number of questions asked over multiple years in the People's Survey provide insights into the way RAMSI's police reform initiatives are perceived by women, men, boys and girls. Every year since 2007 the survey has asked respondents, 'Does the [R]SIPF treat people fairly and with respect?' Responses to this question demonstrate an overall decline in perceptions of RSIPF fairness and respect between 2007 and 2011, although no meaningful analysis of this trend is provided. Examining this data once it is sex- and age-disaggregated provides a more complex picture. Between 2007 and 2008 there was a dramatic drop in the number of women who answered 'yes' to this question, followed by an increase between 2008 and 2010 and a drop again after 2010. For men there was a much more steady decline throughout this entire period. For young women and young men there was a similarly steady decline from 2007 to 2009, then a more positive response in 2010, followed by another decline in 2011 (see Figure 6.1).

When asked about the overall decline, one of my respondents, from the Australian Federal Police, felt that it was an 'unfortunate

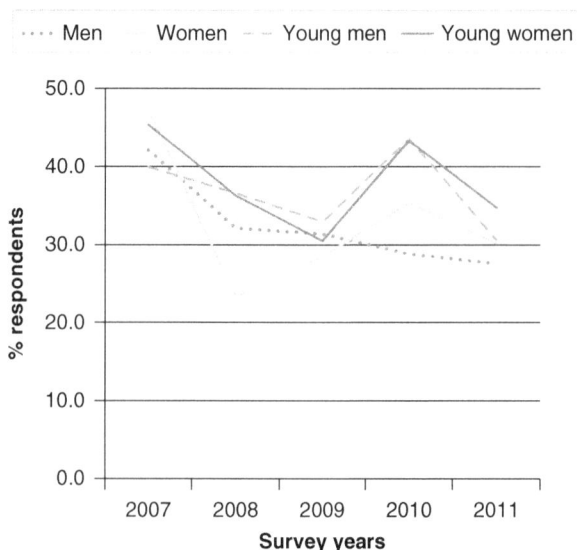

Figure 6.1   Answered 'yes' to the question '*Does the SIPF treat people fairly and with respect?*' for years 2007–2011

consequence' of the presence of the international PPF in the country, as the well trained, equipped and resourced PPF provide a point of comparison that the RSIPF cannot compete with.[47] Conversely, a local respondent felt that the decline could be linked to a 'rough edge' to the new policing image, introduced by the PPF:

> I must admit that that rough edge is probably coming from RAMSI. We are used to community policing here which is quite different to what I'm seeing at the moment ... The approach now is much more focussed on investigating crimes and collecting evidence rather than supporting communities to police themselves. There has been a change from the cordial approach to policing to police officers that are not listening, are perceived as rude and unfriendly, not really caring, with an 'I know it all' attitude. It is a shift to being more masculine.

While both these explanations provide important practical and cultural insights into policing issues that need addressing, neither explain the gendered fluctuations. Understanding the reasons for differential per-spectives is key to turning this data into a meaningful guide for gender sensitive reforms.

In 2011 the survey asked respondents, for the first time, to consider whether the RSIPF had 'improved' over the last five years. Results show that all groups showed high 'no' response rates, which is consistent with the general decline in positive views about the RSIPF shown in Figure 6.1. However, of those who perceived an improvement, adult men outnumbered the other groups, whereas young men (followed by young women) were most likely to respond that the RSIPF had *not* improved (see Figure 6.2). This suggests a critical intersection between age and gender in the experience of law enforcement in Solomon Islands. Given there is a bulging youth population and high rates of youth unemployment and related social problems,[48] this finding raises critical questions about how the RSIPF engages with young men and women, and how the PPF could support more constructive and positive engagement in this regard.

Also indicated in Figure 6.2, women and young women are more likely to answer 'don't know' when asked this question. This could indicate that women and young women have less contact with the police, perhaps because of the decline in community policing. Another reading of this data is that women and young women may feel less safe to rate the performance of the RSIPF. This inference is consistent with

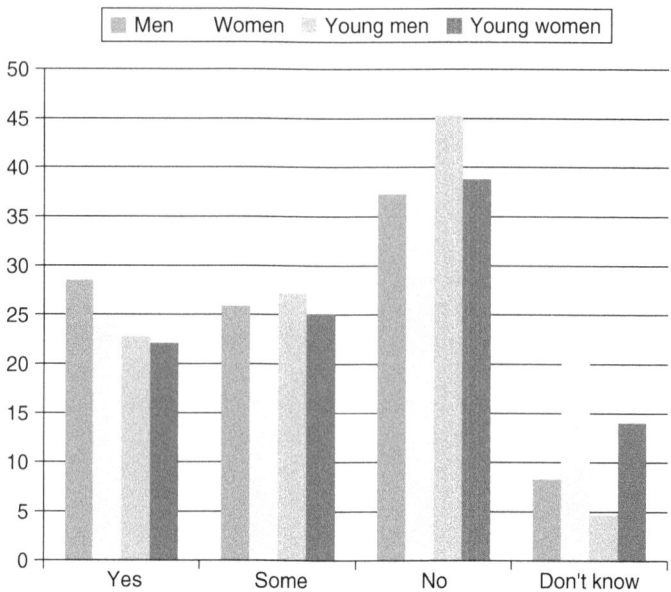

Figure 6.2   Answers to '*Has the RSIPF improved in the past 5 years?*'

earlier data relating to the willingness of respondents to make formal complaints about the RSIPF. In 2006 the People's Survey pilot asked respondents whether they would 'feel safe to make a formal complaint against a [RSIPF] police officer'.[49] Only 52.5 per cent of women and 44 per cent of young women said they would feel safe to make a complaint, compared with 81 per cent of men and 75.1 per cent of young men.[50] This alarming gender gap plainly suggests a police force that is significantly distrusted by women and girls. Unfortunately, the question was not asked again after 2006.

Instead, between 2007 and 2009 this question was revised to ask, 'would you make formal complaint about an RSIPF officer?'[51] This question was not asked after 2009. The 2007–2009 trend data indicates that women and girls are far less likely to make a formal complaint against a police officer than men and boys, although their willingness to make complaints increased modestly over time (as it did for young men). Given the wording of the question, it is also not clear whether the differential responses are because women are beginning to feel safer to make complaints or because they have less reason or cause to make them (that is, due to perceptions that the RSIPF is more reliable). With supplementary qualitative analysis and clearer and more consistent survey questions, results like this could provide a useful evidence base to inform programme design – for example, by justifying additional expenditure on programmes to address the safety concerns that prevent women from making complaints about police.

My final example of missed opportunities to learn from sex-differentiated People's Survey findings relates to Solomon Islander perceptions of safety in their communities. For example, when asked about the law and order situation in their community, women were most likely out of all groups to say 'safe and peaceful' in 2006 (47.5 per cent),[52] yet by 2011 they were least likely to feel this way (28.6 per cent).[53] In contrast, in 2006 young women were least likely to say their community was 'safe and peaceful' (21 per cent),[54] but by 2011 they were more likely to feel this way than adult women and men (31.6 per cent), although only marginally.[55] Again, these trends point to a critical intersection between gender and age in understanding perceptions of safety, and demonstrate continuing acute safety concerns for women and young women at the community level. What is puzzling is the contrast between these results and responses to the question 'Do *you* feel safe in your community?', which was asked for the first time in 2010. The results indicate that the number of young women answering 'sometimes' or 'hardly ever' increased by eight per cent from 2010 to 2012 (with a corresponding decrease in the number of women answering 'always').[56] Why, at a time when more young women feel their communities are safe and peaceful, would less young women feel safe personally? Unpacking the gender dimensions of this apparent disconnect between perceptions of public law and order and personal sense of safety is critical to effectively mainstreaming gender equality through police reform efforts.

As this brief analysis shows, despite some limitations of the survey methodology, including changes to the survey design and questions over the years making analysis of trends difficult, the data collected holds much potential. Tapping into that potential to support gender sensitive mission planning would be a logical, and much overdue, next step for RAMSI, and may also provide valuable insights for other missions.

Incorporation of gender as a cross-cutting theme in RAMSI

Shortly after the first RAMSI People's Survey pilot was published, the Solomon Islands Government and RAMSI began negotiating a *Partnership Framework*, finally agreed in April 2009.[57] A Proposed

Framework Agreement was produced by a team led by the Secretary to Cabinet in the Solomon Islands Government, Ruth Liloqula.[58] Liloqula was of the view that the *Partnership Framework* needed to mainstream gender throughout each pillar (including law and justice), given well documented indicators of women's lack of socio-economic opportunity and subordinate political status in Solomon Islands society:[59]

> Despite what the constitution says, women's status remains low. Not only in the communities but inside the government institutions as well. Women are considered as inferior to men. What really prevents gender mainstreaming is that men see themselves as entitled to have power because of their gender, and their interests take precedence over any other ideas about women and men.[60]

For these reasons, Liloqula argued the *Partnership Framework* needed to have a specific goal relating to women's rights. As a result, the original Proposed Framework Agreement, approved at Solomon Islands Cabinet level, included a clear women's rights goal: '[to] secure the rights of women, thereby creating equal opportunities for all to advance the wellbeing of the nation'.[61] Against this goal indicators were identified relating to gender equality, participation and representation of women, economic empowerment and the reduction of violence against women.[62]

This document was then revised by RAMSI before being endorsed by the Pacific Islands Forum Ministerial Standing Committee in May 2009. In the final version of the *Partnership Framework* the women's rights objective was removed and replaced by a much weaker objective that: '[Solomon Islands Government] policy commitments to gender equality are advanced consistently across government'. There is also a generally worded commitment that:

> RAMSI programs and [Solomon Islands Government] partner agencies jointly agree on relevant gender outcomes from their operations consistent with [Solomon Islands Government] policy and indicators for reporting on progress towards them against a 2009 baseline.[63]

RAMSI has accelerated progress towards implementing a number of gender equality-related initiatives since signing the partnership. Yet, at the time of writing, over four years later, there has been no progress on jointly agreeing these 'relevant gender outcomes' in any of RAMSI's three pillars (law and justice; economic governance and growth; and machinery of government), or in reporting against a 2009 baseline.[64] An independent assessment of RAMSI in 2011 was critical of the gender targets of the *Partnership Framework* because they 'are not underpinned by an overarching concept of what is needed to be achieved in gender and why'.[65] Had the women's rights goal and indicators from the original version been retained in the final *Partnership Framework*, there would have been a much clearer set of gender equality commitments that RAMSI and the Solomon Islands Government could be held accountable to.

Despite this limitation, the 2009 *Partnership Framework* was an improvement on the 2005 Framework as, for the first time, it included 'advancing gender equality' as a cross-cutting theme as well as identifying targets relating to the collection of sex-disaggregated data, gender awareness, inclusive service delivery, gender sensitive complaints mechanisms, reporting and prosecutions of SGBV and gender balance. According to Liloqula, the inclusion of gender as a cross-cutting theme was a contentious issue with RAMSI in negotiations.[66] The Solomon Islands Government team, involved in drafting the document, was adamant that gender issues should be considered across all government programmes and not relegated to the Ministry of Women, Youth and Children's Affairs, which was RAMSI's preference.[67] David Jones, who worked on the finalisation of the *Partnership Framework* from within the PPF in 2009, shared his views on the possible reasons for RAMSI resistance to the focus on gender:

> I think the concern within RAMSI, especially from the law and justice side, was that it was going beyond the original reason for the establishment of RAMSI. Many senior people thought it was stepping outside areas of responsibility and making RAMSI seem like a de-facto government. We'd resisted getting into health, education and major infrastructure for that very reason. Lots of people thought this was Solomon Islands Government sovereign responsibility not RAMSI's. That's the positive way of looking at it. The negative way of looking at it would be to say that, certainly on the security, law and justice side, many people were resistant because they had no idea about how to go about doing something like that.[68]

Liloqula and Jones both believe that the reason gender was included as a cross-cutting theme was due to the push from the Solomon Islands Government team, rather than it being a clear priority for RAMSI, although Liloqula noted internal resistance from parts of government as well, which had to be managed. Jones said that, particularly for members of the PPF, there was very limited understanding of what a gendered approach to capacity building would entail in practice when working alongside their RSIPF colleagues:

> Remember this advisory approach is still quite new for many police. If you ask them to develop a strategy to advance the Solomon Islands Government commitments in relation to CEDAW [*Convention on the Elimination of All Forms of Discrimination against Women*] they go 'what?' If you say that there's a riot happening at a soccer match between Guadalcanal and Malaita they go 'hit the button, we know what to do, we've got a standard operating procedure'.[69]

The inclusion of gender in the *Partnership Framework* has been reported as a catalyst for some positive developments.[70] These include the appointment of a Gender Adviser to RAMSI, some evidence of improved collection of sex-disaggregated data (although this varies widely between programmes) and the conduct of a Gender Stocktake by AusAID for the first time in 2010.[71] The Stocktake[72] assessed RAMSI programmes against the Solomon Islands Government's Gender, Equality and Women's Development Policy, which was developed with funding from RAMSI and other donors, and approved in March 2010.[73] The policy includes five outcomes which relate to improved equitable health and education, improved economic status of women, equal participation of women and men in decision-making and leadership, elimination of violence against women and increased capacity for gender mainstreaming.[74] The Stocktake found that 63 per cent of RAMSI activities were in alignment with the policy, although they were concentrated mainly on the equal participation in decision-making and leadership outcome, which relates to gender balancing and, to a lesser extent, PPF/RSIPF work on eliminating violence against women, which is central to gender mainstreaming.[75]

Despite some promising developments, it is notable that the Gender Stocktake found that 'many staff in both RAMSI and [Solomon Islands Government] were unaware of the incorporation of gender equality within the *Partnership Framework* and felt that they lacked the skill to assess and integrate gender as a cross-cutting issue'.[76] This is indicative of inadequate resourcing and leadership, and possibly also resistance, with respect to gender mainstreaming efforts. Also, in the absence of clear goals and objectives for promoting gender equality across RAMSI, it is not hard to see how well-meaning staff might find it difficult to understand what role they should play.

Conclusion

RAMSI's experience demonstrates just some of the challenges involved in making gender equality a core component of peacekeeping and SSR endeavours, as well as translating formal commitments into good practice on the ground. RAMSI has shown that progressive improvements to gender sensitive assessment, planning and design processes are possible over the life of a mission – from a largely gender-blind approach in the early days to the inclusion of gender as a cross-cutting theme across all of RAMSI's pillars in 2009. However, this advance has been very slow, and there is no doubt that gender equality remains a peripheral consideration in the police reform components of RAMSI.

This case study confirms that a critical success factor is having gender mainstreaming included as an agreed core objective for the mission and, further, that unless this objective is clearly integrated and understood across the mission, police personnel on the ground are likely to see gender as an optional 'add-on'.[77] Failure to set clear expectations and goals also creates the risk that practitioners will actively resist a gender sensitive approach, due to the perception that it goes 'beyond the mission'.[78]

RAMSI's experience also demonstrates that even where there is strong practice around the collection of sex-disaggregated data for reporting purposes, as in the People's Surveys, this data is not necessarily analysed to its fullest potential to feed into programme planning. This is consistent with findings from other post-conflict SSR interventions that gender analysis is rarely systematically used in situation analysis, programme design or evaluations.[79] Unlike other missions though, RAMSI has compiled an impressive sex-, age- and geographically-disaggregated dataset that provides great opportunities for ensuring that programme design and planning is gender sensitive, if it were used for strategic analysis and 'sense-making' rather than just reporting. To make this shift, gender analysis, which promotes gender mainstreaming, must be identified as one of the key objectives of the People's Survey, and its methodology must be revised to enable investigation of multi-year trends.

It is clear that many of the gains in developing more gender sensitive assessment, planning and design processes within RAMSI have been driven by AusAID, key gender 'champions' within Solomon Islands Government and inside the mission itself, and also, no doubt, local women's groups as part of the FemLINKPACIFIC network.[80] It would clearly be beneficial for these actors and agencies to be more involved in planning RAMSI-like missions from the outset – even in their strong operational policing and peacekeeping phases. This conclusion is consistent with research findings that effective gender mainstreaming is much more achievable when gender is considered in early planning stages, to prevent dominant masculine policing cultures from being entrenched within a mission.[81]

While RAMSI has a lot of work to do to bring gender in from the periphery to the core of the mission, some progress has been made – and this progress is cause for hope that the mission will continue to improve its approach to advancing gender equality. As yet though, there is little evidence of improved status of women in Solomon Islands, with persistently high and widespread rates of violence against women and some worrying signs that women's economic and political opportunity may actually be in decline.[82] Ultimately the measure of RAMSI's success in advancing gender equality and gender sensitive police reforms should be an improvement in the status, safety and security of women and girls.

It is clear that, right from the start, missions like RAMSI need to ensure that gender equality is everybody's business, and that technocratic policies and practices are not enough. Effective gender mainstreaming relies on working closely and dynamically with people at the community level, listening to their concerns and involving them in devising better policies and practices to change gendered practices of participation, violence and policing.

Appendix 1: key informant interviews

Interviews for this study were conducted with the following people. Many thanks to the participants of this study for sharing their rich experiences and ideas.

John Roughon – Founder of the Solomon Islands Development Trust (Solomon Islands' largest national NGO) and prominent civil society social commentator in the Solomon Islands. John has had extensive involvement with senior RAMSI personnel throughout the life of the mission. The Solomon Islands Development Trust has also conducted community surveys of public opinion on RAMSI.

David Jones – David worked in the Solomon Islands with RAMSI for the first time in 2005, for six months. He then returned to the Solomon Islands in 2009 working for the first year in the PPF Governance section, where he was involved in negotiations around the Solomon Islands Government/RAMSI Partnership Agreement. He then moved into a direct advisory position within the RSIPF in 2010. David is an unsworn member of the Australian Federal Police International Deployment Group, working as an advisor in the Pacific Police Development Program.

Ruth Liloqula – Ruth was one of the first Solomon Island women to graduate with a university degree. She is a veteran public servant, with a wide experience in all government departments holding very senior positions, including Permanent Secretary to Cabinet. She led the Solomon Islands Government team that drafted the Proposed Partnership Framework with RAMSI.

Abby McLeod – A cultural anthropologist working for the Australian Federal Police International Deployment Group. Abby was a researcher involved in the 'Policing the Neighbourhood' Australian Research Council Linkage project with the International Development Group and has extensive experience researching the gender practice of the Australian Federal Police across the Pacific and in Timor-Leste.

Vandra Harris – Vandra is an expert in civil-military affairs and is an academic working at the Royal Melbourne Institute of Technology (RMIT). Vandra was one of the researchers involved in the 'Policing the Neighbourhood' project and in particular has researched issues of masculinity and women's participation in the Australian Federal Police in the context of Solomon Islands, Papua New Guinea and Timor-Leste.

Sinclair Dinnen – Sinclair is a researcher at Australian National University who was the lead researcher on the 'Policing the Neighbourhood' Australian Research Council Linkage project. He worked in Solomon Islands in 2000, with the Solomon Islands Christian Association, which set up a Peace Office that was facilitating dialogue between the then rival militias.

Denis McDermott – Denis was the Commander of the RAMSI Participating Police Force and Deputy Commissioner of the Royal Solomon Islands Police Force between July 2007 and June 2009. He is now involved in the International Commanders Training Force and working throughout the Pacific in policing capacity building roles.

Notes

1. *Security Council Resolution 1325*, UN Doc. S/RES/1325 (31 October 2000), para. 5.
2. See UN Department of Peacekeeping Operations (DPKO) and UN Department of Field Support (DFS), 'Ten-year impact study on implementation of UN Security Council Resolution 1325 (2000) on women, peace and security in peacekeeping' (DPKO and DFS, 2010), pp. 9–10.
3. DPKO and DFS, 'Ten-year impact study, p. 11.

4. T. Denham, 'Police reform and gender' (Democratic Control of Armed Forces (DCAF), Organization for Security and Co-Operation in Europe (OSCE)/ Office for Democratic Institutions and Human Rights (ODIHR) and United Nations International Research and Training Institute for the Advancement of Women (UN-INSTRAW), 2008), p. 1 n. 4, citing H. Groenewald and G. Peake, 'Police reform through community-based policing: Philosophy and guidelines for implementation' (International Peace Academy, 2004), p. 1.
5. B.K. Greener, *The New International Policing* (Basingstoke: Palgrave Macmillan, 2009), p. 1.
6. See generally A. Goldsmith and S. Dinnen, 'Transnational police building: Critical lessons from Timor-Leste and Solomon Islands', *Third World Quarterly*, Vol. 28, No. 6 (2007) 1091.
7. UN Development Programme (UNDP) and UN Development Fund for Women (UNIFEM), 'Policy briefing paper: Gender sensitive police reform in post conflict societies' (UNDP and UNIFEM, October 2007); A. Korneeva, 'Police reform and gender: Practice note 2' (DCAF, OSCE/ODIHR and UN-INSTRAW, 2008); T. Denham, 'Police reform and gender'; DPKO and DFS, 'DPKO/DFS guidelines: Integrating gender perspectives into the work of United Nations military in peacekeeping missions' (DPKO and DFS, March 2010); and Organisation for Economic Co-Operation and Development (OECD), 'OECD DAC handbook on security sector reform – Section 9: Integrating gender awareness and equality' (OECD, 2009).
8. E. Mobekk, 'Gender, women and security sector reform', *International Peacekeeping*, Vol. 17, No. 2 (2010) 278, p. 282, citing *Securing Peace and Development: The Role of the United Nations in Supporting Security Sector Reform – Report of the Secretary-General*, UN Doc. A/62/659–S/2008/39 (23 January 2008), p. 11.
9. See B.K. Greener, W.J. Fish and K. Tekulu, 'Peacebuilding, gender and policing in Solomon Islands', *Asia Pacific Viewpoint*, Vol. 52, No. 1 (2011) 17, p. 17; J. Corrin, '*Ples bilong mere*: Law, gender and peace-building in Solomon Islands', *Feminist Legal Studies*, Vol. 16, No. 2 (2008) 169, p. 190; C. Benard, 'Assessing the truths and myths of women in war and peace' (Paper presented at the United States Institute of Peace Conference on Perspectives on Grassroots Peacebuilding: The Roles of Women in War and Peace, Washington DC, 14 September 1999); and Mobekk, 'Gender, women and security sector reform', p. 279.
10. M. Bastick and K. Valasek (eds), 'Gender and security sector reform toolkit' (DCAF, ODIHR and UN-INSTRAW, 2008), p. 5.
11. Greener et al., 'Peacebuilding, gender and policing in Solomon Islands', p. 17.
12. Bastick and Valasek, 'Gender and security sector reform toolkit', p. 5.
13 Greener et al., 'Peacebuilding, gender and policing in Solomon Islands', p. 17.
14. Bastick and Valasek, 'Gender and security sector reform toolkit', p. 4, citing *Mainstreaming the Gender Perspective into All Policies and Programmes in the United Nations System: Report of the Secretary-General*, UN Doc. E/1997/66 (12 June 1997).
15. Bastick and Valasek, 'Gender and security sector reform toolkit', box 11.
16. OECD, 'Handbook on security sector reform', p. 4.

17. Bastick and Valasek, 'Gender and security sector reform toolkit', p. 12.
18. Denham, 'Police reform and gender', p. 21.
19. Bastick and Valasek, 'Gender and security sector reform toolkit', p. 16.
20. DPKO and DFS, 'Guidelines: Integrating gender perspectives', p. 27.
21. H. Hudson, 'A bridge too far? The gender consequences of linking security and development in SSR discourse and practice', in A. Schnabel and V. Farr (eds), *Back to the Roots: Security Sector Reform and Development* (Zürich: LIT Verlag, 2012) 77, p. 79.
22. O. Marenin, 'Restoring policing systems in conflict torn nations: Process, problems, prospects' (Occasional Paper No. 7, Geneva Centre for the Democratic Control of Armed Forces, June 2005), p. 39.
23. Mobekk, 'Gender, women and security sector reform', p. 279.
24. Greener et al., 'Peacebuilding, gender and policing in Solomon Islands', p. 24.
25. Oxfam Community Aid Abroad, 'Australian intervention in the Solomons: Beyond Operation Helpem Fren – An agenda for development in the Solomon Islands' (Oxfam, August 2003), p. 1.
26. E. Wainwright, 'How is RAMSI faring? Progress, challenges, and lessons learned' (Australian Strategic Policy Institute, April 2005), p. 2.
27. J. Cockayne, 'Operation Helpem Fren: Solomon Islands, transitional justice and the silence of contemporary legal pathologies on questions of distributive justice' (Working Paper No. 3, Center for Human Rights and Global Justice, New York University School of Law, 2004), p. 7.
28. *Agreement between Solomon Islands, Australia, New Zealand, Fiji, Papua New Guinea, Samoa and Tonga concerning the Operations and Status of the Police and Armed Forces and Other Personnel Deployed to Solomon Islands to Assist in the Restoration of Law and Order and Security*, [2003] ATS 17 (signed and entered into force on 24 July 2003), art. 2 (*RAMSI Treaty*).
29. Ibid., preamble para. 4.
30. T.T. Kabutaulaka, 'Australian foreign policy and the RAMSI intervention in Solomon Islands', *Contemporary Pacific*, Vol. 17, No. 2 (2005) 283, p. 288.
31. See E. Wainwright, 'Our failing neighbour: Australia and the future of Solomon Islands' (Australian Strategic Policy Institute, 2003), p. 13, which made the national security case for Australia's intervention on the basis that Solomon Islands risked becoming a 'petri dish in which transnational and non-state security threats can develop and breed'. This report is widely cited as an influential catalyst for the Australia's decision to intervene in Solomon Islands. See, for example, Oxfam Community Aid Abroad, 'Australian intervention in the Solomons', p. 8; S. Hameiri, 'The region within: RAMSI, the Pacific Plan and new modes of governance in the Southwest Pacific', *Australian Journal of International Affairs*, Vol. 63, No. 3 (2009) 348, p. 349; Goldsmith and Dinnen, 'Transnational police building', p. 1103; and C. Moore, *Happy Isles in Crisis: The Historical Causes for a Failing State in Solomon Islands, 1998–2004* (Canberra: Asia Pacific Press, 2004), pp. 201–204.
32. Interview with John Roughan (3 February 2012).
33. Greener, *The New International Policing*, p. 59.
34. Ibid., p. 59.
35. N. Maclellan, 'Bridging the gap between state and society: New directions for Solomon Islands' (Oxfam Australia and Oxfam New Zealand, July 2006), p. 10.

36. Interview with Sinclair Dinnen (3 February 2012).
37. N.L. Olsen, R. Downing, P. Heijkoop and L. Posner, 'RAMSI 2005/2006 annual performance report' (RAMSI Performance Assessment Advisory Team and CAMRIS International, July 2006), pp. 11–12.
38. AusAID Gender Unit, 'Gender situational analysis – Solomon Islands programs' (AusAID, October 2006), quoted in J. Winter and K. Schofield, 'Annual performance report 2006/2007: A report on the performance of the Regional Assistance Mission to the Solomon Islands' (RAMSI Performance Assessment Advisory Team, July 2007), p. 3.
39. Interview with Ruth Liloquala (5 March 2012).
40. Interview with Abby McLeod (29 February 2012).
41. Ibid.
42. AusAID, 'Solomon Islands transitional country strategy 2006 to mid-2007' (Australian Government, March 2006), p. 15.
43. See ANU Enterprise, 'People's survey 2007' (RAMSI, 2007).
44. Interview with David Jones (7 March 2012).
45. Interview with Ruth Liloquala (5 March 2012).
46. Most of the surveys have a section on 'gender issues' but this only includes basic examples of gender differences in responses, such as 'female respondents were less likely to say they feel safe in their community, household or in Honiara': ANU Enterprise, 'People's survey 2011' (RAMSI, February 2012), p. 159. See also ANU Enterprise, 'People's survey 2010' (RAMSI, April 2011), p. 19.
47. Interview with David Jones (7 March 2012).
48. Commonwealth Secretariat, 'Youth unemployment and social harmony concerns in Solomon Islands talks', *The Commonwealth* (28 October 2006), http://secretariat.thecommonwealth.org/news/152816/152865/155792/youth_unemployment_and_social_harmony.htm (last accessed October 2013).
49.. ANU Enterprise, 'People's survey pilot 2006: Solomon Islands' (RAMSI, 2006), p. 29.
50. ANU Enterprise, 'People's survey pilot 2006', p. 29.
51. ANU Enterprise, 'People's survey 2007', p. 45; ANU Enterprise, 'People's survey 2008' (RAMSI, 2008), p. 52; ANU Enterprise, 'People's survey 2009' (RAMSI, February 2009), p. 113.
52. ANU Enterprise, 'People's survey pilot 2006', p. 21.
53. ANU Enterprise, 'People's survey 2011', p. 79.
54. ANU Enterprise, 'People's survey pilot 2006', p. 21.
55. ANU Enterprise, 'People's survey 2011', p. 79.
56. In 2010, 30.6 per cent of young women answered 'sometimes' and 3.2 per cent answered 'hardy ever'. In 2011, 37 per cent of young women answered 'sometimes' and 4.7 per cent answered 'hardly ever'. See ANU Enterprise, 'People's survey 2010', p. 78; ANU Enterprise, 'People's survey 2011', p. 80.
57. *Partnership Framework between the Solomon Islands Government and Regional Assistance Mission to the Solomon Islands* (endorsed by Pacific Islands Forum Ministerial Standing Committee, 15 May 2009) (*Partnership Framework*).
58. Ruth Liloqula was appointed the first female Secretary to Cabinet in 2007.
59. Solomon Islands ranks in the bottom five countries for women's economic opportunity. See Economist Intelligence Unit, 'Women's economic

opportunity 2012: A global index and ranking from the Economist Intelligence Unit' (*The Economist*, 2012), p. 21. See also Japan International Cooperation Agency, 'Country gender profile: Solomon Islands' (JICA, February 2010); and H. Wallace, 'Paddling the canoe on one side: Women in decision-making in Vanuatu and the Solomon Islands', *Development*, Vol. 54, No. 4 (2011) 505.

60. Interview with Ruth Liloquala (5 March 2012).
61. 'Proposed framework for phase 2: RAMSI Assistance Mission Agreement between Solomon Islands Government and RAMSI' (March 2009), p. 95.
62. Ibid.
63. *Partnership Framework*, pp. 90–91.
64. S. Emmott, M. Barcham and T. Kabutaulaka, 'Annual performance report 2010: A report on the performance of the Regional Assistance Mission to the Solomon Islands' (RAMSI Independent Experts Team, 21 March 2011), p. 23. See also AusAid, 'Regional Assistance Mission Solomon Islands Annual Program Performance Report 2012–13' (AusAID, July 2013).
65. AusAid, 'Regional Assistance Mission'.
66. Interview with Ruth Liloquala (5 March 2012).
67. Ibid.
68. Interview with David Jones (7 March 2012).
69. Ibid.
70. Emmott et al., 'Annual performance report 2010', p. 23.
71. Ibid.
72. This document is classified by the Australian Government (AusAID) and was not able to be obtained for this study.
73. Emmott et al., 'Annual performance report 2010', p. 23.
74. Youth and Children Affairs Ministry for Women, 'Solomon Islands national policy on gender equality and women's development' (Solomon Islands Government, March 2010), p. 2.
75. Emmott et al., 'Annual performance report 2010', p. 23.
76. Ibid.
77. Interview with Ruth Liloquala (5 March 2012).
78. Ibid.; and interview with Vandra Harris (20 February 2012).
79. H. O'Connell, 'What are the opportunities to promote gender equity and equality in conflict-affected and fragile states? Insights from a review of evidence', *Gender & Development*, Vol. 19, No. 3 (2011) 455, p. 462.
80. See S. Bhagwan Rolls, 'Thinking Globally and Acting Locally: Linking Women, Peace and Security in the Pacific', in this volume.
81. V. Harris and A. Goldsmith, 'Gendering transnational policing: Experiences of Australian women in international policing operations', *International Peacekeeping*, Vol. 17, No. 2 (2010) 292, p. 303, citing T. Fitzsimmons, 'The postconflict postscript: Gender and policing in peace operations', in D. Mazurana, A. Raven-Roberts and J. Parpart (eds), *Gender, Conflict, and Peacekeeping* (Lanham: Rowman & Littlefield, 2005) 185, p. 193.
82. See Economist Intelligence Unit, 'Women's economic opportunity 2012'.

Part III
Danger

7
Beyond Stories of Victory and Danger: Resisting Feminism's Amenability to Serving Security Council Politics

Dianne Otto

Introduction

Feminist responses to the Security Council's agenda on women, peace and security, which commenced with the adoption of *Security Council Resolution 1325* (SCR 1325) in 2000,[1] have been overwhelmingly celebratory, although feminist accounts of danger are mounting. While I understand the reluctance to cast a critical gaze over such an avowedly activist project,[2] as it can feel like a betrayal of feminist activism and look like playing into the hands of those who are hostile to feminism, holding back from critical analysis gives credence to the idea that a distinction can be drawn between activism and critique. As Carol Cohn avers, with reference to 'tensions' between academic and activist approaches to SCR 1325, 'perhaps we academics and researchers should slow down, engage in the appreciative aspect of critique and see what we can learn from it, before focussing on its possible dangers or limitations'.[3] She is, I think, reflecting the view that feminist critique is damaging to activism.

While disagreeing with this distinction between activism and scholarly critique, I have struggled to find a grammar that enables me to think and talk about the radical potential of the SCRs on women, peace and security while also acknowledging the many threats they pose to feminist goals and ways of thinking. In securing my own interpolation into the story I tell about the resolutions – as someone who contributes to activist strategising as well as academic critique – I have, in the past, developed an approach that largely follows Cohn's advice, which is to start by celebrating some of the positive effects of the resolutions for women, before turning to my critical analysis.[4] Not surprisingly, this ledger approach of weighing both sides has led me to the conclusion that the resolutions are double-edged, providing, on the one hand, productive 'footholds' for continuing feminist activism and, on the other, a means whereby the Security Council is able to enhance the legitimacy of its post-Cold War, and post-9/11, expanding exercise of unaccountable power in the name of protecting women and their rights.[5] This approach has implicated me in maintaining the narrative of tension between activism and (academic) critique, which has become encoded in the opposition between feminist 'victory' and feminist 'danger' stories about the resolutions, despite the reality that there are activists and academics on both sides of this debate and many participants have a foot in both camps. Treating the resolutions as double-edged has also helped to turn these feminist debates inwards, seriously limiting the frame of transformative vision.

In this chapter I want to move away from weighing the positives and negatives, as demanded by this mode of story-telling, to examine what the two stories have in common. Following the lead of Clare Hemmings, who explores the commonalities in western feminist 'progress' and 'loss' narratives,[6] which are usually read as oppositional, I want to ask what politics of the present are sustained by both the victory and the danger accounts of the resolutions on women, peace and security and, thus, how a transformative feminist project might be better furthered, or at least less hindered, through this engagement with the Security Council.[7] I also want to disavow the distinction between activism and critique that these stories maintain.

In this effort to depart from my ledger approach to analysing the resolutions, I will examine some of the issues and assumptions that are common to both the feminist victory and feminist danger versions of the stories about the resolutions, in order to tease out the larger politics that are being occluded in these debates. In particular, I am interested in examining how various aspects of the resolutions have proved to be so amenable to serving distinctly anti-feminist military and neocolonial projects, and how this amenability might be reduced, which is also a concern of Hemmings.[8] My goal is not to counsel against either victory celebrations or dangerous liaisons, but rather to foster a deeper understanding of how feminist ideas are captured by security institutions and become the tools of powerful actors, in order to explore how this amenability might be countered by telling (and acting upon) different feminist stories.

The politics of the present that I want to examine are those associated with areas of substantial agreement in the two feminist narratives: first, the initial move of selecting the Security Council as a fruitful site for feminist engagement and, second, the use of gender as a synonym for women in the resolutions and the associated idea that being female serves as a collective referent for making positive contributions to peace. I will also briefly discuss a third common thread in these stories, which is that the resolutions, whether understood as victory or danger, are nevertheless worthy of feminist support because they empower grass-roots women's movements and activists. There are many other commonalities, which I do not have room to consider here, including the calls for increased accountability for implementation of the resolutions and the claimed linkage between peace and women's equality. What emerges from my (limited) examination is a shared narrative of 'progress' which is highly amenable to supporting present-day politics of securitised militarism, made more palatable by the gestures towards the inclusion of women, which becomes encoded as a mark of western (civilisational) superiority. In order to reduce this amenability and open new spaces for transformative feminist subjects and projects, I argue that the progress thread embedded in the narratives needs to be abandoned and the feminist perspectives that are silenced, particularly counter-realist, queer and postcolonial feminist perspectives, need to be embraced so that more resistive stories about the resolutions, and the possibilities they offer for transformative change, can be crafted.

The Security Council as a site of feminist engagement

Feminists have long been divided about whether it is possible to promote radical change from within mainstream institutions. In the context of promoting visions of 'feminist' peace, Virginia Woolf famously argued that women can best help prevent war by 'not repeating your [men's] words and following your methods but by finding new words and creating new methods', which is best done by remaining outside the institutions of power,[9] while others have argued that institutional engagement is imperative.[10] Against the backdrop of this history of contention, it is puzzling that there has been so little feminist debate about the wisdom of engagement with the patently undemocratic and secretive Security Council, the seat of power of the world's superpower(s), whose permanent members are also the world's largest arms dealers. Both victory and danger accounts of the resolutions have been primarily concerned with conceptual and policy problems with the resolutions themselves, and the practical issues of their implementation, rather than questioning the extent to which 'words and methods' have been dictated and securitised by the institutional location.[11]

Indeed, the general tenor of the discussion about feminist engagement with the Security Council is infused with the excitement of victory: exhilaration at the audacity of the strategy to carve out a space for feminist activism within the United Nations' (UN) 'most powerful' body,[12] amazement that the 'world's largest international security institution' has acknowledged gender as relevant to 'doing security',[13] and enthusiasm about the new 'political legitimacy' that has been attributed to women's peace activism.[14] As Joan Scott explains, this kind of feminist excitement echoes throughout feminist history in stories of women's transgressive interventions in the public (masculine) realm of politics, operating as a simplifying and unifying fantasy that helps feminism to work as a movement.[15] Little wonder that feminist danger stories on this point are in short supply.[16] Such is the grip of the fantasy of the triumph of transnational feminist activism that the Cold War history of women's issues in the UN providing 'a terrain of superpower struggle' has been quickly forgotten.[17] Feminists simply followed the power, increasingly concentrated in the United States (US)-dominated Security Council since the end of the Cold War,[18] helping to change the nature of the international security agenda, along with many others, including environmentalists seeking action on climate change[19] and even child victims of clergy sexual abuse seeking justice.[20] Rather than questioning what the Security Council has to gain from its new-found feminist alliance, feminists have helped to consolidate its power,[21] even attributing new law-making powers to the Council by claiming that the women, peace and security resolutions are legally binding.[22]

The myopic character of feminist enthusiasm for engaging the power of the Security Council is evident in the recent struggle to counter efforts by some Council members, notably the Russian Federation, China, Pakistan and Colombia, to limit the Council's mandate to address sexual violence to those (conflict-ridden) countries listed as situations on its agenda.[23] This issue arose in debate on the Secretary-General's 2012 report on implementation of the Security Council's women, peace and security resolutions on sexual violence – SCRs 1820, 1888 and 1960.[24] The Secretary-General's report presents 'an agreed working definition' of conflict-related sexual violence, which includes incidents or patterns of sexual violence that 'occur in conflict or post-conflict settings or other situations of concern (for example, political strife)'.[25] The definition also extends to sexual violence that has an 'indirect nexus with the conflict or political strife', including 'a temporal, geographical and/or causal link'.[26] There is no doubt that this definition casts a very wide net, reflecting the claim by many feminists that sexual violence constitutes a continuum spanning both times of peace and armed conflict,[27] but which, if adopted, would give the Council extremely broad powers. Those Security Council members supporting the Secretary-General's broad approach include the United Kingdom, Belgium and France, who cited Egypt and Syria as examples of 'political instability' where the Council should be able to act to counter the 'terrible scourge' of sexual violence.[28] The positions taken in this debate map onto larger geopolitical divisions, illustrating how the question of protecting women from sexual violence provides western powers with a 'feminist' pretext for responding militarily to present-day political realities, as they perceive them, of 'new' wars, 'failed states' and 'terror' – all categories that feminists should be wary of. Yet feminist advocacy appears oblivious to the larger (super)power agendas that the securitisation of women's rights and gender equality is amenable to serving.

The absence of a critical analysis of the Security Council aligns the politics of feminist engagement with the Council with political realism.[29] It is a strategy reliant on hegemonic military and neocolonial power to achieve feminist goals, and endorses 'law-making' by an unrepresentative and secretive political body. Abandoned are feminist commitments to democratic and transparent decision-making, to bottom-up rather than top-down politics, to cooperation rather than power politics, to justice as well as order, and to critiques of imperial, military and unaccountable power. The strategy securitises women's rights, giving priority to militaristic solutions to complex problems.[30] This feminist alliance with the Security Council enables – even encourages – the Council to present itself as a champion of feminist goals and a creator of international law, and endorses the idea that violation of women's rights could provide a trigger for the imposition of sanctions,[31] the collective use of force[32] or a justification for military occupation.[33] This surely gives the Security Council and its hegemonic 'law' too much power, undermining democratic and redistributive politics, and women's agency. As Sheri Gibbings concludes, with the adoption of SCR 1325 the feminist agenda for ending armed conflict and promoting peace became 'the integration of women and a gender perspective' into the existing system of international peace and security,[34] rather than 'finding new words and creating new methods'[35] to transform it.

Utilising gender as a synonym for women and promoting women as peacemakers

At the same time as feminists have resisted working with mainstream peace and security institutions, there have been others seeking the increased participation of women in formal conflict resolution and peacemaking processes. Nearly a century ago, in 1915, The Hague Congress of Women, attended by women's peace activists from both sides of the World War I conflict, passed resolutions to this effect.[36] Numerous commitments by international institutions to enhancing women's participation have since been extracted, including from the Assembly of the League of Nations in 1931[37] and the UN General Assembly in 1972.[38] Needless to say, these pledges have failed spectacularly to translate into changed practice.[39] Yet in the same hopeful spirit as earlier generations of feminists, those lobbying the Security Council to adopt SCR 1325 urged it to recognise the positive contributions that women can and do make to preventing conflict and securing peace.[40] This time, in addition to insisting that women be included in formal conflict-related decision-making processes and recognised as promoters of peace in their local communities, activists set out to counter the Security Council's protective gender script.[41] This script, which emerged explicitly in the wake of the Cold War,[42] put women for the first time on the Security Council's agenda as victims of armed conflict which, as already discussed, supported the new post-Cold War identity of the US, and the west more generally, as the global protector of women (and children).

Like their predecessors, the feminists who urged the Security Council to promote increased participation by women in the prevention and resolution of international disputes met with considerable rhetorical success. The preamble of SCR 1325 makes reference to the importance of women's 'equal participation and full involvement' in the maintenance and promotion of international peace and security, and its first three substantive paragraphs recommend women's 'increased representation' and 'participation' in a wide range of decision-making structures.[43] Other provisions call for support for 'local women's peace initiatives and indigenous processes for conflict resolution'.[44] Yet this potentially more empowering expansion of the Security Council's gender script was also amenable to the US's agenda of presenting itself as the global protector of women. Despite the best intentions of those feminists who pushed for SCR 1325 to foster women's political agency, rather than focus on their victimhood, this additional representation is susceptible to supporting the reinvigoration of conservative gender stereotypes of women as 'natural' peacemakers, limiting women's contributions to feminised topics (such as reintegrating militarised men into peacetime life and assisting victims of sexual violence), and leaving the gendered duality of male competence and female pacifism (and vulnerability) firmly in place. In the view of 'danger' feminists, the nod to increasing women's participation in decision-making quickly became, in practice, an efficiency measure, designed to engage women as 'untapped resources'[45] and thereby improve the effectiveness of the UN's existing conflict resolution and peacebuilding processes, rather than a liberating move for women.

The fears of danger feminists were confirmed when the Security Council largely reverted to its protective script of women as victims of the sexual violence of armed conflict in its second thematic resolution on women, peace and security, SCR 1820, adopted in 2008. In this move, later reaffirmed in SCR 1888, SCR 1960 and SCR 2106, the Security Council resumed its putative role as women's protector, drawing back from the inference that it might be a defender of their political participation and rights. SCR 1820 also perpetuates the mythology that women cannot be both victims and active participants in peacebuilding by stating that 'violence, intimidation and discrimination ... erode women's capacity and legitimacy to participate in post-conflict public life'.[46] Even so, the feminist victory proponents stepped up to celebrate this new move of the Council as necessary to end the impunity that perpetrators of sexual violence during armed conflict enjoy.[47] Among them, Laura Shepherd has argued that SCR 1820 moves further towards women's empowerment than SCR 1325.[48] However, I read these moves differently, as furthering the anti-impunity agenda of international criminal law, which embraces a much more limited notion of women's 'agency' than international human rights law and is restricted to the feminised subject matter of addressing sexual violence. For example, SCR 1820 urges the deployment of more women in peacekeeping troop and police contingents because it will help to 'prevent sexual violence against women and girls'.[49] On the danger side of my earlier ledger, I worried about the broad agenda of SCR 1325 being reduced to the single issue of women's sexual vulnerability and the need for other (implicitly western) women to help rescue them,[50] although the adoption of *Security Council Resolution 1889* in 2010[51] and *Security Council Resolution 2122* in 2013,[52] which both build on the broad agenda of SCR 1325, offers some reassurance in this respect. Further, as Karen Engle argues in this volume, the resolutions make available only two possibilities for women – as either victims or peacemakers.[53] And, as Gibbings finds, even the latter role is severely constrained by the UN's discursive norms of speech and conduct, which make it impossible for women with 'angry' anti-imperial and anti-militarist views to be 'heard' within the terms of the Security Council's women, peace and security agenda.[54] This last point also throws many hopeful claims including that the resolutions at least provide important leverage for local and transnational women's movements to pursue their own feminist politics, emanating from both feminist camps, into serious doubt – an issue that I return to below.

Here, I want to focus on what neither victory nor danger feminists have found problematic with the representations of gender, which is the singular focus of these resolutions on 'women' – whether as participants in conflict-related decision-making or as victims of sexual violence. While the Security Council has not shied away from the terminology of 'gender', as in its expression of willingness to 'incorporate a gender perspective into peacekeeping operations' in SCR 1325,[55] the term is used throughout the women, peace and security framework as a synonym for women. Few feminists have been troubled by this orientation, despite the importance of gender as a social category in feminist thought and the recognition of the interdependence of notions of masculinity and femininity and their hierarchical relationship. Understanding gender as a social category, rather than moored in biology, is what makes feminist change possible. It seems rather obvious that the gendered qualities that are associated with men, as well as with women, need to fundamentally shift if security institutions are ever to demilitarise, and if women and men are ever to enjoy equal political participation in all of its senses. In the context of the women, peace and security agenda, this means that men too must be engaged as peacemakers and recognised as potential victims of sexual violence, if the conservative moorings of biological determinism, which support the gendered grammars of war and peace, strength and vulnerability, are ever to be dislodged.

Further, as emphasised by queer feminists, gender should not be understood as a stable social category that can be directly read onto sexed bodies. Instead, gender is dynamic, complex and unpredictable,[56] or 'performative' as Judith Butler describes it.[57] Importantly, this means that gender identity and/or expression is not limited to a male/female binary or to the presumption of normative heterosexuality that the binary supports.[58] Denaturalising gender enables the recognition of third, in-between, trans, transient and other genders, and of non-heteronormative practices of sexuality.[59] Confining gender to women, as in the Security Council's resolutions, makes it possible to ignore all the gender-related security issues that do not directly impact on 'women'. For example, the targeting of individuals who do not conform to traditional gender roles – such as attacks on *meti* (effeminate males or transgendered people) during the conflict in Nepal – and the bartering of the rights of sexual minorities, as well as women's rights, in efforts to appease local militias, as in the Swat Valley in Pakistan – are excluded from the women, peace and security agenda.[60] Failing to link women's struggles for equality with the struggles of other gender groups enables vulnerable and biologically determinist stereotypes of women to thrive, aiding the dominance of protection issues, which serves the interests of the permanent members of the Security Council[61] and weakens the empowerment aspects of the resolutions.

Feminists, from both the victory and danger camps, also seem untroubled by the way that the category of 'women' in the resolutions is presented as universal and self-evident. Being female is assumed to be a primary identification and collective referent capable of mobilising (all) women in the cause of peace and enabling 'women's security issues' to be addressed through the increased participation of women in decision-making. It seems that the exclusionary and imperial effects of universal categories, argued so cogently by critical and postcolonial feminists,[62] have (again?) been put aside. Hemmings notices a similar propensity in her analysis of the recent rise of 'material feminisms' that claim to have taken the exclusionary problems of essentialism on board and, subsequently, 'moved on' to addressing more substantive concerns.[63] Treating 'gender' as the locus of transformative change, in isolation from other intersecting vectors of power and authority, such as economic status, nationality, race, ethnicity, religion and sexuality, makes the Security Council's resolutions on women, peace and security, and the feminism they embrace, particularly amenable to the service of western, neo-imperial power. While strategic essentialism may at times be defensible, it has the propensity to harden into uncritical acceptance, perpetuating inequality, hierarchising difference and working against transformative change.

Conclusions

Before coming to my conclusions about what politics of the present are sustained by the common threads in the victory and danger stories about the resolutions that I have outlined, and how more resistive feminist accounts that are less amenable to institutional capture might be crafted, I want to briefly reflect on another commonality – the claim that the resolutions have fostered women's grassroots activism. Many accounts of local activists managing to breathe life into the resolutions have been offered as evidence of this progressive potential: as providing a lever to demand women's participation in peace negotiations,[64] to ensure women's rights are recognised in new constitutions,[65] and to gain support for local women's projects.[66] Women's groups in Nepal seem to have been particularly adept at utilising SCR 1325 for their own ends,[67] while Women in Black in Serbia have used the resolution to support their attempts to foster a feminist reconceptualisation of security.[68] The reassurance offered by these stories is that, despite their institutional lineage of hegemonic power, the resolutions can nevertheless offer a means of 'finding new words and creating new methods'.

Yet, on closer inspection, much of the activism by local women's organisations has involved raising awareness about the resolutions and lobbying governments and UN agencies to implement them, rather than using them as a means to support locally resonant community-controlled peacebuilding work, outside the discursive constraints of the resolutions.[69] A six-country field study, which sought women's views about the relevance and impact of SCR 1325, found that civil society organisations, despite security threats and few resources, 'have been the engine behind the UNSCR 1325 movement',[70] but noted 'the pressure to adopt the women, peace and security agenda and be seen to be "doing something"', which means groups 'are basically repackaging existing programmes under the UNSCR 1325 umbrella, but the substance is not necessarily well-adapted or tied to ongoing policy processes'.[71] As has already been noted, the women, peace and security agenda, at least in its present manifestation, does not present opportunities for women's movements pursuing more radical change by challenging colonialism and neoliberal economics. But the situation is even worse if women's grassroots struggles are compelled to reinvent themselves in liberal, technocratic or legalistic terms, or otherwise be discredited.[72] This state of affairs places a huge burden on local activists to deliver a feminist result that is recognisable as such by the Security Council, which threatens to undermine and disempower women's grassroots movements for peace – the very subjects of feminism's transformative hope.

So, how does the story I am telling about the resolutions conclude? My argument is that too much of the feminist analysis of the Security Council's women, peace and security agenda, including my own, has been structured by the assumed differences and tensions between feminist 'victory' and 'danger' chronicles. This narrative structure has turned the discussion inwards, and the efforts by protagonists to distance themselves from the type of feminism they associate with the 'other' camp have prevented the stories' common threads from surfacing and being given the attention they need. The points of agreement in the stories that I have discussed – that the Security Council is a fruitful site for feminist engagement and that the use of gender as a synonym for women is productive for feminist ends – are crying out for critical attention, but have been occluded by the focus on points of difference. The story of commonality, at least as I have told it, points to an underlying continuity between feminist assumptions and those of the Security Council – a very uncomfortable discovery. This discovery points to the need for narratives that help us to understand how feminism is bound up in global relations of power and to acknowledge the continuing work some feminisms do in projecting western superiority.[73] In the absence of this deeper analysis, the feminisms of activism and critique, and of celebration and danger, are highly amenable to capture by discourses of military security and the exceptionalisms they justify. The narrative of feminist 'progress', whether cast in terms of celebration or danger, is especially suited to masking the military logic of international security that generates and relies upon women's inequality and marginalisation, in the west as well as outside it. And finally, I think my story of commonality demands that feminist analyses of power (including the power of law) need to extend beyond seeking to reposition women. Transformative change relies on feminist analysis of the relationships between women and other genders (including men) and, further, on working with gender as an 'analytic category' that does a great deal of work in signifying and shoring up other relations of inequitable power.[74]

Ultimately, it is not enough that the resolutions prompt some new openings for women's participation, increase the pressure to reduce conflict-related sexual violence and grant some long-overdue recognition to local women's projects aimed at peacemaking and peacebuilding. This is not to say that these are not worthwhile achievements. Rather, it is to argue that, as feminists, we cannot afford to separate activism and (academic) critique, as encoded in the tensions between the victory and danger stories of the resolutions. It is a false dichotomy that deprives feminists of the tools we need to promote transformative change. Activism is a form of critique, and critique – even academic critique – is a form of activism. Without feminist stories that expose feminism's amenability to the service of hegemonic power, we are powerless to resist it.

Notes

Many thanks to Candice Parr for her invaluable research assistance.

1. *Security Council Resolution 1325*, UN Doc. S/RES/1325 (31 October 2000) (SCR 1325).
2. F. Hill, M. Aboitiz and S. Poehlman-Doumbouya, 'Nongovernmental organizations' role in the buildup and implementation of Security Council Resolution 1325', *Signs: Journal of Women in Culture and Society*, Vol. 28, No. 4 (2003) 1255.
3. C. Cohn, H. Kinsella and S. Gibbings, 'Women, peace and security: Resolution 1325', *International Feminist Journal of Politics*, Vol. 6, No. 1 (2004) 130, p. 139.
4. D. Otto, 'Power and danger: Feminist engagement with international law through the UN Security Council', *Australian Feminist Law Journal*, Vol. 32 (2010) 97.
5. Ibid.
6. C. Hemmings, *Why Stories Matter: The Political Grammar of Feminist Theory* (Durham: Duke University Press, 2011), pp. 11–12.
7. I do not want to suggest that Hemmings' 'progress' and 'loss' narratives translate directly into the 'victory' and 'danger' versions of feminist stories about the Security Council's resolutions on women, peace and security. Rather, it is her method of looking for continuities in purportedly competing feminist accounts that I am adopting.
8. Hemmings, *Why Stories Matter*, pp. 131–159.
9. V. Woolf, *Three Guineas* (New York: Harcourt, Brace and Company, first published in 1938, 1966 ed.), p. 143.
10. H. Charlesworth, 'Transforming the united men's club: Feminist futures for the United Nations', *Transnational Law and Contemporary Problems*, Vol. 4, No. 2 (1994) 421.
11. See, for example, N. Pratt and S. Richter-Devroe, 'Introduction: Critically examining UNSCR 1325 on women, peace and security', *International Feminist Journal of Politics*, Vol. 13, No. 4 (2011) 489; and C. Chinkin and H. Charlesworth, 'Building women into peace: The international legal framework', *Third World Quarterly*, Vol. 27, No. 5 (2006) 937.
12. See, for example, the response of activists at the International Women's Tribune Centre, in D. Otto, 'The exile of inclusion: Reflections on gender issues in international law over the last decade', *Melbourne Journal of International Law*, Vol. 10, No. 1 (2009) 11.
13. Cohn et al., 'Women, peace and security', p. 139.
14. E. Rehn and E.J. Sirleaf, *Women, War, Peace: The Independent Experts' Assessment on the Impact of Armed Conflict on Women and Women's Role in Peace-Building* (New York: UNIFEM, 2002), p. 3.
15. J.W. Scott, *The Fantasy of Feminist History* (Durham: Duke University Press, 2011), pp. 55–59.
16. However, I do not mean to suggest there are no such stories. See, for example, S. Gibbings, 'No angry women at the United Nations: Political dreams and the cultural politics of United Nations Security Council Resolution 1325', *International Feminist Journal of Politics*, Vol. 13, No. 4 (2011) 522.

17. C. Harrington, 'Resolution 1325 and post-Cold War feminist politics', *International Feminist Journal of Politics*, Vol. 13, No. 4 (2011) 557, p. 558.
18. M. Koskenniemi, 'The police in the temple – Order, justice and the UN: A dialectical view', *European Journal of International Law*, Vol. 6, No. 3 (1995) 325.
19. K.T. Litfin, 'Constructing environmental security and ecological interdependence', *Global Governance*, Vol. 5, No. 3 (1999) 359.
20. B. Zwartz, 'Push to make church inquiry global', *The Age* (Australia) (18 December 2012) 2: 'Australia should use its seat on the United Nations security Council to push for a UN inquiry into how the Catholic Church moves paedophile priests from First to Third World countries to avoid investigation, the state inquiry into clergy sex abuse heard on Monday'.
21. See further N. Krisch, 'International law in times of hegemony: Unequal power and the shaping of the international legal order', *European Journal of International Law*, Vol. 16, No. 3 (2005) 369; and D. Otto, 'The Security Council's alliance of "gender legitimacy": The symbolic capital of Resolution 1325', in H. Charlesworth and J. Coicaud (eds), *Fault Lines of International Legitimacy* (New York: Cambridge University Press, 2010) 239.
22. See, for example, Cohn et al., 'Women, peace and security', p. 132. While under Article 25 of the *Charter of the United Nations*, opened for signature on 26 June 1945, 1 UNTS XVI (entered into force on 24 October 1945) (UN Charter), UN member states agree to carry out the 'decisions' of the Security Council, including those not adopted under the Council's Chapter VII powers, the non-binding language of the 'women, peace and security' resolutions indicates that they are not intended to be binding, and are therefore not 'decisions'.
23. *Security Council Meeting 6772: Women, Peace and Security, Report of the Secretary-General on Conflict-Related Sexual Violence*, UN Doc. S/PV.6722 (23 February 2012), pp. 15, 22, 24.
24. *Security Council Resolution 1820*, UN Doc. S/RES/1820 (19 June 2008) (SCR 1820); *Security Council Resolution 1888*, UN Doc. S/RES/1888 (30 September 2009) (SCR 1888); and *Security Council Resolution 1960*, UN Doc. S/RES/1960 (16 December 2010) (SCR 1960). The US played a key role in the passage of all three of these protective resolutions, serving its turn as the rotating President of the Council at the time each was adopted. A fourth resolution on sexual violence has been adopted since then, sponsored by the United Kingdom during its Council Presidency, *Security Council Resolution 2106*, UN Doc. S/RES/2106 (24 June 2013) (SCR 2106).
25. *Conflict-Related Sexual Violence: Report of the Secretary-General*, UN Doc. A/66/657–S/2012/33 (13 January 2012), para. 1.
26. Ibid.
27. See, for example, C.A. MacKinnon, 'Crimes of war, crimes of peace', in S. Shute and S. Hurley (eds), *On Human Rights: The Oxford Amnesty Lectures* (New York: Basic Books, 1993) 83.
28. *Security Council Meeting 6772: Women, Peace and Security, Report of the Secretary-General on Conflict-Related Sexual Violence*, UN Doc. S/PV.6722 (23 February 2012), pp. 16, 21, 28.
29. For an early feminist critique of realism, see J.A. Tickner, 'Hans Morgenthau's principles of political realism: A feminist reformulation', *Millennium: Journal of International Studies*, Vol. 17, No. 3 (1988) 429.

30. N.F. Hudson, 'Securitizing women's rights and gender equality', *Journal of Human Rights*, Vol. 8, No. 1 (2009) 53.
31. SCR 1820, para. 5; and SCR 1888, para. 10.
32. SCR 1820, para. 1; SCR 1888, para. 1; and SCR 1960, para. 1. See further G. Heathcote, 'Feminist politics and the use of force: Theorising feminist action and Security Council Resolution 1325', *Socio-Legal Review*, Vol. 7 (2011) 23.
33. See, for example, the reference to SCR 1325 in the resolution adopted by the Security Council which provided belated endorsement to the invasion and occupation of Iraq by the US and its allies in 2003: *Security Council Resolution 1483*, UN Doc. S/RES/1483 (23 May 2003).
34. Gibbings, 'No angry women at the United Nations', p. 533.
35. Woolf, *Three Guineas*, p. 143.
36. 'Resolutions Adopted by the International Congress of Women at The Hague, 1 May, 1915', reproduced in J. Addams, E.G. Balch and A. Hamilton, *Women at the Hague: The International Congress of Women and Its Results* (New York: Humanity Books, first published in 1916, 2003 ed.) appendix 3, pp. 123–30 (Hague Resolutions).
37. The *Spanish Resolution*, so-called because it was introduced by the Spanish delegation, was adopted by the 12th Assembly of the League of Nations on 24 September 1931. It read: 'The Assembly, convinced of the great value of the contribution of women to the work of peace and the good understanding between the nations, which is the principle aim of the League of Nations, requests the Council to examine the possibility of women cooperating more fully in the work of the League'.
38. *General Assembly Resolution 3010 (XXVII)*, UN Doc. A/RES/3010(XXVII) (18 December 1972), proclaiming 1975 as International Women's Year, and promising 'intensified action ... to recognize the importance of women's increasing contribution to the development of friendly relations and cooperation among States and to the strengthening of world peace': at para. 2(c).
39. For further discussion, see D. Otto, 'A sign of "weakness"? Disrupting gender certainties in the implementation of Security Council Resolution 1325', *Michigan Journal of Gender and Law*, Vol. 13, No. 1 (2006) 113, pp. 128–138.
40. S. Gibbings, *Governing Women, Governing Security: Governmentality, Gender-Mainstreaming and Women's Activism at the UN* (MA Thesis, York University, 2004), p. 52.
41. Gibbings, 'No angry women at the United Nations', p. 529.
42. *Security Council Resolution 798*, UN Doc. S/RES/798 (18 December 1992) was the first Security Council resolution to make a reference to women: '*Appalled* by the reports of the massive, organised and systematic detention and rape of women, in particular Muslim women, in Bosnia and Herzegovina' (emphasis original).
43. SCR 1325, preamble.
44. Ibid., para. 8(b).
45. C. Cohn, 'Mainstreaming gender in UN security policy: A path to political transformation?', in S. Rai and G. Waylen (eds), *Global Governance: Feminist Perspectives* (Basingstoke: Palgrave Macmillan, 2008) 185, p. 201.
46. SCR 1820, preamble para. 11.
47. S. Cook, 'Security Council Resolution 1820: On militarism, flashlights, raincoats and rooms with doors – A political perspective on where it came from

and what it adds', *Emory International Law Review*, Vol. 23, No. 1 (2009) 125; Human Rights Watch, 'UN: Finally, a step toward confronting rape in war' (Press Release, 18 June 2008); and PeaceWomen, 'Feature analysis: Security Council Resolution 1820: A move to end sexual violence in conflict', *1325 PeaceWomen E-Newsletter*, No. 102 (June 2008) 5.

48. L.J. Shepherd, 'Sex, security and superhero(in)es: From 1325 to 1820 and beyond', *International Feminist Journal of Politics*, Vol. 13, No. 4 (2011) 504, pp. 507–508.

49. SCR 1820, para. 8. See further SCR 1888, preamble para. 15; SCR 1960, pre-amble para.16, operative para. 15; and SCR 2106, para. 14.

50. Otto, 'The Security Council's Alliance', pp. 23–25. A good example of this kind of imperial feminism is N.D. Kristof and S. WuDunn, *Half the Sky: Turning Oppression into Opportunity for Women Worldwide* (New York: Random House, 2009).

51. *Security Council Resolution 1889*, UN Doc. S/RES/1889 (5 October 2009).

52. *Security Council Resolution 2122*, UN Doc. S/RES/2122 (18 October 2013).

53. K. Engle, 'The Grip of Sexual Violence: Reading UN Security Council Resolutions on Human Security', in this volume.

54. Gibbings, 'No angry women at the United Nations'.

55. SCR 1325, para. 5.

56. Scott, *The Fantasy of Feminist History*, pp. 11–15.

57. J. Butler, *Gender Trouble: Feminism and the Subversion of Identity* (New York: Routledge, 1990), p. 140.

58. B. Cossman, 'Gender performance, sexual subjects and international law', *Canadian Journal of Law and Jurisprudence*, Vol. 15, No. 2 (2002) 281.

59. S. Monro, 'Transgender: Destabilising feminisms?', in V.E. Munro and C.F. Stychin (eds), *Sexuality and the Law: Feminist Engagements* (Abingdon: Routledge-Cavendish, 2007) 125.

60. These examples are cited in *Report of the Special Rapporteur on the Promotion and Protection of Human Rights and Fundamental Freedoms while Countering Terrorism*, UN Doc. A/64/211 (3 August 2009), paras 23, 36.

61. S. Basu, 'Permanent Security Council members and resolutions on women, peace and security', *e-International Relations* (31 October 2012), http://www.e-ir.info/2012/10/31/permanent-security-council-members-and-occasional-resolutions-on-women-and-peace-and-security (last accessed October 2013).

62. R. Kapur, 'The tragedy of victimization rhetoric: Resurrecting the "native" subject in international/post-colonial feminist legal politics', *Harvard Human Rights Journal*, Vol. 15 (2002) 1; J. Oloka-Onyango and S. Tamale, '"The personal is political" or why women's rights are indeed human rights: An African perspective on international feminism', *Human Rights Quarterly*, Vol. 17, No. 4 (1995) 691; A.K. Wing (ed.), *Global Critical Race Feminism: An International Reader* (New York: New York University Press, 2000).

63. Hemmings, *Why Stories Matter*, pp. 99–104.

64. *Women and Peace and Security: Report of the Secretary-General*, UN Doc. S/2010/498 (28 September 2010), paras 15, 16.

65. Ibid., para. 69.

66. See S. Bhagwan Rolls, 'Thinking Globally and Acting Locally: Linking Women, Peace and Security in the Pacific', in this volume.

67. CARE, 'From resolution to reality: Lessons learned from Afghanistan, Nepal and Uganda on women's participation in peacebuilding and post-conflict governance' (CARE International, 2011), p. 27; and M. Owen, 'Widowhood issues in the context of United Nations Security Council Resolution 1325', *International Feminist Journal of Politics*, Vol. 13, No. 4 (2011) 616.

68. L. McLeod, 'Configurations of post-conflict: Impacts of representations of conflict and post-conflict upon the (political) translations of gender security within UNSCR 1325', *International Feminist Journal of Politics*, Vol. 13, No. 4 (2011) 594, pp. 601–603.

69. V. Farr, 'UNSCR 1325 and women's peace activism in the Occupied Palestinian Territory', *International Feminist Journal of Politics*, Vol. 13, No. 4 (2011) 539.

70. S.N. Anderlini, 'What the women say: Participation and UNSCR 1325 – A case study assessment' (International Civil Society Action Network and Massachusetts Institute of Technology Center for International Legal Studies, October 2010), p. 42. The places of study were Aceh, Columbia, Liberia, Palestine/Israel, Sri Lanka and Uganda.

71. Ibid., p. 43.

72. S. Richter-Devroe, '"Here it's not about conflict resolution – we can only resist": Palestinian women's activism in conflict resolution and non-violent resistance', in N. Al-Ali and N. Pratt (eds), *Women and War in the Middle East* (London: Zed Books, 2009) 158.

73. See further J.K. Puar, *Terrorist Assemblages: Homonationalism in Queer Times* (Durham: Duke University Press, 2007).

74. J.W. Scott, 'Gender: A useful category of historical analysis', in *Gender and the Politics of History* (New York: Columbia University Press, revised ed., 1999) 28.

8
Security Council Resolution 1325: A Tool for Conflict Prevention?

Felicity Ruby

Introduction

The debate on *Security Council Resolution 1325* (SCR 1325) when it was adopted in 2000,[1] and its follow-up over the years since then, has brought into sharper focus the enormous potential contribution of women as stakeholders of peace, disarmament and conflict prevention. The result has been a greater awareness of the gender dimensions of security issues, and conflict and post-conflict situations, throughout the international community. Even the North Atlantic Treaty Organization is convening workshops on the significance of SCR 1325 to its work.[2] As Director of the Women's International League for Peace and Freedom (WILPF) at the time of SCR 1325's adoption, based in the New York office, I participated in the transnational advocacy network that brought it into being. A website I started soon after it was adopted, in order to monitor its implementation, continues to be widely used.[3] As noted across this collection, in the international policy world and in the community of non-governmental organisations (NGOs), the gender and security nexus is enjoying attention as never before. Indeed, the Security Council has adopted several follow-up resolutions since 2008.[4] Collapsed into the short hand of four numbers '1325' – 10 preambular paragraphs and 18 operational paragraphs – represents a good chunk of WILPF's almost 100 years of international activism for peace. Yet I am bit frustrated with SCR 1325 and how it has been worked with, or used, since its adoption.

SCR 1325 – so what?

An earlier title I had for this chapter was '1325: So what?' It is certainly not living up to my visions of it when I helped push women, peace and security onto the Security Council agenda over 13 years ago. Perhaps some of my assessment is unfair – I leave it to you to decide. I think that SCR 1325 should at least be able to bear scrutiny in such a comfortable place as this edited collection. I have been asked really hard questions about it by people who have been in much harsher places and can justifiably feel a lot more than frustrated. I will start by sharing one story because it will perhaps put us in a suitable frame of mind to talk about women and war, and to stop glossing over what war *is*. I want to question the exhilaration and empowerment that many of us felt when the Security Council finally caught up to what every single other part of the institution of the United Nations (UN) seemed to already understand, and appeared to take gender seriously as an issue in its work. I want to question the claim that so many of us made at the time, that the adoption of SCR 1325 meant the Security Council had finally recognised – what WILPF and the broader women's movement had been banging on about since the turn of the last century – that militarism and armed conflict are completely at odds with the goals of gender equality and international peace and freedom.

Here is one of the stories I want to share. Some women from the Democratic Republic of the Congo (DRC) were in New York in 2003. They were trying to wake people up to what was happening in their country, the size of Western Europe, where at that point two million people had died. The women were telling stories to a room full of people at the UN, including many members of the Security Council, who acted as if they were shocked and made all the right noises about the urgency of bringing the conflict to an end. As women working for peace, members of WILPF have heard many women's stories of war. We make time to listen and we believe them. It is why we are activists and continue to organise. The stories we hear at WILPF usually fit into our larger analytical framework, confirming and deepening nearly a century of WILPF study and campaigning to raise awareness of the political, economic, social and psychological causes of war. Yet these stories will still unzip your soul, surgically remove your solar plexus and unleash a fountain of tears, as this one did to me. One of the DRC women described being forced to cook the organs of her husband for his killers, who had killed him after they had forced him to watch her being raped. She then asked me, 'and what can your little resolution do for me after that?' She had a good question because the answer was actually nothing. For her, nothing could heal her trauma or bring back her husband. I felt then, and continue to feel today, that unless SCR 1325 can be used to prevent that happening to another woman, the answer to the 'so what' question is that SCR 1325 is of very limited utility.

When I moved on from the WILPF office to work at the United Nations Development Fund for Women (UNIFEM) in 2003, I had the opportunity to travel to Colombia and Bougainville to help women there to utilise SCR 1325, and I felt again and again the stinging realisation that it was of little use. I arrived so full of the theory, so full of great ideas – nice, fresh, clean ideas on paper[5] – hoping that SCR 1325 could make a difference to rebuilding amid the continuing terrible effects of armed conflict. My conclusion was then, and remains now, that we have to have much higher ambitions for SCR 1325 and learn how to use it to *prevent* armed conflict, and to stop conflict eruption, escalation and continuing re-emergence. So I want to make the case for 'so what' given the realities of armed conflict, which seem always to involve an inherently unlawful explosion of systematic cruelty, that is calculated and premeditated, the brunt of which is born by women in so many ways. Unless SCR 1325 can be used to prevent war, it is in danger of never living up to all of our cheerleading and, believe me, I have done my fair share of leaping around about SCR 1325.

In addition to the 'so what' question, I also often ask myself, when faced with a perplexing situation in WILPF, 'so what would Jane do about this situation?' And by this I am thinking of Jane Addams, the founding President of WILPF, a Nobel Peace Prize laureate in 1931, and someone that J. Edgar Hoover declared to be the 'most dangerous woman in America' because she was of the ruling class and she was talking about real change and about ending war.[6] She came from a comfortable background, but chose to put herself in uncomfortable situations – political, economic and social – to stand, march and work with working-class and impoverished women. She was constantly questioning how justice would come about and her books are a testament to the discomfort of her struggles to promote transformative change.[7] So I will try to postulate about what Jane would do with SCR 1325 if she were with us now.

I think Jane would likely counsel that SCR 1325 is a tool, and that much depends on how we use it. She would ask us what we want to do with this tool. Is it a tool to put a spanner in the works? Is it a tool to take apart and then to rebuild? Is it a tool to create something new? Is it a tool to extend the Security Council's understanding of its mandate to include WILPF and our issues? Is it a tool to prevent armed conflict and eliminate militarism?

To date, there are perhaps four main ways that SCR 1325 has served as a tool for its advocates: as a key, an action tool, an educational tool and a shaming tool. Women's NGOs have successfully employed SCR 1325 as a multifaceted tool, yet at the same time institutional opposition and resistance continues to frustrate the transformation of the tool into effective strategies to counter militarism, promote peace and realise women's substantive equality.

As a 'key tool' SCR 1325 opens doors for women to get their issues onto the agenda in peace negotiations, in policy setting forums and, in a very small way, in the Security Council, with varying levels of success. That this has occurred in Northern Ireland, Kenya and in some negotiations on the DRC is not insignificant. Yet as time goes by, we can see that the operation of SCR 1325 as a door-opening key turns out to be the exception rather than the rule. In 2012, the Secretary-General reported that of the nine peace agreements that were signed in 2011, only two contained women, peace and security provisions.[8] Further, of the 14 peace processes that were underway in 2011, only four of the negotiating party delegations included a woman.[9] Despite the words on paper, which recognise the importance of women's participation, the overall picture is one of lack of political will and inaction.

Women have used SCR 1325 as an 'action tool' by insisting that implementation and monitoring mechanisms be put in place. The Security Council has called on states to implement SCR 1325, including through the development of National Action Plans (NAPs) or other national-level strategies.[10] In 2013, 38 national governments had approved NAPs and others were in the drafting phase.[11] The NAPs are supposed to ensure that gender issues are integrated into peacemaking and peacebuilding policymaking processes, from the initial drafting of a policy through to its delivery, whether that be in the form of making statements, providing aid and technical assistance, participating in peacekeeping, and so on.

In addition, women have used SCR 1325 as an 'education tool' to help people understand security through a gender lens. One example of long-overdue gender awareness is the adoption of a resolution on women and disarmament by the UN General Assembly's First Committee on peace and security, which marked the first time it had discussed issues related to gender or women in the 65 years of its existence.[12] Another example is the acknowledgement that weapons can have a gender-differentiated impact, despite not distinguishing between women and men, and that there are gender differences in how they are used and by whom.[13] This awareness filtered through into discussions during drafting of the *Arms Trade Treaty* aimed at regulating the international trade in conventional arms, adopted in 2013,[14] and the *Cluster Munitions Treaty* aimed at eliminating the use of cluster munitions, adopted in 2008,[15] which both include gender components. In these examples, SCR 1325 operated like a wedge to lock in acknowledgment of gender perspectives for long enough that they came to be incorporated in some way.

Finally, I have seen SCR 1325 used by women as a 'shaming tool' in an attempt to embarrass those who have made commitments and yet have not followed through with deeds and money, and to shame their government representatives into listening to them – 'EVEN the Security Council gets it, why can't you?'

So yes, SCR 1325 has been a tool that has, in some respects, created some new ways of understanding and pursuing international peace and security. But are we using it as a conflict prevention tool? SCR 1325 contains language about women's important role in conflict prevention,[16] but have women's peace activists, including WILPF and PeaceWomen, brought life to that language and sought ways to use it to challenge war and militarism per se? To demand a radical rethinking of what collective security really is? To promote further feminist analyses of how and why wars start and endure? To expose how the war system works, who benefits from it and how the global trade in weapons makes armed conflict inevitable? I think we have been insufficiently imaginative and ambitious when it comes to utilising SCR 1325 as a tool for conflict prevention.

SCR 1325 and conflict prevention

Very often we have been too caught up using SCR 1325 as a tool to improve the situation of women in peacekeeping operations (which it is); or as a lever for increasing the number of women in UN posts and in peace negotiations (it is also about this); or as a means of demanding an end to impunity for sexual violence in armed conflict and its aftermath (again, this is part of it). While these are incredibly important issues, I think we can address them in more powerful ways by using SCR 1325 to prevent armed conflict at its sources, including the sources of monetary support and the sources of weapons used to wage war. Particularly poignant for me was the observation of a close WILPF friend that the early WILPF women spoke *as* women about *everything* – including country situations, security concepts, military spending, as well as theories like deterrence. We need to ask how the Security Council has become the centre of our attention and why are we only talking about women when pre-1325 we also spoke about disarmament and conflict prevention. SCR 1325 must be developed as a tool to question the taken-for-granted militarised culture of international security, the human lives, money and other valuable resources that are wasted on military security – especially on weapons – weapons to kill, mutilate, humiliate and destroy. Globally, just six states export 74 per cent of the world's weapons – United States (US), Russia, Germany, United Kingdom (UK), China and France[17] – and of these states, all but Germany hold permanent seats on the Security Council. I do not think SCR 1325 has been used enough as a tool for conflict prevention. It could be used in all of WILPF's campaigns against weapons, in all of the feminist campaigns against armed conflict, and I think it should be. It is time for us to dare to be more political and to engage in large numbers, as feminists, in 'hard' security issues, especially the prevention of armed conflict and the elimination of weapons, with more confidence and determination.

This edited collection has come about because women's groups are trying and pushing and working to make a difference, usually on a shoestring budget, with hardly any financial resources or media coverage. We have some good reasons to celebrate our collective endurance and solidarity, our networks and our achievements. We also have some very good reasons to be alarmed at how the practice of collective security is unfolding, despite the adoption of SCR 1325. The small, sometimes medium gains we have made as WILPF, in collaboration with many others as peace women, need to be seen in the larger context, in a tense and frightening world of increasing military expenditure and investment in war, where armed conflict is still resorted to as a means to resolve international and domestic disputes. Carl von Clausewitz once said that war is the 'continuation of politics by other means',[18] which in John Horne's adaption became 'war is masculinity by other means'.[19] If only SCR 1325 was bringing some gender wisdom to the world of peace and security thinking and action. As you read these words, Gaza and the West Bank continue to be brutally occupied. As you read these words, the violence in the DRC continues, on and on. The conflict-related deaths in Afghanistan also continue and women's rights remain circumscribed and under threat, with Taliban-controlled regions retaining restrictions on female mobility in public space, including access to education and health services.[20] Military intervention did not achieve much for Afghan women, if indeed anything. We witnessed instead the instrumentalisation of women's rights and SCR 1325 to justify the military force and the violence that it unleashed.[21] The rhetoric of women's rights that accompanied the use of force in Afghanistan in 2001, and since, demonstrates how SCR 1325 can be dangerously manipulated and how feminist actors were not astute or united enough to challenge women's rights and aspirations being misused – once again – as an instrument of policy, as a symbol to justify and encourage war. We have to reclaim SCR 1325 as a tool for feminist purposes and work with it harder, stronger, differently.

The same instrumentalisation happened with Iraq – SCR 1325 became a tool in support of war, rather than a tool to prevent it.[22] The violence in Iraq also continues, on and on, and insecurity persists after foreign troops have left. The 2003 military action led to thousands and thousands of civilian deaths in Iraq and yet for some, perhaps many, the Iraqi intervention by the US, UK and their 'coalition of the willing' was not a failure. Billions and billions and billions of US dollars have been distributed through no-bid contracts, often immune from audit.[23] To my mind, this is organised crime; an organised crime against humanity in Iraq and an organised crime in the shape of corporate welfare.

Let's take a minute to think about those billions of dollars. If you count, one-two-three-four … two hundred … twenty two thousand and one … all the way to one million, it would take 11.5 days without stopping to eat, drink or sleep. To count to one billion, one-two-three … four hundred million, twenty eight thousand, two hundred and three … it would take 32 years of non-stop counting. From the first day of the year 2008, one billion seconds earlier was the year 1961. One billion minutes ago was the beginning of the Common Era. One billion hours ago human ancestors were living in the Stone Age. One billion days ago no animal walked upright, and the earth was mostly populated with crawling, swimming beings. And today we talk in terms of trillions – units of one thousand billion. At a global level for 2012, military spending is estimated to be over US\$1.7 trillion dollars. This is over 600 times the UN core budget. Annual global military spending amounts would fund the UN for over 3000 years at its current budget. It seems especially apt to reflect on the immensity of dollars spent given the so-called global economic crisis of 2008 and the money that has been used to try to prop up free market capitalism and the tiny amounts that women's rights advocates work with on our projects.

It also seems apt if we again turn to asking what Jane would do, because she talked a lot about 'bread and roses' as she sought to improve the lives of the poverty-stricken immigrants and forgotten citizens of Chicago – where she basically started the profession of progressive social work.[24] Jane Addams focussed on the economics of war and made the nexus with the economics of peace. I do not think Jane would be disparaging about SCR 1325, not at all. It would be more her way to advise us use whatever tools we have, to welcome every millimetre of movement forward. But I also think she would use SCR 1325 like a sail, to get the ship pointed towards The Hague of her imagination, the city of peace, international law and negotiated settlement of international disputes. She would surely not view SCR 1325 as an end in itself, but as a means towards the ending of war itself and, in the meantime, a focus for protesting against and challenging the legitimacy of armed conflict as it rages. She would also have used SCR 1325 to highlight how much armed conflicts cost financially, in addition to their cost in human lives and opportunities, and propose better ways for the funds to be spent. Jane would stretch SCR 1325 to its limits.

If Jane had been around in 2000, I think she would have said *yes and* when will you get on with a resolution on men, peace and security? I have drafted some of what it might say:

The United Nations Security Council,

urges Member States to ensure decreased over-representation of men at all decision-making levels in national, regional and international institutions and mechanisms for the prevention, management and resolution of conflict;

urges the Secretary-General to appoint less men as special representatives and envoys to pursue good offices on his behalf, until there is 50-50 gender representation;

calls on Member States to stop putting forward male candidates to the Secretary-General for appointment as special representatives and envoys;

calls on all parties to armed conflict to take urgent measures to adopt peaceful measures to resolve their disputes, including the immediate cessation of rape and sexual abuse, ensuring that all offenders are prosecuted and providing reparations to all victim/survivors; and

undertakes to dramatically reduce weapons production and military expenditure by its permanent members, and actively work towards global disarmament by the year 2020.

Jane would have urged us to resist the use of SCR 1325 as a means to merely make war safer for women (as if that was possible), and to reject its translation into a list of bureaucratic performance indicators which encourage a 'tick the box' approach,[25] to taking into account the diversity and breadth of women's experiences of armed conflict and welcome their many transformative contributions to peace, including to conflict prevention and its resolution.

Conclusion

It is genuine human security that we want to achieve – by way of disarmament, conflict prevention, an equitable international economic order and transformed gender relations – not merely the adoption of a series of Security Council resolutions. If SCR 1325 helps us work towards these goals, then fine, but if it means that our primary focus is on elite actors, usually men in suits, sitting around a table in New York, and not women in situations of armed conflict, then we are in danger of betraying our own goals. If we are to realise the full potential of SCR 1325, and stay true to the hopeful women who have worked tirelessly to advance these goals for at least the last century, we have to ensure that the stories and faces of women affected by armed conflict are shaping our responses, not the elite actors far removed from the everyday realities of conflict. We have to find a way to allow diverse actors to speak and to be heard. We also need to conceptualise and articulate feminist perspectives on these 'hard' big-picture security issues, to enter into and fire debates about weapons and militarism. Until we do, we are not living up to the aspirations that drove the campaign to have SCR 1325 adopted. SCR 1325 is about human rights, and it is also about responsibilities. Currently, there is a great deal of emphasis on the Security Council once a year, in October, when SCR 1325 has its anniversary, with NGOs pleading again for women to have some democracy; for training so local women can be informed about and contribute to policy and practice related to security issues; and for measures that will make peacekeeping safer for women. As long as we do only this, we are serving the institutional instrumentalisation of SCR 1325, rather than making it work for our goals.

We have to remember that SCR 1325 is our tool, the tool of women's peace activists and human rights NGOs. It was our idea, not the Security Council's, and it is our efforts that have given it life since its adoption.[26] If we cannot use this tool to participate in the 'big' security debates, and to challenge the 'inevitability' of the militarised framework of international peace and security, its foundation and structure, then what are we doing? This is what WILPF is all about – finding the facts and the figures and the fury – the heart-felt fury about needless waste and death – to organise, to mobilise to prevent armed conflicts and to rescue everyone's future from the profit margins, hip pockets and mindsets of economic rationalists and military security thinking. Before 2000, it seemed impossible that the Security Council would pay any attention to women other than as the inevitable victims of armed conflict who needed to be rescued and protected by the Council. The adoption of SCR 1325 was indeed a watershed, and there is much to celebrate with this achievement. But we also have to use it to challenge the underpinnings of marketised and militarised international peace and security. This involves having the courage not only to talk about the importance of the contributions that women can make, but to make these many contributions actually happen and matter. It involves taking up the responsibility to speak as women about the hard security issues. The Security Council continues to define security in a very narrow military way, and fails to see that bombs, guns and landmines provide no answer to deepening (feminised) poverty, increased environmental risks of tsunamis, hurricanes and floods, spreading violence against women, viral pandemics and acute water shortages. These are our real security threats. These threats can be addressed, but only if the human and economic resources currently going into weapons and war are redirected. We need to use SCR 1325 to redefine international peace and collective security, and the means whereby they are attained.

Notes

Many thanks to Dianne Otto who helped me put this chapter together from my notes.

1. *Security Council Resolution 1325*, UN Doc. S/RES/1325 (31 October 2000) (SCR 1325).
2. 'Promoting women's roles in peace and security', *North Atlantic Treaty Organization*, http://www.nato.int/cps/en/natolive/91057.htm (last accessed October 2013).
3. *PeaceWomen*, a project of the WILPF, http://www.peacewomen.org (last accessed October 2013).
4. *Security Council Resolution 1820*, UN Doc. S/RES/1820 (19 June 2008); *Security Council Resolution 1888*, UN Doc. S/RES/1888 (30 September 2009); *Security Council Resolution 1889*, UN Doc. S/RES/1889 (5 October 2009); *Security Council Resolution 1960*, UN Doc. S/RES/1960 (16 December 2010) (SCR 1960); *Security Council Resolution 2106*, UN Doc. S/RES/2106 (24 June 2013); and *Security Council Resolution 2122*, UN Doc. S/RES/2122 (18 October 2013).

5. See, for example, F. Hill, M. Aboitz and S. Poehlman-Doumbouga, 'Nongovernmental organizations' role in the buildup and implementation of Security Council Resolution 1325', *Signs: Journal of Women in Culture and Society*, Vol. 28, No. 4 (2003) 1255.

6. M. Fullilove, 'Images in psychiatry: Jane Addams, 1860–1935', *American Journal of Psychiatry*, Vol. 155, No. 6 (1998) 828.

7. See, for example, J. Addams, *Peace and Bread in Time of War* (Urbana: University of Illinois Press, first published in 1922, 2002 ed.).

8. *Report of the Secretary-General on Women and Peace and Security*, UN Doc. S/2012/732 (2 October 2012), para. 19, box 9.

9. Ibid., para. 18, box 8.

10. See, for example, *Statement by the President of the Security Council*, UN Doc. S/PRST/2004/40 (28 October 2004); and *Statement by the President of the Security Council*, UN Doc. S/PRST/2005/52 (27 October 2005).

11. See 'National Action Plans', *PeaceWomen*, http://www.peacewomen.org/pages/about-1325/national-action-plans-naps (last accessed October 2013).

12. *Women, Disarmament, Non-Proliferation and Arms Control*, UN Doc. A/RES/65/69 (13 January 2011).

13. See, for example, 'Gender', *United Nations Office for Disarmament Affairs*, http://www.un.org/disarmament/HomePage/gender/gender.shtml (last accessed October 2013).

14. *Arms Trade Treaty*, UN Doc. A/RES/67/234 B (2 April 2013), (opened for ratification 3 June 2013), preamble para. 10, art. 7(4).

15. *Convention on Cluster Munitions*, opened for signature on 3 December 2008, 48 ILM 354 (entered into force on 1 August 2010), preamble para. 8, arts 5(1), 6(7), 7(1)(k).

16. SCR 1325, para. 1.

17. 'Shocking facts: Scale and impact of the arms trade', *Amnesty International* (27 June 2012), http://www.amnesty.org.au/armstrade/comments/29065 (last accessed October 2013).

18. C. von Clausewitz, *On War* (Oxford: Oxford University Press, 2008) [trans. of: *Vom kriege*, first published in 1832)].

19. J. Horne, 'Masculinity in politics and war in the age of nation-states and world wars, 1850–1950', in S. Dudink, K. Hageman and J. Tosh (eds), *Masculinities in Politics and War: Gendering Modern History* (Manchester: Manchester University Press, 2004) 22.

20. Amnesty International, 'Afghanistan: Don't trade away women's human rights' (AI Doc. 11/007/2011, August 2011).

21. Laura Bush launched the President George W Bush's 'women's rights' campaign in Afghanistan on the President's weekly radio address, 17 November 2001, see D. Stout, 'A nation challenged: The First Lady; Mrs Bush cites women's plight under the Taliban', *The New York Times* (18 November 2001) 4.

22. Iraqi women were heralded by the US Administration as promoters of freedom and democracy, in support of the invasion of Iraq in 2003, see P.J. Dobriansky, T. Gilly, Z. Al-Suwaij, M. Alattar and E. Naama, 'Human rights and women in Iraq: Voices of Iraqi women', *US Department of State Archive* (6 March 2003), http://2001-2009.state.gov/g/rls/rm/2003/18477.htm (last accessed in October 2013).

23. R. Berrios, 'Government contracts and contractor behaviour', *Journal of Business Ethics* Vol. 63, No. 2 (2006) 119, pp. 121–122, 125.
24. J. Addams, *Newer Ideals of Peace* (Urbana: University of Illinois Press, first published in 1907, 2007 ed.).
25. See, for example, SCR 1960, para. 8.
26. D. Otto, 'A sign of "weakness"? Disrupting gender certainties in the implementation of Security Council Resolution 1325', *Michigan Journal of Gender and Law*, Vol. 13, No. 1 (2006) 113.

9
Increasing Women's Presence in Peacekeeping Operations: The Rationales and Realities of 'Gender Balance'

Olivera Simić

Introduction

Between 1948, when the United Nations (UN) Security Council established its first peacekeeping operation (PKO),[1] and the end of the Cold War, few women were deployed as peacekeepers,[2] as the operations performed largely military functions and did not have much interaction with the local population in host countries. However, since the end of the Cold War there has been a proliferation of PKOs across the globe and their mandates have rapidly expanded, well beyond purely military goals. Peacekeeping now involves diplomatic, civilian, police and military personnel in a wide range of activities, including conflict prevention, peace enforcement, peacebuilding, peacemaking and humanitarian operations. PKOs have become, in every sense, multidimensional interventions.[3] Increasingly ambitious peacebuilding activities have led to many more direct interactions between PKO personnel and the local population.

Although the issue of 'gender (im)balance' should have been a concern to PKOs from the start, given the *Charter of the United Nations'* (UN Charter) commitment to women's equality,[4] the change in their nature, scope and mandate has raised the issue of gender balance more intensely. The large presence of women in post-conflict countries, who are often involved in grassroots post-reconstruction activities, has become an important facet of contemporary PKOs. The calls for an increased number of women in PKOs became more insistent with the adoption of UN *Security Council Resolution 1325* (SCR 1325),[5] which 'urges the Secretary-General to seek to expand the role and contribution of women in UN field-based operations, and especially among military observers, civilian police, human rights and humanitarian personnel'.[6]

It is now seen as a problem that women have been denied equal access and participation in peacekeeping, despite the fact that women have always made up the majority of those who remain in the aftermath of armed conflict. To address this concern, feminists have used SCR 1325 to lobby for better representation of women in peacemaking, peace-keeping and peacebuilding processes.

Even before the adoption of SCR 1325, pressure was mounting for the UN Department of Peacekeeping Operations (DPKO) to adopt more serious measures to advance gender balance in all facets of peacekeeping missions.[7] However, it was not until 2005 that the DPKO made a formal commitment to gender equality, which included the goal of achieving 50/50 gender balance in civilian professional posts at all levels in the 'near future'.[8] As for police contingents, in 2010 the DPKO set a target for women of 20 per cent by 2014,[9] and undertook to continue working to increase the presence of women in military contingents without set-ting a specific target. According to the DPKO, 'gender balance refers to the degree to which men and women hold the full range of positions in a society or organization'.[10] The need to achieve greater parity between the number of women and men in PKOs, according to the DPKO, is based on the UN goal of gender equality, that is, equality between women and men.[11]

Although the DPKO suggests that 'gender balance is critical to the attainment of gender equality',[12] I argue that feminist goals are endan-gered if gender equality is conflated with gender balance. Gender equal-ity requires that women and men enjoy equal rights, responsibilities and opportunities, which demands transformative change in the way that gender has been conceived[13] – a much more ambitious project than simply increasing the presence of women in existing masculinist institutions. The achievement of gender equality requires both gender balance and gender mainstreaming, but current DPKO policies seem to focus only on gender balance. It is assumed that once gender balance is achieved, gender equality, including the full participation of women in peacekeeping, will be achieved as well.

Despite many appeals from the Security Council to states, UN agencies and private entities involved in peacekeeping to increase the number of females in PKOs,[14] even the conservative targets set by the DPKO are a long way from realisation. Although the 1990s saw a slow increase in female military presence in PKOs, in 2007 women still constituted less than two per cent of military personnel, with that figure rising slightly to 3.33 per cent in 2010.[15] As of June 2012, only 1,354 of the 14,098 UN police were women (9.6 per cent), and only 2,164 of the 81,443 military troop personnel were female (2.66 per cent).[16] So far, the main strategy for increasing the number of police and military women in PKOs has been through the deployment of 'female only' units.

Although the DPKO has promoted a number of other reforms aimed at incorporating a gender perspective into PKOs, including the establishment of mechanisms to focus exclusively on gender issues such as gender units, gender advisors and gender focal points, and the provision of gender awareness training to peacekeeping personnel, my focus in this chapter is on its efforts to improve gender balance by increasing the number of women police serving in PKOs.[17] The chapter begins by critically assessing the official rationales provided for increasing the number of female peacekeepers. The realities to date are then discussed, highlighting the disconnection between the official rationales and the on-the-ground experience. Finally, the chapter argues that the gender balance agenda is endangering what feminists had hoped to achieve with SCR 1325. The chapter concludes that gender balance has been a tokenistic exercise by the DPKO, and argues that instead, PKOs need to deploy more women and men who are committed to gender mainstreaming, to making this operational on the ground and to ensuring it is backed up by institutional structures and policies. Only then will the full and equal participation of women in peacekeeping, and in the communities they help to reconstruct, become possible.

The rationale for gender balance

Although the DPKO has actively promoted gender reform by calling for more women to be deployed in PKOs, it has little or no influence over the personnel recruited by the police- and troop-contributing countries. Indeed, whether the DPKO can meet the gender balance targets it has set depends on the contributing countries. It depends, firstly, on the political will and capacity to recruit more women into national military and police forces and, secondly, on the will to then deploy them in PKOs. The power to achieve the gender-balanced targets thus lies in the hands of the contributing countries and, in particular, their national recruitment policies. The UN Secretary-General, Ban Ki-moon, weighed in by launching a campaign in August 2009 that promoted an increase in the number of women peacekeepers in military contingents to ten per cent – and, following the DPKO, in police units to 20 per cent – by 2014.[18] However, he acknowledged that achieving these goals depended on 'the will of the [contributing] countries'.[19] This public recognition of the role that the contributing countries play in determining who is deployed allows the UN to implicitly distance itself from any responsibility, if its targets are not achieved.

As of January 2012, the three main contributing countries were Pakistan, Bangladesh and India, who together provide almost 35 per cent of the overall military and police contingents.[20] That the initiative to create all-female peacekeeping units has come from these countries is then not surprising. In 2007, the first all-female police contingent from India was deployed in Liberia. Since then, three more women's police units have been deployed – a Bangladeshi unit in Haiti, a Samoan unit in Timor Leste and a Rwandan unit in Sudan.[21] However, the deployment of all-female police units, rather than integrating women into existing units, could be seen as a way to avoid changing the masculine police and military cultures of PKOs. Deployment in single-sex units means women work separately from men, and enables them to be treated as an adjunct to them. These units therefore give a false impression that PKOs are becoming more inclusive of women. This method of increasing the number of female peacekeepers ensures that there is little, if any, impact on the male-dominated culture of the PKO as a whole.

The primary rationale for the inclusion of more women in PKOs has been that their presence will help to reduce the incidence of widespread sexual exploitation and abuse. They have been perceived primarily as a task force to combat sexual violence. Indeed, one of the main reasons that the DPKO decided to deploy an all-female police unit from Bangladesh in Haiti was because 'reports of sexual violence in the camps for internally displaced persons abound'.[22] The Security Council has also adopted this rationale in its women, peace and security resolutions on combating sexual violence. In *Security Council Resolution 1820* (SCR 1820), for example, troop- and police-contributing countries are encouraged to consider taking steps to prevent sexual violence, 'including wherever possible the deployment of a higher percentage of women peacekeepers or police'.[23] The Secretary-General has also recently stated that women peacekeepers 'would be useful for [encouraging] women in conflict areas to report on sexual abuse and harassment'.[24]

However, this rationale is motivated more by the need for a 'quick fix' to solve the UN's reputational problems than by a desire to address the problem of sexual violence in PKOs because of the impact on victims, as I have argued elsewhere.[25] Acting on the calls for the deployment of more women peacekeepers has come largely as a response to the UN's damaged image, following disturbing reports of the involvement of peacekeepers in sexual exploitation and abuse.[26] So, the push for more women peacekeepers is fuelled by the expectation that they will salvage the UN's good reputation by taking on the responsibility for preventing sexual exploitation and abuse of local women by other (assumed male) peacekeepers.

It has also been asserted, by feminist scholars and the media, that women peacekeepers will be better than men at dealing with local women. Gordana Odanovic, for example, argues that women peace-keepers will be more sensitive to the needs and problems that local women experience in their communities, in particular when it comes to their experiences of sexual and physical violence.[27] Similarly, Judith Hicks Stiehm contends that women are 'perceived as more empathic' to other women, are likely to have easier 'access to host-country women' and will be more adept at 'defusing tension rather than trying to control events'.[28] These claims are made without any empirically based evidence and thus rely solely on gender stereotypes.[29] Yet commentators continue to make statements about the necessity of deploying more women based on essentialist assumptions about women (and men). This promotes an 'add women and stir' approach,[30] which leaves women's inequality unquestioned and unchallenged. The President of Liberia, Ellen Sirleaf Johnstone, has been reported as saying that women bring to the task of peacekeeping 'extra sensitivity and more caring', characteristics 'that come from being a mother, taking care of a family, being concerned about children, managing the home'.[31] Her claims are based on gender stereotypes about women and men, implicitly assuming that all women are 'naturally' sensitive and maternal, while men are not. Maternalist narratives also reinforce the stereotype that women are inherently more peaceful than men and therefore more suited to promoting peace activities.[32]

There is another underlying rationale for the deployment of more women peacekeepers, which assumes that female peacekeepers, especially from the global south, will be predisposed to empathising with their 'sisters' in the countries to which they are deployed.[33] It is assumed that because of their similar colonial histories, and perhaps socio-economic backgrounds, female peacekeepers and local women will naturally gravitate towards each other. However, this too relies on totalising gender stereotypes of women from the global south, completely ignoring their diversity and the part played by other hierarchies of power, such as race, ethnicity, religion, sexuality and so on.

These rationales for improving gender balance in PKOs, which rely fundamentally on gender (and racial) stereotypes of women and men, reinforce a gendered division of labour in PKOs. They suggest that women can do what male peacekeepers cannot – offer care, empathise with and relate to local women. The implication is that men are freed of these responsibilities, since they are better assumed by women. As a consequence, local women's issues are perhaps even more likely to be neglected, and women peacekeepers end up bearing a double burden – of responsibility as soldiers and police, as well as of responsibility as 'women' – while men are let off the hook. The work of challenging gender stereotypes, so crucial to gender mainstreaming and to building peace, is left completely unaddressed. These stereotypes also support the perception that female peacekeepers are the best suited to handle health care and other humanitarian and social dimensions of missions.[34] As Kathleen Jennings argues, these representations are telling us not what women are capable of doing, but confine women – even as peacekeepers – to traditional gender roles.[35]

In sum, gender stereotypes are relied upon to promote gender balance in PKOs. The rationales for including more women are essentialist in their nature and erroneously assume that achieving numerical targets women in PKOs will achieve gender equality too. Women are deployed in PKOs on the hypothesis that they will be committed to working with local women, above all to prevent sexual abuse committed by peacekeepers and local men. The rationales assume that women will value their connection with other women over all other considerations, and that men are incapable of developing productive and respectful working relations with women. There is also a disconnection between the rationales and the realities on the ground, once female peacekeepers are deployed in PKOs, as I will now explore.

The realities of female peacekeepers' experiences on the ground

PKOs have been, and still are, very much 'boy's clubs' operating in a predominantly masculine environment. Female peacekeepers who join the 'club' to work as police officers and soldiers find that they are nevertheless expected to act in 'feminine' ways. The official rationale for their participation relates to their assumed *feminine* characteristics (emotional, caring and tender), while the requirements of their jobs as police and soldiers require attributes that are perceived as *masculine* (tough, strong and brave). They are expected, on one hand, to be maternal, asexual and nurturing, while on the other hand, they are required to serve as well-trained, competent soldiers and police. These expectations clash. As Gerard DeGroot notes, the gendered stereotypes, which have previously excluded women from a range of roles in peace and armed conflict, have now been used to justify women's inclusion in those same roles.[36] There is also the compounding problem that, when women do not conform to gender-role stereotypes, and even when they do, they are more likely to be harassed in male-dominated fields like the military and police.[37] As a result, female peacekeepers often find themselves in an impossible situation: how can they live up to the DPKO's gendered expectations and yet successfully perform their jobs in the masculine environment in which PKOs operate, and in which they have chosen to participate?

As a measure of the importance of demonstrating that they can do the same work as men, female peacekeepers are often addressed by their female superiors in a distinctly masculine language. For example, Monia Gusain, the sergeant in command of all Indian female peacekeepers, calls her subordinates 'my men'.[38] Similarly, Sunita Dhundia, battalion commander of the first Indian all-female police unit in Liberia says, 'my girls know the hazards of the call of duty – they have to do it, they're soldiers'.[39] These statements demonstrate the overwhelming need to fit into the masculine peacekeeping milieu, rather than seeking to change it in any way by, for example, promoting the idea that all police and soldiers should be more responsive to local women's concerns.

It is apparent that many women peacekeepers prefer to embrace masculine norms over prescribed female gender roles. Indeed, it is unlikely that they even have this choice since they have to conform or they are unlikely to succeed in being a soldier or police officer. As DeGroot argued a decade ago, in the military there is a widely held belief that women are 'genetically programmed for a caring role' and cannot acquire impulses necessary for effective soldiering.[40] Often male norms and attitudes are taken as a point of departure: they provide a normative framework for conduct and self-definition within the peacekeeping culture, which women are often keen to embrace. For example, Sergeant Dora Dordoye, a physical instructor in Liberia, reported: 'What men can do in every activity or in any force, I can also do it'.[41] Similarly, a Bosnian female peacekeeper stated: 'I believe that a gender balance should not be the only reason to deploy female officers to a mission or position. As for male officers – proper skills, attitudes and behaviours are necessary and should be the primary reason for appointing someone'.[42] These statements suggest that female peacekeepers are strongly committed to being treated the same as men. Yet, they face significant obstacles to enjoying equality on the ground. As an Australian female police officer stated, 'I wouldn't be included in operations just because they thought that I might get hurt or might, for instance, break a nail ... I'm a police officer, I can get out there'.[43] Rather than breaking down the stereotypes, it seems that female peacekeepers, whether they are serving in all-women units or not, continue to face exclusion or are limited from performing some peacekeeping tasks because of their gender. The official rationales for gender balance are actually working against challenging such entrenched attitudes.

On the ground, the underlying assumption that female peacekeepers will be committed to improving the lives of local women in host states is clearly debunked. As Liora Sion's research shows, female military peacekeepers do not join the army as 'a result of a women's liberation motivation'.[44] They tend to be conservative in their ideological attitudes, and many hold the masculinist traditions of the military in high regard. Women (like men), from the global south as elsewhere, see joining a peacekeeping unit as a good employment opportunity, a chance to improve their career prospects and increase their incomes.[45] Yet, as Marsha Henry argues, the fact that peacekeeping militaries, including women, are largely coming from the global south has an exploitative dimension. The prospect of earning up to three times their usual monthly salary as peacekeepers, despite performing functions that western militaries do not want to assume, is seen by many as a financially rewarding commitment.[46] Women in the global south, likely to be even more affected by precarious work and low wages than men, would perhaps be even keener than men to serve in PKOs.[47] Therefore, while the deployment of all-female military and police units may be one way to address the extreme under-representation of women from developing and least developed countries in UN operations,[48] they reveal more about peacekeeping economies than about serious efforts to achieve gender balance.

Other research on female peacekeepers also confirms that, rather than being interested in local women's issues, women (like men) are drawn to peacekeeping by the prospects of good money and career advancement. Ulrike Baumgarter finds that gender advisors based at DPKO are not part of a women's movement, and nor do they identify themselves as feminists.[49] Further, according to the 2010 survey by the UN International Research and Training Institute for the Advancement of Women, some of the main incentives for women to join PKOs were similar to those of their male colleagues – the desire to further one's career (reported as the top reason); economic benefits; an altruistic goal of bringing peace to a war-torn society; an interest in sharing experiences and meeting colleagues from other countries; or simply the wish to work and live in an international environment.[50] None of the female peacekeepers who responded to the survey identified, as their motivation, the desire to learn more about and support local women. And we may ask – why should they? Why is there an assumption that international female peacekeepers want first and foremost to help their 'sisters in need'?

Finally, on a practical level, it is well known that military peacekeepers are strongly discouraged from mixing socially with the local population, and so are confined to their barracks when they are not working. It is not clear then how female military peacekeepers could have access to host-country women, beyond their policing and military functions, when their movements outside of their compounds are significantly restricted. I would further argue there is really no evidence to suggest that female peacekeepers are inclined to establish and sustain such contacts.

The efforts towards achieving gender balance are also seen by some men as directly affecting (reducing) their opportunities.[51] Marisa Silvestri asserts that integrating women into contemporary police forces may be perceived as 'a threat to men's definition of their work, their occupational culture, their social status, and their self-image as "real men"'.[52] While it is true that rising female participation within policing and army contingents has the potential to challenge the notion of policing and soldiering as men's work, this needs to be welcomed rather than feared.[53] However, there has been little institutional acknowledgement of the importance of changing men's socially constructed perceptions of themselves and their female colleagues, without which it is likely that such change will continue to be viewed negatively and even resisted. It is clear that if this issue is not given full attention, and efforts at gender balance are not supported by robust gender mainstreaming strategies that work against the perpetuation of gender stereotypes, there is little hope that the incorporation of female peacekeepers can result in any substantial change in the masculine framework of PKOs, let alone in their work with local communities.

Thus, there is a glaring gap between official policies and rationales for gender balance and the realities on the ground. Although women have gained increased access to policing and military jobs in PKOs, they struggle with competing expectations based on gender stereotypes. They have often found themselves in a contradictory position, trying to fulfil the expectations put on their shoulders by the DPKO, many of their male colleagues and even themselves, yet remaining marginal and undervalued as a result of the unchallenged masculine culture of PKOs.

What happened to gender mainstreaming and the goal of women's equality?

Although SCR 1325 has been widely praised as a 'significant success story for gender mainstreaming',[54] a number of feminists have been more critical of this claim. For instance, in the view of Women in Black Belgrade, the principle of gender equality has been used to 'militarise females', while SCR 1325 has been used as a tool to justify increasing the number of women in PKOs.[55] In their view, SCR 1325 has paved the way for more women to be brought into the military, under the pretext of 'gender equality'. They also observe that SCR 1325 is primarily applied to developing countries, and so-called transitional countries, which for them confirms its 'hegemonic character', as 'an instrument of militarization and patriarchalization of society',[56] rather than as an instrument of women's liberation.

Many other feminists have argued that simply increasing women's presence in PKOs will not necessarily change the peacekeeping culture of hyper-masculinity or bring about institutional transformation.[57] The UN agenda to deploy more women is seen as harbouring two problematic assumptions – that women are more peaceful than men; and that achieving gender balance in PKOs will promote a wider gender mainstreaming agenda.[58] Dianne Otto has also raised concerns about the claimed feminist 'achievements' in international law, arguing that the Security Council has to be pushed to go 'beyond tokenistic participation' and towards 'embrac[ing] an agenda of women's substantive equality'.[59] As Sandra Whitworth points out, the UN's work on gender mainstreaming has tended to focus not on gender relations, but on the ways in which women are different to men, both in terms of their particular vulnerabilities in situations of armed conflict and in terms of their potential contribution to peacekeeping efforts.[60] As a result, gender mainstreaming in the context of PKOs has been largely driven by prevailing stereotypical assumptions about masculinity and femininity,[61] which can be seen in the project of improving their gender balance, as I have argued.

The conclusion to draw is more than clear: that despite its presentation as an important tool for mainstreaming gender issues in PKOs, engagement with SCR 1325 by the UN Secretariat and DPKO has so far been confined to a tokenistic commitment to working towards gender balance. There needs to be a concerted effort to revive the original aspirations of the proponents of the Security Council's women, peace and security agenda, to learn the lessons of the salutary story of gender balance and renew our efforts to halt the dangers brought by spreading militarism and its patriarchal norms.

Conclusion

The invitation for more women to join PKOs relies on gender stereotypes, rather than challenging them. In the context of PKOs, gender continues to be seen as a woman's issue, and the idea of gender balance has replaced the more substantive goal of gender mainstreaming. Gender balance in PKOs has been adopted by the UN as a key public relations strategy to be seen to be addressing sexual violence. It has also served to limit the impact and vision of SCR 1325. Aiming for an increase in the number of women in PKOs does not necessarily challenge women's inequality. Paradoxically, it may even reinforce women's inequality by its reliance on gender stereotypes and by putting more demands on women peacekeepers than on men.

By pushing for gender balance, the DPKO gives the impression that gender-related peace and security issues can be addressed by simply increasing the number of women, who will then attend to women's concerns. Gender balance is presented as the solution to the violence, confrontation and conflict, especially of a sexual nature, that may arise in PKOs. In reality, it endangers the transformative vision of gender equality. Women's participation is reduced to achieving their descriptive (quantitative) presence, rather than ensuring their substantive (qualitative) contributions to change. Measures that may be capable of bringing substantive change to the gendered practices of peacekeeping military and police contingents, and to local women's and men's lives, are neatly avoided.

The mere presence of women peacekeepers will not, by itself, change the gender hierarchies and the macho culture deeply embedded in the military and policing cultures that dominate PKOs. The rationale for increasing the number of women peacekeepers in PKOs must be rethought. What is needed are the political commitment and concrete policies to turn an agenda of gender balance into meaningful participation by women in transforming peacekeeping cultures, so that they become an exemplar of women's equality, including in their interactions with the communities they are sent to protect. International and domestic policies and practices need to change to support an increase in the number of peacekeepers, both women and men, who are committed to changing gender inequality in the institutions for which they work, as well as in the local communities they support. Clearly, a mere increase in the number of women peacekeepers will not bring about the transformative structural and institutional change hoped for by those who lobbied for the adoption of SCR 1325.

Notes

I would like to thank Dianne Otto for her invaluable editing assistance.

1. The UN Truce Supervision Organization, established by the Security Council in the Middle East in 1948: *Security Council Resolution 50*, UN Doc. S/RES/50–S/801 (29 May 1948).
2. In the 32 years between 1957 and 1989, a total of only 20 women served as UN peacekeepers. DPKO, 'Women in peacekeeping', *United Nations Peacekeeping*, http://www.un.org/en/peacekeeping/issues/women/women-inpk.shtml (last accessed October 2013).
3. The term 'peace support operations' has been used since the 1990s to describe multidimensional peace operations. However, I will use the term 'peacekeeping operations' (PKOs) to refer to all peacekeeping missions from 1948 to the present.
4. *Charter of the United Nations*, opened for signature on 26 June 1945, 1 UNTS XVI (entered into force on 24 October 1945) (UN Charter) declares the UN's ambition to 'reaffirm faith in fundamental human rights, in the dignity and worth of the human person, in the equal rights of men and women': at preamble.
5. *Security Council Resolution 1325*, UN Doc. S/RES/1325 (31 October 2000) (SCR 1325).
6. Ibid., para. 4.
7. *Windhoek Declaration* (Windhoek, Namibia, 31 May 2000), reproduced in 'Appendix 1', *International Peacekeeping*, Vol. 8, No. 2 (2001) 115, including the *Namibia Plan of Action on Mainstreaming a Gender Perspective in Multidimensional Peace Support Operations*: at p. 116; and *Comprehensive Review of the Whole Question of Peacekeeping Operations in All Their Aspects: Letter Dated 12 July 2000 from the Permanent Representative of Namibia to the United Nations Addressed to the Secretary-General*, UN Doc. A/55/138–S/2000/693 (14 July 2000).
8. 'Commitment to gender equality', *United Nations Department of Field Support, Logistics Support Division* (2008), https://www.lsd.unlb.org/Shared%20 Documents/womenatlsd.aspx (last accessed October 2013); and *Improvement of the Status of Women in the United Nations System*, UN Doc. A/Res/59/164 (10 February 2005).
9. DPKO, 'Ten year impact study of implementation of UN Security Council Resolution 1325 (2000) on women, peace and security in peacekeeping' (DPKO, 2010), p. 27.
10. DPKO, 'Mainstreaming a gender perspective in multidimensional peace operations' (DPKO, July 2000), p. 69.
11. Ibid., p. 69.

12. 'Commitment to gender equality', *United Nations Department of Field Support, Logistics Support Division* (2008), https://www.lsd.unlb.org/Shared%20 Documents/womenatlsd.aspx (last accessed October 2013).

13. *Convention on the Elimination of All Forms of Discrimination against Women*, opened for signature on 1 March 1980, 1249 UNTS 13 (entered into force on 3 September 1981), especially art. 5.

14. SCR 1325, para. 4; *Security Council Resolution 1820*, UN Doc. S/RES/1820 (19 June 2008) (SCR 1820), para. 8; *Security Council Resolution 1889*, UN Doc. S/RES/1889 (5 October 2009), paras 1, 4; and *Security Council Resolution 2122*, UN Doc. S/RES/2122, (18 October 2013) (SCR 2122), paras 7(c), 9.

15. DPKO and UN Office of Military Affairs (OMA), 'Statistical report on female military and police personnel in UN peace operations prepared for the 10th anniversary of the SCR1325' (DPKO and OMA, 2010).

16. DPKO, 'Gender statistics by mission: For the month of June 2012' (June 2012), http://www.un.org/en/peacekeeping/resources/statistics/gender. shtml (last accessed October 2013). When it comes to senior posts in PKOs, the situation is even more concerning, with only seven women so far having been appointed as Special Representatives of the Secretary-General and only one as Deputy Special Representative of the Secretary-General.

17. T.M. Fapohunda, 'Integrating women and gender issues in peace development', *International Journal of Peace and Development Studies*, Vol. 2, No. 6 (2011) 162, p. 163.

18. 'Gender: Women UN peacekeepers – More needed', *IRIN Humanitarian News and Analysis* (20 May 2010), http://www.irinnews.org/Report/89194/ GENDER-Women-UN-peacekeepers-more-needed (last accessed October 2013).

19. Ibid.

20. Center on International Cooperation, *Annual Review of Global Peace Operations 2012* (Boulder: Lynne Rienner, 2012). This has been a trend for the last decade or so.

21. Rwanda is also one of the top six troop-contributing countries: DPKO and UN Department of Public Information, *Background Note: UN Peacekeeping*, UN Doc. DPI/2429/Rev.15 (June 2012), p. 2.

22. 'Gender: Women UN peacekeepers – more needed', *IRIN Humanitarian News and Analysis* (20 May 2010), http://www.irinnews.org/Report/89194/ GENDER-Women-UN-peacekeepers-more-needed (last accessed October 2013).

23. SCR 1820, para. 8. See further *Security Council Resolution 1888*, UN Doc. S/RES/1888 (30 September 2009), preamble para. 15; *Security Council Resolution 1960*, UN Doc. S/RES/1960 (16 December 2010), preamble para.16, operative para. 15; *Security Council Resolution 2106*, UN Doc. S/RES/2106 (24 June 2013), para. 14; and SCR 2122, para. 9.

24. I. Lutfia, 'Indonesia wants more female UN peacekeepers', *JakartaGlobe* (23 March 2012), http://www.thejakartaglobe.com/archive/indonesia-wants-more-female-un-peacekeepers/506456/ (last accessed October 2013).

25. O. Simić, 'Does the presence of women really matter? Towards combating male sexual violence in peacekeeping operations', *International Peacekeeping*, Vol. 17, No. 2 (2010) 188, p. 196.

26. D. Otto, 'Making sense of zero tolerance policies in peacekeeping sexual economies', in V.E. Munro and C.F. Stychin (eds), *Sexuality and the Law: Feminist Engagements* (Abingdon: Routledge-Cavendish, 2007) 259.
27. G. Odanović, 'Participation of women in UN peacekeeping operations', *Western Balkans Security Observer*, Vol. 5, No. 16 (2010) 70, p. 73.
28. J.H. Stiehm, 'United Nations peacekeeping: Men's and women's work', in M.K. Meyer and E. Prügl (eds), *Gender Politics in Global Governance* (Lanham: Rowman & Littlefield, 1999) 41, p. 56.
29. For an alternative view, see J. True, 'The Political Economy of Gender in UN Peacekeeping', this volume.
30. J. Valenius, 'A few kind women: Gender essentialism and Nordic peacekeeping operations', *International Peacekeeping*, Vol. 14, No. 4 (2007) 510, p. 517.
31. D. Carvajal, 'Women put own stamp on mission in Liberia', *The New York Times* (23 March 2010) 12.
32. S. Ruddick, 'Maternal thinking', *Feminist Studies*, Vol. 6, No. 2 (1980) 342.
33. M. Henry, 'Peacexploitation? Interrogating labor hierarchies and global sisterhood among Indian and Uruguayan female peacekeepers', *Globalizations*, Vol. 9, No. 1 (2012) 15, p. 25.
34. Lutfia, 'Indonesia wants more female UN peacekeepers'.
35. K.M. Jennings, 'Women's participation in UN peacekeeping operations: Agents of change or stranded symbols?' (Norwegian Peacebuilding Resource Centre, September 2011), p. 7.
36. G.J. DeGroot, 'A few good women: Gender stereotypes, the military and peacekeeping', *International Peacekeeping*, Vol. 8, No. 2 (2001) 23, p. 24.
37. J.L. Berdahl, 'Harassment based on sex: Protecting social status in the context of gender hierarchy', *Academy of Management Review*, Vol. 32, No. 2 (2007) 641.
38. Ibid.
39. 'India to send all-women peacekeeper force to Liberia', *DNA* (15 September 2006), http://www.dnaindia.com/india/report_india-to-send-all-women-peacekeeper-force-to-liberia_1053109 (last accessed October 2013).
40. DeGroot, 'A few good women', p. 22.
41. United Nations, 'Women in peacekeeping: The power to empower', *YouTube*, http://www.youtube.com/watch?v=vAuFQj9xBYc (last accessed October 2013).
42. F. Bertolazzi, 'Women with a blue helmet: The integration of women and gender issues in UN peacekeeping missions' (Working Paper Series, UN International Training Institute for the Advancement of Women, 2010), p. 17.
43. Quoted in V. Harris and A. Goldsmith, 'Gendering transitional policing: Experiences of Australian women in international policing operations', *International Peacekeeping*, Vol. 17, No. 2 (2010) 292, p. 300.
44. L. Sion, 'Peacekeeping and the gender regime: Dutch female peacekeepers in Bosnia and Kosovo', *Journal of Contemporary Ethnography*, Vol. 37, No. 5 (2008) 561, p. 568.
45. Henry, 'Peacexploitation?', p. 19.
46. 'How peacekeeping works', *BBC News* (17 April 2007), http://news.bbc.co.uk/2/hi/6524867.stm (last accessed October 2013).

47. There are global estimates of the gender pay gap. Women are paid 17 per cent less than their male counterparts: S. Scarpetta and P. Swaim (eds), 'OECD employment outlook' (OECD, 2008).

48. United Nations General Assembly, *Improvement of the Status of Women in the United Nations System*, UN Doc. A/Res/59/164 (10 February 2005).

49. U. Baumgärtner, 'Learning to speak a "masculine" language: Rationalization of gender equality in the United Nations peacekeeping bureaucracy' (Paper presented at the International Studies Association Annual Conference, New Orleans, 2010), p. 22, cited in Jennings, 'Women's participation in UN peacekeeping operations', p. 4 n. 11.

50. Bertolazzi, 'Women with a blue helmet', p. 13.

51. J.H. Stiehm, 'Women, peacekeeping and peacemaking: Gender balance and mainstreaming', *International Peacekeeping*, Vol. 8, No. 2 (2001) 39, p. 42.

52. M. Silvestri, *Women in Charge: Policing, Gender and Leadership* (Cullompton: Willan, 2003), p. 38.

53. T. Prenzler and H. Hayes, 'Measuring progress in gender equity in Australian policing', *Current Issues in Criminal Justice*, Vol. 12, No. 1 (2000) 20, p. 22.

54. J. True, 'Mainstreaming gender in global public policy', *International Feminist Journal of Politics*, Vol. 5, No. 3 (2003) 368, p. 373.

55. L. Mladjenovic, 'Massive rape as part of war strategy' (Conference Report, Sarajevo, Bosnia and Herzegovina, 9–10 March 2012) (on file with author).

56. Mladjenovic, 'Massive rape as part of war strategy'.

57. Stiehm, 'Women, peacekeeping and peacemaking'; Simić, 'Does the presence of women really matter?'; Jennings, 'Women's participation in UN peacekeeping operations'; Henry, 'Peacexploitation?'.

58. Simić, 'Does the presence of women really matter?'.

59. D. Otto, 'Power and danger: Feminist engagement with international law through the UN Security Council', *Australian Feminist Law Journal*, Vol. 32 (2010) 97, p. 107.

60. S. Whitworth, *Men, Militarism and UN Peacekeeping: A Gendered Analysis* (London: Lynne Rienner, 2004), pp. 119–150.

61. DeGroot, 'A few good women'; and Simić, 'Does the presence of women really matter?'.

Part IV
Silences

10
Systemic Silencing: Addressing Sexual Violence against Men and Boys in Armed Conflict and its Aftermath

Chloé Lewis

Introduction

Feminist international legal scholarship is conventionally aimed at addressing the androcentric bias of international law. Its starting point, therefore, is that women have been and continue to be excluded from international law vis-à-vis both its emancipatory and protective potential. As Elisabeth Evatt states in her foreword to Hilary Charlesworth and Christine Chinkin's seminal treatise, *The Boundaries of International Law*, international law 'shows little concern for women, their interests and their special vulnerabilities'.[1] However, in light of the proliferation of international laws, policies and programmes addressing conflict-related sexual violence over the course of the last two decades, this chapter seeks to add nuance to this claim. More specifically and towards this end, this chapter explores the silencing of male 'victimhood'[2] within mainstream international sexual violence discourse.

Conventional analyses of gender, armed conflict and peacekeeping habitually emphasise the vulnerabilities of women and girls, and their vulnerabilities to sexual violence in particular. They tend, therefore, to presuppose and reproduce gendered assumptions that pit women as the inevitable victim, while men are represented as a 'monolithic perpetrator class'.[3] While a number of feminist scholars have problematised the emphasis on female sexual vulnerability in armed conflicts,[4] notions of male sexual victimhood remain peripheral and relatively unexplored. Against this backdrop, I critically examine international materials and documentation pertaining to conflict-related sexual violence, and find that they produce and rely on three representations of men and masculinities: the 'Male Perpetrator', the 'Strategic Ally' and the elusive 'Male Victim Subject'. In doing so, I seek to demonstrate the limited legal, conceptual and programmatic spaces available to males within international sexual violence discourse,[5] emphasising the dominance of the 'Male Perpetrator' and the concomitant *repress*-entation[6] of the 'Male Victim Subject'.

With this aim in mind, this chapter proceeds in three sections. First, I provide a brief background to developments vis-à-vis responses to conflict-related sexual violence within the international community[7] and illustrate the parallel marginalisation of male victims. Secondly, I embed my analysis within critical legal feminist literature before I introduce the three male personas that emerge from mainstream sexual violence discourse, demonstrating the resilience of the male perpetrator/female victim binary underpinning all three figures. The final section offers some tentative reflections on three possible avenues, and the implications thereof, to promote more gender-inclusive approaches to international protection from sexual violence in armed conflict. The aim of this discussion is not to draw attention and resources away from female survivors. Instead, by drawing out these three male personas, my goal is to problematise the limited spaces available to males and to stress the need for a more sustained focus on male-directed sexual violence within international sexual violence discourse and programmatic responses. This analysis is, paradoxically, rendered all the more critical in light of recent developments within the women, peace and security (WPS) agenda, not least with respect to the adoption of *Security Council Resolution 2106* (SCR 2106)[8]: the first of the WPS resolutions to make explicit reference to men and boys, including to male-directed sexual violence. Rather than signalling a concrete shift in understandings of conflict-related sexual violence, however, and as highlighted throughout this chapter, widespread change to policies and practices, beyond this particular resolution, remains necessary.

Setting the scene: tracing male-directed sexual violence in armed conflict

Sexual violence in conflict is a phenomenon which, since the 1990s, has gained increasing prominence on the international human rights and humanitarian agendas. Sexual violence prevention and response have developed into a key sector of humanitarian and peacekeeping operations, constituting its own mode of discourse with supporting institutions, vocabulary, scholarship and doctrines.[9] The adoption of *Security Council Resolution 1325* (SCR 1325)[10] marked a significant turning point in this regard. Effectively re-conceptualising conflict-related sexual violence as an international security concern, rather than an exclusively humanitarian one, SCR 1325 placed the issue within the realm of high politics.[11]

The United Nations (UN) Secretary-General has since established the UN Action to Stop Sexual Violence in Conflict (UN Action), uniting the work of 13 UN agencies in addressing conflict-related sexual violence[12] and efforts to confront sexual violence in conflicts are also emerging at the governmental level of certain states. For instance, following United States (US) Secretary of State Hilary Clinton's highly publicised visit to the Eastern region of the Democratic Republic of the Congo (DRC) in 2011, the US State Department pledged US$17 million to 'assist female victims of sexual violence in DRC'.[13] In May 2012, the United Kingdom Government launched its Preventing Sexual Violence Initiative (PSVI), aiming to 'replace the culture of impunity with one of deterrence' by, inter alia, establishing a team of experts to deploy to conflict-affected areas; building a global partnership to prevent sexual violence; and increasing funding to UN Action.[14]

Given that sexual (and gender-based) violence was scarcely on the international agenda two decades ago, these developments are undoubtedly remarkable. Their focus, however, remains predominantly on sexualised violence perpetrated against women and girls, and rarely includes sexual violence targeting men and boys.[15] Paradoxically, there has in recent years been a marked shift towards 'engaging men and boys' in efforts to prevent and respond to sexual (and gender-based) violence. Yet, as I will argue, these male-inclusive strategies tend to reaffirm the female victim/male perpetrator paradigm, continuing to exclude males *qua* victims/survivors. This enduring exclusion is especially disconcerting given the mounting evidence of male-directed sexual violence, which has now been identified in over 25 armed conflicts in the last decade alone.[16] This emerging recognition notwithstanding, quantitative and qualitative data documenting this phenomenon nevertheless remains sparse.[17] According to Chris Dolan – Director of the Refugee Law Project based in Kampala, Uganda – male-directed sexual violence remains akin to an 'urban legend'.[18] The paucity of data is partly due to under-reporting by survivors, but is also partly attributable to a failure by researchers and practitioners to ask males about their experiences of violence, and of sexual violence in particular.[19]

The limited data that is available includes a 2010 study, assessing the prevalence of conflict-related sexual violence and its impact on physical and mental health in Eastern DRC, which found that 23.6 per cent of male respondents had experienced sexual violence, with 'rape' reported in 20.8 per cent of cases.[20] Prompted by these findings and seeking to further contribute to the evidence of male sexual violence in conflict-affected settings, Mervyn Christian and his colleagues investigated the effects of male sexual and gender-based violence (SGBV) on survivors, their families and communities in South Kivu, in Eastern DRC. Although tangential to their particular research focus, participants reported that international non-governmental organisations (NGOs) active in the region do not address male-directed SGBV.[21] Dolan supports this finding, describing the issue as 'systematically silenced' [22] by international organisations. The 2012 Human Security Report echoes Dolan's view, asserting that the needs of male survivors are 'systematically ignored'[23] and subsequently points to the insufficient and inequitable nature of policy responses that result.[24] Indeed, the 2008 independent evaluation of the UN High Commissioner for Refugees' (UNHCR) policies and programmes geared towards preventing and responding to SGBV concluded that 'the sexual abuse of boys and men is often neglected, under-reported and hardly addressed by any of UNHCR's programmes'.[25]

This backdrop notwithstanding, a number of noteworthy advances have occurred since. The UN Secretary-General, for instance, categorically incorporates male survivors within the definition of conflict-related sexual violence used in his recent annual reports on this issue[26] and states that male-directed sexual violence must be 'addressed at all levels as part of a comprehensive approach to protecting civilians'.[27] In August 2012, UNHCR published its first guidelines on working with men and boys as survivors of SGBV in displacement contexts. The document offers insights into the risks of male-directed SGBV during all stages of forced displacement, enumerates key indicators and emphasises the need for inclusivity in understandings of and responses to SGBV in UNHCR's programmes.[28] Finally, SCR 2106 adopted in June 2013, acknowledges that, while disproportionately affecting women and girls, sexual violence in armed conflict and post-conflict 'also affect[s] men and boys'.[29]

These (very) recent developments mark a potentially significant shift within the international community towards more gender-inclusive approaches to conflict-related sexual violence prevention and protection. However, if these are to translate into meaningful change for the lived experiences of male victims/survivors, understanding how, and to what effect, male-directed sexual violence has been silenced by the international community remains an important starting point. Towards building this understanding, the next section examines recurring tropes of masculinity embedded within mainstream sexual violence discourse which reflect and reinforce gendered assumptions that, to date, have functioned to restrict the conceptual, legal and programmatic spaces available to males within this context.

(Re-)reading international sexual violence discourse

Feminist engagements with international law are, for obvious reasons, primarily concerned with the ways in which women have been 'excluded, marginalised, silenced, misrepresented, patronised, or victimised by [international] institutions'.[30] That 'women' must be the sole subjects of feminist international legal scholarship and activism is, however, a notion that is gradually being contested.[31] Despite this, there remains an absence of critical interrogations of representations of men and masculinities in international law and practice. Underlining the importance of such an exercise, Dianne Otto contends that, because of their interdependence, 'feminist campaigns will never succeed unless they take account of both male and female subjectivities'.[32] With this insight in mind, the remainder of this section draws out three recurring tropes of masculinity embedded within mainstream sexual violence discourse: the 'Male Perpetrator', the 'Strategic Ally' and the elusive 'Male Victim Subject'.

The following analysis examines selected materials that constitute, and are in turn constituted by, mainstream sexual violence discourse and attendant practices, including Security Council resolutions on WPS;[33] the UN Secretary-General's reports on conflict-related sexual violence;[34] institutional and organisational reports and guidelines for practice in the fields of SGBV prevention and response;[35] UNHCR Executive Committee Notes;[36] the UN Women Global Virtual Knowledge Centre on Ending Violence against Women and Girls;[37] and NGO campaigns and evaluations.[38] These materials, produced at different times since the 1990s, embody shifting facets of mainstream sexual violence discourse, in particular with respect to representations of men and boys. It is important to note at the outset that I do not conceive of the three male figures that I present as a typology or as exhaustive. Instead, by drawing out these recurring tropes, I wish to show how they function to define and restrict spaces available to males within conflict-related sexual violence discourse and programmatic responses.

Not surprisingly, the 'Male Perpetrator' is *a priori* the most evident of the three male personas, principally because 'men' have habitually and historically been identified as the primary perpetrators of sexual violence. As feminist Susan Brownmiller emphatically stated, 'rape is nothing more or less than a conscious process of intimidation by which *all* men keep *all* women in a state of fear'.[39] Whilst an extreme and profoundly essentialist view, it is one that continues to reverberate implicitly, and at times explicitly, within international sexual violence discourse.

Until recently, men were rarely explicitly discussed with regard to sexual violence. Instead, men and boys existed as a background presence, that is, as presumed perpetrators.[40] For instance, *Security Council Resolution 1820* (SCR 1820), the first to focus entirely on sexual violence in conflict and post-conflict, refers to 'women and girls' 13 times, exclusively as victims of sexual violence. Men and boys, however, are not mentioned. The taken-for-granted presence of the male perpetrator figure relies on the understanding of sex/gender as a dualism in which women and men are defined in relation, and even in opposition, to each other.[41] According to this prevailing logic, if women are the victims, men are (assumedly) the perpetrators. This particular reading of the absence of men in SCR 1820, generally reflected in the broader WPS framework, is not an especially or innovative one.[42] Existing analyses have not, however, discussed how the tacit yet pervasive presence of the male perpetrator, as counterpart to 'the female victim', functions to eclipse male victimhood.

Moreover, in addition to emerging implicitly, the 'Male Perpetrator' appears more concretely within mainstream sexual violence discourse. It is not uncommon to find a less extreme adaption of Brownmiller's polemic within institutional documentation and practice guidelines. The report from the Inter-Agency Standing Committee's 'Lessons Learned' conference, for instance, states that: 'The bottom line is that gender-based violence is predominately men's violence towards women and children ... (Of course, not all men are perpetrators of violence)'.[43] Indeed, the notion that most cases of SGBV involve a female victim/survivor and a male perpetrator is one that is emphasised and re-emphasised in SGBV documentation, usually to justify female-specific responses.[44]

The perpetual repetition of the 'women-as-victims' and 'men-as-perpetrators' binary, combined with the longstanding silence around male victimhood, effectively leaves the gendered paradigm unquestioned. The prevalence of the 'Male Perpetrator' figure thus limits the construal of men and masculinities, directly informing the construction and implementation of policies to prevent and respond to sexual violence. This is reflected, for instance, in female-specific service provision as well as in the development of the (male) 'Strategic Ally'.

The 'Strategic Ally' is a more recent addition to international sexual violence discourse, emerging as a product of the turn towards engaging men and boys in promoting gender equality.[45] To this extent, sexual violence is generally no longer viewed as solely a 'women's issue'. Part of the rationale behind such male-inclusive strategies is, according to UNHCR, to overcome the perception held by some men, in refugee settings for instance, that the goal of gender equality and SGBV prevention is to 'empower women to dominate men and to discriminate against men'.[46] It is thus proposed that bringing in men as 'allies' will help mitigate male resentment over female-focussed policies and programmes, while still engendering positive change for women and girls.[47] A further premise underpinning this shift is based on men's assumed status as 'the perpetrator, the problem and the power-holder'.[48] In effect, as 'the gatekeepers of the current gender order',[49] gender equality and eliminating violence against women cannot be achieved without the active participation of men.[50] This notion is echoed in SCR 2106 which affirms the 'enlistment of men and boys' as 'central to long-term efforts to prevent sexual violence in conflict and post-conflict situations'.[51]

In this vein, the Programming Modules of UN Women's Global Virtual Knowledge Centre to End Violence against Women, developed by UN Women in 2012, are instructive. The online resource centre is designed for policymakers and practitioners working in the sector, and aims to make evidence-based programming guidance and evaluation tools accessible to users.[52] The opening paragraph of the module on men and boys states that '[v]iolence against women and girls is rooted in widely-accepted gender norms about men's authority and use of violence to exert control over women'; as such, given that 'the primary perpetrators of violence against women and girls are men … prevention efforts must engage them'.[53] The module further asserts that 'many men in society, if provided with information and sensitization about the issue [of SGBV], represent untapped but *potentially influential allies* in the struggle to end violence against women, within their families, communities and decision-making circles'.[54] The possibility of male victimhood, however, is not acknowledged. Rather, male perpetration of violence against women and girls is presented as the masculine norm to be altered by sensitisation and, ultimately, by 'redefining manhood'.[55]

This idea of (re)defining 'manhood' and 'masculinity' to promote gender equality and prevent sexual (and gender-based) violence has influenced a number of initiatives. The 'Vrai Djo' (Real Man) campaign launched by Search for Common Ground in the DRC offers an apt example in this regard. Through a series of scenario-based short films and audio recordings which probe 'Omoni vrai djo?' (Is he a real man?), the campaign aims to contribute to changing male attitudes and behaviour towards women in the country by promoting 'positive male role models'.[56] One of the clips shows a rural Congolese woman harvesting in a field. She suddenly experiences stomach pain and falls to the ground. She is found by two uniformed male soldiers. The dramatic change in the tone of the music, and the unmistakable fright in her eyes, make the viewer keenly aware that she fears that she is about to be raped. Instead, one of the soldiers extends his hand to her and they both escort her back to her husband. The closing scene of the video then features a Congolese celebrity, Celeo Scram, who challenges the (perceived) inevitability of male-perpetrated sexual violence by asking 'Omoni vrai djo?'

The 'Strategic Ally' in sexual violence discourse, policies and programmes is therefore predicated on men's 'instrumentalist capacity' as agents of change in reducing male-on-female sexual violence, rather than as possible victims thereof.[57] Viewed in this way, the 'Strategic Ally' is, like the 'Male Perpetrator', positioned in contradistinction to the 'oppressed' and 'victimised' female. In essence, therefore, strategies geared towards engaging men and boys as allies in efforts to reduce sexual violence serve to reinforce the assumption that men are inevitably the perpetrators, and rarely, if at all, the victims.

Yet, it would be incorrect to suggest that the international community has been completely silent about male-directed sexual violence. Frequently, however, the possibility of male sexual victimisation is (foot)noted and is subsequently absented from the main text, rendering the 'Male Victim Subject' something of a disappearing or elusive 'Other'.

It was therefore a surprise to find that the UNHCR Executive Committee *Note on Certain Aspects of Sexual Violence against Refugee Women*, published in 1993, recognised that males can also be targeted at every stage of the so-called refugee cycle. The *uni*-gendered[58] title of the Note notwithstanding, the Executive Committee's recognition of male-directed sexual violence in 1993 is in itself remarkable, especially when considered against the backdrop of silence characterising the issue. What is more remarkable, however, is that it is action-orientated. The Note states that measures to protect and respond to female survivors 'must also include provisions for men and boys in similar circumstances'.[59] As Sandesh Sivakumaran observes, whilst language that recognises male victims sometimes appears in the descriptive sections of legal and policy documents, they tend to disappear in the sections devoted to measures of implementation, where female-specific language remains the norm.[60] Yet, even the seemingly robust reference to the need for male-inclusive service provision included in the Note has thus far not translated into effective policy or practice on the ground. As observed by the independent evaluation of UNHCR's SGBV programmes mentioned earlier, male-directed sexual violence is 'neglected, under-reported and hardly addressed by any of UNHCR's programmes'.[61]

Indeed, the *repress*-entation of male victimhood at the operational stages remains commonplace, as evident in more recent international reports on addressing sexual violence and exemplified in the UN Secretary-General's first report on conflict-related sexual violence.[62] While gender-inclusive[63] in a number of important respects, the report nevertheless emphasises the deployment of *Women's* Protection Advisers (WPAs) (my emphasis), as mandated by *Security Council Resolution 1888* and *Security Council Resolution 1960* (SCR 1960), as well as SCR 2106. According to the report, their mandate is to 'strengthen the monitoring and reporting, prevention and response to conflict-related sexual violence against women, men and children'.[64] Despite this inclusive mandate, maintaining the *uni*-gendered language of the title is problematic for at least two reasons. First, the appellation excludes males from the protective ambit of WPAs, reinforcing the already deep-seated idea that conflict-related sexual violence is a women's issue and, thus, that only women need support and protection. Secondly, and not unrelatedly, subsuming the protection of male survivors under the rubric of 'women's protection' functions to reify the emasculation – real or perceived – of male survivors.

In light of prevailing attitudes pitting victimhood as antithetical to masculinity,[65] the emasculation of the victim is widely recognised as being at once a motivation for the perpetration of male-directed sexual violence and a characteristic element of the lived experiences of male survivors.[66] The female-specified designation of WPAs affirms this stigma and further alienates male survivors, potentially rendering them (even) less likely to seek or receive assistance.

A more inclusionary title, such as 'Sexual Violence Protection Advisers', would avoid these pitfalls, reflect the broader ambit of their stated mandate and, crucially, would reinforce the seemingly emergent shift towards male-inclusivity rather than undermine it. That a gender-specific title was adopted not only reflects the entrenched nature of assumptions of female victimhood, but also demonstrates how difficult it is to introduce male victimhood into mainstream sexual violence discourse in any meaningful and substantive way.

This difficulty is further underscored when we examine the frequent use of gendered pronouns to refer to victims and perpetrators. Whilst there are some indications that this is becoming less common, gendered pronouns remain an important mechanism through which the 'Male Victim Subject' is *repress*-ented in sexual violence discourse. Indeed, feminist scholars and activists have long been attentive to the exclusionary effects of the use of male pronouns in continually reconstituting the androcentric bias of international law and policy. It is therefore essential to consider how pronouns may likewise function in reverse within conventionally female-centric spaces, such as sexual violence.

Linguistically speaking, pronouns indicate, reproduce and normalise the gendered assumptions underlying a discourse;[67] in this case, that women are the victims and men are the perpetrators. Thus, the discursive power of these indexical signs should not be discounted. The 1995 UNHCR publication *Sexual Violence against Refugees: Guidelines on Prevention and Response* illustrates this point well. Despite the acknowledgement that '[v]ery little is known about the true incidence of sexual violence against male refugees', the Guidelines go on to state that: 'The pronouns in these Guidelines in relation to victims of sexual violence are phrased in the feminine voice and the pronouns in relation to perpetrators are phrased in the masculine voice'.[68] Similarly, the updated 2003 version of the Guidelines recognise that 'men and boys are *often* the victims of sexual violence',[69] but nevertheless, as an 'acknowledgement' that 'statistics confirm that the majority of victim/survivors are women and girls ... the Guidelines use feminine pronouns to describe victims/survivors'.[70] The point is made almost verbatim in the report of the Inter-Agency Standing Committee's 'Lessons Learned' conference, which recognises 'that males are often survivors of sexual violence; however, the majority of survivors of sexual and gender-based violence are female', thus, '[f]or simplicity, pronouns used in these recommendations are in the feminine voice'.[71] Notwithstanding the acknowledgement of male victimhood in these documents, the use of feminine pronouns in relation to victims *ipso facto* functions to write out the 'Male Victim Subject' almost instantaneously.

In this respect, Jacques Derrida's notion of 'disappearance' is especially useful in accounting for the elusive presence of the 'Male Victim Subject' within international sexual violence discourse. In Derrida's terms, the initial reference to male victims/survivors of sexual violence can be understood as a 'trace' within the text, which disappears to become a 'lost presence'.[72] Its disappearance hinders the reader's ability to understand the meaning or implications of the trace as it remains 'inaccessible and impenetrable'.[73] Instead, the disappearance of the 'Male Victim Subject' *repress*-ents male victimhood as an exception to a well-established rule and, in turn, reinforces the underlying female victim/male perpetrator narrative. His 'lost presence', moreover, reifies the *in*-significant status accorded to male victimhood given that, in Derrida's words, '[a] nothing *itself* is determined by disappearing'.[74]

By identifying three recurring representations of men and masculinities within international sexual violence discourse, this section sought to highlight the dominance of the 'Male Perpetrator', increasingly of the 'Strategic Ally', alongside the concomitant *repress*-entation of the 'Male Victim Subject'. In the next section, I consider three possible ways of overcoming the systematic silencing of male sexual victimisation within mainstream sexual violence discourse so as to promote more inclusive approaches towards collective security.

Building on the traces of the elusive 'male victim subject'

As mentioned above, there have been some important discursive developments drawing attention to male-directed sexual violence in conflict and post-conflict settings. However, these developments have yet to translate into definitive and consistent international policy and service delivery. Acknowledging that men and boys are often victims of sexual violence in conflict settings while doing justice to the (likely) reality that females are disproportionately affected is no simple feat. In this section, I explore three avenues through which the traces of the 'Male Victim Subject' might be built on to counter his disappearance and promote more inclusive approaches to protection in conflict-affected settings.

The first possible approach might be a 'gender-separate'[75] one, supported, for instance, by a 'Brother' resolution[76] to supplement the seven WPS 'Sister' resolutions. Recognising the ways in which men and boys are also adversely impacted in contexts of armed conflict and forced displacement, such a resolution would promote a more complex understanding of gender within the WPS framework. Male gendered harms might include conscription into armed forces and militias, long-term detention and, indeed, male-directed sexual violence. By particularising the masculine subject in international sexual violence discourse, a gender-separate approach might help disrupt entrenched assumptions underpinning contemporary sexual violence discourse by presenting males as possible targets of gendered harms in ways that give rise to human rights claims. This might conceivably go some way to preventing the disappearance of male (sexual) harms in conflict and post-conflict affected settings.

One of the dangers of a 'Brother' resolution, however, is that it may promote an 'artificially sex-bifurcated treatment of rape [and sexual violence more widely]'.[77] This could reinforce a dualistic model of gender in which the protection of men and women in armed conflict is viewed as a 'contest' between mutually exclusive claims,[78] problematically sustaining depictions of gender relations as competitive or zero-sum. Relatedly, a male-specific resolution could lead to women's re-marginalisation within the very spaces carved out by decades of feminist activism to address their exclusion from international human rights and humanitarian law.[79] This concern is expressed by a UNHCR Gender Official, who noted that 'as soon as you stop talking about women, women are forgotten'.[80] Whilst responding to female and male survivors need not be viewed as mutually exclusive, the weight of such concerns renders the adoption of a 'Brother' resolution problematic, if not unhelpful.

A second possible strategy to build on the traces of the 'Male Victim Subject' might be to adopt a *gender-neutral approach*, which would discursively disassociate the women-as-victims and men-as-perpetrators equation. This is, in fact, the approach adopted by the International Criminal Court, which defines the perpetrators and victims of rape in gender-neutral terms.[81] Gender-neutrality appears to be graining traction in more recent WPS resolutions. SCR 1960, for instance, refers more inclusively to the 'protection of civilians' from sexual violence in armed conflicts, and makes only three references to the qualifier 'in particular women and children', more common in previous resolutions.[82] As observed by R. Charli Carpenter, however, the extent to which the term 'civilian' is considered gender-neutral is questionable as it is often associated with women and children, and not adult males.[83] Nevertheless, a gender-neutral approach could prima facie unsettle the assumed naturalness of the female victim/male perpetrator dichotomy, allowing for the 'Male Victim Subject' to be recognised substantively.

Yet, as Noelle Quénivet notes, gender-neutrality might be resisted on the basis that it 'obscures the reality that an overwhelming majority of rape victims are women'.[84] Thus, echoing fears discussed with regard to a 'Brother' resolution, gender-neutrality may also lead to female victims/survivors again being marginalised. Whilst these concerns may have some merit, and maintaining a focus on female (sexual) victimisation in conflict is important, it must not be at the cost of silencing the sexual violence experienced by men and boys. Moreover, given the embedded feminisation of notions of 'victimhood' and 'vulnerability', and the masculine associations of 'perpetrator', it is perhaps more likely that gender-neutrality might reinforce rather than dismantle the female victim/male perpetrator equation discussed throughout this chapter. This approach might, as a consequence, inadvertently (re)produce the silence around male victimhood and may not, therefore, represent the most effective avenue for promoting male-inclusivity.

A third possibility for building on the traces of the 'Male Victim Subject' might be to adopt a *gender-equal* instrument whereby both males and females are included as putative victims. Dustin Lewis posits that the explicit recognition of male victims of sexual violence in international law and policy must, 'at a minimum, be the initial step in providing enhanced protection',[85] suggesting that this would encourage humanitarian workers and doctors working in conflict-affected areas to recognise and better respond to male-directed sexual violence.[86] Moreover, this approach might have the added value of positioning male and female victims/survivors as equally worthy of international protection, which might also help challenge harmful stereotypes surrounding masculinity that contribute to under-reporting.

This strategy could, however, tacitly suggest that conflict-related sexual violence is a 'shared' or 'homogenous' experience regardless of the victim's, or indeed the perpetrator's, gender. This may have the (unintended) effect of concealing male and female specificities in motivating and experiencing sexual violence. This could hamper prevention efforts that seek to adopt a root-causes approach to eliminating the causes of, and factors that contribute to, conflict-related sexual violence.[87]

Interestingly, SCR 2106 brings together the gender-neutral and gender-equal approaches to a certain degree. As noted above, the resolution incorporates a fleeting reference to male survivors and is, on the whole, relatively gender-neutral, urging, for instance, the provision of 'non-discriminatory and comprehensive health services' for survivors in its operative clauses.[88] This assumedly includes non-discrimination on the basis of gender. However, these moves are relatively minor and overall SCR 2106 still reinforces the masculine tropes discussed above. The reference to male survivors appears only in the preamble, while the operative clauses use both gender-neutral and, in some instances, female-specific language. The disappearance of the 'Male Victim Subject' in the operative part of SCR 2106 therefore confirms his continuing presence–absence.

Furthermore, while the language in SCR 2106 generally aligns with a trend towards gender-neutrality vis-à-vis sexual violence, examining the Security Council debate that preceded its adoption is instructive.

Nineteen (brief) references were made to men and boys *qua* victims/survivors over the course of the 60 statements made by state representatives. In contrast, and with varying degrees of substance, 325 references were made to female victims/survivors. It is evident, therefore, that the focus remains overwhelmingly centered on women as victims and, by extension, on men as (potential) perpetrators.[89]

The three possibilities I have explored – the gender-separate, the gender-neutral and the gender-equal approaches – each offer possible pathways for building on the traces of the 'Male Victim Subject' to enhance the recognition and protection of male survivors of conflict-related sexual violence. They each, however, also raise a myriad of *problématiques* to be carefully considered before adopting, or even advocating, a particular approach.

While this discussion has centred exclusively on gender, wider exploration is also needed to account for the ways in which intersecting social hierarchies, including race, ethnicity and sexuality, are represented in discourses of international protection. It is necessary, moreover, to probe in greater depth the role of normative constructions of masculinity and femininity, as well as the possible role of homophobia, in accounting for the reluctance on the part of the international community to address male-directed sexual violence in a meaningful way.[90] Intersecting factors and normative expectations may also contribute to the perpetration of male-directed sexual violence, as well as the reluctance of male survivors to seek support.[91] Additionally, male survivors themselves might not embrace such an approach as notions of 'victimhood' are commonly perceived as incompatible with masculinity/ies. This is reflected in an International Organization for Migration report on male victims of trafficking, whose authors note that 'the social construction of "victimhood" may be problematic for some men to accept and apply to their situation'.[92] This raises important questions as to whose interests are represented in the production of international (legal) documents on conflict-related sexual violence; whose vocabulary of sexual victimisation is adopted; and whose claims to 'authority' are recognised and privileged.

Nevertheless, at the very least, explicit and sustained *writing in* of male sexual victimisation to international sexual violence discourse remains necessary to unsettle the systematic silencing of male-directed sexual violence. Whilst it is equally evident that this will not provide a panacea for ensuring the prevention of and protection against male-directed sexual violence in conflict and its aftermath, the importance of international law as a site of 'discursive struggle' and 'normative challenge'[93] renders it a potent starting point.

Conclusions

Building on the work of critical feminist scholars, this chapter set out to explore the *repress*-entation of the 'Male Victim Subject' within international sexual violence discourse. Since the adoption of SCR 1325, conflict-related sexual violence has increasingly become a priority within the international community. These advances have, however, presupposed a female victim/male perpetrator dichotomy, systematically silencing male survivors. Notwithstanding increasing, although ad hoc, recognition of male-directed sexual violence at the international institutional level, it has yet to translate into tangible policy and programmatic changes on the ground. Seeking to illuminate this *problématique*, this chapter identified the contours of three recurring representations of men and masculinities that restrict the conceptual, legal and programmatic spaces available to men and boys within mainstream sexual violence discourse, namely to the 'Male Perpetrator', the 'Strategic Ally' and the (disappearing) 'Male Victim Subject'.

This analysis thus underscores the need for more explicit and sustained recognition of male sexual violence within international law and policy. How such inclusivity should be achieved, however, remains unclear. By tentatively exploring three possible avenues for building on the traces of the 'Male Victim Subject' – the gender-separate, gender-neutral and gender-equal approaches – this chapter also highlighted some of the implications of each strategy, to be considered before pursuing any particular one. This uncertainty notwithstanding, Cynthia Enloe famously stated that the role of the 'curious feminist' is to illuminate those at the 'margins, silences and bottom rungs'.[94] Viewed in this light, expanding feminist agendas to include the silenced phenomenon of male-directed sexual violence appears to be entirely consistent with this core feminist principle.

Notes

My deepest thanks and gratitude are due to Dr Fiddian-Qasmiyeh and Professor Dianne Otto for their unfailing support and for offering such clarity in times of conceptual chaos.

1. E. Evatt, 'Foreword', in H. Charlesworth and C. Chinkin, *The Boundaries of International Law: A Feminist Analysis* (Manchester: Manchester University Press, 2000), p. x.
2. The term 'victim' 'connotes powerlessness and stigmatisation': UNHCR, 'Sexual and gender-based violence against refugees, returnees and internally displaced persons: Guidelines for prevention and response' (UNHCR, May

2003), p. 6. Thus, I generally use the term 'survivor' in recognition of the agency and resilience of individuals who have experienced sexual violence. However, I use the term 'victim' vis-à-vis the under-representation of male survivors, as it is the idea of perceiving men as 'victims' that appears to jar. I place the term in quotation marks not to 'call into question the urgency or credibility of [male "victimhood"] as a political issue, but rather to show that the way [its] materiality is circumscribed is fully political': J. Butler, 'Contingent foundations: Feminism and the question of "postmodernism"', in S. Seidman (ed.), *The Postmodern Turn: New Perspectives on Social Theory* (Cambridge: Cambridge University Press, 1994) 153, p. 170.

3. L. Stemple, 'Male rape and human rights', *Hastings Law Journal*, Vol. 60, No. 3 (2009) 605, p. 635.

4. See, for example, African Rights, *Rwanda: Not So Innocent – When Women Become Killers* (London: African Rights, 1995); M. Alison, *Women and Political Violence: Female Combatants in Ethno-National Conflict* (Abingdon: Routledge, 2009); and C.O.N. Moser and C.F. Clark (eds), *Victims, Perpetrators or Actors? Gender, Armed Conflict, and Political Violence* (London: Zed Books, 2001).

5. I use this term to refer specifically to discourses surrounding international *conflict-related sexual* violence and use it interchangeably with 'mainstream sexual violence discourse'.

6. This concept is borrowed from E. Fiddian-Qasmiyeh, 'Concealing violence against women in Sahrawi refugee camps: The politicisation of victimhood', in H. Bradby and G.L. Hundt (eds), *Global Perspectives on War, Gender and Health: The Sociology and Anthropology of Suffering* (Farnham: Ashgate, 2010) 99.

7. The focus of this chapter is primarily on United Nations entities and implementing partners, however, this analysis may also be relevant to other international and regional bodies.

8. *Security Council Resolution 2106*, UN Doc. S/RES/2106 (24 June 2013) (SCR 2106).

9. According to Said, these form four core components of all discourses: E.W. Said, *Orientalism* (London: Penguin Books, first published 1978, 2003 ed.), p. 2.

10. *Security Council Resolution 1325*, UN Doc. S/RES/1325 (31 October 2000) (SCR 1325).

11. R.C. Carpenter, 'Recognizing gender-based violence against civilian men and boys in conflict situations', *Security Dialogue*, Vol. 37, No. 1 (2006) 83, p. 85.

12. 'About UN Action', *Stop Rape Now: UN Action against Sexual Violence in Conflict*, http://www.stoprapenow.org/about (last accessed October 2013). See also K. Engle, 'The Grip of Sexual Violence: Reading UN Security Council Resolutions on Human Security', in this volume.

13. United States Government Accountability Office, 'The Democratic Republic of the Congo: Information on the rate of sexual violence in war-torn Eastern DRC and adjoining countries' (Report to Congressional Committees No. GAO-11-702, July 2011).

14. United Kingdom Government, 'Preventing sexual violence initiative', *UK.GOV* (12 December 2012), https://www.gov.uk/government/policies/preventing-conflict-in-fragile-states--2/supporting-pages/preventing-sexual-violence-initiative (last accessed October 2013).

15. E. Rowley, C. Garcia-Moreno and E. Dartnall, 'Executive summary: Research themes and questions to guide research on sexual violence in conflict and post-conflict settings' (Sexual Violence Research Initiative, 2012), p. 2.
16. United Nation Office for the Coordination of Humanitarian Affairs (OCHA), 'Discussion Paper 2: The nature, scope and motivation for sexual violence against men and boys in armed conflict' (Paper presented at the UN OCHA Research Meeting on the Use of Sexual Violence in Armed Conflict: Identifying Gaps in Research to Inform More Effective Interventions, 26 June 2008), p. 1.
17. It is important to note that until the 1990s, concrete data on sexual violence perpetrated against women and girls in armed conflicts was similarly sparse. As noted by Carol Harrington, 1989 marked a 'striking change in documen-tation and analysis of the problem': C. Harrington, *The Politicization of Sexual Violence: From Abolitionism to Peacekeeping* (Farnham: Ashgate, 2010), p. 1. Susan Brownmiller remarks that 'serious historians have rarely bothered to document specific acts of rape in warfare': S. Brownmiller, *Against Our Will: Men, Women and Rape* (New York: Simon and Schuster, 1975), p. 40.
18. C. Dolan, quoted in N. Bennett, '"Changing gender norms is essential for peacebuilding in Congo'", *The Guardian* (20 October 2010), http://www.guardian.co.uk/world/2010/oct/20/congo-gender (last accessed October 2013).
19. See, for example, C. Clark, 'Gender-based violence research initiatives in refugee, internally displaced, and post-conflict settings: Lessons learned' (Rosemarie Rogers Working Paper No. 17, Massachusetts Institute of Technology, April 2003), p. 23; F. Roth, T. Guberek and A.H. Green, 'Using quantitative data to assess conflict-related sexual violence in Colombia: Challenges and opportunities' (Corporación Punto de Vista and Benetech, 2011), p. 56.
20. K. Johnson, J. Asher, M. Kisielewski, L. Lawry, R. Ong, B. Rughita and J. Scott, 'Association of sexual violence and human rights violations with physical and mental health in territories of the Eastern Democratic Republic of the Congo', *Journal of the American Medical Association*, Vol. 304, No. 5 (2010) 553, p. 557. For further quantitative data on levels of male sexual violence in conflict and post-conflict settings, see, for example, M. Nagai, G. Burnham, U. Karunakara and E. Rowley, 'Violence against refugees, non-refugees and host populations in Southern Sudan and Northern Uganda', *Global Public Health*, Vol. 3, No. 3 (2008) 249; Stemple, 'Male rape and human rights'; and *Conflict-Related Sexual Violence: Report of the Secretary-General*, UN Doc. A/66/657–S/2012/33 (13 January 2012).
21. M. Christian, G. Burnham, N. Glass, S. Octave and P. Ramazani, 'Sexual and gender based violence against men in the Democratic Republic of the Congo: Effects on survivors, the families and the community', *Medicine, Conflict and Survival*, Vol. 27, No. 4 (2011) 227, p. 242.
22. W. Storr, 'The rape of men', *Observer Magazine* (17 July 2011) 36, p. 41.
23. A. Mack (ed.), *Human Security Report 2012: Sexual Violence, Education, and War – Beyond the Mainstream Narrative* (Vancouver: Human Security Press, 2012), p. 44.
24. Mack (ed.), *Human Security Report 2012*, p. 45.
25. S. Rothkegel, E. Engelhardt-Wendt, R. Hennig, J. Papy, J. Poluda, B. Weyermann and C. Wonani, 'Evaluation of UNHCR's efforts to prevent and

respond to sexual and gender-based violence in situations of forced displacement' (UNHCR, 2008), p. 8.

26. *Report of the Secretary-General: Conflict-Related Sexual Violence*, UN Doc. A/66/657–S/2012/33 (13 January 2012), p. 3; and *Report of the Secretary-General: Sexual Violence in Conflict*, UN Doc. A/67/792–S/2013/149 (14 March 2013), p. 2.

27. *Report of the Secretary-General: Conflict-Related Sexual Violence*, UN Doc. A/66/657–S/2012/33 (13 January 2012), p. 3.

28. UNHCR, 'Working with men and boy survivors of sexual and gender-based violence in forced displacement' (Need to Know Guidance No. 4, UNHCR, 2012).

29. SCR 2106, para. 6.

30. V. Munro, *Law and Politics at the Perimeter: Re-Evaluating Key Feminist Debates in Feminist Theory* (Oxford: Hart, 2007), p. 12, quoted in A. Edwards, *Violence against Women under International Human Rights Law* (Cambridge: Cambridge University Press, 2010), pp. 2–3.

31. See, for example, N.E. Dowd, 'Masculinities and feminist legal theory', *Wisconsin Journal of Law, Gender & Society*, Vol. 23, No. 2 (2008) 201; N. Levit, 'Feminism for men: Legal ideology and the construction of maleness', *UCLA Law Review*, Vol. 43, No. 4 (1996) 1037; D. Otto, 'Disconcerting "masculinities": Reinventing the gendered subject(s) of international human rights law', in D. Buss and A. Manji (eds), *International Law: Modern Feminist Approaches* (Oxford: Hart, 2005) 105.

32. D. Otto, 'Lost in translation: Re-scripting the sexed subjects of international human rights law', in A. Orford (ed.), *International Law and its Others* (Cambridge: Cambridge University Press, 2006) 318, p. 354.

33. SCR 1325; *Security Council Resolution 1820*, UN Doc. S/RES/1820 (19 June 2008) (SCR 1820); *Security Council Resolution 1888*, UN Doc. S/RES/1888 (30 September 2009) (SCR 1888); *Security Council Resolution 1889*, UN Doc. S/RES/1889 (5 October 2009) (SCR 1889); *Security Council Resolution 1960*, UN Doc. S/RES/1960 (16 December 2010) (SCR 1960); SCR 2106; *Security Council Resolution 2122*, UN Doc. S/RES/2122 (18 October 2013) (SCR 2122).

34. *Report of the Secretary-General: Conflict-Related Sexual Violence*, UN Doc. A/66/657–S/2012/33 (13 January 2012).

35. UNHCR, 'Prevention and response to sexual and gender-based violence in refugee situations' (Inter-Agency Lessons Learned Conference Proceedings, Geneva, 27–29 March 2001); UNHCR, 'Sexual violence against refugees: Guidelines on prevention and response' (UNHCR, March 1995); UNHCR, 'Sexual and gender-based violence against refugees, returnees and internally displaced persons'; UNHCR, 'UNHCR handbook for the protection of women and girls' (UNHCR, January 2008); D. Buscher, 'Masculinities: Male roles and male involvement in the promotion of gender equality – A resource packet' (Women's Commission for Refugee Women and Children (now Women's Refugee Commissions (WRC)), September 2005); and WRC, 'Redefining manhood, rebuilding nations: How men can empower women to lift post-conflict communities' (WRC, August 2007).

36. UNHCR Executive Committee, *Note on Certain Aspects of Sexual Violence against Refugee Women*, UN Doc. A/AC.96/822/Corr.1 (19 October 1993).

37. 'About', *Virtual Knowledge Centre to End Violence against Women and Girls*, http://www.endvawnow.org/en/about (last accessed October 2013).

38. For example, Search for Common Ground Democratic Republic of Congo, 'Final report: "Vrai djo" project' (Report submitted to the Foreign & Commonwealth Office of the British Government, May – June 2011).
39. Brownmiller, *Against Our Will*, p. 15.
40. R.W. Connell, *The Role of Men and Boys in Achieving Gender Equality*, UN Doc. EGM/Men-Boys-GE/2003/BP (17 October 2003), p. 11.
41. Otto, 'Lost in translation', p. 320.
42. See, for example, A. Barrow, 'UN Security Council Resolutions 1325 and 1820: Constructing gender in armed conflict and international humanitarian law', *International Review of the Red Cross*, Vol. 92, No. 877 (2010) 221; and P. Scully, 'Vulnerable women: A critical reflection on human rights discourse and sexual violence', *Emory International Law Review*, Vol. 23, No. 1 (2009) 113, p. 118.
43. UNHCR, 'Prevention and response to sexual and gender-based violence in refugee situations'.
44. UNHCR, 'Sexual and gender-based violence against refugees, returnees and internally displaced persons', pp. 14, 37; UNHCR, 'Handbook for the protection of women and girls', p. 201; and UNHCR, 'Sexual violence against refugees', p. 3.
45. Connell, *The Role of Men and Boys in Achieving Gender Equality*. See also A. Greig and J. Edström, 'Mobilising men in practice: Challenging sexual and gender-based violence in institutional settings – Tools, stories, lessons' (Institute of Development Studies, January 2012); M. Kaufman, 'Sexual violence in conflict and post-conflict: Engaging men and boys' (Advocacy Brief, MenEngage and United Nations Population Fund, July 2012); and Buscher, 'Masculinities'.
46. UNHCR, 'Handbook for the protection of women and girls', p. 55.
47. Ibid., p. 58; and Buscher, 'Masculinities', p. 15.
48. Connell, *The Role of Men and Boys in Achieving Gender Equality*, p. 11.
49. WRC, 'Redefining manhood, rebuilding nations', p. 15.
50. Ibid.
51. SCR 2106, preamble para. 5.
52. 'About', *Virtual Knowledge Centre to End Violence against Women and Girls*, http://www.endvawnow.org/en/about (last accessed October 2013).
53. A. Guedes, 'Men and Boys' (Knowledge Module, United Nations Development Fund for Women and Men Engage, January 2012), p. 4.
54. Ibid. (emphasis added).
55. WRC, 'Redefining manhood, rebuilding nations'.
56. Search for Common Ground Democratic Republic of Congo, 'Final report: "Vrai djo" project'.
57. Stemple, 'Male rape and human rights', p. 624.
58. My thanks and gratitude are due to Qasmiyeh for introducing me to this analytical concept.
59. UNHCR Executive Committee, *Note on Certain Aspects of Sexual Violence*, p. 5.
60. S. Sivakumaran, 'Lost in translation: UN responses to sexual violence against men and boys in situations of armed conflict', *International Review of the Red Cross*, Vol. 92, No. 877 (2010) 259, p. 267. For an alternative analysis, see Engle, 'The Grip of Sexual Violence'.
61. Rothkegel et al., 'Evaluation of UNHCR's efforts', p. 8.
62. *Report of the Secretary-General: Conflict-Related Sexual Violence*, UN Doc. A/66/657–S/2012/33 (13 January 2012).

63. By gender-inclusivity, I refer to the inclusion of males and females as possible targets of conflict-related sexual violence within the Secretary-General's definition and reporting of the phenomenon. See *Report of the Secretary-General: Conflict-Related Sexual Violence*, UN Doc. A/66/657–S/2012/33 (13 January 2012), p. 4.

64. *Report of the Secretary-General: Conflict-Related Sexual Violence*, UN Doc. A/66/657–S/2012/33 (13 January 2012), p. 4.

65. See, for example, R. Surtees, 'Trafficking of men – A trend less considered: The case of Belarus and Ukraine' (Migration Research Series No. 36, International Organization for Migration, 2008).

66. J. Gettleman, 'Symbol of unhealed Congo: Male rape victims', *The New York Times* (5 August 2009) 1.

67. E. Pirovolakis, *Reading Derrida and Ricoeur: Improbable Encounters between Deconstruction and Hermeneutics* (Albany: State University of New York Press, 2010), p. 88.

68. UNHCR, 'Sexual and gender-based violence against refugees, returnees and internally displaced persons', p. 3.

69. Ibid., p. 6 (emphasis added).

70. UNHCR, 'Sexual and gender-based violence against refugees, returnees and internally displaced persons'.

71. UNHCR, 'Prevention and response to sexual and gender-based violence in refugee situations', p. 69.

72. G.C. Spivak, 'Translator's preface', in J. Derrida, *Of Grammatology* (G.C. Spivak trans., Baltimore: Johns Hopkins University Press, 1997) ix, p. xvi [trans. of *De la grammatologie* (first published 1967)].

73. J. Derrida, *Writing and Difference* (A. Bass trans., London: Routledge & Kegan Paul, 1997), p. 69 [trans. of *L'écriture et la différence* (first published 1967)].

74. Ibid., p. 8 (emphasis in original).

75. Term borrowed from T. Shand, M. Herstad, P. Pawlak, T. Paine, J. Khanyile and S. Tall, *Good Practice Brief on Male Involvement in GBV Prevention and Response in Conflict, Post-Conflict and Humanitarian Crisis Settings in Sub-Saharan Africa* (Cape Town: Sonke Gender Justice Network, 2013), p. 19.

76. My thanks are due to Dr Fiddian-Qasmiyeh for this especially fitting term.

77. Stemple, 'Male rape and human rights', p. 646.

78. H. Durham and K. O'Byrne, 'The dialogue of difference: Gender perspectives on international humanitarian law', *International Review of the Red Cross*, Vol. 92, No. 877 (2010) 31, p. 49.

79. Otto, 'Lost in translation', p. 350.

80. Carpenter, 'Recognizing gender-based violence', p. 99.

81. See, for example, V. Oosterveld, 'Prosecution of gender-based crimes in international law', in D. Mazurana, A. Raven-Roberts and J. Parpart (eds), *Gender, Conflict, and Peacekeeping* (Lanham: Rowman & Littlefield, 2005) 67, p. 73.

82. SCR 1960, preamble paras. 2, 3, 10.

83. R.C. Carpenter, *'Innocent Women and Children': Gender Norms and the Protection of Civilians* (Aldershot: Ashgate, 2006), p. 2. See also Sivakumaran, 'UN responses to sexual violence against men and boys in situations of armed conflict', p. 270.

84. N.N.R. Quénivet, *Sexual Offenses in Armed Conflict & International Law* (Ardsley: Transnational Publishers, 2005), p. 15. See also, for example,

T. Gillespie, 'Rape crisis centres and "male rape": A face of the backlash', in M. Hester, L. Kelly and J. Radford (eds), *Women, Violence and Male Power: Feminist Activism, Research and Practice* (Buckingham: Open University Press, 1996) 148.
85. D. Lewis, 'Unrecognized victims: Sexual violence against men in conflict settings under international law', *Wisconsin International Law Journal*, Vol. 27, No. 1 (2009) 1, p. 48.
86. Ibid., pp. 48–49.
87. UNHCR, 'Sexual and gender-based violence against refugees, returnees and internally displaced persons', p. 5.
88. SCR 2106, para. 19.
89. Although principally focussed on women's participation, SCR 2122 makes no reference to men and boys and thus further affirms the female-centred focus of the WPS agenda.
90. S. Sivakumaran, 'Male/male rape and the "taint" of homosexuality', *Human Rights Quarterly*, Vol. 27, No. 4 (2005) 1274.
91. Discussions beginning to address some of these questions include, A. del Zotto and A. Jones, 'Male-on-male sexual violence in wartime: Human rights' last taboo?' (Paper presented at the Annual Convention of the International Studies Association, New Orleans, 23–27 March 2002); Sivakumaran, 'Male/male rape and the "taint" of homosexuality'; and Sivakumaran, 'UN responses to sexual violence against men and boys in situations of armed conflict'.
92. Surtees, 'Trafficking of men – A trend less considered', p. 13.
93. R. Kapur, 'The tragedy of victimization rhetoric: Resurrecting the "native" subject in international/post-colonial feminist legal politics', *Harvard Human Rights Journal*, Vol. 15 (2002) 1, p. 32, cited in Otto, 'Lost in translation', p. 356.
94. C. Enloe, *The Curious Feminist: Searching for Women in a New Age of Empire* (Berkeley: University of California Press, 2004), pp. 19–42.

11
Security Council Resolution 1325: Age and Gender in Conflict and the Future of Feminist Activism

Cara Gleeson, Sharna de Lacy, May Maloney and Fiona McAlpine

Introduction

The contributors to this collection have raised important questions about how gender relates to international law, conflict and peacekeeping. They have asked us to consider how (and why) an increased focus on women in matters of peace and security has centred on the female as 'victim' at the expense of women as 'agents'. The authors have challenged feminist scholars and activists to change the peace and conflict conversation by leveraging *Security Council Resolution 1325*[1] (SCR 1325) as a tool to re-envision peacekeeping operations;[2] to (re)engage as feminists with the 'hard' security debate;[3] to shed greater light on women's experience of conflict and peace; and to work towards the implementation of regional action plans.[4]

This chapter also highlights SCR 1325 as a tool for change and asks readers to question not only how gender relates to conflict and peacekeeping but also how age intersects with gender in this discourse. We argue that an examination of the intersection of age and gender is often absent from demographic studies of conflict, which centre on young men and are often silent about young women, and that age/gender intersectionality needs to be considered in all peace and conflict literature, and activism, if we are to address the desires and experiences of women across their life cycles. We are acutely aware that young women's life chances are also shaped by other characteristics such as race, ethnicity, socio-economic position, sexuality and disability, creating a more complex picture than we are able to draw. However, by examining the intersectionality of age and gender, with particular regard to young women and their role in peace activism, peacebuilding and the promotion of collective security, we hope to make a start. We argue that age reveals a differential experience that warrants attention, just as gender plays a significant role in power relations and experience of conflict. We want to promote greater intergenerational dialogue to begin to address the erasure of young women from demographic studies of conflict, from accounts of feminist peace activism and from among those we consider to be agents of peacemaking and peacebuilding.

Young women occupy a relatively invisible space within the women, peace and security discourse leaving a lacuna yet to be examined with rigour by feminist scholars and activists and by international institutions. While some activists and non-governmental organisations (NGOs) have started research in this area, young women themselves are often not included in the development of new policies or research priorities, and research-funding priorities remain largely centred on demographic studies of young men in conflict.

The transition from childhood to adulthood differs dramatically around the world, but everywhere it has distinct gendered dimensions. It is during this period that gender roles harden, and societal expectations and opportunities for young women and men begin to diverge. This chapter applies a 'gender lens' (which refers to differential masculine and feminine roles and experiences) in its analysis, finding that most demographic studies of 'youth' in conflict centre on the masculine experience and young male violence in particular. Those studies that do include young women centre only on their 'reproductive' role, or characterise them as merely passive victims. We seek to make visible the need for discussion of the particular and varied experiences and social contributions of young women in conflict and in peacetime.

While drawing on current literature on youth and conflict, peacebuilding and the prevention of conflict, this chapter also relies on preliminary research that the authors conducted as members of Young Women's International League for Peace and Freedom (YWILPF) Australia in 2012. The research documents the experiences of five young women connected to the researchers through their involvement in the global network of Women's International League for Peace and Freedom (WILPF) organisations. Their experiences are accompanied by the observations of the authors.[5] The young women interviewed for this research are from Colombia, Nigeria, Afghanistan (currently living in Europe), the United States (US) and Sweden. Due to the small scale of the research and limited resources, these interviews were conducted via email and/or Skype. The young women answered a set of brief open-ended questions devised by the researchers on international security, what SCR 1325 means to them and their experiences as young women activists. Originally seven young women were approached to participate, with the final five being selected through availability.

While this approach was adequate for explorative research, there were many limitations within the methodology, and the research exposed areas that require further examination. The passive nature of the research, undertaken via email, meant there was little opportunity for the participants to contribute outside the parameters of the original brief interview questions. Each participant was in isolation from the others, which did not allow for the sharing of experiences and learning that can facilitate deeper reflection and research. There was insufficient time to examine the cross-cultural and linguistic differences in definitions of security, feminism and activism. A participatory methodology, bringing together young women from around the world for longer discussions, would likely bring richer data. By giving voice to the young women interviewed, we hope to broaden the discussion on women, peace and security, and demonstrate the contributions young women are already making to this area of work.

Defining youth

According to the United Nations Development Programme (UNDP), almost half of the world's population is under the age of 25. People in this age group are clearly stakeholders in addressing many of the critical social, economic and security issues facing the world today.[6] Yet a persistent challenge confronting peace, conflict and feminist studies on youth is defining who 'youth' are. The United Nations (UN) General Assembly, in declaring 1985 to be International Youth Year, defined 'youth' as persons between 15 and 24 years of age. The UN has subsequently affirmed this definition, while recognising that the meaning of the term 'youth' varies in different societies and that definitions of youth may change over time with the circumstances of that society.[7] In Australia, the terms 'youth' and 'young people' are used interchangeably within government departments and programmes to refer to people between the ages of 12 and 25; but outside the public sector (including within YWILPF) the term may extend to those up to 30 or 35.

A problem of using age as an indicator is that age ranges continue to differ across definitions. Joy, of WILPF Nigeria, one of the newest WILPF sections, states 'ninety per cent of our members are young women between the ages of 36 and below ... this is quite impressive'.[8] In contrast, the Nigerian public health sector defines young people as being aged between 10 and 24 years, while in broader national Nigerian policies on youth they are defined as being aged 18–35 years.[9] In customary systems in Nigeria, the idea of 'youth' is likely to be very different, and may not exist at all. Clearly, the age specification for 'young' varies within and between nations.

Moving beyond the arbitrariness of definitions based on numerical age, 'youth' and 'young' are words often used to denote a transitional period in a person's life, which may be long or short, that is 'intrinsically linked with the idea of transition from childhood to adulthood'.[10] Emphasis on the notion of 'transition' as opposed to age specificity enables us to engage the meaning of 'youth' as it may apply across different settings and to the individual. While Alex de Waal convincingly argues that 'the concept of youth is a western concept and a political construct',[11] we find it useful, nevertheless, to locate the transitional period or point (from childhood to adulthood) where gender norms are more firmly instantiated. As the UNDP in its paper *Youth and Violent Conflict* elaborates:

> The transition from childhood to adulthood has a crucial gender dimension. During this stage, societal expectations and personal aspirations of young men and young women begin to diverge. Youth is often the time [or moment] when 'the world expands for boys and contracts for girls.' Girls begin to experience new restrictions and the attitudes, behaviour, conduct and, in particular, the sexuality of young women begin to be more closely watched, even 'policed'. Cultural norms dictate that females are sheltered at the stage of puberty, for reasons such as purity and marriageability, stigma and family reputation. … There seems to be a perception that youth, as a status, is more relevant for boys than for girls.[12]

While we acknowledge that there may be vast differences between western and non-western assumptions about youth, including about whether it is based on age or biological development, the intersection of gender and age provides a useful point or moment in time that marks significant gender divergence between boys and girls and entrenchment of social gender constructs. As such, our 'gender lens' must be sensitive to life stages if we are to fully understand and respond to gender discrimination as it presents and is embedded throughout a woman's life cycle.

As mentioned, the focus of the gender/youth intersection in this chapter is on young women. However this is not to detract from the importance of acknowledging and investigating other intersections, such as the experiences of women in all age stages, or on young men and boys, who also experience the entrenchment of harmful 'masculinities', and face particular barriers to participation in decision-making structures and distinct forms of discrimination in peacekeeping and peacebuilding communities. Throughout this chapter, we look at the problematic of 'youth' and the issues that arise with the absence of young women's voices in demographic studies and, thus, more broadly. We also use the term 'young women' in relation to the feminist peace activists who participated in this research, who are 36 years or younger, and who are members of WILPF.

Women, peace and security

Here, we examine SCR 1325 as a tool for young women activists. We show that although the resolution makes no explicit reference to the intersection of age and gender, young women are using it as a tool for raising awareness, for advocacy and to attempt to hold their governments to account.

Just as we know that women can experience conflict differently to men, age can present another set of variables that reveal differential experiences in conflict, peacebuilding and the prevention of conflict. SCR 1325 makes references to 'women and girls' a number of times, calling for recognition of their specific experiences, needs, rights, protection and participation in conflict prevention, resolution and recovery.[13] Subsequent women peace and security resolutions have also made reference to 'women and girls', most frequently in the context of sexual violence.[14] These references to 'girls' have generally been dealt with by linking child protection activities, and the UN *Convention on the Rights of the Child* (CRC),[15] with the women, peace and security agenda.[16] Such linkages are really only acknowledging the protection needs of girls. What they fail to take account of is the situation of young women, in that critical period of transition in the life cycle, who do not just have protection needs, but are actively engaging in life and need to be included in any agenda for change. For instance, the specific circumstances of young women are difficult to locate under the CRC or SCR 1325. Marc Sommers believes that the reason young women and men do not have an institutionalised mechanism, such as a counterpart to the CRC for youth, is due to the difficulty in defining who they are, especially across cultures and diverse circumstances.[17]

The gender mainstreaming machinery adopted by the UN High Commissioner for Refugees (UNHCR) offers a fruitful acknowledgement of the many elements that define people's experiences in its *Age, Gender and Diversity Policy*.[18] This policy – which was informed by academic efforts in Latin America to identify the differential experiences and impacts of forced displacement on individuals and communities[19] – was finalised in 2011, and offers a lens through which to look at the intersectionality of gender, age and other diversity factors. The perceived need for such a policy is evidence that gender alone is not a sufficient analysis though which to understand and respond to people's needs and experiences in the context of conflict and recovery. To gain a more thorough understanding of the social complexities and power dynamics – before, during and after conflict – requires a deeper consideration of the intersections of age and gender, as well as other factors that inform experiences, such as ethnicity, disability, family composition or sexual orientation.

Drawing from this, it is evident that young women, like other age and gender cohorts, have particular experiences of conflict and therefore bring unique perspectives and their own modes of agency to the table, especially when considering collective security. Young women are community members, and may be breadwinners, future political leaders, mothers or primary caregivers, and their contributions are vital to prospects for peacebuilding and development. Importantly, young women also represent future directions for feminism and peace activism, translating and shaping the feminist agenda for a new generation. Their participation in all parts of society is a necessary antecedent to the prevention and resolution of conflict. Yet young women are rarely consulted in peacekeeping operations, peacebuilding activities and peace negotiations. As Joy from Nigeria stated, 'you [as a young woman] hardly get access to decision makers, and you have to contend with sometimes very disheartening treatment from fellow activists'.[20] Young women are too often viewed, like 'girls', principally as 'victims' or, at best, passive recipients of assistance, who have little to say about their future or the future of their society.

Research has shown that rehabilitation strategies in post-conflict communities often fail to see young women's roles during conflict and thus target reintegration of young men. This is evident in *Bush Wives and Girl Soldiers*, where Chris Coulter collates the experiences of female combatants sourced from a year and a half of interviews in post-civil war Sierra Leone.[21] During the war, rebels would visit villages to kidnap or coerce girls and young women to join them, who would then serve with the rebel groups by working in their camps, as cooks and porters, and often at high risk of sexual violence, as well as training as fighters. Coulter explains that, although adjustment back into post-conflict village life can be a difficult task for rebels of all genders, the experiences of women were ignored, despite being able to provide valuable insights about recovery and peacebuilding.

Aisling Swaine and Thomas Feeny's research into the experiences of young women in Kosovo echoes these findings. Young women often found relief from their feelings of destitution and anger by becoming active participants in the resistance, taking up arms and joining the guerrilla camps.[22] Brigitte Sørensen argues that the social reintegration needs of those who, through the upheaval of conflict, challenged gender stereotypes are yet to be recognised by conflict recovery policy:

> The reconfiguration of gender roles and positions is an integral part of the challenge of rebuilding war-torn societies. It is important for policy makers and operational actors in national governments and aid organisations to understand the complex ways gender and rebuilding interact.[23]

Sørensen's research points to the need for a much deeper gender analysis of the impact of armed conflict, one which treats gender as a fluid category and does not confine its understanding to only male and female.

Just as feminists have argued that women should not be assumed to be vulnerable simply because of their gender, youth is not 'necessarily [a] critical determinant of vulnerability'.[24] Jo Boyden and Joanna de Berry make this point, arguing that 'even when profoundly distressed or troubled, the young frequently exercise remarkable resilience'.[25] In these accounts, young women's agency and resilience, as well as their vulnerability, are important experiences that need to be acknowledged and addressed. It is young women who are best positioned to identify the issues that they face and how they might best be addressed, and therefore they need to be actively included in peace and security discussions.

Yet, the young women in our research spoke of being ignored at first, when speaking up about security and peace in their communities, as their age and gender often defined them as having no 'legitimate' voice on such matters. When asked how SCR 1325 impacted their activism, interviewees overwhelmingly considered it to be an effective tool to leverage and legitimate participation in women's rights, peace and security advocacy. Joy noted that 'SCR 1325 means that women now have a voice and a platform to actively lobby for equitable treatment, a place at the decision-making table, and in the promotion of women's rights'.[26] For Aaquila,[27] in the context of feminist advocacy for peace in Afghanistan and Europe, SCR 1325 and the women, peace and security agenda provide 'a kind of hold, a good general tool for us as women and others to inform what we want and what our rights are'.[28]

As a tool SCR 1325, combined with its follow-up resolutions,[29] is multifaceted. On the one hand SCR 1325 was used by the young women in our case study to empower and educate themselves, and to demonstrate that the UN Security Council supports – even requires – their participation and values their contribution in post-conflict communities. Joy provided the example of 'Miss 1325 Nigeria', a project launched in April 2012, in which Miss 1325 is selected to 'be an ambassador for peace in Nigeria. She would carry the campaign to the grassroots and all over. We believe this will make the resolution more real and understandable'.[30] On the other hand, SCR 1325 has been used by young women as an advocacy tool. As Joy explains:

> SCR 1325 means that we now have a very important tool to hold our government accountable and to advocate for policies and programmes that are gender responsive. It also means that I have the right as a [young] woman to actively participate in all peace processes and that the sky is my limit as long as I am willing to fly high enough.[31]

They have effectively used SCR 1325 to advocate for institutional change and to persuade governments to increase the participation of young women in peacebuilding activities.

In non-conflict situations, SCR 1325 has been used by young activists to the same ends, as evident in YWILPF Australia's submission to the Australian Government National Action Plan on Women, Peace and Security, which called for recognition to the changing roles and needs of women across their life spans and for young women's representation on civil society advisory mechanisms.[32] Interestingly the submission and subsequent roundtables began an advocacy discourse between YWILPF and the Australian Government. Young activists, then, have identified SCR 1325 as a tool for advocacy and accountability, and young women have used the resolution as an entry card to the discussion table and to show that they should be heard in peace negotiations and peacebuilding.

Youth, conflict and peace

While the previous section focuses on seeing and including young women in the women, peace and security agenda, and in utilising its accompanying tools, particularly the SCRs, this section demonstrates the need to include young women in research and policy development about the role of youth in conflict and in peacebuilding. By understanding youth as a period of transition, during which gender roles are consolidated, we may also better understand how experience of armed conflict impacts on young people, and particularly on young women, and start to value their potential contribution to discussion and activism relating to women, peace and security. As Josefine in Sweden said, '[t]he true peacekeepers are those who build lasting peace. Not the ones that may perhaps be able to quench violence with violence'.[33]

During conflict there is often movement and fluidity in social norms. As a consequence, groups within a society, such as young people and women, may frequently find themselves in non-traditional situations. As Boyden and de Berry find:

> Social constructs like child, youth and family, and practices in child rearing and childcare come to acquire new meanings and functions. As the circumstances and contributions of children and adults, girls and boys, and men and women are altered, so are the definitions and expectations of childhood, youth, adulthood, girlhood, boyhood and other social categories.[34]

For young people, the breakdown in security comes during a stage of transition. Schools may be closed or destroyed, leaving young people without access to education at a critical period of their development. After conflict ends, there are usually limited opportunities to return to education or training, which are likely to be taken up by young men. Therefore for young women, this loss may be a permanent setback in societies that value an investment in their education only up until a certain age. Young women's lack of education can have broader repercussions for national development and for the attainment of sustainable peace. As such, while young people of all genders may be encouraged to assume active roles during conflict or during periods of escalation, they, like women, are often dismissed once informal agitation turns to 'real' business, or the conflict reaches the point of peace negotiations. This provides one reason why stories from young women remain relatively unheard and their contributions to the peaceful future of their communities are not valued.

Furthermore, too often in the context of conflict young people are limited by contradicting stereotypes of being either active security threats or passive victims.[35] The concept of youth as an active security threat is recognised widely throughout the west by reference to the 'youth bulge' theory, which was developed in the 1980s by a visiting geographer to the US Central Intelligence Agency.[36] This theory implies that an increased risk of violent conflict accompanies a high youth cohort within a society, and conceptualises the prevalence of such youth as a 'ticking time bomb'. A 'youth bulge' is said to be present where more than 30 per cent of the population is between 15 and 24 years old.[37]

Seeing a large population of young people as a social and security threat is problematic in at least three key ways. First, it overlooks the fact that demography is not in itself the cause of conflict. The causes are complex. There are many factors recognised as potentially increasing the risk of violence, including political, economic and social and cultural factors.[38] The presence of a youth bulge has, in practice, proved an insufficient predictor of conflict. Indeed, the growing evidence base derived from feminist international relations and security scholarship, overwhelmingly suggests that the best predictor of violent conflict is gender inequality.[39] As Cynthia Enloe has argued, we must adopt a 'feminist curiosity', to render the invisible lives of women visible and to seriously examine their experiences in spheres of security and international relations.[40] Enloe's work has exposed the centrality of gender to unequal power relations, militarism and conflict.

A youth bulge is a demographic characteristic that preceded conflict in some countries with recent violence – namely Rwanda, Burundi, Nigeria, Ethiopia, the Democratic Republic of the Congo, Somalia, Sudan and Nepal. However, there are a number of other countries with similar numbers of young people that have not experienced recent violence, including Malawi, Botswana, Benin, Belize and Bangladesh. Additionally, Sri Lanka, Colombia and Bosnia-Herzegovina have experienced relatively recent armed conflicts but do not have a high youth population. What such countries do have in common is a high level of structural gender inequality.[41] Thus, while youth populations may have some impact on the form and extent of armed conflict, it is an insufficient predictor. As it has been noted, there is scant attention paid to the intersectionality of age and gender in security scholarship. However, the effects of conflict on young people warrant closer investigation, particularly in regard to how they may be exploited by state actors and non-state groups for political purposes, and how this differentially affects young men and young women.

The second way that the youth bulge thesis is problematic is that it perpetuates the idea that youth are responsible for conflict, and that the nature of such responsibility is based on (male) gender. Anne Hendrixson demonstrates that the youth bulge idea has been extended to the field of 'strategic demography', which uses population character-istics such as age, ethnicity, geographic location and numbers to help locate terrorist threats.[42] Pointing to the utilisation of the youth bulge theory by western states, particularly the US, to justify their foreign policy interventions, Hendrixson notes that this use of the theory per-petuates a stereotyped notion of 'young men as explosively violent and young women as explosively fertile', ready to produce the next genera-tion of angry young men. She concludes that the theory 'disrespects the younger generation, underestimates its potential and leaves it deval-ued'.[43] Moreover, by perpetuating such gendered stereotypes, the youth bulge theory delegitimises the potential for young women and men to contribute to peace in their societies.

The third problem with the youth bulge theory is that the gendered stereotypes that it espouses are deployed in policy, programming and research on youth and conflict. This plays out in post-conflict spaces where young women, even combatants, are erased as participants in conflict precisely because this disrupts the stereotyped expectations of the theory, which is that young women are reproductive, or victims, or both. As Coulter observes, this is an additional explanation for the failure to develop programmes to reintegrate female combatants, given they do not fit the youth bulge gender dichotomy.

Young women as peace activists

Placing greater emphasis on youth participation and engagement would provide expanded potential for peacebuilding and conflict prevention. Just as women's participation was recognised as crucial to peacebuild-ing through the passing of SCR 1325, we must recognise that youth participation is inextricably linked to prospects for sustainable peace and development. Young people, including young women, whose expe-riences are absent or stereotyped in conflict discourse, must 'be recog-nized as agents of change, as potential spoilers but also as key makers and guarantors of peace'.[44] Long lasting peace rests on their engagement in and acceptance of the peace negotiation process.[45]

As elaborated in the preceding discussion, the young women inter-viewed for this research use SCR 1325 as a tool to spur other young women into political participation and to open doors to forums in which they hope to participate. Josefine, in discussing the importance of participation as an aspect of the women, peace and security agenda, pointed out that while participation was recognised by SCR 1325 due to civil society's role in its creation, the later resolutions (in particular SCRs 1820, 1888 and 1960) were developed institutionally, within the male-dominated UN system, without the same level of input from civil society, and consequently failed to recognise the importance of participation.[46] The failure of the participational aspects of SCR 1325 to take root, particularly in regard to peace negotiations and access to decision-making roles, and the failure of the follow-up resolutions that focus on sexual violence to emphasise participation, may shed light on why young women, at least in our study, have not taken the other resolutions up as a tool.

Siobhán McEvoy-Levy, in 2001, highlighted the need for the 'the powers that be' to properly integrate politically active and pro-peace youth into peace and peacebuilding processes, and provide them with ownership of the process to ensure they will hold carriage of it.[47] These processes need to be actively representative of young women or they risk perpetuating the status quo seen in peace talks to date. Additionally, attention should be paid to bringing those men and women 'on board' who are opposed to or ambivalent about the peace process, if peace is to be sustainable.[48] Ximena from Colombia has been using SCR 1325 to promote peacemaking in this way: 'I think that peacemaking is process for all of life, in which you must believe to continue, and to motivate more people to be involved'.[49]

Globally, women are still largely excluded from formal institutions that shape security policy. Felicity Ruby, in her contribution to this collection, points to the various ways in which women's civil society has successfully used SCR 1325 as an advocacy tool, but underscores a failure to use it to bring women into peace negotiations, to address substantive equality or use it as a tool for conflict prevention.[50] To counter this, Ruby argues that we need to be more creative with SCR 1325 and the women, peace and security agenda as tools to (re)engage in 'hard security' issues as women; to demand a radical rethinking of collective security; and to dismantle the systems which perpetuate and profit from war. Yet access to positions of influence in security and foreign policy institutions remains subject to a gendered 'glass ceiling'. For activists in the US, engagement with SCR 1325 has provided a platform to lobby for real participation and access to decision-making roles that attempt to shape security policy, not just internationally, but also in domestic debates, as Sydney recounts:

In the United States, the resolution has been interpreted largely in an international way. While I think that some of the issues brought up in 1325 are focused on conditions that do not concretely exist in the United States, I believe that our government could interpret the resolution differently to include domestic application of its core ideas. In particular, women's political participation could be greatly improved.[51]

There is clearly a need for increased feminist activism to gain entry to the domestic security debates, and young women's activism needs to be supported.

In Sweden, young women are seeking to support other young women to engage in peace processes, through direct involvement and lobbying for change from within domestic affairs through professional structures that young women may have gained access to, thanks to current and previous generations of women's rights activists. Josefine noted this when she said:

> I think it is easier for this generation of women (speaking from a Swedish perspective) to talk about power structure(s) without needing to hold on to the idea of women as peaceful by nature. We also bring a new kind of professionalism. Many are trained or educated on working with lobbying and other ways of influencing the political agenda.[52]

Linking this activism and lobbying to hard security debates is an area for more action.

While it should be acknowledged that advocacy and lobbying knowledge is often conveyed to young women advocates by former young women advocates, Josefine's comment shows the ongoing need to adapt and develop multiple lobbying techniques to advance the feminist agenda. However, there is a perception among many young people, at least in the west, that the battle for women's equality has been won. Sydney, for example, notes:

> In the US younger individuals consider gender equality an issue of the past, and feminism therefore a whiny, overdone, controlling movement today. A barrier that I have personally faced in activism is age discrimination from other activists. There is definitely a reluctance to allow the involvement of or give responsibility to younger individuals.[53]

Therefore, young activists must struggle to convince other young women of feminism's continued relevance, in addition to struggling to claim space for meaningful involvement among older generations of feminists.

Our interviews show that young women globally are active in peace and security debates, although they face many struggles, and despite their relative invisibility in international law, in policy, in research, in demographic studies and in some forms of activism. Increasingly, too, young women are globally connected and engaged with one another, through new information technologies, partnerships and coalitions. Young feminist activists often know each other's views and opinions and share similar objectives. However, the capacity of institutions – such as civil society, security institutions and state structures – to incorporate young women's views remains woefully inadequate.

Arguably, SCR 1325 has provided a vehicle for peace activism and a new focal point for feminist engagement among the young women who have been drawn to it as a tool. Although the text of SCR 1325 refers to 'women and girls' and neglects diversity factors, some of the feminist groups have made attempts to address the lack of young women's voices in the women, peace and security arena. The establishment of YWILPF in 2005 is one such example. Josefine explained the relevance of SCR 1325 to WILPF's work:

> It means that WILPF's agenda since 1915, a hundred years later made it all the way to the UN Security Council's agenda. It means recognition of the tireless work that is being done by women around the world, and it means a small step towards a change in how the international community aims to work.[54]

As a constituent part of the historically significant women's peace organisation WILPF, YWILPF members have been heavily involved in SCR 1325 activism, while also recognising the great efforts of feminist peace activists of preceding generations.

SCR 1325 is the result of decades of feminist peace advocacy, and holds the potential to unite the many forms of women's rights advocacy in efforts towards peace and disarmament. For the young women interviewed here, the transformational aspects of SCR 1325 include its usefulness as a way to highlight the need to include young women and girls in the conversation, and to treat them as agents of policy and post-conflict reconstruction, not solely as victims. Experiences are shaped by age as well as gender – and for this to be adequately understood and reflected in security policy, young men and women must be included as participants and partners in peace. That young women are taking up the women, peace and security agenda, and its tools, demonstrates that the women, peace and security agenda can be a site for greater cross-generational dialogue amongst women. The experiences of women peace activists – whether working in conflict or post-conflict situations; or outside these settings in an environment of peace; or in countries that are playing a role in conflicts elsewhere – are inevitably framed by a diversity of local factors. Across contexts, however, it is clear that young women share a common struggle in making their agency visible to policymakers and to other activists, as activists and decision-makers, not only as carers, underpaid labour and bearers of future generations. There is a need for us all to consider the intersection of age and gender, to ensure the participation of young women and to increase their opportunities to contribute to conflict prevention, resolution and recovery efforts.

Conclusion

This chapter has considered the experiences of young WILPF women from Nigeria, Colombia, Sweden, Afghanistan, the US and Australia, in the context of their work as activists towards creating secure and peaceful futures. Noting the limited literature and research on young women in the security context, YWILPF Australia has attempted to shine light on young women's experiences and to challenge their neglect by researchers with some preliminary research, examining what young women can contribute to collective security and peacebuilding activities. As the literature shows, 'much less scholarly attention has been awarded to the peacebuilding activities of youth than to their violence',[55] and more attention has been paid to young men rather than young women.

The experience of having their everyday lives transformed into a battlefield means that young men's and women's life trajectories change drastically. Young people, female and male, may assume any number of roles in conflict, by necessity or by choice, including as combatants and/or as peacebuilders. However youth are not a homogenous group; there is a predetermined path neither of victimhood, nor of violent or peaceful opposition. What is clear is that in order to attain sustainable peace, young people must be part of the conversation and part of the action in the processes of negotiating and building it.

On the ground, women's rights and humanitarian organisations need to incorporate age and gender analysis in their programme development and evaluation, drawing on standards such as the UNHCR's *Age, Gender and Diversity Policy*,[56] to take meaningful steps to include young women in the development of programmes targeted to young people. At an international level, the authors do not support the idea of a specific young women's SCR, not least because of the many issues associated with cross-cultural definitions of youth and the need for other intersectional considerations as well. However, it is imperative that a broader interpretation of the subjects of SCR 1325 is adopted, beyond women and girls. Civil society can take the lead by including young people in their work, particularly in peacebuilding activities. YWILPF presents one means to encourage and promote the inclusion of young people, and there are many other examples of good practice globally, such as FemLINKPACIFIC, where the intersection of age and gender is mainstreamed across the organisation's practice and in specific youth-targeted programmes.[57]

In this chapter, we have explored the silencing and erasure of young women in feminist peace activism. We have attempted to show that the intersection of age and gender is an important consideration when looking at experiences of conflict. We have focussed on young women, who are too often invisible, compared to their male counterparts, to show that, despite the barriers, young women are present and active, and they take on a diversity of social roles. However, their experiences are not visible in international law or in the security discourse or debate. Often, young women's roles are stereotyped, as demonstrated by the 'youth bulge' theory which, despite its essentialisms, influences policy, programming and funding priorities that perpetuate the exclusion of young women from reintegration programmes, from peace negotiations and from other institutions. Yet despite their exclusion, young women are remarkably active. The young women connected through the WILPF network have been using SCR 1325 as a tool for change and as a means to connect with the wider feminist movement.

Felicity Ruby urges us to think more creatively about using SCR 1325,[58] and we, the authors, hope that we have contributed to changing the conversation, and to creating an agenda for young women's inclusion that is attentive to the persistent and prevalent silences. An important aspect of this is international intergenerational solidarity amongst women peace activists that embraces the intersection of age and gender as a consideration in all of our work.

Notes

Presently, the Young Women's International League for Peace and Freedom (YWILPF) Australia is a small but passionate group of young women volunteering our time to work on issues of peace and security. We invite readers with stories or experiences to share to contact us, as YWILPF is committed to providing a space for these experiences to be heard and promoted. YWILPF is part of WILPF Australia and membership is open. If interested, please contact ywilpfaustralia@gmail.com or see http://ywilpf.wordpress.com. We would also like to thank Grace Jennings-Edquist, Dianne Otto and Gina Heathcote for their editing assistance.

1. *Security Council Resolution 1325*, UN Doc. S/RES/1325 (31 October 2000) (SCR 1325).
2. See L.J. Shepherd, 'The Road to (and from) "Recovery": A Multidisciplinary Feminist Approach to Peacekeeping and Peacebuilding', in this volume.
3. See F. Ruby, '*Security Council Resolution 1325*: A Tool for Conflict Prevention?', in this volume.
4. For the latter two points, refer to S. Bhagwan Rolls, 'Thinking Globally and Acting Locally: Linking Women, Peace and Security in the Pacific', in this volume.
5. All authors of the chapter are young Australian women who have been involved in peace activism for a number of years.
6. M. Ebata, V. Izzi, A. Lenton, E. Ngjela, E. and P. Sampson, 'Youth and violent conflict: Society and development in crisis?' (UNDP, 2006).
7. *Implementation of the World Programme of Action for Youth to the Year 2000 and Beyond: Report of the Secretary-General*, UN Doc. A/56/180 (12 July 2001).
8. Joy, WILPF Nigeria, young woman research participant.
9. United Nations Population Fund (UNFPA), 'Nigeria Adolescents population: Selected socio-demographic variables' (UNFPA Nigeria, 2006).
10. Ebata et al., 'Youth and violent conflict', pp. 17–18.
11. Ibid., p. 16.
12. Ibid., p. 17.
13. SCR 1325, paras 8(a), 8(c), 9, 10, 11, 12, 14, 16 and 17.
14. See, for example, *Security Council Resolution 1820*, UN Doc. S/RES/1820 (19 June 2008) (SCR 1820), paras 3, 4, 5, 8, 9, 10, 14 and 15.
15. *Convention on the Rights of the Child*, opened for signature on 20 November 1989, 1577 UNTS 3 (entered into force on 2 September 1990).
16 'Peacebuilding – Emerging issues: Youth, gender and the changing nature of armed conflict', *Peacebuild* (February 2008), http://www.peacebuild.ca/en/peacebuilding-resources/publications-links/peacebuilding (last accessed October 2013).
17. M. Sommers, 'Youth and conflict: A brief review of available literature' (US Agency for International Development, 2006), p. 5.
18. More information can be found at 'UNHCR age, gender and diversity policy', *UNHCR: The UN Refugee Agency* (1 June 2011), http://www.unhcr.org/4e7757449.html (last accessed October 2013).
19. See, for example, the discussion of El Enfoque Diferencial in D. Meertens, 'Género, desplazamiento, derechos', in M. Nubia Bello (ed.), *Desplazamiento*

Forzado. Dinámicas de Guerra, Exclusión y Desarraigo (Bogotà: Universidad Nacional de Colombia, 2004) 197.

20. Joy, WILPF Nigeria.
21. C. Coulter, *Bush Wives and Girl Soldiers: Women's Lives through War and Peace in Sierra Leone* (Ithaca: Cornell University Press, 2011).
22. A. Swaine and T. Feeny, 'A neglected perspective: Adolescent girls' experiences of the Kosovo conflict of 1999', in J. Boyden and J. de Berry (eds), *Children and Youth on the Frontline: Ethnography, Armed Conflict and Displacement* (New York: Berghahn Books, 2004) 63.
23. B. Sørensen, 'Women and post-conflict reconstruction: Issues and sources' (WSP Occasional Paper No. 3, United Nations Research Institute for Social Development, 1998), p. ii.
24. J. Boyden and J. de Berry, *Children and Youth on the Frontline* (New York: Berghahn Books, 2004), p. xvii.
25. Boyden and Berry, *Children and Youth on the Frontline*, p. xvii.
26. Joy, WILPF Nigeria.
27. Not her real name.
28. Aaquila, Afghanistan and Europe, young woman research participant.
29. SCR 1820; *Security Council Resolution 1888*, UN Doc. S/RES/1888 (30 September 2009); *Security Council Resolution 1889*, UN Doc. S/RES/1889 (5 October 2009); *Security Council Resolution 1960*, UN Doc. S/RES/1960 (16 December 2010); and *Security Council Resolution 2106*, UN Doc. S/RES/2106 (24 June 2013).
30. Joy, WILPF Nigeria.
31. Ibid.
32. YWILPF Australia, 'YWILPF Australia submission – Australian Draft National Action Plan on: Women, Peace and Security' (YWILPF Australia, 2011).
33. Josefine, WILPF Sweden, young woman research participant.
34. Boyden and de Berry, *Children and Youth on the Frontline*, p. xviii.
35. Sommers, 'Youth and conflict', p. 5.
36. A. Hendrixson, 'Angry young men, veiled young women: Constructing a new population threat' (Briefing No. 34, The Corner House, December 2004), p. 2.
37. Hendrixson, 'Angry young men, veiled young women', p. 2; and L. McLean Hilker and E. McAslan Fraser, 'Youth exclusion' (Social Development Direct, April 2009) annex, p. 19.
38. McLean Hilker and Fraser, 'Youth exclusion', annex, p. 12.
39. See, for example, V.M. Hudson, B. Ballif-Spanvill, M. Caprioli, C.F. Emmett and R. McDermott, 'The heart of the matter: The security of women and the security of states', *International Security*, Vol. 33, No. 3 (2008) 7; M. Caprioli, B. Ballif-Spanvill, C. Emmett, V.M. Hudson, R. McDermott and S.M. Stearmer, 'Walking a fine line: Addressing issues of gender with WomanStats' (Paper presented at the Annual International Studies Association Conference, Chicago, 27 January 2007); V.M. Hudson, 'Sex, war, and peace: Rank, and winter on rank', *Political Psychology*, Vol. 31, No. 1 (2010) 33; and M.G. Marshall and D.M. Marshall, 'Gender empowerment and the willingness of states to use force' (Occasional Paper Series No. 2, Centre for Systematic Peace, February 1999), p. 2.

40. C. Enloe, *Globalization and Militarism: Feminists Make the Link* (Lanham: Rowman & Littlefield, 2007).
41. V.M. Hudson, B. Ballif-Spanvill, M. Caprioli and C.F. Emmett, *Sex and World Peace* (New York: Columbia University Press, 2012).
42. Hendrixson, 'Angry young men, veiled young women', p. 1.
43. Ibid., p. 16.
44. 'Peacebuilding – Emerging issues: Youth, gender and the changing nature of armed conflict', *Peacebuild* (February 2008), p. 9, http://www.peacebuild.ca/en/peacebuilding-resources/publications-links/peacebuilding (last accessed October 2013).
45. S. McEvoy-Levy (ed.), *Troublemakers or Peacemakers? Youth and Post-Accord Peace Building* (Notre Dame: University of Notre Dame Press, 2006), p. 5.
46. Josefine, WILPF Sweden.
47. S. McEvoy-Levy, 'Youth as social and political agents: Issues in post-settlement peace building' (Occasional Paper No. 21, Kroc Institute for International Peace Studies, December 2001), p. 33.
48. Ibid., p. 33.
49. Ximena, WILPF Colombia, young woman research participant.
50. Ruby, *'Security Council Resolution 1325'*.
51. Sydney, United States WILPF, young woman research participant.
52. Josefine, Sweden WILPF.
53. Ibid.
54. Josefine, WILPF Sweden.
55. McEvoy-Levy, *Troublemakers or Peacemakers?*, p. 25.
56. 'UNHCR age, gender and diversity policy', *UNHCR: The UN Refugee Agency* (1 June 2011), http://www.unhcr.org/4e7757449.html (last accessed October 2013).
57. See Bhagwan Rolls, 'Thinking Globally and Acting Locally'. See also *FemLINKPACIFIC* (2007), http://www.femlinkpacific.org.fj (last accessed October 2013).
58. Ruby, *'Security Council Resolution 1325'*.

12
The Political Economy of Gender in UN Peacekeeping
Jacqui True

Introduction

In his 2010 report on women's participation in peacekeeping and peacebuilding, the United Nations (UN) Secretary-General Ban Ki-moon stated that 'ensuring women's participation in [peacekeeping] and peacebuilding is not only a matter of women and girl's rights. Women are crucial partners in shoring up the two major pillars of lasting peace: economic recovery and social cohesion, and political legitimacy'.[1] Implicit in this statement is the assumption that constructing security in formerly war-torn, conflict-affected countries involves socio-economic as well as political-military transformation. Yet in UN peacekeeping missions there is typically a major disconnect between the political-military and the socio-economic stabilisation pillars of international security. The lack of integration of these core dimensions of 'security' has had a disproportionately negative impact on women's rights in post-conflict societies. Military security, the reinstatement of political order and the rule of law are enacted without consideration of their social and economic impacts and prioritised over social and economic aspects of security. Moreover, peacekeeping missions do little to create livelihoods and economic opportunities for girls and women or enhance their survival strategies after conflict.

Addressing pre-existing gender inequalities between men and women is officially 'mainstreamed' as a key objective within the mandate of UN peace operations. Yet this objective is undermined by the political economy context, which reinforces structural gender inequalities between men and women in employment, the informal economy and participation in decision-making roles. It is further undermined, as feminist international relations scholars have made visible, by the peacekeeping sex industry, which like that on foreign military bases, involves expatriate and wealthy local men using their disproportionate economic power to purchase exploitative sexual services from women and girls.[2] A gender perspective is necessarily to illuminate the relational basis of women's oppression and inequality with men. But gender-based oppression and inequality affect men – especially marginalised, 'feminised' groups of men and boys – as well as women. In post-conflict contexts, for example, where there are usually few income-generating alternatives, international peace operations create both economic opportunity and exploitation.

In this chapter I argue that significant attention by all actors must be paid to economic as well as political empowerment in the reconstruction of post-conflict societies. This is not a prescription for 'gender mainstreaming' grafted onto security interventions that maximise the role of the market and minimise the role of the state in economic recovery. Reconceptualising peace operations through a feminist political economy framework means transforming the underlying structures of socio-economic inequality that affect women's and men's differential insecurity and vulnerability to violence and poverty after conflict. These gendered structures prevent women in particular from participating as equals with men in all aspects of peace processes. To the study of peacekeeping, the chapter contributes a feminist political economy perspective that takes into account the material as well as the cultural and normative basis of gender inequalities and of insecurity, including all forms of gender-based violence. Following Paul Higate and Marsha Henry, I conceptualise gender relations as 'characterized by negotiation, bargaining and exchange between different actors'; men and women positioned variously within constructions of masculinities and femininities 'with different[ial] access to economic and social [and political] power' that these imply.[3] Such a political economy definition and approach to lived gender relations requires that we address physical/political and economic/livelihood insecurities as part of the same framework for bringing about peace.

The first part of this chapter examines the lack of coherence between the political and economic security pillars of peacekeeping and peacebuilding, even within efforts to mainstream gender in peace operations. The second part of the chapter examines the gendered impact of this dissonance, and the socio-economic marginalisation experienced by women in post-conflict societies that constrains their equal participation with men in peace and security. A major contributing factor to women's marginalisation after conflict is their experience of gendered economic discrimination, exploitation and violence in the security sector and the economic sphere. I conclude the chapter by highlighting two approaches that have the potential to transform gendered inequalities in post-conflict settings by integrating the political and economic security pillars of peace operations.

The gap between the political and economic security pillars of peacekeeping

In effect, most UN peacebuilding missions have given primacy to re-establishing law and order (the military/political security pillar) rather than restoring women and men's livelihoods (the economic security pillar) after conflict. This failure to integrate the economic and political pillars of security is reflected in the UN Security Council Resolutions on women, peace and security, beginning with *Security Council Resolution 1325* (SCR 1325) in 2000,[4] which establish the framework for mainstreaming gender equality goals in international peacekeeping.

With SCR 1325, the Security Council recognised the urgent need to end ongoing violations of women's human rights during and after conflict. That resolution stressed 'the importance of [women's] equal participation and full involvement in all efforts for the maintenance and promotion of peace and security, and the need to increase their role in decision-making with regard to conflict prevention and resolution'.[5] SCR 1325 calls for the integration of gender across UN security policy and UN Department of Peacekeeping Operations (DPKO) operations, including the need for better representation and participation of women, gender analysis and sex-disaggregated data and research on peace operations. The DPKO is expected to promote, facilitate, support and monitor the incorporation of a gender perspective in its peacekeeping operations and country missions, which requires gender training for peacekeeping operations and gender-mainstreamed demobilisation programmes for security and military personnel.[6] Member states are expected to adopt national action plans that coordinate the promotion of SCR 1325 at all levels and across relevant policy areas, and include specific measures, clear targets and benchmarks for full implementation by 2015.[7]

In June 2008, the Security Council further reaffirmed its commitment to SCR 1325's implementation and adopted *Security Council Resolution 1820* (SCR 1820) calling for states to end the widespread and/or systematic use of sexual violence as an instrument of conflict.[8] However, in both SCR 1325 and SCR 1820 gender mainstreaming is chiefly limited to the inclusion of women's issues, such as 'women's role in peace-building', 'the protection of women' and 'women and girls affected by armed conflict'.[9] Conceptually, at least, women and girls remain passive victims protected by male soldiers, militarised states and their male representatives on the Security Council. Such victimhood denies women the agency extended by other parts of SCR 1325, perpetuating the stereotype of women as non-violent peacemakers and men as violent aggressors.

Importantly, from a feminist political economy perspective, the two resolutions are silent about the gendered socio-economic inequalities that make women more vulnerable during conflict and post-conflict situations, exclude them from participation in security decision-making, and reinforce a culture of impunity for egregious violence against women. Adopted in 2009, *Security Council Resolution 1889* (SCR 1889) for the first time mentions the need to support women's socio-economic rights in post-conflict settings[10] but, even so, provides no specific mechanisms or plan of action for realising these rights through peacekeeping and peacebuilding institutions. Most recently, the pre-amble to *Security Council Resolution 2122* (SCR 2122) recognises that 'sustainable peace requires an integrated approach based on coherence between political, security, development, human rights, including gender equality, and rule of law and justice activities' as well as 'the need to address the gaps and strengthen links between the UN peace and security in the field, human rights and development work as a means to address root causes of armed conflict and threats to the security of women and girls'.[11] These references open some belated opportunities for the integration of the socio-economic aspects of 'security' into the women, peace and security framework.

Potentially revolutionary, SCR 1325 and SCR 1820 acknowledge the role of women in peace and security, and contain mandates for ensuring women's equal participation in protection; in peace processes and post-conflict reconstruction; and in prevention of violence. Putting SCR 1325 into practice by promoting women's participation in peace processes, however, depends on efforts to change the gendered social and economic inequalities that currently constrain their participation and underlie their vulnerability in conflict and post-conflict settings. Yet to date, peacekeeping missions have done little to address the economic and social dimensions of women's empowerment, despite SCR 1889 and policy frameworks such as the United Nations Development Programme (UNDP) Eight Point Agenda for Women's Empowerment and Gender Equality in Crisis Prevention and Recovery[12] and the UN

Peacebuilding Commission's Declaration recognising women's economic empowerment contributes greatly to the stabilisation and prosperity of societies after conflict.[13]

Analysis of the allocation of donor state funding for peace operations shows a disproportionate focus on political security and humanitarian assistance, with the assumption that later assistance would focus on economic security and development.[14] Significant resources have been allocated to security sector reform; disarmament; demobilisation and reintegration in post-conflict countries; and the law and justice sector more generally, as well as some immediate humanitarian needs. At least 60 per cent of peacebuilding budgetary allocations have gone toward the salaries of military contractors serving as UN peacekeepers.[15]

In a 2010 report, the UNDP conducted a gender-specific budget analysis to reveal the gendered priorities of peacebuilding.[16] While the attention to gender equality and women's needs was low priorities in the overall peacebuilding budgets of 12 post-conflict countries, the least attention to gender issues was evident in spending on economic recovery and infrastructure, demonstrating the lack of integration and bias toward political/military security even in gender-mainstreamed programmes.

At the same time, this UNDP report reviewed economic reconstruction aid to four post-conflict countries (Timor-Leste, Sierra Leone, Kosovo and South Sudan), addressing the economic security pillar of peace operations, and found there had been only very limited resources allocated to promote gender equality or women's specific needs.[17] In the Post-Conflict Needs Assessments less than five per cent of activities and only three per cent of budget lines mentioned either gender equality or women's needs. Yet in all four post-conflict countries, critical gender gaps between women and men existed, including, for example, with respect to access to education and health, access to water for domestic consumption, to agricultural inputs and access to economic opportunities.[18] Women were also excluded from the planning of economic reconstruction in Sierra Leone, Timor-Leste, Kosovo and South Sudan. This UNDP evaluation found that none of the countries had an economic policy adviser with gender budget analysis training and skills.[19]

The challenge for the UN is to bridge the gap between the interdependent political and economic security pillars of peacekeeping in order to achieve the protection, participation and prevention goals of the SCRs on women, peace and security and create gender-equal and lasting peace. Women's capacity to access economic resources after conflict affects their access to justice and physical security. If key economic and social rights such as those to land and housing, to transact in one's own legal name, to equality in marriage, to employment opportunities and equal pay and to freedom of mobility are not secured early enough after conflict, then many women who are already poor and marginalised will be denied opportunities for both economic and political participation in peace and reconstruction.

The impact of the political and economic security gap on women

Compared with men, women experience greater negative effects and fewer benefits from the political/military model of peacebuilding intervention focussed on establishing order through formal legal and political institutions. This model's neglect of economic rights and of reparations for wartime losses of property, losses of income and injuries, including sexual and gender-based violence, severely limits women's engagement in peace processes. In particular, the absence of legal reform to recognise women's inheritance, land and property rights, and lack of funding for implementing individual or collective reparations for women survivors of war/conflict, disproportionately affects the economic livelihoods of widows, female heads of households, young women and former female combatants. For women survivors of sexual and gender-based violence, recovery, protection and prevention of future violence are 'often tied to their ability to move on and generate incomes for themselves and children'.[20] In spite of this, the direction of resources to legal justice remedies for violence, consistent with the emphasis on political security and judicial process over economic security, may inadvertently marginalise women's basic needs.

The political security approach to peacebuilding cannot and does not address the often dire economic situation after conflict that commonly brings corruption and criminality. Marginalised groups of women experience extreme income inequality, working in the informal economy and most precarious employment positions in the labour market. And they suffer from pre-conflict legacies of poor investment in gender-equal economic and social development with respect to education, health, housing, food security, water, property and land rights. In fact, post-conflict conditions tend to exacerbate women's already unequal economic and social status relative to men. The 2011 World Bank Development Report concurs that while the impact of armed conflict falls directly on young males, who are the majority of fighting forces, women and children suffer disproportionately from war's indirect effects.[21] Analysing adult mortality as a result of armed conflict, political scientists Quan Li and Ming Wen find that, over time, women's mortality attributable to war is as high as men's, due to war's lingering social and economic effects.[22] Increases in female heads of households, gender discrimination and preference for men in employment, exploitation in incipient sex industries, female displacement and resettlement in urban slums and gender bias in disarmament, demobilisation and reintegration (DDR) processes are all part of a pattern of gendered marginalisation after conflict, discussed further below. This marginalisation is compounded by the push to return to the 'normal' gender division of labour, in both the domestic and public spheres.

Increases in female-headed households

One of the impacts of the disproportionate numbers of men killed in conflict is the increase in female heads of households solely responsible for their family's survival. At the same time the women providers have often lost assets, employment and their access to education as a result of the conflict and are therefore at greater risk of poverty. They may be forced into risky income generation activities, such as exploitative sex work, with heightened vulnerability to violence, in order to feed their families. In post-genocide Rwanda, for example, the 70 per cent of households headed by females fell into poverty at greater rates than male-headed households precisely because they had lost their access to or ownership of land.[23] Land was either transferred to a son or other male relative, or sold for survival reasons.[24] Tilman Bruck and Marc Votknecht, analysing women's relative economic position before and after violent conflict, find that the interruption of schooling, especially secondary schooling, affects girls more than boys and has a long-term impact on their economic well-being.[25]

Traditional gender divisions of labour within family households persist as well. Schindler finds that in areas where there is a shortage of male partners, young, unmarried women still engage in traditional feminine activities conforming to gender stereotypes (although, interestingly, she finds less gendered allocation of labour within female-headed households).[26] And despite the near gender balance in parliamentary politics in Rwanda, the societal gender imbalance in power is manifested in the high incidence of rape of young girls and of domestic violence, with nine out of ten women reporting that their husbands had forced them to have sexual intercourse – considered rape in most countries – in the period 1998–2003 following the genocidal conflict.[27] This is not to say that there have not been some advances for some women and girls in post-genocide Rwanda. Some female small landholders and entrepreneurs have gained new-found rights to land and property and equal inheritance. Girls have also shot ahead in the education system, where previously over 40 per cent of women were illiterate.[28] The experience in Rwanda demonstrates that there are important opportunities for improving the political, economic and social status of citizens, and women citizens particularly, during the rebuilding of societies after crises.

Gender discrimination in post-conflict employment

Another contributor to women's economic and social marginalisation after conflict is the gender discrimination they experience in post-conflict employment. Women's participation in the labour market often increases for survival reasons after conflict. This is termed the 'added worker effect' by economists to explain the increases in the labour supply of married women when their husbands are killed in conflict (or become unemployed) – based on the historical, but disputable, assumption that married women's employment is always secondary to their partner's.[29] But women face discrimination in seeking formal employment because of the preference for male employees and the focus on reintegration of male combatants, as well as women's typically lower levels of skill and education than men in conflict-affected countries. Women's self-employment and informal sector business activities, such as prostitution and market trade, also increase after conflict, possibly in response to the lack of other employment opportunities. These precarious forms of work heighten their economic and physical insecurity.

In the early phases of state-building, it is common to create mass employment opportunities for men, such as road-building and housing construction, which typically offer quick employment to large numbers of men. Few women have held decision-making positions in reconstruction or state-building agencies in post-conflict countries. Despite a UN directive in Timor-Leste that women should be 30 per cent of all national and district hiring within every classification/level of employment, this commitment was not realised.[30] Women were likewise excluded from the planning of economic reconstruction in Sierra Leone, Timor-Leste, Kosovo and South Sudan.[31] Not surprisingly, since few women have been involved in decisions about economic reconstruction, mass employment opportunities for women that are culturally acceptable have typically not been planned or implemented. For instance, in the first years of the Afghan reconstruction, external actors had a limited vision of women's economic activity, such as in the form of sewing projects.[32] Yet where economic programmes are initiated, equitable inclusion of women and men is essential. Consultation with women prior to job allocation can help determine areas of cultural sensitivity. Sanam Naraghi Anderlini explains that, in Afghanistan, women would be ostracised if they engage in road-building, but in Kenya it is acceptable.[33] In Nepal, women have been traditionally involved in heavy construction work, so they should have equal opportunity to access construction jobs.[34] Moreover, in many settings men and women grow different crops or have different responsibilities regarding animal husbandry. Without knowledge of these local practices, or with assumptions based on pre-conflict times, humanitarian and development interventions may be ineffective. They can accentuate existing social and economic gender inequalities and in so doing, heighten women's vulnerability to insecurity and violence.

Exploitative peacekeeping sex industry

Peacekeeping economies are constructed on the basis of gendered divisions of labour, and women and girls are disproportionately employed in the service, sex and entertainment industries, attending to the demands of male expatriates, local elites and criminals with economic power. Within these sectors, the cases of Kosovo and Bosnia show that positions of power, ownership and influence, especially in those industries controlled by organised crime, tend to be occupied by men, with women's participation concentrated in the middle or lowest levels.[35] Although perceived as only temporary, peacekeeping sex industries typically outlast the formal post-peacekeeping mission, shaping gendered economic and social power relations in the long term.

In Bosnia and Herzegovina and Kosovo the infrastructure developed for prostitution during the peacekeeping period has endured, as has the demand created by the large international presence and organised crime involvement in illegal trafficking.[36] People become used to earning money through jobs created by the sex industry. Ten years after the Bosnian conflict, government trafficking data shows that women continue to be both imported and exported, albeit with the number of foreign women decreasing and the number of Bosnian victims increasing significantly.[37] These numbers reflect the economic desperation and lack of alternative economic opportunities that many women face. The UN response has been to enforce a zero tolerance policy on sexual relationships between peacekeepers and locals, and a code of conduct for peacekeepers that treats sexual misconduct as an exceptional occurrence, rather than a political economy based on unequal gendered social relations.[38] This policy approach deals with the issue of sexual exploitation and abuse on 'an individual level, with application and sanctions restricted to UN personnel'.[39] Administrative rules and regulations, however, cannot eliminate the economic incentives for sex work and for the culture of violence against women.

Disproportionate female displacement

As well as experiencing poverty, employment discrimination and exploitation, women are more likely than men to be displaced after conflict. Displaced households are often forced to migrate to urban or border areas, and among them, female-headed households are disproportionately represented. These households lose significant assets, as well as access to social networks, which contribute to their poverty and thus vulnerability to violence.[40] They may end up living in squatter settlements or slums where access to resources such as water, sanitation, firewood and food is minimal. Typically, the responsibility for procuring these basic needs is relegated to women and girls. Having to travel in unfamiliar territory beyond the confines of their community, they are especially vulnerable to sexual violence, including gang rape. These experiences have been documented in the case of approximately 25,000 people displaced by conflict and ethnic violence between Malaitan and Guadalcanese groups in the Solomon Islands from 1998 to 2003, who now live in slums near Honiara, the capital. In those slums there is no access to adequate sanitation, a reliable water supply or safety. Solomon Islands women bear the burden of collecting water for their families. As many as two-thirds of women and girls have encountered gender-based and sexual violence (including gang rape) while travelling to fetch water or use latrines.[41]

Gender bias in DDR programmes

Although the violence experienced by internally displaced people is particularly rife, female combatants who stay in their home villages after war frequently experience social and economic marginalisation due to pervasive gender bias in DDR programmes that target the needs of male combatants.[42] Scholars of gender and post-conflict studies argue that the return to normalcy after armed conflict limits the potential for women's economic and political empowerment. As in previous experiences of the aftermath of war and revolution, contemporary conflict-affected societies expect that women will revert to traditional domestic roles subordinate to men.[43] Male combatants who return to civilian life frequently express a sense of entitlement to being the breadwinners, employees, managers and property owners. However, women combatants – often economically driven to join armed groups in the first place – suffer not only gender-based violence but also economic marginalisation after conflict.[44]

Soldiers who are no longer able to wield small arms in public may use them as an expression of their power in the domestic realm in acts of violence against intimate partners or other family members.[45] The public reintegration of soldiers into peacetime civilian life often does not help with their adjustment to private family relationships destabilised by war. For example, during the war in South Sudan, daughters became economic bargaining chips, increasing forced and early marriage, as well as rape within marriage and domestic violence.[46] Childbearing was also considered a patriotic obligation for women in the struggle for self-determination. These gendered experiences and pervasive gender-based violence have resulted in many men having a sense of entitlement to sexual services, both inside and outside marriage, after the end of conflict.

The gender bias and discrimination in post-conflict societies explored above show how the failure to address social and economic rights has particularly detrimental impacts on women's security. The tension between the military/political and economic security pillars of peace operations needs to be resolved in more integrated frameworks for action, post-conflict financing and needs assessments, as well as more effective gender mainstreaming programmes on the ground. The focus of SCR 2122 on facilitating women's full participation and protection within 'wider post-conflict reconstruction processes where these are mandated tasks within the mission' acknowledges the need for greater integration, and must be welcomed.[47] Conceiving political stability and socio-economic development as separate may advance the security and rights of some groups, but it cannot advance women's security and rights, given the disproportionate poverty and discrimination they experience, especially in post-conflict settings.

Mainstreaming gender and integrating political and economic security in peace operations

International actors – the UN and donor states, as well as the World Bank, International Monetary Fund and the regional development banks – are responsible for helping to bring economic as well as political stability to conflict-affected countries. These actors must support the realisation of fundamental economic and social rights for women and men as a precursor to their full participation and successful forging of gender-inclusive peace. Two examples illustrate how gendered inequalities in post-conflict settings can be transformed by integrating political and economic security within approaches to peacebuilding – putting women in charge of security and recognising gendered harms in reparations programmes.

Putting women in charge of security

One approach to altering endemic cultures of violence and gendered divisions of labour in peacekeeping economies simultaneously is to recruit and train women for decision-making positions across public and private sectors, but crucially in senior positions relating to the protection and physical security of citizens. From a political economy perspective, the singular focus on law and justice, and instituting liberal democratic institutions, typically overlooks the unequal power relations in the economy and society that fuel gendered violence to start with. Yet reforming the security sector by putting women in charge can begin to unsettle some of those power relations by increasing the employment opportunities open to women and publically sanctioning their equal social status. Liberia is considered 'good practice' by the UN because women without arms played a major role in negotiating the peace between warring parties and have subsequently, under the leadership of Africa's only woman president, Ellen Johnson Sirleaf, hosted the first UN female peacekeeping police unit from India in 2007 and, until recently, the only woman UN envoy, the UN Mission in Liberia Special Representative to the Secretary-General Ellen Margrethe Løj.[48] Women stood up – Christians and Muslims together – to confront warlords and government forces terrorising Liberians, and as a result they brought down a dictator after a 14-year struggle.[49] Following an impasse in six-week-long peace talks in 2003, and violence perpetrated against civilians by all parties, women activists involved in the Women's Mass Action for Peace barricaded negotiating teams in the meeting rooms, demanding a complete solution within two weeks. They also demanded that no warlords be included in the transitional government. Their actions broke the deadlock and agreement was reached within the two weeks.[50]

Since then, Liberian women have begun to assume formal positions in the security sector for protecting human rights. This change is starting to have an impact on the social and economic empowerment of all women across Liberian society.[51] For example, the presence of the all-female (Indian) police unit, now replaced by a Ghanaian unit seconded from the African Union, inspired Liberian women to join the local police force, with the number of women officers in Liberia's own police force rising to 15 per cent.[52] There is increased reporting of gender-based violence because women who were targeted in the civil war, or suffered abuse in fighting forces, are more comfortable reporting these crimes to women. Girls' enrolment in school has also increased, and observers have noted that girls have been inspired by the female faces they see in the police and security sector and see greater future employment opportunities available to them.[53] Moreover, there have been decreases in the rate of sexual abuse and exploitation. Yet Liberia still needs to attend to integrating women and girl fighters into national programmes for disarmament, demobilisation, reinsertion and reintegration.[54] Female former combatants can be marginalised, rejected from new security structures, and forced into sexually exploitative income generation work where the risk of ongoing violence is great. Yet these women often have useful skills to bring to peacebuilding and a commitment to the betterment of their communities.

Even while the outcomes are gradual in Liberia, they are altering the local political economy by redressing the socio-economic power imbalance between women and men. If the UN expects to see a significant change in gendered peacekeeping economies, including decreases in the cases of HIV/AIDS; in the number of brothels around peacekeeping bases; and in the number of babies fathered and abandoned by peacekeepers after their mission comes to an end, then putting women in charge of the security sector is essential.

Reparations for gender-equal development

A second approach to mainstreaming gender socio-economic equality in peace operations is to design reparations programmes for gendered harms in order to develop the economic and political capacities and livelihoods of women and girls. By conceptualising reparations for gross violence and mass violations of human rights in a development framework, and not merely as a legal justice approach to righting previous wrongs to individuals or restoring the pre-harm situation, we can potentially affect the gendered inequalities in access to resources and status that create women's post-conflict marginalisation. Such an approach is suggested by SCR 2122 when it recalls the relevance of 'provisions of international law on the right to reparations for violations of individual rights'.[55] Ruth Rubio-Marin shows how, in their modest contribution to democracy-building, reparations help to either reinforce or subvert some of the pre-existing structural gender inequalities that are commonly built into the social tissue of civil society resulting in women's systematic discrimination.[56]

Focussing on reparations shifts our attention away from the overwhelming attention given to criminal justice and what to do with the perpetrators, toward the victims of violence and how to assist them to reclaim their lives and potentialities.[57] Shifting the focus from individual to collective reparations also helps us to address violent social structures and thus the prevention of future violence. And finally, designing reparations programmes that address community development in a future-oriented way is a crucial strategy for addressing the unequal gender dimensions of recovery and peacebuilding, especially given women's increased socio-economic activities at the community level after conflict, when many have become the sole breadwinners for their families.

In Timor-Leste, where 40 per cent of the population lives in poverty, the Truth and Reconciliation Commission (known by its Portuguese acronym CAVR) framed reparations and its recommendations in broad recovery terms with key measures for women.[58] Recognising that many victims, especially of sexual violence, will not come forward publicly, CAVR defined beneficiaries as not only those who appeared before it at the time, but also those identified over a two-year period following the commission's end. About 25 per cent of those who made statements to the commission were women. This is significantly more than can have been expected to speak up had CAVR not quite so consciously created a gender-sensitive space. To prevent gender bias, CAVR also instituted a quota system for reparations, ensuring that 30 per cent of the total compensation was set aside for women victims, widows, children and other family members harmed by the death or torture of their husbands, fathers and brothers, taking into account both primary and secondary harms.[59] Social services, material support and economic empowerment through livelihood activities, group counselling and community education, were all conceived as reparations programmes. Though they have largely failed to be implemented, women-friendly recommendations that emerged from the CAVR process included support to single mothers and victims of sexual violence and scholarships for their children; support for the disabled, widows and torture victims; and support to the most affected communities. Specific measures were suggested to encourage women's participation. For example, scholarship fund programmes were tied to provision of services to women, so that in coming forward for their children, the women would benefit, too. Public education programmes addressing attitudes to violence and to women were recommended alongside victim counselling services and other measures.[60]

Securing women's land and property rights must be a major focus of post-conflict peacebuilding and could be addressed through collective reparations. Among other things, there is evidence that women's enjoyment of stronger socio-economic rights is a major deterrent to violence against women, levelling the playing field with men, allowing women to protect and depend upon themselves.[61]

Conclusion

The current disconnect between the political and economic aspects of security has serious, long-term consequences for women's rights, for gender mainstreaming in peace operations and for the prevention of conflict. Women's capacity to participate in peacebuilding is closely linked to their enjoyment of economic security and rights. Poverty – as well as unequal gender norms, impunity for and fear of violence – prevents women from participating in post-conflict decision-making and constrains their contributions to the long-term recovery of their society. Only by attending to economic and social rights within peace missions, integrated with efforts to build political and military order, will the foundations for gender-equal, sustainable peace be laid.

Notes

1. *Report of the Secretary-General: Women's Participation in Peacebuilding*, UN Doc. A/65/354–S/2010/466 (7 September 2010), para. 7.
2. S. Whitworth, *Men, Militarism and UN Peacekeeping: A Gendered Analysis* (Boulder: Lynne Rienner, 2004); and C. Enloe, *Bananas, Beaches and Bases: Making Feminist Sense of International Politics* (London: Pandora, 1989).
3. P. Higate and M. Henry, 'Engendering (in)security in peace support operations', *Security Dialogue*, Vol. 35, No. 4 (2004) 481, p. 482.
4. *Security Council Resolution 1325*, UN Doc. S/RES/1325 (31 October 2000) (SCR 1325).
5. Ibid., preamble.
6. See, for example, *System-Wide Action Plan for the Implementation of Security Council Resolution 1325 (2000)*, UN Doc. S/2005/636 (10 October 2005) annex, p. 18. See also '2008–2009 UN System-wide action plan for the implementation of Resolution 1325 (2000) on women, peace and security: DPKO', *Inter-Agency Network on Women and Gender Equality*, http://www.un.org/womenwatch/ianwge/taskforces/wps/implementation_review_20082009.html (last accessed October 2013).
7. See, for example, the following statements by the President of the Security Council: UN Doc. S/PRST/2007/5 (7 March 2007), p. 2; UN

Doc. S/PRST/2007/40 (24 October 2007), p. 2; and UN Doc. UN Doc. S/PRST/2010/22 (26 October 2010), p. 2. See also N. Zakharova, 'Women and peace and security: Guidelines for national implementation' (UN Women, 2012).

8. *Security Council Resolution 1820*, UN Doc. S/RES/1820 (19 June 2008) (SCR 1820).

9. SCR 1325, preamble; and SCR 1820, preamble.

10. *Security Council Resolution 1889*, UN Doc. S/RES/1889 (5 October 2009) (SCR 1889), para. 10.

11. *Security Council Resolution 2122*, UN Doc. S/RES/2122 (18 October 2013) (SCR 2122), preamble paras 11 and 14 respectively.

12. United Nations Development Programme (UNDP), 'Eight point agenda for women's empowerment and gender equality in crisis prevention and recovery' (UNDP, 2010).

13. United Nations Peacebuilding Commission, 'Declaration of the High-level Ministerial Event on Women's economic empowerment for peacebuilding', UN Doc. PBC/7/OC/3 (26 September 2013).

14. UNDP, 'The price of peace: Financing for gender equality in post-conflict reconstruction' (Synthesis Report, UNDP, October 2010).

15. Ibid.

16. Ibid.

17. Ibid.

18. Ibid., p. 35.

19. Ibid.

20. S.N. Anderlini, 'WDR gender background paper' (World Bank, February 2010), p. xiv; 'DRC: Sexual violence prevention and re-integration funding "falls through cracks"', *IRIN Humanitarian News and Analysis* (4 November 2009), http://www.irinnews.org/Report/86865/DRC-Sexual-violence-prevention-and-re-integration-funding-falls-through-cracks (last accessed October 2013).

21. World Bank, 'World development report 2011: Conflict and development' (World Bank, 2011).

22. Q. Li and M. Wen, 'The immediate and lingering effects of armed conflict on adult mortality: A time-series cross-national analysis', *Journal of Peace Research*, Vol. 42, No. 4 (2005) 471. For example, the risk of death and disability from infectious diseases rises sharply in conflict-affected countries, and women and children are the majority of long-term victims: H.A. Ghobarah, P. Huth and B. Russett, 'Civil wars kill and maim people – Long after the shooting stops', *American Political Science Review*, Vol. 97, No. 2 (2003) 189.

23. H. Rombouts, 'Women and reparations in Rwanda: A long path to travel', in R. Rubio-Marin (ed.), *What Happened to the Women? Gender and Reparations for Human Rights Violations* (New York: Social Science Research Council, 2006) 194, p. 205.

24. See P. Justino and P. Verwimp, 'Poverty dynamics, violent conflict, and convergence in Rwanda', *Review of Income and Wealth*, Vol. 59, No. 1 (2013) 66, based on panel data on Rwanda following the same households before and after conflict. Similar results have been found for Mozambique: T. Brück and K. Schindler, 'Smallholder land access in post-war Northern Mozambique', *World Development*, Vol. 37, No. 8 (2009) 1379; and T. Bundervoet,

'Estimating poverty in Burundi' (HiCN Working Paper No. 20, University of Sussex, October 2006).

25. T. Brück and M. Vothknecht, 'Impact of violent conflicts on women's economic opportunities', in K. Kuehnast, C. de Jonge Outdraat and H. Hernes (eds), *Women and War: Power and Protection in the 21st Century* (Washington DC: United States Institute of Peace Press, 2011) 85, pp. 107–108.

26. K. Schindler, 'Who does what in a household after genocide? Evidence from Rwanda' (HiCN Working Paper No. 90, University of Sussex, December 2010).

27. International Committee of the Red Cross, *Report on Violence against Women from 1998–2003* (Kigali: Ministry of Gender and Family Promotion, 2004). Heidy Rombouts stresses that 'the weak structural position of women in society has had an impact on the degree and forms of violence women experience, such as sexual violence, both in times of peace and war': Rombouts, 'Women and reparations in Rwanda', p. 205. Moreover, she argues that violence has been used as a tool to oppose women's emancipation in postgenocide Rwandan society.

28. Rombouts, 'Women and reparations in Rwanda'; and S. Boseley, 'Rwanda: A revolution in rights for women', *The Guardian* (29 May 2010), http://www.theguardian.com/world/2010/may/28/womens-rights-rwanda (last accessed October 2013).

29. See N. Menon and Y. van der Meulen Rodgers, 'War and women's work: Evidence from the conflicts in Nepal' (HiCN Working Paper No. 104, University of Sussex, October 2011).

30. H. Charlesworth, 'Worlding women in international law', in B. D'Costa and K. Lee-Koo (eds), *Gender and Global Politics in the Asia-Pacific* (New York: Palgrave, 2009) 19, pp. 23–24.

31. UNDP, 'The price of peace'.

32. C. Bernard, K. Corde, S.G. Jones, O. Oliker, B.K. Stearns and C.Q. Thurston, *Women and Nation-Building* (Santa Monica: RAND Corporation, 2008).

33. Anderlini, 'WDR gender background paper'.

34. Ibid.

35. K.M. Jennings and V. Nikolić-Ristanović, 'UN peacekeeping economies and local sex industries: Connections and implications' (MICROCON Research Working Paper No. 176, Institute of Development Studies, University of Sussex, September 2009); and 'Human trafficking FAQs: Who are the victims and culprits of human trafficking?', *United Nations Office on Drugs and Crime* (2013), http://www.unodc.org/unodc/en/human-trafficking/faqs.html (last accessed October 2013).

36. M. Hajdinjak, 'Smuggling in Southeast Europe: The Yugoslav Wars and the development of regional criminal networks in the Balkans' (CSD Report No. 10, Center for the Study of Democracy, 2002); D. Pallen, 'Sexual slavery in Bosnia: An externality of the market', *Swords and Ploughshares*, Vol. 13, No. 1 (2003) 27; and M. Pugh, 'Peacekeeping and critical theory', *International Peacekeeping*, Vol. 11, No. 1 (2004) 39.

37. Jennings and Nikolić-Ristanović, 'UN peacekeeping economies'.

38. See O. Simić, 'Does the presence of women really matter? Towards combating male sexual violence in peacekeeping operations', *International Peacekeeping*, Vol. 17, No. 2 (2012) 188; D. Otto, 'Making sense of zero

tolerance policies in peacekeeping sexual economies', in V.E. Munro and C.F. Stychin (eds), *Sexuality and the Law: Feminist Engagements* (Abingdon: Routledge-Cavendish, 2007) 259.

39. Jennings and Nikolić-Ristanović, 'UN peacekeeping economies', p. 20.
40. See A.M. Ibáñez and A. Moya, 'The impact of intra-state conflict on economic welfare and consumption smoothing: Empirical evidence for the displaced population in Colombia' (HiCN Working Paper No. 23, Institute of Development Studies, University of Sussex, 2006).
41. Amnesty International, '"Where is the dignity in that?" Women in Solomon Islands slums denied sanitation and safety' (Amnesty International, September 2011).
42. M.H. Mackenzie, *Female Soldiers in Sierra Leone: Sex, Security, and Post-Conflict Development* (New York: New York University Press, 2012).
43. L. Handrahan, 'Conflict, gender, ethnicity and post-conflict reconstruction', *Security Dialogue*, Vol. 35, No. 4 (2004) 429; D. Pankhurst, 'The gendered impact of peace', in M. Pugh, N. Cooper and M. Turner (eds), *Whose Peace? Critical Perspectives on the Political Economy of Peacebuilding* (Basingstoke: Palgrave, 2008) 30; and M. Turshen, 'The political economy of violence against women during armed conflict in Uganda', *Social Research*, Vol. 67, No. 3 (2000) 803.
44. J. Annan, C. Blattman, K. Carlson and D. Mazurana, 'Civil war, reintegration, and gender in Northern Uganda', *Journal of Conflict Resolution*, Vol. 55, No. 6 (2011) 877. Annan et al. analyse the gender differences in the post-conflict impacts of war and reintegration on Lord's Resistance Army soldiers in Uganda with a quantitative dataset building on earlier qualitative studies. During conflict they found that 'unlike males … females have few civilian opportunities and so they see little adverse economic impact of recruitment' into the armed group (p. 877). Negative economic effects persist in the post-conflict period for soldiers, especially where opportunities for schooling and work experience have been lost. Males returning from the Lord's Resistance Army were well behind their peers. But this is not the case for most females, however, who appear to have had few economic opportunities prior to and during the conflict if they were not abducted. See also D. Mazurana and K. Carlson, 'War slavery: The role of children and youth in fighting forces in sustaining armed conflicts and war economies in Africa', in D. Žarkov (ed.), *Gender, Violent Conflict, and Development* (New Delhi: Zubaan Books, 2008) 205.
45. See V. Farr, H. Myrttinen and A. Schnabel (eds), *Sexed Pistols: The Gendered Impacts of Small Arms and Light Weapons* (New York: United Nations University Press, 2009); and C. Cockburn, *Antimilitarism: Politics and Gender Dynamics of Peace Movements* (Basingstoke: Palgrave Macmillan, 2012).
46. UNDP, The price of peace', p. 27.
47. SCR 2122, para. 4.
48. N. Popovic, 'Women, peace and security in Liberia: Supporting the implementation of Resolution 1325 in Liberia' (Background Paper, UN-INSTRAW, March 2009), p. 10. A second woman UN envoy, Ameenah Haq, has since 2010 been appointed to oversee UN operations in Timor-Leste.
49. D. Aker and J. Freeman, 'For real global security, put women in their place – At the negotiating table', *The Christian Science Monitor* (3 December

2010), http://www.csmonitor.com/Commentary/Opinion/2010/1203/For-real-global-security-put-women-in-their-place-at-the-negotiating-table (last accessed October 2013).

50. See the 2008 film *Pray the Devil Back to Hell*, http://www.praythedevilbackto-hell.com (last accessed October 2013).

51. See, for example, K. Cordell, 'Gender mainstreaming in peacekeeping operations – Liberia 2003–2009: Best practices report' (UNMIL, September 2010); and S. Willett, 'Introduction: Security Council Resolution 1325: Assessing the impact on women, peace and security', *International Peacekeeping*, Vol. 17, No. 2 (2010) 142.

52. Women make up just nine per cent of the 14,000 police officers and two per cent of the 85,000 military personnel in UN peace operations. The UN has set the goal of 20 per cent female participation in police/military personnel operations by 2014: see UN Department of Public Information, 'United Nations in global effort to increase number of female police in peacekeeping operations' (Press release No. PKO/218, WOM/1751, United Nations, 7 August 2009).

53. Cordell, 'Gender mainstreaming in peacekeeping operations', p. 43. At the end of the civil war, women's employment in the government sector was very low, representing 0.8 per cent in the judiciary, 5.3 per cent in bureaus and agencies and 10.3 per cent in ministries: World Bank, African Development Bank and International Finance Corporation, 'Joint country assistance strategy for the Republic of Liberia for the period FY09–FY11' (Report No 47928-LR, World Bank, 2009), para. 57. See also T. Ford and S. Morris, 'India's female peacekeepers inspire Liberian girls', *Visionews. net* (October 2010), http://www.visionews.net/india´s-female-peacekeepers-inspire-liberian-girls (last accessed October 2013). For an alternative view, see O. Simić, 'Increasing Women's Presence in Peacekeeping Operations: The Rationales and Realities of "Gender Balance"', this volume.

54. Annan et al., 'Civil war, reintegration, and gender in Northern Uganda'; S. McKay and D. Mazurana, 'Where are the girls? Girls fighting forces in Northern Uganda, Sierra Leone and Mozambique: Their lives during and after war' (International Centre for Human Rights and Democratic Development, 2004); and Multi-Country Demobilization and Reintegration Program and United Nations Development Fund for Women, 'Workshop report: Taking a gender perspective to strengthen the multi-country demo-bilization and reintegration program (MDRP) in the Great Lakes Region' (Kigali, Rwanda, 31 October – 2 November 2005).

55. SCR 2122, para. 13.

56. R. Rubio-Marin, 'The gender of reparations: Setting the agenda', in R. Rubio-Marin (ed.), *What Happened to the Women?* 20, p. 25.

57. Ibid., pp. 23–24.

58. Comissão de Acolhimento, Verdade e Reconciliação (Commission for Truth, Reception and Reconciliation), 'Chega! The report of the Commission for Reception, Truth and Reconciliation in Timor-Leste' (CAVR, 2005).

59. Potential gender inequalities in reparations programmes could readily be institutionalised if, for instance, the programmes considered land owner-ship, the number of dependents (that is, head-of-household status) and the loss of opportunity and income in ascertaining compensation given

the gender discrimination in these rights and status prior to conflict: see R. Rubio-Marin (ed.), *What Happened to the Women?*.

60. G. Wandita, K. Campbell-Nelson and M.L. Pereira, 'Learning to engender reparations in Timor-Leste: Reaching out to female victims', in R. Rubio-Marin (ed.), *What Happened to the Women?* 284.

61. See B. Agarwal and P. Pradeep, 'Toward freedom from domestic violence', *Journal of Human Development*, Vol. 8, No. 3 (2007) 359, pp. 359–379; and J. True, *The Political Economy of Violence against Women* (New York: Oxford University Press, 2012).

Part V
Conclusions

13
Concluding Remarks: Establishing Common Ground between Feminism and the Military

Judith Gardam and Dale Stephens

Introduction

The symposium on which this collection of chapters is based brought together feminist scholars and activists with representatives of the military of both sexes. It seemed fitting in this concluding chapter to focus on achieving a productive exchange of ideas between these two seemingly disparate sets of viewpoints. Consequently, what follows primarily reflects a conversation between feminism and the military. It inevitably has somewhat of an international humanitarian law focus as both of the authors, one a feminist academic lawyer and the other a former naval legal officer and now an academic, specialise in this particular field.

This approach has not allowed us to do justice to the rich and diverse voices of the symposium and we have not attempted to do so. What we have tried to achieve in our selective treatment is to frame our remarks to be in keeping with the four themes that emerged from the symposium and are reflected in the collection – namely 'shame', 'hope', 'danger' and 'silences' – but not necessarily from the same perspective as the other contributors.

The key to any successful dialogue is to locate common ground and that has been our aim in our choice of themes. For example, both the feminist and the soldier have a stake in the topic of sexual violence against women (and men) in times of armed conflict and share the difficulty in arriving at a consensus in their ranks as to how to confront the issue. Similarly, both sides to the debate are concerned with the casualties of armed conflict, although as we will see for different reasons and not necessarily with the same outcome in mind.

265

Many of the other contributors to this work may well share the view of Ann Scales that militarism and the military are in 'fundamental symbiosis with gender oppression', a view that does not immediately conjure up a productive dialogue.[1] Any debate about peacebuilding, collective security, gender and *Security Council Resolution 1325* (SCR 1325),[2] however, necessarily involves the military and paramilitaries who are essential components of this nexus. Consequently, despite the potential hazards of such an engagement, establishing a better understanding between these two traditional antagonists may prove fruitful. A feminist dialogue with the military also serves as a case study of the complexities of such interchanges where the stakes can be literally a matter of life and death for those involved.

The structure of our chapter is, first, to identify and comment from our respective perspectives on some crosscutting themes of the symposium. The majority of the themes identified are not in themselves new concerns, but fresh light was shone on their detail. The symposium also showcased some new voices entering the debate, in particular the 'silence' about sexual violence against men in times of armed unrest. These ideas provide an opportunity for self-reflection, one of the core strengths of feminism but also a potential site for the stagnation of debate. We provide a few thoughts on the need to be inclusive, and to ensure that a particular theme contributes to achieving transformative outcomes for women and does not serve as a 'dangerous' distraction.

Second, we turn the focus of our exchange of ideas to two recent United States (US) military initiatives. We describe the new approach to counterinsurgency (COIN) warfare as exemplified in the *Counterinsurgency Field Manual* (COIN Manual) of the US Army and Marine Corps.[3] This approach, centred on securing civilians, underpinned coalition efforts in both Iraq and Afghanistan[4] and our particular interest is the balance between civilian casualties and force protection explicit in COIN and the philosophy that underpins it. We then turn to the combatant. As part of their gender mainstreaming action plan in response to SCR 1325, North Atlantic Treaty Organization (NATO) forces in Afghanistan have been including Female Engagement Teams (FETs) in their operations, comprised of women soldiers. The use of FETs must surely attract the attention of feminists and soldiers alike, whether favourably or otherwise, and we reflect a little on the possibilities inherent in this initiative. We see both these developments as reflecting the collection theme of 'hope' in the sense that the powerful imperative of force protection, prioritised over civilian protection, that plays out in targeting and operational decisions may be loosened somewhat, and that perhaps the use of FETs might make a difference for women on the ground.

Crosscutting themes: something old and something new

As is the case with many international feminist get-togethers there was a notable underlying tension in the symposium presentations between the search for ideological coherence from within the academy and the rather world-weary call from those who deal with the reality for women in the field, to just get on with the task in hand without being so precious about the implications of what we do. Also lurking not so quietly behind all the discussions was the influence of so-called 'governance feminism' out of the US that sees some feminists now wielding unprecedented levels of power in international institutions.[5] This view, however, fails to resonate with others who regard this way of thinking as a dangerous diversion from attempts to break down systemic power.

Part of the ennui activists' experience stems from what some may see as the paralysing impact of one of the symposium themes. A major preoccupation in recent feminist international law scholarship is how the international efforts of the last decade or so to confront sexual violence against women in times of armed conflict, and in its aftermath, are based on protective stereotypes of women and bound up with notions of shame. It is feared that the feminist vision of empowering women and achieving transformative change that is at the heart of SCR 1325 has been consistently undermined by the perpetuation of the image of women as powerless victims who are unable to exercise any control over their lives, a theme picked up and explored in the first section of this book.[6] Speakers at the symposium also rightly cautioned that we see only part of the picture if we do not take into account the intersection of gender and ethnicity that is a characteristic of much sexual violence in modern conflicts.[7]

By far the majority of these misgivings are associated with recent developments in the criminal enforcement of the provisions of international humanitarian law dealing with sexual violence against women in armed conflict. There now exists a thriving area of 'respectable' international criminal law scholarship (both feminist and non-feminist) focussing on this issue, and unprecedented advances have been made in the interpretation and enforcement of the relevant provisions of international humanitarian law.[8] How to view these advances and, moreover, how they were achieved have pitted feminists against each other and the fallout of the differences on this topic continues to the present day.[9]

It is not possible to do justice in the space available to what are complex ideological positions that have characterised the debate amongst feminists as to how the law should deal with sexual violence against women in times of armed conflict. For some feminists these developments in international criminal law characterise the impact of sexual violence on women as a 'fate worse than death' and as nothing short of calamitous, resulting inevitably in a life lived in shame and disgrace.[10] However, such an approach, it is argued, essentialises women's experience of sexual violence in armed conflict and, amongst other things, hampers the feminist end-game of empowering women by imposing on them, whether they like it or not, the stereotypical feminine characteristics of vulnerability, helplessness and lack of agency. Consequently, from this perspective, we do a disservice to women by insisting that sexual violence necessarily has this far-reaching impact.

A component of these concerns is that what is seen as shameful is intrinsically associated with the gendered notion of femininity. Over the centuries women, to different degrees but within all cultures, have been valued for their chastity and modesty.[11] Once this is perceived as lost through rape or sexual violence in armed conflict, so the argument goes, they become worthless and, what is more, are often rejected by the community to which they belong.[12] To what extent this in fact occurs, and how feminists should respond to it, is controversial.[13] Without entering into the specifics of this debate, it is important to acknowledge that it was not women that established this paradigm of shame, although they are frequently deeply implicated in its maintenance, but the patriarchal system of which they are a part. Nevertheless, feminists should reflect carefully on whether their achievements in this area (and they are considerable) further perpetuate and reinforce this vision of women and what other possible strategies may be available to them.

Not everyone is comfortable with a strategy that questions the extent of the impact of sexual violence in armed conflict on women. The emphasis on women's agency in particular concerns many feminists as they see it as a distraction from the issue of systemic power and who exercises it.[14] There is certainly a need to be context-specific when ideas of agency are under discussion as agency has many aspects. It is one thing to advocate women's political agency in terms of participating in conflict resolution and post-conflict reconstruction initiatives but quite another to promote their sexual agency in times of armed conflict, particularly where the issue presents in terms of consent to sexual relations with one's captors. In such situations women are often extremely vulnerable and frequently helpless, and lack the resources to exercise agency.

This is all well and good, but how productive in real terms are these feminist debates? There are other related concerns from this focus on sexual violence arguably more far-reaching and of which sexual violence in armed conflict is just a symptom. Certainly, elements of the sexual violence agenda perpetuate and reinforce a limited vision of women and all too frequently present women as powerless victims with sexual violence as their inevitable fate. However, in doing so, sexual violence agendas deflect attention from the myriad other pressing issues, in terms of the protection of their economic, social and cultural rights, that women face during and after armed conflict that, if not caused by endemic discrimination, are certainly exacerbated by it.

The so-called progress on the prosecution of sexual violence during armed conflict also gives credence to the claim that women are now being taken seriously by the international legal regime. But are they? As Hilary Charlesworth has observed in the context of the inclusion of women in human rights institutions, it is easy to be 'dazzled' by appearances.[15]

Another side effect of the focus on sexual violence against women is apparently to hide the extent and ways in which men experience such violence during times of armed conflict. This line of inquiry is linked to the idea that initiatives over the last decade or so to confront the impact of armed conflict on women civilians are, so to speak, sucking the oxygen from the air and serving to obscure what happens to male civilians.[16] This is a topic that must particularly resonate with the military and male combatants since the 2006 events of Abu Ghraib. There has been, from time to time, considerable attention paid to the issue of sexual violence against female prisoners of war primarily in support of the argument that women have no place in combat roles.[17] However, the treatment of Iraqi detainees at Abu Ghraib showcased the potential dangers for male prisoners of war. Predictably in some quarters the blame for these events was sheeted home to feminism.[18]

There has been some response from the military as to how to deal with the issue of sexual violence against combatants generally. The Australian Defence Force has a progressive unisex approach to confronting the possibility that its forces may be subjected to sexual violence upon capture.[19] By way of contrast, the US apparently has no particular training in place as to how these issues should be dealt with and the prevailing military culture is not seen as sympathetic to such an initiative.[20]

From a feminist perspective there are a number of questions here that really go to the heart of what the feminist project is about or perhaps, more accurately, what it is not about. Addressing the impact of armed conflict on men is a perfectly respectable and necessary area of scholarship and activism, but is it feminist? For a start, one should not be misled by the number and topics of United Nations (UN) resolutions and the high profile UN rape campaigns[21] into thinking that anything has changed for women as a result of all this activity. The statistics on sexual violence against women in armed conflict remain catastrophic and there seems little sign of progress. Certainly, the fact that sexual violence against men in armed conflict is paid scant attention must be acknowledged. It is also true that feminists have devoted a great deal of effort to overcoming women's traditional reluctance to discuss sexual violence in armed conflict. Their approach to this task is regarded as tantamount to zealotry in some quarters.[22] Yet it is important to consider if these achievements are really a reflection of feminist power in determining the agenda. In our view, feminists and feminist action are not responsible for this silence over male experiences of sexual violence in armed conflict. There is no evidence to support the argument that the much-vaunted successes in bringing the issue of sexual violence against women to the attention of the UN and the international community generally, and to the forefront of developments in international criminal law, have thrust the topic in relation to men into the shade.

There is a need to look a little further to understand more fully why there is comparative silence about sexual violence against men in times of armed conflict. Feminist international lawyers have used to good effect the methodology of identifying the silences of their discipline and how revealing these are about the influence of gender. There seems to be a tendency, however, to forget that gender does not equate only with women.[23] Searching for its influence will also throw light on the construct of masculinity that condemns many men to play out limiting and stereotypical roles in society. As is seen in the debates over sexual violence against women in times of armed conflict, the idea of 'shame' is at the centre of how these events are perceived and dealt with. A parallel question is how gender and the notion of shame contribute to the response to sexual violence against men. As with sexual violence against women, the prevailing cultural context where this silence occurs and the factors of race and ethnicity, as well as gender, add layers of complexity to the analysis. Nevertheless, seemingly in all cultures it is both honourable and manly to suffer during periods of armed conflict, but only in certain ways. Death, injury, disablement and certain types of torture during armed conflict carry no sense of shame with them, quite the reverse. They are accepted as part of the price that is paid for tolerating a system of resolving disputes by forceful means. But being subjected to sexual violence carries a strong stigma of shame in most cultures and has a distinct gendered impact on men as well as women. In the view of one male US soldier,

> [i]f it would have happened to me, rape I mean, I probably wouldn't be here today; I probably would have done something to get myself killed ... But if for some strange reason I survived, I would never tell anyone, no one, never. To me, that's the worst thing that a guy could have done to him.[24]

Perhaps herein lies part of the explanation as to why the issue of sexual violence against men has been neglected.

Every now and then there will be events, like the role of women in the treatment of detainees at Abu Ghraib, that require feminists to pause and reflect on the ethics of their project. But at the end of the day, in the words of Gina Heathcote, 'we need to acknowledge that feminism is not an endless opening up of ideas, but rather a method that has an empirical link to the real world harm that many women encounter daily and globally'.[25] At the same time, however, the present conversation between feminism and the military is premised on gender and this takes us necessarily beyond a focus purely on women. How far feminist approaches should proceed with the process of acknowledging and apprehending male experiences of harm during armed conflict and its aftermath is another question.

Out from the shadows: women civilians/combatants

The second area in which we find common space for conversations between feminist and military interests is in relation to the issue of the casualties of armed conflict and in particular the question of so-called collateral casualties. As one would expect, the respective feminist and military perspectives and priorities on this issue are at first glance far apart. The COIN in Iraq, however, has seen traditionally opposing priorities move somewhat closer together through changes in military strategy and tactics that may lead to positive outcomes for both sides of the current debate.[26] Another military initiative that is worth some reflection, and which may serve the interests of feminists and the military in times of armed conflict and its aftermath, is the NATO gender mainstreaming initiative of using FETs in Afghanistan.

Counterinsurgency warfare and force protection

> Because the civilian is fundamental to the COIN mission, force protection must now give way.[27]

Traditionally the priority of the military is to minimise force casualties. 'During peace operations of the 1990s, force protection effectively became part of the mission, privileging the soldier over the civilian'.[28] For military actors this is common sense if one's focus is achieving military victory. Feminists, in contrast, focus on the protection of the civilian population where by far the majority of women are located. Consequently, one of the criticisms by feminist international humanitarian law scholars of the way in which armed conflict is conducted is that the protection of the civilian population is always assumed to be subsidiary to 'force protection'.[29] Such an assumption has considerable influence on how the fundamental international humanitarian law principle of proportionality is applied. Proportionality requires a balance to be struck between the anticipated military advantage of a particular attack and the perceived number of incidental civilian casualties thereof. If force protection is a priority of those making the calculation, it will assume more significance in the assessment of the military advantage component of the equation and the consequent downplay of the risk of collateral (or civilian) casualties.

The new approach to force protection in COIN warfare, as one might expect, is based on pragmatism. Under COIN, it is argued that the assumption of increased tactical risk will lead to a reduction in strategic risk. In other words, lowering force protection in the short term, although it may lead to more immediate military casualties, is more likely to result in winning the war, which is measured less in terms of insurgent casualties than in a reduction of civilian casualties and a correlative investment in the legitimacy of the host government. Surely this must constitute a win for both the soldier and the feminist.[30]

There are, however, inevitably negative aspects to such an initiative. For example, the US 2007 so-called 'surge'[31] in the number of troops in Iraq that implemented the COIN strategy relied on the cooption of local tribal leaders to achieve its military success. It is reported that such a strategy led to increased violence and discriminatory acts against the local female population.[32] But it is also the case that the soldier paid a high price in terms of military casualties. Hence, one of the 'paradoxes' highlighted in the COIN Manual is that '[t]he more successful the counterinsurgency is, the less force can be used and the more risk must be accepted'.[33] The COIN doctrine knowingly places greater physical risk on counterinsurgent forces. It concedes that choices will need to be made that will result in higher casualties of soldiers. This is the foreseeable cost of demonstrably protecting civilians so as to provide both security and political space to enable the legitimacy of the host government to properly develop. These truisms necessarily test resolve[34] as well as public expectation. It is clearly evident that coalition military casualties rapidly escalated under the COIN doctrine in Iraq. Military casualties (deaths) during the entire Iraq campaign were higher in 2007 than in any other year (961)[35] and the April, May and June 2007 monthly death counts, when the COIN doctrine was primarily being implemented, were among the highest on record.[36] Conversely, from an all-time high in February 2007, Iraqi civilian deaths due to the armed conflict actually began a steady but decisive and dramatic decline.[37]

COIN itself recognises '[t]his disturbing implication [increased own force casualties] forms the subtext of criticism from conventional military circles ... And maybe the doctrine's political Achilles' heel as well'.[38] Moreover, for COIN to work there has to be a relatively stable, functional and legitimate government in place with a genuine commitment to addressing the problem of insurgency. COIN is based on the assumptions that it is possible to 'win the hearts and minds of the people' and that the mission cannot hope to succeed unless the government enjoys the respect of a significant section of the population. Accordingly, COIN has proved to be a considerable success in Iraq after the 2003 armed conflict but has not been seen as appropriate for conditions that have prevailed in Afghanistan since the 2001 invasion. COIN does, nonetheless, demonstrate that traditional conceptions of war fighting can be decisively re-imagined as circumstances require. It is significant that during the implementation of the COIN strategy, contemporary military journals disclosed a fascination by military operators with the implications of force, in terms of psychological, sociological and anthropological effects, as a means to fulfilling mission accomplishment goals.[39] Such a focus obviously offers a key opportunity for greater social and gender input into military planning processes: a development that both feminist and military actors need to reflect upon and consider further.

Female Engagement Teams in Afghanistan

The NATO gender mainstreaming initiative to develop FETs is distinct in a number of ways. The FETs do not just sit back at headquarters and play token roles,[40] nor is their focus on responding to sexual violence against women. They are involved in actual military operations in support of infantry units in the field, including information gathering, weapon searches and the distribution of humanitarian assistance.[41] It is reported that this strategy has 'enhanced operational effectiveness through "improved information gathering, enhanced credibility and better force protection"'.[42]

Once again we see a dovetailing of interests. It is not, of course, the prospect of improved military efficiency from these initiatives that would hold particular interest for feminists but their by-product; the potential for increasing the visibility of women and their needs during and in the aftermath of armed conflict. Thus it has been reported that FETs can gain direct access to women in Afghan communities that is unavailable to their male colleagues. Consequently, they can assist in the equal implementation of the requirements of international humanitarian law that deal with essential supplies and services.[43] One should not, however, see such developments as the start of a brave new world. There is reportedly some resistance to such undertakings at the battlefield command level and some military commanders see little or no value in engaging with Afghan women.[44]

The use of FETs also highlights the vexed question of how to best accommodate the woman combatant into the structure of the military. One of the earliest debates involving feminism and the military was the issue of the right of women to serve in combat positions. This is an acutely divisive topic for both feminist and military actors. Not only do their respective viewpoints on the role of women frequently differ, but there is no consensus within their own ranks as to how this question is best resolved.

Traditionally, competent performance of duties when on active service is a relevant consideration when assessing promotion prospects within the military, and to deny these possibilities to women is discriminatory. Slowly but surely, however, women are gaining access to roles in the military forces of many states that were previously denied to them. For example, in September 2011 the Australian Minister for Defence announced that the Government had formally agreed to the removal of gender restrictions from Australian Defence Force combat roles. This decision is to be implemented over the next five years.

The equality argument, however, for the participation of women in the military will not resonate with all feminists. Some have difficulty in reconciling the need to ensure that women have equal opportunity within this institution in order to meet their legitimate expectations for career advancement with the fact that this institution can be for some a toxic environment in which to work and live.[45] Moreover, many feminists would see their efforts better directed towards demilitarisation rather than increasing the number of women in the military. As Felicity Ruby (formerly Hill), prior director of the Women's International League for Peace and Freedom (WILPF), argues in her criticism of how SCR 1325 has been used: 'I think it is time for us to dare to be more political, the key [is] to enter in numbers, as women, to what is called the "hard security issues" with more confidence and determination. That is the peacekeeping I am interested in – not seeing more women in uniforms. Militarising more women was never my goal'.[46] Sari Kuovo agrees and questions whether it is consistent with broader feminist goals to take on the issue of gender equality within the military without considering the institutions in question.[47]

The equality argument for women's participation in the military is however preferable to the nowadays largely discredited view that women will have a positive effect on the prevailing ethos of this institution. Such an approach is based on the stereotypical and limiting assumption that women are more peace-loving; cooperative; and peace-building by nature than men.[48]

Conclusion

This chapter reflects an unusual collaboration, indeed perhaps an unprecedented one, between military and feminist perspectives. It was also a way out, for a short time for one of the authors, of the feminist dilemma of always 'talking to ourselves'. What has been gained is significant; namely a better understanding. Perhaps we are not as far apart as one might initially think. There is recognition that the increasing involvement of traditional military forces in such activities as peacekeeping, stabilisation and reconstruction operations and counterinsurgency requires fundamental change: '[r]evised military skills – requires "un warrior" type command skills; "emotional intelligence, empathy with one's opponents, tolerance, patience, subtlety, sophistication, nuance and political adroitness"'.[49] The parallel between this description and the stereotypical attributes of women will not be lost on many and takes us to the centre of conversations about the receptiveness of military structures to feminist dialogues on gender. It is also the case that the counterinsurgency in Iraq had lost its way until high-level US military officials initiated consultations with, amongst others, a female human rights lawyer, with the COIN Manual as the result.[50]

The participation of women in all aspects of peace and security processes is integral to SCR 1325. This must include wherever women choose to have their voices heard, whether it be at the peace table or in the front line of military operations. The COIN and FETs examples indicate that such voices may well trigger further meaningful conversation between the feminist and the soldier.

Notes

1. A. Scales, 'Militarism, male dominance and law: Feminist jurisprudence as oxymoron', *Harvard Women's Law Journal*, Vol. 12 (1989) 25.
2. *Security Council Resolution 1325*, UN Doc. S/RES/1325 (31 October 2000).
3. United States Department of the Army, *The US Army/Marine Corps: Counterinsurgency Field Manual* (Chicago: University Chicago Press, 2007).
4. S. Sewall, 'Introduction to the University of Chicago print edition: A radical field manual', in United States Department of the Army, *Counterinsurgency Field Manual* (Chicago: University Chicago Press, 2007) xxi, p. xxv: 'The field manual makes securing the civilian, rather than destroying the enemy, their top priority'.
5. See, for example, J. Halley, 'Rape at Rome: Feminist interventions in the criminalization of sex-related violence in positive international criminal law', *Michigan Journal of International Law*, Vol. 30, No. 1 (2008) 1.
6. See, for example, K. Engle, 'Feminism and its (dis)contents: Criminalizing wartime rape in Bosnia and Herzegovina', *The American Journal of International Law*, Vol. 99, No. 4 (2005) 778, pp. 780, 794–797, 806–807; K. Engle, 'Judging sex in war', *Michigan Law Review*, Vol. 106, No. 6 (2008) 941; R. Kapur, 'The tragedy of victimization rhetoric: Resurrecting the "native" subject in international/post-colonial feminist legal politics', *Harvard Human Rights Journal*, Vol. 15 (2002) 1; and Otto's critique of the thematic resolutions of the Security Council on women peace and security: 'Power and danger: Feminist engagement with international law through the UN Security Council', *Australian Feminist Law Journal*, Vo. 32 (2010) 97.
7. D.E. Buss, 'The curious visibility of wartime rape: Gender and ethnicity in international criminal law', *Windsor Yearbook of Access to Justice*, Vol. 25, No. 1 (2007) 3; and Engle, 'Judging sex in war'.
8. See, for example, C. Chinkin, 'Feminist reflections on international criminal law', in A. Zimmermann (ed.), *International Criminal Law and the Current Development of Public International Law* (Berlin: Duncker & Humblot, 2003) 125.
9. J. Gardam, 'A new frontline for feminism and international humanitarian law', in V. Munro and M. Davies (eds), *The Ashgate Research Companion to Feminist Legal Theory* (UK: Ashgate, 2013) 217.
10. Engle, 'Feminism and its (dis)contents'; and Engle, 'Judging sex in war'.
11. S. Kouvo, 'Taking women seriously? Conflict, state-building and gender in Afghanistan', in S. Kouvo and Z. Pearson (eds), *Feminist Perspectives on Contemporary International Law: Between Resistance and Compliance?* (Oxford: Hart, 2011) 159, p. 162, discussing the concept of honour in Afghan tribal culture.

12. See, for example, D. Otto, A. Javate De Dios, V. Nainar and L. Vichuta, 'Panel statement for the Asia-Pacific women's regional hearing on gender-based violence in conflict' (Phnom Penh, Cambodia, 10–11 October 2012), p. 6, referring to the 'profound stigma that is often associated with being a survivor of sexual violence'.
13. See, for example, Engle, 'Feminism and its (dis)contents', pp. 791–792, for a discussion of differing views of the impact of rape in Islamic culture.
14. See, for example, Kouvo, 'Taking women seriously?'; M. Grahn-Farley, 'The politics of inevitability: An examination of Janet Halley's critique of the criminalisation of rape as torture', in S. Kouvo and Z. Pearson (eds), *Feminist Perspectives on Contemporary International Law: Between Resistance and Compliance?* (Oxford: Hart, 2011) 109.
15. H. Charlesworth, 'Talking to ourselves? Feminist scholarship in international law', in S. Kouvo and Z. Pearson, *Feminist Perspectives on Contemporary International Law: Between Resistance and Compliance?* (Oxford: Hart, 2011) 17, p. 23.
16. R.C. Carpenter, *'Innocent Women and Children': Gender, Norms and the Protection of Civilians* (Aldershot: Ashgate, 2006).
17. See E. Sciolino, 'Female POW is abused, kindling debate', *The New York Times* (29 June 1992) 1.
18. See, for example, J. Wheeler, 'Take it like a man', *Washington Times* (20 May 2004), http://www.washingtontimes.com/news/2004/may/20/20040520-083647-9853r/?page=all (last accessed October 2013). For a feminist assessment, see C. Enloe, 'Wielding masculinity inside Abu Ghraib: Making feminist sense of an American military scandal', *Asian Journal of Women's Studies*, Vol. 10, No. 3 (2004) 89.
19. This instruction is traditionally undertaken as a standard module during pre-deployment training for Australian Defence Force members.
20. Information supplied to the authors by Colonel Jody Prescott (retired), US Army.
21. See, for example, *Stop Rape Now: UN Action against Sexual Violence in Conflict*, http://www.stoprapenow.org (last accessed October 2013).
22. Engle, 'Feminism and its (dis)contents', p. 794.
23. See, for example, H. Charlesworth, 'Not waving but drowning: Gender mainstreaming and human rights in the United Nations', *Harvard Human Rights Journal*, Vol. 18 (2005) 1.
24. Sciolino, 'Female POW is abused, kindling debate'.
25. Email discussion with Judith Gardam and Dale Stephens, on file.
26. See generally D. Stephens, 'Counterinsurgency and stability operations: A new approach to legal interpretation, in the war in Iraq: A legal analysis', *US Naval War College International Law Studies*, Vol. 86 (2010) 289.
27. Sewall, 'Introduction: A radical field manual', p. xxix.
28. Ibid.
29. J. Gardam, 'Gender and non-combatant immunity', *Transnational Law and Contemporary Problems*, Vol. 3, No. 2 (1993) 345; and J. Gardam and M. Jarvis, *Women, Armed Conflict and International Law* (The Hague: Kluwer Law International, 2001), pp. 117–122.
30. For an alternative reading, see L. Khalili, 'Gendered practices of counterinsurgency', *Review of International Studies*, Vol. 37, No. 4 (2011) 1471.

31. The 'surge' strategy was announced by President Bush on 10 January 2007. See President George W. Bush, 'President's address to the nation', *The White House: President George W. Bush* (Archive) (10 January 2007), http://georgewbush-whitehouse.archives.gov/news/releases/2007/01/20070110-7.html (last accessed October 2013).

32. D. Otto, 'Remapping crisis through a feminist lens', in S. Kouvo and Z. Pearson (eds), *Feminist Perspectives on Contemporary International Law: Between Resistance and Compliance* (Oxford: Hart, 2011) 75, pp. 87–88.

33. United States Department of the Army, *Counterinsurgency Field Manual*, pp. 48–9 para. 1-151.

34. 'Resolve' is identified in many accounts of COIN as being the key counter-insurgent vulnerability. See, for example, J. Molan, 'Thoughts of a practitioner', *Australian Army Journal*, Vol. 5, No. 2 (2008) 215, p. 220.

35. See *icasualties.org: Iraq Coalition Casualty Count – Operation Iraqi Freedom*, http://icasualties.org/Iraq/index.aspx (last accessed October 2013).

36. Ibid.

37. Ibid.

38. Sewall, 'Introduction: A radical field manual', p. xxix.

39. A random sample includes G. Reynolds, 'Embracing complexity: An adaptive effect approach to the conflict in Iraq', *Australian Army Journal*, Vol. 3, No. 3 (2006) 129; J. Kiszely, 'Post-modern challenges for modern warriors', *Australian Army Journal*, Vol. 5, No. 2 (2008) 177; R. Noble, '"Beyond cultural awareness": Anthropology as an aid to the formulation of military strategy in the twenty-first century', *Australian Army Journal*, Vol. 6, No. 2 (2009) 65.

40. This appears to be the case with the Gender Adviser appointed under Bi-SC Directive 40-1 (NATO, 2009): J.M. Prescott, 'NATO gender mainstreaming and the feminist critique of the law of armed conflict', *Georgetown Journal of Gender and the Law*, Vol. 14, No. 1 (2013) 83, p. 116 n. 242 and accompanying text.

41. M. Pottinger, H. Jilani and C. Russo, 'Half-hearted: Trying to win Afghanistan without Afghan women', *Small Wars Journal* (18 February 2010), http://smallwarsjournal.com/jrnl/art/trying-to-win-afghanistan-without-afghan-women (last accessed October 2013).

42. Prescott, 'NATO gender mainstreaming', citing S. Dharmanpuri, 'Just add women and stir?', *Parameters*, Vol. 41, No. 1 (2011) 56, p. 56.

43. Pottinger et al., 'Half-hearted', p. 7. See, for example, *Geneva Convention Relative to the Protection of Civilian Persons in Time of War*, opened for signature on 12 August 1949, 75 UNTS 287 (entered into force on 21 October 1950), art. 55, which provides for humanitarian assistance to civilians in occupied territories.

44. Pottinger et al., 'Half-hearted'.

45. In November 2012 the Australian Government announced a judicial enquiry into the sexual abuse and other misconduct in the Australian Defence Force. See L. Vasek and B. Nicholson, 'Judicial enquiry, apology for defence force sex abuse cases', *The Australian* (26 November 2012), http://www.theaustralian.com.au/national-affairs/defence/judicial-inquiry-apology-for-australian-defence-force-sex-abuse-cases/story-e6frg8yo-1226524035737 (last accessed October 2013).

46. F. Hill, 'How Resolution 1325 came about and what we hoped it would achieve: A retrospective view' (Paper presented at the International Symposium on Peacekeeping in the Asia-Pacific: Gender Equality, Law and Collective Security, Melbourne Law School, 19–20 April 2012). See also F. Ruby, '*Security Council Resolution 1325*: A Tool for Conflict Prevention?', in this volume.
47. Kouvo, 'Taking women seriously?'.
48. H. Charlesworth, 'Are women peaceful? Reflections on the role of women in peace-building', *Feminist Legal Studies*, Vol. 16, No. 3 (2008) 347; O. Simić, 'Increasing Women's Presence in Peacekeeping Operations: The Rationales and Realities of "Gender Balance"', this volume.
49. Kiszely, 'Post-modern challenges for modern warriors', p. 177.
50. See Sewall, 'Introduction: A radical field manual'.

Bibliography

Articles, chapters and books

Addams, J., *Newer Ideals of Peace* (Urbana: University of Illinois Press, first published on 1907, 2007 ed.).

———, *Peace and Bread in Time of War* (Urbana: University of Illinois Press, first published on 1922, 2002 ed.).

African Rights, *Rwanda: Not So Innocent – When Women Become Killers* (London: African Rights, 1995).

Aganthangelou, A.M. and Ling, L.H.M., *Transforming World Politics: From Empire to Multiple Worlds* (London: Routledge, 2009).

Agarwal, B. and Pradeep, P., 'Toward freedom from domestic violence', *Journal of Human Development*, Vol. 8, No. 3 (2007) 359.

Alison, M., *Women and Political Violence: Female Combatants in Ethno-National Conflict* (Abingdon: Routledge, 2009).

Annan, J., Blattman, C., Carlson, K. and Mazurana, D., 'Civil war, reintegration, and gender in Northern Uganda', *Journal of Conflict Resolution*, Vol. 55, No. 6 (2011) 877.

Anthony, W., 'Recovery from mental illness: The guiding vision of the mental health service system in the 1990s', *Psychosocial Rehabilitation Journal*, Vol. 16, No. 4 (1993) 11.

Barnidge, R.P., 'The due diligence principle under international law', *International Community Law Review*, Vol. 8, No. 1 (2006) 81.

Barrow, A., 'UN Security Council Resolutions 1325 and 1820: Constructing gender in armed conflict and international humanitarian law', *International Review of the Red Cross*, Vol. 92, No. 877 (2010) 221.

Bassiouni, M.C., 'International recognition of victims' rights', *Human Rights Law Review*, Vol. 6, No. 2 (2006) 203.

Bell, C. and O'Rourke, C., 'Peace agreements or pieces of paper? The impact of UNSC Resolution 1325 on peace processes and their agreements', *International and Comparative Law Quarterly*, Vol. 59, No. 4 (2010) 941.

Berdahl, J.L., 'Harassment based on sex: Protecting social status in the context of gender hierarchy', *Academy of Management Review*, Vol. 32, No. 2 (2007) 641.

Bernard, C., Corde, K., Jones, S.G., Oliker, O., Stearns, B.K. and Thurston, C.Q., *Women and Nation-Building* (Santa Monica: RAND Corporation, 2008).

Berrios, R., 'Government contracts and contractor behaviour', *Journal of Business Ethics* Vol. 63, No. 2 (2006) 119.

Boutros-Ghali, B., *An Agenda for Peace: Preventative Diplomacy, Peacemaking and Peace-Keeping* (New York: United Nations, 1992).

Boyden, J. and de Berry, J., *Children and Youth on the Frontline* (New York: Berghahn Books, 2004).

Braithwaite, J., Charlesworth, H., Dunn, L. and Reddy, P., *Reconciliation and Architectures of Commitment: Sequencing Peace in Bougainville* (Canberra: ANU E Press, 2010).

Brown, W., *Regulating Aversion: Tolerance in the Age of Identity and Empire* (Princeton: Princeton University Press, 2006).

Brownmiller, S., *Against Our Will: Men, Women and Rape* (New York: Simon and Schuster, 1975).

Brück, T. and Schindler, K., 'Smallholder land access in post-war Northern Mozambique', *World Development*, Vol. 37, No. 8 (2009) 1379.

Brück, T. and Vothknecht, M., 'Impact of violent conflicts on women's economic opportunities', in K. Kuehnast, C. de Jonge Outdraat and H. Hernes (eds), *Women and War: Power and Protection in the 21st Century* (Washington DC: United States Institute of Peace Press, 2011) 85.

Buergenthal, T., 'To respect and ensure: State obligations and permissible derogations', in L. Henkin (ed.), *The International Bill of Rights: The Covenant on Civil and Political Rights* (New York: Columbia University Press, 1981) 72.

Burke, R., 'Status of forces deployed on UN peacekeeping operations: Jurisdictional immunity', *Journal of Conflict & Security Law*, Vol. 16, No. 1 (2011) 63.

———, 'Attribution of responsibility: Sexual abuse and exploitation, and effective control of blue helmets', *Journal of International Peacekeeping*, Vol. 16, No. 1–2 (2012) 1.

Buss, D.E., 'The curious visibility of wartime rape: Gender and ethnicity in international criminal law', *Windsor Yearbook of Access to Justice*, Vol. 25, No. 1 (2007) 3.

Butler, J., *Gender Trouble: Feminism and the Subversion of Identity* (New York: Routledge, 1990).

———, 'Contingent foundations: Feminism and the question of "postmodernism"', in S. Seidman (ed.), *The Postmodern Turn: New Perspectives on Social Theory* (Cambridge: Cambridge University Press, 1994) 153.

Carpenter, R.C., *'Innocent Women and Children': Gender Norms and the Protection of Civilians* (Aldershot: Ashgate, 2006).

———, 'Recognizing gender-based violence against civilian men and boys in conflict situations', *Security Dialogue*, Vol. 37, No. 1 (2006) 83.

Center on International Cooperation, *Annual Review of Global Peace Operations 2012* (Boulder: Lynne Rienner, 2012).

Chandler, D., 'Race, culture and civil society: Peacebuilding discourse and the understanding of difference', *Security Dialogue*, Vol. 41, No. 4 (2010) 369.

Chandler, J., 'Taim bilong ol Meri?: A new agenda in PNG', *Griffith Review*, Vol. 40 (2013) 66, http://griffithreview.com/images/stories/edition_articles/ed40_pdfs/jo%20chandler%20-%20taim%20bilong%20ol%20meri.pdf (last accessed October 2013).

Charlesworth, H., 'Transforming the united men's club: Feminist futures for the United Nations', *Transnational Law and Contemporary Problems*, Vol. 4, No. 2 (1994) 421.

———, 'Not waving but drowning: Gender mainstreaming and human rights in the United Nations', *Harvard Human Rights Journal*, Vol. 18 (2005) 1.

———, 'Are women peaceful? Reflections on the role of women in peace-building', *Feminist Legal Studies*, Vol. 16, No. 3 (2008) 347.

———, 'Worlding women in international law', in B. D'Costa and K. Lee-Koo (eds), *Gender and Global Politics in the Asia-Pacific* (New York: Palgrave, 2009) 19.

———, 'Talking to ourselves? Feminist scholarship in international law', in S. Kouvo and Z. Pearson, *Feminist Perspectives on Contemporary International Law: Between Resistance and Compliance?* (Oxford: Hart, 2011) 17.

Charlesworth, H., and Wood, M., 'Women and human rights in the rebuilding of East Timor', *Nordic Journal of International Law*, Vol. 71, No. 2 (2002) 325.

Chinkin, C., 'Feminist reflections on international criminal law', in A. Zimmermann (ed.), *International Criminal Law and the Current Development of Public International Law* (Berlin: Duncker & Humblot, 2003) 125.

Chinkin, C. and Charlesworth, H., 'Building women into peace: The international legal framework', *Third World Quarterly*, Vol. 27, No. 5 (2006) 937.

Christian, M., Burnham, G., Glass, N., Octave, S. and Ramazani, P., 'Sexual and gender based violence against men in the Democratic Republic of the Congo: Effects on survivors, the families and the community', *Medicine, Conflict and Survival*, Vol. 27, No. 4 (2011) 227.

Cockburn, C., *Antimilitarism: Politics and Gender Dynamics of Peace Movements* (Basingstoke: Palgrave Macmillan, 2012).

Cohn, C., 'Mainstreaming gender in UN security policy: A path to political transformation?', in S. Rai and G. Waylen (eds), *Global Governance: Feminist Perspectives* (Basingstoke: Palgrave Macmillan, 2008) 185.

Cohn, C., Kinsella, H. and Gibbings, S., 'Women, peace and security: Resolution 1325', *International Feminist Journal of Politics*, Vol. 6, No. 1 (2004) 130.

Cook, S., 'Security Council Resolution 1820: On militarism, flashlights, raincoats, and rooms with doors – A political perspective on where it came from and what it adds', *Emory International Law Review*, Vol. 23, No. 1 (2009) 125.

Corrin, J., '*Ples bilong mere*: Law, gender and peace-building in Solomon Islands', *Feminist Legal Studies*, Vol. 16, No. 2 (2008) 169.

Cossman, B., 'Gender performance, sexual subjects and international law', *Canadian Journal of Law and Jurisprudence*, Vol. 15, No. 2 (2002) 281.

Costin, L.B., 'Feminism, pacifism, internationalism and the 1915 International Congress of Women', *Women's Studies International Forum*, Vol. 5, No. 3–4 (1982) 301.

Coulter, C., *Bush Wives and Girl Soldiers: Women's Lives through War and Peace in Sierra Leone* (Ithaca: Cornell University Press, 2011).

Crawford, N.C., 'The passion of world politics: Propositions on emotion and emotional relationships', *International Security*, Vol. 24, No. 4 (2000) 116.

Darby, P., 'Rolling back the frontiers of empire: Practising the postcolonial', *International Peacekeeping*, Vol. 16, No. 5 (2009) 699.

Davidson, L., 'Recovery, self management and the expert patient: Changing the culture of mental health from a UK perspective', *Journal of Mental Health*, Vol. 14, No. 1 (2005) 25.

Davies, M., 'Feminism and the flat law theory', *Feminist Legal Studies*, Vol. 16, No. 3 (2008) 281.

Davis, A.Y., 'A vocabulary for feminist praxis: On war and radical critique', in R.L. Riley, C.T. Mohanty and M.B. Pratt (eds), *Feminism and War: Confronting US Imperialism* (London: Zed Books, 2008) 19.

De Schutter, O., 'Globalization and jurisdiction: Lessons from the *European Convention on Human Rights*', *Baltic Yearbook of International Law*, Vol. 6 (2006) 185.

DeGroot, G.J., 'A few good women: Gender stereotypes, the military and peacekeeping', *International Peacekeeping*, Vol. 8, No. 2 (2001) 23.

Dennis, M., 'Application of human rights treaties extraterritorially to detention of combatants and security internees: Fuzzy thinking all around?', *ILSA Journal of International & Comparative Law*, Vol. 12, No. 2 (2006) 459.

Derrida, J., *Writing and Difference* (A. Bass trans., London: Routledge & Kegan Paul, 1997) [trans. of *L'écriture et la différence* (first published on 1967)].

Douglas, S., Farr, V., Hill, F. and Kasuma, W., 'Case study: Bougainville – Papua New Guinea', in S. Douglas and F. Hill (eds), *Getting It Right, Doing It Right: Gender and Disarmament, Demobilization and Reintegration* (New York: United Nations Development Fund for Women, 2004) 20, p. 23.

Dowd, N.E., 'Masculinities and feminist legal theory', *Wisconsin Journal of Law, Gender & Society*, Vol. 23, No. 2 (2008) 201.

Duffey, T., 'United Nations peacekeeping in the post-Cold War world', *Civil Wars*, Vol. 1, No. 3 (1998) 1.

Durham, H. and O'Byrne, K., 'The dialogue of difference: Gender perspectives on international humanitarian law', *International Review of the Red Cross*, Vol. 92, No. 877 (2010) 31.

Edwards, A., *Violence against Women under International Human Rights Law* (Cambridge: Cambridge University Press, 2010).

Engle, K., 'Feminism and its (dis)contents: Criminalizing wartime rape in Bosnia and Herzegovina', *American Journal of International Law*, Vol. 99, No. 4 (2005) 778.

———, 'Judging sex in war', *Michigan Law Review*, Vol. 106, No. 6 (2008) 941.

———, 'Self-critique, (anti) politics and criminalization: Reflections on the history and trajectory of the human rights movement', in J. M. Beneyto and D. Kennedy (eds), *New Approaches to International Law: The European and American Experiences* (The Haag: TMC Asser Press, 2012) 41.

Engle, K. and Lottman, A., 'The force of shame', in C. McGlynn and V.E. Munro (eds), *Rethinking Rape Law: International and Comparative Perspectives* (New York: Routledge, 2010) 76.

Enloe, C., *Bananas, Beaches and Bases: Making Feminist Sense of International Politics* (London: Pandora, 1989).

———, *Maneuvers: The International Politics of Militarizing Women's Lives* (Berkeley: University of California Press, 2000).

———, *The Curious Feminist: Searching for Women in a New Age of Empire* (Berkeley: University of California Press, 2004).

———, 'Wielding masculinity inside Abu Ghraib: Making feminist sense of an American military scandal', *Asian Journal of Women's Studies*, Vol. 10, No. 3 (2004) 89.

———, *Globalization and Militarism: Feminists Make the Link* (Lanham: Rowman & Littlefield, 2007).

Evatt, E., 'Foreword', in H. Charlesworth and C. Chinkin, *The Boundaries of International Law: A Feminist Analysis* (Manchester: Manchester University Press, 2000) ix.

Fapohunda, T.M., 'Integrating women and gender issues in peace development', *International Journal of Peace and Development Studies*, Vol. 2, No. 6 (2011) 162.

Farr, V., 'UNSCR 1325 and women's peace activism in the Occupied Palestinian Territory', *International Feminist Journal of Politics*, Vol. 13, No. 4 (2011) 539.

Farr, V., Myrttinen, H. and Schnabel, A. (eds), *Sexed Pistols: The Gendered Impacts of Small Arms and Light Weapons* (New York: United Nations University Press, 2009).

Fiddian-Qasmiyeh, E., 'Concealing violence against women in Sahrawi refugee camps: The politicisation of victimhood', in H. Bradby and G.L. Hundt (eds), *Global Perspectives on War, Gender and Health: The Sociology and Anthropology of Suffering* (Farnham: Ashgate, 2010) 99.

Fierke, K.M., 'Bewitched by the past: Social memory, trauma and international relations', in D. Bell (ed.), *Memory, Trauma and World Politics: Reflections on the*

Relationship between Past and Present (Basingstoke: Palgrave Macmillan, 2006) 116.

――――, 'Whereof we can speak, thereof we must not be silent: Trauma, political solipsism and war', *Review of International Studies*, Vol. 30, No. 4 (2004) 471.

Franke, K., 'Theorizing yes: An essay on feminism, law, and desire', *Columbia Law Review*, Vol. 101, No. 1 (2001) 181.

Fullilove, M., 'Images in psychiatry: Jane Addams, 1860–1935', *American Journal of Psychiatry*, Vol. 155, No. 6 (1998) 828.

Fung, L., 'Engendering the peace processes: Women's role in peacebuilding', in H. Durham and T. Gurd (eds), *Listening to the Silences: Women and War* (Leiden: Brill, 2005) 225–237.

Garasu, L., 'The role of women in promoting peace and reconciliation', in A. Carl and L. Garasu (eds), *Weaving Consensus: The Papua New Guinea – Bougainville Peace Process* (London: Conciliation Resources in collaboration with BICWF, 2002) 28.

Gardam, J., 'Gender and non-combatant immunity', *Transnational Law and Contemporary Problems*, Vol. 3, No. 2 (1993) 345.

――――, 'A new frontline for feminism and international humanitarian law', in V. Munro and M. Davies (eds), *The Ashgate Research Companion to Feminist Legal Theory* (UK: Ashgate, 2013) 217.

Gardam, J. and Jarvis, M., *Women, Armed Conflict and International Law* (The Hague: Kluwer Law International, 2001).

Garrett, J., 'UNEP to help Bougainville manage clean up of Rio Tinto mine', *Radio Australia* (23 September 2013), http://www.radioaustralia.net.au/pacific/2013-09-04/unep-to-help-bougainville-manage-cleanup-of-rio-tinto-mine/1185677 (last accessed October 2013).

Ghobarah, H.A., Huth, P. and Russett, B., 'Civil wars kill and maim people – Long after the shooting stops', *American Political Science Review*, Vol. 97, No. 2 (2003) 189.

Gibbings, S., *Governing Women, Governing Security: Governmentality, Gender-Mainstreaming and Women's Activism at the UN* (MA Thesis, York University, 2004).

――――, 'No angry women at the United Nations: Political dreams and the cultural politics of United Nations Security Council Resolution 1325', *International Feminist Journal of Politics*, Vol. 13, No. 4 (2011) 522.

Gillespie, T., 'Rape crisis centres and "male rape": A face of the backlash', in M. Hester, L. Kelly and J. Radford (eds), *Women, Violence and Male Power: Feminist Activism, Research and Practice* (Buckingham: Open University Press, 1996) 148.

Goldsmith, A. and Dinnen, S., 'Transnational police building: Critical lessons from Timor-Leste and Solomon Islands', *Third World Quarterly*, Vol. 28, No. 6 (2007) 1091.

Goodman, M.K. and Barnes, C., 'Star/poverty space: The making of the "development celebrity"', *Celebrity Studies*, Vol. 2, No. 1 (2011) 69.

Grahn-Farley, M., 'The politics of inevitability: An examination of Janet Halley's critique of the criminalisation of rape as torture', in S. Kouvo and Z. Pearson (eds), *Feminist Perspectives on Contemporary International Law: Between Resistance and Compliance?* (Oxford: Hart, 2011) 109.

Greener, B.K., Fish, W.J. and Tekulu, K., 'Peacebuilding, gender and policing in Solomon Islands', *Asia Pacific Viewpoint*, Vol. 52, No. 1 (2011) 17.

Greener, B.K., *The New International Policing* (Basingstoke: Palgrave Macmillan, 2009)

Grewal, I., *Transnational America: Feminisms, Diasporas, Neoliberalisms* (Durham: Duke University Press, 2005).

Hakana, H., Ninnes, P. and Jenkins, B. (eds), *NGOs and Post-Conflict Recovery: The Leitana Nehan Women's Development Agency Bougainville* (Canberra: ANU E Press, 2006).

Hall, S. and O'Hara, J., 'The narrative construction of reality: An interview with Stuart Hall', *Southern Review*, Vol. 17, No. 1 (1984) 3.

Halley, J., 'Rape at Rome: Feminist interventions in the criminalization of sex-related violence in positive international criminal law', *Michigan Journal of International Law*, Vol. 30, No. 1 (2008) 1.

Hameiri, S., 'The region within: RAMSI, the Pacific Plan and new modes of governance in the Southwest Pacific', *Australian Journal of International Affairs*, Vol. 63, No. 3 (2009) 348.

Hampson, F.J., 'The relationship between international humanitarian law and human rights law from the perspective of a human rights treaty body', *International Review of the Red Cross*, Vol. 90, No. 871 (2008) 549.

Handrahan, L., 'Conflict, gender, ethnicity and post-conflict reconstruction', *Security Dialogue*, Vol. 35, No. 4 (2004) 429.

Harrington, C., *The Politicization of Sexual Violence: From Abolitionism to Peacekeeping* (Farnham: Ashgate, 2010).

———, 'Resolution 1325 and post-Cold War feminist politics', *International Feminist Journal of Politics*, Vol. 13, No. 4 (2011) 557.

Harris, V. and Goldsmith, A., 'Gendering transitional policing: Experiences of Australian women in international policing operations', *International Peacekeeping*, Vol. 17, No. 2 (2010) 292.

Heathcote, G., 'Feminist politics and the use of force: Theorising feminist action and Security Council Resolution 1325', *Socio-Legal Review*, Vol. 7 (2011) 23.

———, *The Law on the Use of Force: A Feminist Analysis* (Abingdon: Routledge, 2011).

———, 'Naming and shaming: Human rights accountability in Security Council Resolution 1960 (2010) on women, peace and security', *Journal of Human Rights Practice*, Vol. 4, No. 1 (2012) 82.

Hegarty, D. and Regan, A., 'Peacebuilding in the Pacific Islands: Lessons from Bougainville, Solomon Islands and Fiji', in Centre for Humanitarian Dialogue, *Handbook on Conflict and Mediation in Asia* (Geneva: Centre for Humanitarian Dialogue, 2006) 57.

Hemmings, C., *Why Stories Matter: The Political Grammar of Feminist Theory* (Durham: Duke University Press, 2011).

Henry, M., 'Peacexploitation? Interrogating labor hierarchies and global sisterhood among Indian and Uruguayan female peacekeepers', *Globalizations*, Vol. 9, No. 1 (2012) 15.

Higate, P., *Gender and Peacekeeping Case Studies: The Democratic Republic of the Congo and Sierra Leone* (Pretoria: Institute for Security Studies, 2003).

Higate, P. and Henry, M., 'Engendering (in)security in peace support operations', *Security Dialogue*, Vol. 35, No. 4 (2004) 481.

Hill, F., Aboitiz, M. and Poehlman-Doumbouya, S., 'Nongovernmental organizations' role in the buildup and implementation of Security Council Resolution 1325', *Signs: Journal of Women in Culture and Society*, Vol. 28, No. 4 (2003) 1255.

Horne, J., 'Masculinity in politics and war in the age of nation-states and world wars, 1850–1950', in S. Dudink, K. Hageman and J. Tosh (eds), *Masculinities in Politics and War: Gendering Modern History* (Manchester: Manchester University Press, 2004) 22.

Hudson, H., 'A bridge too far? The gender consequences of linking security and development in SSR discourse and practice', in A. Schnabel and V. Farr (eds), *Back to the Roots: Security Sector Reform and Development* (Zürich: LIT Verlag, 2012) 77.

Hudson, N.F., 'Securitizing women's rights and gender equality', *Journal of Human Rights*, Vol. 8, No. 1 (2009) 53.

Hudson, V.M., 'Sex, war, and peace: Rank, and winter on rank', *Political Psychology*, Vol. 31, No. 1 (2010) 33.

Hudson, V.M., Ballif-Spanvill, B., Caprioli, M. and Emmett, C.F., *Sex and World Peace* (New York: Columbia University Press, 2012).

Hudson, V.M., Ballif-Spanvill, B., Caprioli, M., Emmett, C.F. and McDermott, R., 'The heart of the matter: The security of women and the security of states', *International Security*, Vol. 33, No. 3 (2008) 7.

Hutchings, K., 'Feminist ethics and political violence', *International Politics*, Vol. 44, No. 1 (2007) 90.

———, 'Cognitive short cuts', in J.L. Parpart and M. Zalewski (eds), *Rethinking the Man Question: Sex, Gender and Violence in International Relations* (London: Zed Books, 2008) 23.

Hutchison, E., 'Trauma and the politics of emotions: Constituting identity, security and community after the Bali Bombing', *International Relations*, Vol. 24, No. 1 (2010) 65.

Hutchison, E. and R. Bleiker, 'Emotional reconciliation: Reconstituting identity and community after trauma', *European Journal of Social Theory*, Vol. 11, No. 3 (2008) 385.

International Committee of the Red Cross, *Report on Violence against Women from 1998–2003* (Kigali: Ministry of Gender and Family Promotion, 2004).

Jabri, V., 'Feminist ethics and hegemonic global politics', *Alternatives*, Vol. 29, No. 3 (2004) 265.

Johnson, K., Asher, J., Kisielewski, M., Lawry, L., Ong, R., Rughita, B. and Scott, J., 'Association of sexual violence and human rights violations with physical and mental health in territories of the Eastern Democratic Republic of the Congo', *Journal of the American Medical Association*, Vol. 304, No. 5 (2010) 553.

Justino, P. and Verwimp, P., 'Poverty dynamics, violent conflict, and convergence in Rwanda', *Review of Income and Wealth*, Vol. 59, No. 1 (2013) 66.

Kabutaulaka, T.T., 'Australian foreign policy and the RAMSI intervention in Solomon Islands', *Contemporary Pacific*, Vol. 17, No. 2 (2005) 283.

Kandiyoti, D., 'Between the hammer and the anvil: Post-conflict reconstruction, Islam and women's rights', *Third World Quarterly*, Vol. 28, No. 3 (2007) 503.

Kanetake, M., 'Whose zero tolerance counts? Reassessing a zero tolerance policy against sexual exploitation and abuse by UN peacekeepers', *International Peacekeeping*, Vol. 17, No. 2 (2010) 200.

Kapur, R., 'The tragedy of victimization rhetoric: Resurrecting the "native" subject in international/post-colonial feminist legal politics', *Harvard Human Rights Journal*, Vol. 15 (2002) 1.

Kapur, R., *Erotic Justice: Law and the New Politics of Postcolonialism* (London: Glasshouse Press, 2005).

Khalili, L., 'Gendered practices of counterinsurgency', *Review of International Studies*, Vol. 37, No. 4 (2011) 1471.

Kinsella, H.M., *Image before the Weapon: A Critical History of the Distinction between Combatant and Civilian* (Ithaca: Cornell University Press, 2011).

Kiszely, J., 'Post-modern challenges for modern warriors', *Australian Army Journal*, Vol. 5, No. 2 (2008) 177.

Knox, J.H., 'Horizontal human rights law', *The American Journal of International Law*, Vol. 102, No. 1 (2008) 1.

Koskenniemi, M., 'The police in the temple – Order, justice and the UN: A dialectical view', *European Journal of International Law*, Vol. 6, No. 3 (1995) 325.

Kouvo, S., 'Taking women seriously? Conflict, state-building and gender in Afghanistan', in S. Kouvo and Z. Pearson (eds), *Feminist Perspectives on Contemporary International Law: Between Resistance and Compliance?* (Oxford: Hart, 2011) 159.

Krisch, N., 'International law in times of hegemony: Unequal power and the shaping of the international legal order', *European Journal of International Law*, Vol. 16, No. 3 (2005) 369.

Kristof, N.D. and WuDunn, S., *Half the Sky: Turning Oppression into Opportunity for Women Worldwide* (New York: Random House, 2009).

Lancaster, R.N., *Sex Panic and the Punitive State* (Berkeley: University of California Press, 2011).

Lasslett, K., 'State terror and the Bougainville conflict', *International State Crime Initiative*, multimedia installation, http://www.statecrime.org/testimony project/bougainville (last accessed October 2013).

Lawson, R., 'Life after *Bankovic*: On the extraterritorial application of the *European Convention on Human Rights*', in F. Coomans and M. Kamminga (eds), *Extraterritorial Application of Human Rights Treaties* (Antwerp: Intersentia, 2004) 83.

Leach, P., 'Beyond the Bug River: New approaches to redress by the ECHR', *European Human Rights Law Review*, Vol. 10 (2005) 148.

Lester, H. and Gask, L., 'Delivering medical care for patients with serious mental illness or promoting a collaborative model of recovery?', *British Journal of Psychiatry*, Vol. 188, No. 5 (2006) 401.

Levit, N., 'Feminism for men: Legal ideology and the construction of maleness', *UCLA Law Review*, Vol. 43, No. 4 (1996) 1037.

Lewis, D., 'Unrecognized victims: Sexual violence against men in conflict settings under international law', *Wisconsin International Law Journal*, Vol. 27, No. 1 (2009) 1.

Li, Q. and Wen, M., 'The immediate and lingering effects of armed conflict on adult mortality: A time-series cross-national analysis', *Journal of Peace Research*, Vol. 42, No. 4 (2005) 471.

Litfin, K.T., 'Constructing environmental security and ecological interdependence', *Global Governance*, Vol. 5, No. 3 (1999) 359.

Littler, Jo, 'Introduction: Celebrity and the transnational', *Celebrity Studies*, Vol. 2, No. 1 (2011) 1.

Lofton, K. and Weber, B.R., 'The legacies of Oprah Winfrey: Celebrity, activism and reform in the twenty-first century', *Celebrity Studies*, Vol. 3, No. 1 (2012) 104.

Loucaides, L., 'Determining the extra-territorial effect of the *European Convention*: Facts, jurisprudence and the *Banković* case', *European Human Rights Law Review*, No. 4 (2006) 391.

Mack, A. (ed.), *Human Security Report 2012: Sexual Violence, Education, and War – Beyond the Mainstream Narrative* (Vancouver: Human Security Press, 2012).

Mackenzie, M.H., *Female Soldiers in Sierra Leone: Sex, Security, and Post-Conflict Development* (New York: New York University Press, 2012).

MacKinnon, C.A., 'Crimes of war, crimes of peace', in S. Shute and S. Hurley (eds), *On Human Rights: The Oxford Amnesty Lectures* (New York: Basic Books, 1993) 83.

Mazurana, D. and Carlson, K., 'War slavery: The role of children and youth in fighting forces in sustaining armed conflicts and war economies in Africa', in D. Žarkov (ed.), *Gender, Violent Conflict, and Development* (New Delhi: Zubaan Books, 2008) 205.

McClain, L. and Grossman, J. (eds), *Gender Equality: Dimensions of Women's Equal Citizenship* (Cambridge: Cambridge University Press, 2009).

McCormack, T., '*Their* atrocities and *our* misdemeanours: The reticence of states to try their "own nationals" for international crimes', in M. Lattimer and P. Sands (eds), *Justice for Crimes against Humanity* (Oxford: Hart, 2003) 107.

McEvoy-Levy, S. (ed.), *Troublemakers or Peacemakers? Youth and Post-Accord Peace Building* (Notre Dame: University of Notre Dame Press, 2006).

McGoldrick, D., 'Extraterritorial application of the Covenant on Civil and Political Rights', in F. Coomans and M. Kamminga (eds), *Extraterritorial Application of Human Rights Treaties* (Antwerp: Intersentia, 2004) 41.

McLeod, L., 'Configurations of post-conflict: Impacts of representations of conflict and post-conflict upon the (political) translations of gender security within UNSCR 1325', *International Feminist Journal of Politics*, Vol. 13, No. 4 (2011) 594.

Meertens, D., 'Género, desplazamiento, derechos', in M. Nubia Bello (ed.), *Desplazamiento Forzado. Dinámicas de Guerra, Exclusión y Desarraigo* (Bogotà: Universidad Nacional de Colombia, 2004) 197.

Meron, T., 'Extraterritoriality of human rights treaties', *The American Journal of International Law*, Vol. 89, No. 1 (1995) 78.

Milanovic, M., *Extraterritorial Application of Human Rights Treaties: Principles and Policy* (Oxford: Oxford University Press, 2011).

Miller, S.K., 'Accountability for the conduct of UN-mandated forces under international human rights law: A case study concerning sexual abuse of the UN Mission in the Democratic Republic of the Congo (MONUC)', in R. Arnold and G.-J.A. Knoops (eds), *Practice and Policies of Modern Peace Support Operations under International Law* (Ardsley: Martinus Nijhoff, 2006) 261.

Mobekk, E., 'Gender, women and security sector reform', *International Peacekeeping*, Vol. 17, No. 2 (2010) 278.

Molan, J., 'Thoughts of a practitioner', *Australian Army Journal*, Vol. 5, No. 2 (2008) 215.

Monro, S., 'Transgender: Destabilising feminisms?', in V.E. Munro and C.F. Stychin (eds), *Sexuality and the Law: Feminist Engagements* (Abingdon: Routledge-Cavendish, 2007) 125.

Moore, C., *Happy Isles in Crisis: The Historical Causes for a Failing State in Solomon Islands, 1998–2004* (Canberra: Asia Pacific Press, 2004) .

Moran, M.H., 'Gender, militarism and peace-building: Projects of the postconflict moment', *Annual Review of Anthropology*, Vol. 39 (2010) 261.

Moser, C.O.N. and Clark, C.F. (eds), *Victims, Perpetrators or Actors? Gender, Armed Conflict, and Political Violence* (London: Zed Books, 2001).

Murray, J., 'Who will police the peace-builders? The failure to establish account-ability for the participation of United Nations civilian police in the trafficking of women in post-conflict Bosnia and Herzegovina', *Columbia Human Rights Law Review*, Vol. 34, No. 2 (2003) 475.

Nagai, M., Burnham, G., Karunakara, U. and Rowley, E., 'Violence against refugees, non-refugees and host populations in southern Sudan and northern Uganda', *Global Public Health*, Vol. 3, No. 3 (2008) 249.

Nash, J.C., 'Re-thinking intersectionality', *Feminist Review*, Vol. 89 (2009) 1.

Nesiah, V., 'Discussion lines on gender and transitional justice: An introductory essay reflecting on the ICTJ Bellagio Workshop on Gender and Transitional Justice', *Columbia Journal of Gender and Law*, Vol. 15, No. 3 (2006) 799.

Ní Aoláin, F., 'Women, security, and the patriarchy of internationalized transitional justice', *Human Rights Quarterly*, Vol. 31, No. 4 (2009) 1055.

Ní Aoláin, F., Chan, N. and Haynes, D.F., *On the Frontlines: Gender, War and the Post-Conflict Process* (New York: Oxford University Press, 2011).

Noble, R., '"Beyond cultural awareness": Anthropology as an aid to the formulation of military strategy in the twenty-first century', *Australian Army Journal*, Vol. 6, No. 2 (2009) 65.

O'Connell, H., 'What are the opportunities to promote gender equity and equality in conflict-affected and fragile states? Insights from a review of evidence', *Gender & Development*, Vol. 19, No. 3 (2011) 455.

Odanović, G., 'Participation of women in UN peacekeeping operations', *Western Balkans Security Observer*, Vol. 5, No. 16 (2010) 70.

Office of the Special Adviser on Gender Issues and Advancement of Women, *Gender Mainstreaming: An Overview* (New York: United Nations, 2002).

Oloka-Onyango, J. and Tamale, S., '"The personal is political" or why women's rights are indeed human rights: An African perspective on international feminism', *Human Rights Quarterly*, Vol. 17, No. 4 (1995) 691.

Oosterveld, V., 'Prosecution of gender-based crimes in international law', in D. Mazurana, A. Raven-Roberts and J. Parpart (eds), *Gender, Conflict, and Peacekeeping* (Lanham: Rowman & Littlefield, 2005) 67.

Otto, D., 'Disconcerting "masculinities": Reinventing the gendered subject(s) of international human rights law', in D. Buss and A. Manji (eds), *International Law: Modern Feminist Approaches* (Oxford: Hart, 2005) 105.

———, 'A sign of "weakness"? Disrupting gender certainties in the implementation of Security Council Resolution 1325', *Michigan Journal of Gender and Law*, Vol. 13, No. 1 (2006) 113.

———, 'Lost in translation: Re-scripting the sexed subjects of international human rights law', in A. Orford (ed.), *International Law and its Others* (Cambridge: Cambridge University Press, 2006) 318.

———, 'Making sense of zero tolerance policies in peacekeeping sexual economies', in V.E. Munro and C.F. Stychin (eds), *Sexuality and the Law: Feminist Engagements* (Abingdon: Routledge-Cavendish, 2007) 259.

———, 'The sexual tensions of UN peacekeeping operations: A plea for "sexual positivity"', *Finnish Yearbook of International Law*, Vol. 18 (2007) 33.

———, 'The exile of inclusion: Reflections on gender issues in international law over the last decade', *Melbourne Journal of International Law*, Vol. 10, No. 1 (2009) 11.

———, 'Power and danger: Feminist engagement with international law through the UN Security Council', *Australian Feminist Law Journal*, Vol. 32 (2010) 97.

———, 'The Security Council's alliance of "gender legitimacy": The symbolic capital of Resolution 1325', in H. Charlesworth and J. Coicaud (eds), *Fault Lines of International Legitimacy* (New York: Cambridge University Press, 2010) 239.

———, 'Remapping crisis through a feminist lens', in S. Kouvo and Z. Pearson (eds), *Feminist Perspectives on Contemporary International Law: Between Resistance and Compliance* (Oxford: Hart, 2011) 75.

Owen, M., 'Widowhood issues in the context of United Nations Security Council Resolution 1325', *International Feminist Journal of Politics*, Vol. 13, No. 4 (2011) 616.

Pallen, D., 'Sexual slavery in Bosnia: An externality of the market', *Swords and Ploughshares*, Vol. 13, No. 1 (2003) 27.

Pankhurst, D., 'The gendered impact of peace', in M. Pugh, N. Cooper and M. Turner (eds), *Whose Peace? Critical Perspectives on the Political Economy of Peacebuilding* (Basingstoke: Palgrave, 2008) 30.

Parashar, S., 'Embodied "otherness" and negotiations of difference', *International Studies Review*, Vol. 13, No. 4 (2011) 696.

Peck, J., 'Looking a gift horse in the mouth': Oprah Winfrey and the politics of philanthropy', *Celebrity Studies*, Vol. 3, No. 1 (2012) 106.

Pirovolakis, E., *Reading Derrida and Ricoeur: Improbable Encounters between Deconstruction and Hermeneutics* (Albany: State University of New York Press, 2010).

Pottinger, M., Jilani, H. and Russo, C., 'Half-hearted: Trying to win Afghanistan without Afghan women', *Small Wars Journal* (18 February 2010), http://smallwarsjournal.com/jrnl/art/trying-to-win-afghanistan-without-afghan-women (last accessed October 2013).

Pratt, N. and Richter-Devroe, S., 'Introduction: Critically examining UNSCR 1325 on women, peace and security', *International Feminist Journal of Politics*, Vol. 13, No. 4 (2011) 489.

Prenzler, T. and Hayes, H., 'Measuring progress in gender equity in Australian policing', *Current Issues in Criminal Justice*, Vol. 12, No. 1 (2000) 20.

Prescott, J.M., 'NATO gender mainstreaming and the feminist critique of the law of armed conflict', *Georgetown Journal of Gender and the Law*, Vol. 14, No. 1 (2013) 83.

Puar, J.K., *Terrorist Assemblages: Homonationalism in Queer Times* (Durham: Duke University Press, 2007).

Puechguirbal, N., 'Discourse on gender, patriarchy and Resolution 1325: A textual analysis of UN Documents', *International Peacekeeping*, Vol. 17, No. 2 (2010) 172.

Pugh, M., 'Peacekeeping and critical theory', *International Peacekeeping*, Vol. 11, No. 1 (2004) 39.

———, 'Local agency and political economies of peacebuilding', *Ethnicities and Nationalism*, Vol. 11, No. 2 (2011) 308.

Pupavac, V., 'War on the couch: The emotionology of the new international security paradigm', *European Journal of Social Theory*, Vol. 7, No. 2 (2004) 149.

Quénivet, N.N.R., *Sexual Offenses in Armed Conflict & International Law* (Ardsley: Transnational Publishers, 2005).

———, 'The role of the International Criminal Court in the prosecution of peacekeepers for sexual offences', in R. Arnold (ed.), *Law Enforcement within the Framework of Peace Support Operations* (Leiden: Martinus Nijhoff, 2008) 399.

Rai, S.M., *The Gender Politics of Development: Essays in Hope and Despair* (London: Zed Books, 2008).

Ramon, S., Healy, B. and Renouf, N., 'Recovery from mental illness as an emergent concept and practice in Australia and the UK', *International Journal of Social Psychiatry*, Vol. 53, No. 2 (2007) 108.

Rehn, E. and Sirleaf, E.J., *Women, War, Peace: The Independent Experts' Assessment on the Impact of Armed Conflict on Women and Women's Role in Peace-Building* (New York: UNIFEM, 2002).

Reynolds, G., 'Embracing complexity: An adaptive effect approach to the conflict in Iraq', *Australian Army Journal*, Vol. 3, No. 3 (2006) 129.

Richmond, O.P., *Maintaining Order, Making Peace* (Basingstoke: Palgrave Macmillan, 2002)

———, 'Resistance and the post-liberal peace', *Millennium: Journal of International Studies*, Vol. 38, No. 3 (2010) 665.

Richter-Devroe, S., '"Here it's not about conflict resolution – We can only resist": Palestinian women's activism in conflict resolution and non-violent resistance', in N. Al-Ali and N. Pratt (eds), *Women and War in the Middle East* (London: Zed Books, 2009) 158.

Roberts, G. and Wolfson, P., 'The rediscovery of recovery: Open to all', *Advances in Psychiatric Treatment*, Vol. 10, No. 1 (2004) 37.

Robinson, F., 'Stop talking and listen: Discourse ethics and feminist care ethics in international political theory', *Millennium: Journal of International Studies*, Vol. 39, No. 3 (2011) 845.

Rombouts, H., 'Women and reparations in Rwanda: A long path to travel', in R. Rubio-Marin (ed.), *What Happened to the Women? Gender and Reparations for Human Rights Violations* (New York: Social Science Research Council, 2006) 194.

Rowe, P., *The Impact of Human Rights Law on Armed Forces* (Cambridge: Cambridge University Press, 2006).

Roxstrom, E., Gibney, M. and Einarsen, T., 'The NATO bombing case (*Banković et al. v. Belgium et al.*) and the limits of western human rights protection', *Boston University International Law Journal*, Vol. 23, No. 1 (2003) 55.

Rubin, G.S., 'Thinking sex: Notes for a radical theory of the politics of sexuality', in C.S. Vance (ed.), *Pleasure and Danger: Exploring Female Sexuality* (Boston: Routledge & Kegan Paul, 1984) 267.

Rubio-Marin, R., 'The gender of reparations: Setting the agenda', in R. Rubio-Marin (ed.), *What Happened to the Women? Gender and Reparations for Human Rights Violations* (New York: Social Science Research Council, 2006) 20.

——— (ed.), *What Happened to the Women? Gender and Reparations for Human Rights Violations* (New York: Social Science Research Council, 2006).

Ruddick, S., 'Maternal thinking', *Feminist Studies*, Vol. 6, No. 2 (1980) 342.

Rupp, L., *Worlds of Women: The Making of an International Women's Movement* (Princeton: Princeton University Press, 1997).

Said, E.W., *Orientalism* (London: Penguin Books, first published on 1978, 2003 ed.).

Santhebennur, M., 'UN to assist in Bougainville mine remediation', *Australian Mining* (5 September 2013), http://www.miningaustralia.com.au/news/ unitednationstoassistinbougainvillemineremediation (last accessed October 2013).

Scales, A., 'Militarism, male dominance and law: Feminist jurisprudence as oxymoron', *Harvard Women's Law Journal*, Vol. 12 (1989) 25.

Scheinin, M., 'Extraterritorial effect of the *International Covenant on Civil and Political Rights*', in F. Coomans and M. Kamminga (eds), *Extraterritorial Application of Human Rights Treaties* (Antwerp: Intersentia, 2004) 73.

Scott, J.W., 'Gender: A useful category of historical analysis', in *Gender and the Politics of History* (New York: Columbia University Press, revised ed., 1999) 28.

———, *The Fantasy of Feminist History* (Durham: Duke University Press, 2011).

Scully, P., 'Vulnerable women: A critical reflection on human rights discourse and sexual violence', *Emory International Law Review*, Vol. 23, No. 1 (2009) 113.

Sewall, S., 'Introduction to the University of Chicago print edition: A radical field manual', in United States Department of the Army, *The US Army/Marine Corps: Counterinsurgency Field Manual* (Chicago: University Chicago Press, 2007) xxi.

Shand, T, Herstad, M., Pawlak, P., Paine, T., Khanyile, J. and Tall, S., *Good Practice Brief on Male Involvement in GBV Prevention and Response in Conflict, Post-Conflict and Humanitarian Crisis Settings in Sub-Saharan Africa* (Cape Town: Sonke Gender Justice Network, 2013).

Shepherd, L.J., *Gender, Violence and Security: Discourse as Practice* (London: Zed Books, 2008).

———, 'Power and authority in the production of United Nations Security Council Resolution 1325', *International Studies Quarterly*, Vol. 52, No. 2 (2008) 383.

———, 'Sex, security and superhero(in)es: From 1325 to 1820 and beyond', *International Feminist Journal of Politics*, Vol. 13, No. 4 (2011) 504.

———, *Gender, Violence and Popular Culture: Telling Stories* (London: Routledge, 2013).

Silvestri, M., *Women in Charge: Policing, Gender and Leadership* (Cullompton: Willan, 2003).

Simić, O., 'Rethinking "sexual exploitation" in UN peacekeeping operations', *Women's Studies International Forum*, Vol. 32, No. 4 (2009) 288.

———, 'Does the presence of women really matter? Towards combating male sexual violence in peacekeeping operations', *International Peacekeeping*, Vol. 17, No. 2 (2012) 188.

———, *Regulation of Sexual Conduct in UN Peacekeeping Operations* (New York: Springer, 2012).

Sion, L., 'Peacekeeping and the gender regime: Dutch female peacekeepers in Bosnia and Kosovo', *Journal of Contemporary Ethnography*, Vol. 37, No. 5 (2008) 561.

Sirivi, J.T. and Havini, M.T., *As Mothers of the Land: The Birth of the Bougainville Women for Peace and Freedom* (Canberra: Pandanus Books, 2004).

Sivakumaran, S., 'Male/male rape and the "taint" of homosexuality', *Human Rights Quarterly*, Vol. 27, No. 4 (2005) 1274.

———, 'Sexual violence against men in armed conflict', *European Journal of International Law*, Vol. 18, No. 2 (2007) 253.

———, 'Lost in translation: UN responses to sexual violence against men and boys in situations of armed conflict', *International Review of the Red Cross*, Vol. 92, No. 877 (2010) 259.

Skogly, S.I., 'Extraterritoriality: Universal human rights without universal obligations?', in S. Joseph and A. McBeth (eds), *Research Handbook on International Human Rights Law* (Cheltenham: Edward Elgar, 2010) 71.

Solangon, S. and Patel, P., 'Sexual violence against men in countries affected by armed conflict', *Conflict, Security & Development*, Vol. 12, No. 4 (2012) 417.

Spivak, G.C., 'Translator's preface', in J. Derrida, *Of Grammatology* (G.C. Spivak trans., Baltimore: Johns Hopkins University Press, 1997) ix [trans. of *De la grammatologie* (first published on 1967)].

Stemple, L., 'Male rape and human rights', *Hastings Law Journal*, Vol. 60, No. 3 (2009) 605.

Stephens, D., 'Counterinsurgency and stability operations: A new approach to legal interpretation, in the war in Iraq: A legal analysis', *US Naval War College International Law Studies*, Vol. 86 (2010) 289.

Stiehm, J.H., 'United Nations peacekeeping: Men's and women's work', in M.K. Meyer and E. Prügl (eds), *Gender Politics in Global Governance* (Lanham: Rowman & Littlefield, 1999) 41.

———, 'Women, peacekeeping and peacemaking: Gender balance and mainstreaming', *International Peacekeeping*, Vol. 8, No. 2 (2001) 39.

Swaine, A. and Feeny, T., 'A neglected perspective: Adolescent girls' experiences of the Kosovo conflict of 1999', in J. Boyden and J. de Berry (eds), *Children and Youth on the Frontline: Ethnography, Armed Conflict and Displacement* (New York: Berghahn Books, 2004) 63.

Sylvester, C., *Feminist Theory and International Relations in a Postmodern Era* (Cambridge: Cambridge University Press, 1994).

Tickner, J.A., 'Hans Morgenthau's principles of political realism: A feminist reformulation', *Millennium: Journal of International Studies*, Vol. 17, No. 3 (1988) 429.

———, *Gender in International Relations: Feminist Perspectives on Achieving Global Security* (New York: Columbia University Press, 1992).

True, J., 'Mainstreaming gender in global public policy', *International Feminist Journal of Politics*, Vol. 5, No. 3 (2003) 368.

———, *The Political Economy of Violence against Women* (New York: Oxford University Press, 2012).

Turshen, M., 'The political economy of violence against women during armed conflict in Uganda', *Social Research*, Vol. 67, No. 3 (2000) 803.

United States Department of the Army, *The US Army/Marine Corps: Counterinsurgency Field Manual* (Chicago: University Chicago Press, 2007).

Valenius, J., 'A few kind women: Gender essentialism and Nordic peacekeeping operations', *International Peacekeeping*, Vol. 14, No. 4 (2007) 510.

Vance, C.S., 'Epilogue', in C.S. Vance (ed.), *Pleasure and Danger: Exploring Female Sexuality* (Boston: Routledge & Kegan Paul, 1984) 431.

von Clausewitz, C., *On War* (M. Howard and P. Perat trans., Oxford: Oxford University Press, 2008) [trans. of *Vom kriege* (first published on 1832)].

Wallace, H., 'Paddling the canoe on one side: Women in decision-making in Vanuatu and the Solomon Islands', *Development*, Vol. 54, No. 4 (2011) 505.

Wandita, G., Campbell-Nelson, K. and Pereira, M.L., 'Learning to engender reparations in Timor-Leste: Reaching out to female victims', in R. Rubio-Marin (ed.), *What Happened to the Women? Gender and Reparations for Human Rights Violations* (New York: Social Science Research Council, 2006) 284.

Whitworth, S., *Men, Militarism and UN Peacekeeping: A Gendered Analysis* (Boulder: Lynne Rienner, 2004).

Willett, S., 'Introduction: Security Council Resolution 1325: Assessing the impact on women, peace and security', *International Peacekeeping*, Vol. 17, No. 2 (2010) 142.

Wills, S., *Protecting Civilians: The Obligations of Peacekeepers* (Oxford: Oxford University Press, 2009).

Wiltsher, A., *Most Dangerous Women: Feminist Peace Campaigners of the Great War* (London: Pandora Press, 1985).

Wing, A.K. (ed.), *Global Critical Race Feminism: An International Reader* (New York: New York University Press, 2000).

Wolfers, E.P., '"Joint creation": The *Bougainville Peace Agreement* – And beyond', in A. Carl and L. Garasu (eds), *Weaving Consensus: The Papua New Guinea – Bougainville Peace Process* (London: Conciliation Resources in collaboration with BICWF, 2002) 44.

Woolf, V., *Three Guineas* (New York: Harcourt, Brace and Company, first published on 1938, 1966 ed.).

Zalewski, M., 'Well, what is the feminist perspective on Bosnia?', *International Affairs*, Vol. 71, No. 2 (1995) 399.

——, '"All these theories yet the bodies keep piling up": Theories, theorists, theorising', in S. Smith, K. Booth and M. Zalewski (eds), *International Theory: Positivism and Beyond* (Cambridge: Cambridge University Press, 1996) 340.

Zembylas, M., 'The politics of trauma: Empathy, reconciliation and peace education', *Journal of Peace Education*, Vol. 4, No. 2 (2007) 207.

——, 'The politics of shame in intercultural education', *Education, Citizenship and Social Justice*, Vol. 3, No. 3 (2008) 263.

Report

Amnesty International, 'Bougainville: The forgotten human rights tragedy' (AI Doc. ASA/34/01/97, 26 February 1997).

——, '"Where is the dignity in that?" Women in Solomon Islands slums denied sanitation and safety' (AI Doc. ASA 43/001/2011, September 2011).

——, 'Afghanistan: Don't trade away women's human rights' (AI Doc. ASA 11/007/2011, August 2011).

Anderlini, S.N., 'WDR gender background paper' (World Bank, February 2010).

——, 'What the women say: Participation and UNSCR 1325 – A case study assessment' (International Civil Society Action Network and Center for International Legal Studies, Massachusetts Institute of Technology , October 2010).

ANU Enterprise, 'People's survey pilot 2006: Solomon Islands' (RAMSI, 2006).

——, 'People's survey 2007' (RAMSI, 2007).

——, 'People's survey 2008' (RAMSI, 2008).

——, 'People's survey 2009' (RAMSI, February 2009).

——, 'People's survey 2010' (RAMSI, April 2011).

——, 'People's survey 2011' (RAMSI, February 2012).

AusAID, 'Regional Assistance Mission Solomon Islands Annual Program Performance Report 2012–2013' (AusAID, July 2013).

Baaz, M.E. and Stern, M., 'The complexity of violence: A critical analysis of sexual violence in the Democratic Republic of Congo (DRC)' (Working Paper on Gender-Based Violence, Swedish International Development Cooperation Agency, May 2010).

Bastick, M. and Valasek, K. (eds), 'Gender and security sector reform toolkit' (DCAF, ODIHR and UN-INSTRAW, 2008).

Bertolazzi, F., 'Women with a blue helmet: The integration of women and gender issues in UN peacekeeping missions' (Working Paper Series, UN-INSTRAW, 2010).

Bundervoet, T., 'Estimating poverty in Burundi' (HiCN Working Paper No. 20, University of Sussex, October 2006).

Buscher, D., 'Masculinities: Male roles and male involvement in the promotion of gender equality – A resource packet' (D. Quick ed., WCRW C, September 2005).

CARE, 'From resolution to reality: Lessons learned from Afghanistan, Nepal and Uganda on women's participation in peacebuilding and post-conflict governance' (CARE International, 2011).

Clark, C., 'Gender-based violence research initiatives in refugee, internally displaced, and post-conflict settings: Lessons learned' (Rosemarie Rogers Working Paper No. 17, Massachusetts Institute of Technology, April 2003).

Cockayne, J., 'Operation Helpem Fren: Solomon Islands, transitional justice and the silence of contemporary legal pathologies on questions of distributive justice' (Working Paper No. 3, Center for Human Rights and Global Justice, New York University School of Law, 2004).

Comissão de Acolhimento, Verdade e Reconciliação (Commission for Truth, Reception and Reconciliation), 'Chega! The report of the Commission for Reception, Truth and Reconciliation in Timor-Leste' (CAVR, 2005).

Csáky, C., 'No one to turn to: The under-reporting of child sexual exploitation and abuse by aid workers and peacekeepers' (Save the Children UK, 2008).

Denham, T., 'Police reform and gender' (DCAF, OSCE/ODIHR and UN-INSTRAW, 2008).

Economist Intelligence Unit, 'Women's economic opportunity 2012: A global index and ranking from the Economist Intelligence Unit' (*The Economist*, 2012).

Emmott, S., Barcham, M. and Kabutaulaka, T., 'Annual performance report 2010: A report on the performance of the Regional Assistance Mission to the Solomon Islands' (RAMSI Independent Experts Team, 21 March 2011).

Greig, A. and Edström, J., 'Mobilising men in practice: Challenging sexual and gender-based violence in institutional settings – Tools, stories, lessons' (Institute of Development Studies, January 2012).

Hajdinjak, M., 'Smuggling in Southeast Europe: The Yugoslav Wars and the development of regional criminal networks in the Balkans' (CSD Report No. 10, Center for the Study of Democracy, 2002).

Ibáñez, A.M. and Moya, A., 'The impact of intra-state conflict on economic welfare and consumption smoothing: Empirical evidence for the displaced population in Colombia' (HiCN Working Paper No. 23, Institute of Development Studies, University of Sussex, 2006).

Japan International Cooperation Agency, 'Country gender profile: Solomon Islands' (Japan International Cooperation Agency, February 2010).

Jennings, K.M., 'Women's participation in UN peacekeeping operations: Agents of change or stranded symbols?' (Norwegian Peacebuilding Resource Centre, September 2011).

Jennings, K.M. and Nikolić-Ristanović, V., 'UN peacekeeping economies and local sex industries: Connections and implications' (MICROCON Research

Working Paper No. 176, Institute of Development Studies, University of Sussex, September 2009).

Korneeva, A., 'Police reform and gender: Practice note 2' (Geneva Centre for the Democratic Control of Armed Forces, Office for Democratic Institutions and Human Rights and UN International Research and Training Institute for the Advancement of Women, 2008).

Maclellan, N., 'Bridging the gap between state and society: New directions for Solomon Islands' (Oxfam Australia and Oxfam New Zealand, July 2006).

Marenin, O., 'Restoring policing systems in conflict torn nations: Process, problems, prospects' (Occasional Paper No. 7, Geneva Centre for the Democratic Control of Armed Forces, June 2005).

Marshall, M.G. and Marshall, D.M., 'Gender empowerment and the willingness of states to use force' (Occasional Paper Series No. 2, Centre for Systematic Peace, February 1999).

McEvoy-Levy, S., 'Youth as social and political agents: Issues in post-settlement peace building' (Occasional Paper No. 21, Kroc Institute for International Peace Studies, December 2001).

McKay, S. and Mazurana, D., 'Where are the girls? Girls fighting forces in Northern Uganda, Sierra Leone and Mozambique: Their lives during and after war' (International Centre for Human Rights and Democratic Development, 2004).

McLean Hilker, L. and McAslan Fraser, E., 'Youth exclusion' (Social Development Direct, April 2009).

Menon, N. and van der Meulen Rodgers, Y., 'War and women's work: Evidence from the conflicts in Nepal' (HiCN Working Paper No. 104, University of Sussex, October 2011).

Mladjenovic, L., 'Massive rape as part of war strategy' (Conference Report, Sarajevo, Bosnia and Herzegovina, 9–10 March 2012).

Multi-Country Demobilization and Reintegration Program and United Nations Development Fund for Women, 'Workshop report: Taking a gender perspective to strengthen the multi-country demobilization and reintegration program (MDRP) in the Great Lakes Region' (Kigali, Rwanda, 31 October – 2 November 2005).

Olsen, N.L., Downing, R., Heijkoop, P. and Posner, L., 'RAMSI 2005/2006 annual performance report' (RAMSI Performance Assessment Advisory Team and CAMRIS International, July 2006).

Organisation for Economic Co-Operation and Development, 'OECD DAC handbook on security sector reform – Section 9: Integrating gender awareness and equality' (OECD, 2009).

Oxfam Community Aid Abroad, 'Australian intervention in the Solomons: Beyond Operation Helpem Fren – An agenda for development in the Solomon Islands' (Oxfam, August 2003).

Pacific Cooperation Foundation, 'Stories from Bougainville Participants' (Bougainville – New Zealand Track II Dialogue: 'Women and Land', 28–29 June 2010), http://www.pcf.org.nz/documents/Stories%20from%20 Bougainville%20Participants.pdf (last accessed October 2013).

Papua New Guinea National Council of Women, 'The CEDAW shadow report on the status of women in Papua New Guinea and the autonomous region of Bougainville' (PNG National Council of Women, 2010) 1–46, http://www. iwraw-ap.org/resources/pdf/46_shadow_reports/G2L/Papua_New_Guinea/ CEDAW_SHADOW_REPORT.pdf (last accessed October 2013).

Roth, F., Guberek, T. and Green, A.H., 'Using quantitative data to assess conflict-related sexual violence in Colombia: Challenges and opportunities' (Corporación Punto de Vista and Benetech, 2011).

Rowley, E., Garcia-Moreno, C. and Dartnall, E., 'Executive summary: Research themes and questions to guide research on sexual violence in conflict and post-conflict settings' (Sexual Violence Research Initiative, 2012).

Scarpetta, S. and Swaim, P. (eds), 'OECD employment outlook' (OECD, 2008).

Schindler, K., 'Who does what in a household after genocide? Evidence from Rwanda' (HiCN Working Paper No. 90, University of Sussex, December 2010).

Search for Common Ground Democratic Republic of Congo, 'Final report: "Vrai djo" project' (Report submitted to the Foreign & Commonwealth Office of the British Government, May – June 2011).

Sommers, M., 'Youth and conflict: A brief review of available literature (US Agency for International Development, 2006).

Surtees, R., 'Trafficking of men – A trend less considered: The case of Belarus and Ukraine' (Migration Research Series No. 36, International Organization for Migration, 2008).

United States Government Accountability Office, 'The Democratic Republic of the Congo: Information on the rate of sexual violence in war-torn eastern DRC and adjoining countries' (Report to Congressional Committees No. GAO-11-702, July 2011).

Wainwright, E., 'Our failing neighbour: Australia and the future of Solomon Islands' (Australian Strategic Policy Institute, 2003).

——, 'How is RAMSI faring? Progress, challenges, and lessons learned' (Australian Strategic Policy Institute, April 2005).

Winter, J. and Schofield, K., 'Annual performance report 2006/2007: A report on the performance of the Regional Assistance Mission to the Solomon Islands' (RAMSI Performance Assessment Advisory Team, July 2007).

Women's Commission for Refugee Women and Children, 'Redefining manhood, rebuilding nations: How men can empower women to lift post-conflict communities' (WCRWC, August 2007).

Women's International League for Peace and Freedom, 'From impunity to accountability: Ending impunity for sexual and gender based violence in conflict and post-conflict settings' (WILPF, June 2011).

World Bank, 'World development report 2011: Conflict and development' (World Bank, 2011).

World Bank, African Development Bank and International Finance Corporation, 'Joint country assistance strategy for the Republic of Liberia for the period FY09–FY11' (Report No 47928-LR, World Bank, 2009).

Youth and Children Affairs Ministry for Women, 'Solomon Islands national policy on gender equality and women's development' (Solomon Islands Government, March 2010).

Cases

Aksoy v. Turkey [1996] VI Eur. Court HR 2260.

Al-Saadoon v. United Kingdom (Admissibility) (2009) 49 EHRR SE11.

Al-Skeini v. United Kingdom (European Court of Human Rights, Grand Chamber, Application No. 55721/07, 7 July 2011).

Andreou v. Turkey (Admissibility) (European Court of Human Rights, Chamber, Application No. 45653/99, 3 June 2008).

Armed Activities on the Territory of the Congo (Democratic Republic of the Congo v. Uganda) (Judgment) [2005] ICJ Rep. 168.

Banković v. Belgium (Admissibility) [2001] XII Eur. Court HR 333.

Coard v. United States (Inter-American Commission on Human Rights, Report No. 109/99, Case No. 10.951, 29 September 1999).

Cyprus v. Turkey (1982) 4 EHRR 482.

Cyprus v. Turkey (Admissibility) (1975) 2 Eur. Comm. HR 125.

Hess v. United Kingdom (1975) 2 Eur. Comm. HR 72.

Ilaşcu v. Moldova (2004) 40 EHRR 46.

Isaak v. Turkey (European Court of Human Rights, Chamber, Application No. 44587/98, 24 June 2008).

Issa v. Turkey (Merits) (2005) 41 EHRR 27.

Jiménez v. Ecuador (Inter-American Commission on Human Rights, Report No. 107/01, Case No. 11.542, 11 October 2001).

Legal Consequences for States of the Continued Presence of South Africa in Namibia (South West Africa) notwithstanding Security Council Resolution 276 (1970) (Advisory Opinion) [1971] ICJ Rep. 16.

Legal Consequences of the Construction of a Wall in the Occupied Palestinian Territory (Advisory Opinion) [2004] ICJ Rep. 136.

Loizidou v. Turkey (Merits) (1997) 23 EHRR 513.

Loizidou v. Turkey (Preliminary Objections) (1995) 310 Eur. Court HR (ser. A).

Lordos v. Turkey (Just Satisfaction) (European Court of Human Rights, Chamber, Application No. 15973/90, 10 January 2012).

Prosecutor v. Akayesu (Judgement) (International Criminal Tribunal for Rwanda, Trial Chamber I, Case No. ICTR-96-4-T, 2 September 1998).

Rodríguez v. Honduras (Inter-American Court of Human Rights (ser. C) No. 4, 29 July 1988).

Solomou v. Turkey (European Court of Human Rights, Chamber, Application No. 36832/97, 24 June 2008).

W.M. v. Denmark (1992) 73 Eur. Comm. HR 193.

X and Y v. The Netherlands (1985) 91 Eur. Court HR (ser. A).

Treaties

African Charter on Human and Peoples' Rights, opened for signature on 27 June 1981, 1520 UNTS 217 (entered into force on 21 November 1986).

Agreement between Solomon Islands, Australia, New Zealand, Fiji, Papua New Guinea, Samoa and Tonga concerning the Operations and Status of the Police and Armed Forces and Other Personnel Deployed to Solomon Islands to Assist in the Restoration of Law and Order and Security, [2003] ATS 17 (signed and entered into force on 24 July 2003).

Charter of the United Nations, opened for signature on 26 June 1945, 1 UNTS XVI (entered into force on 24 October 1945).

Convention against Torture and Other Cruel, Inhuman or Degrading Treatment or Punishment, opened for signature on 10 December 1984, 1465 UNTS 85 (entered into force on 26 June 1987).

Convention for the Protection of Human Rights and Fundamental Freedoms, opened for signature on 4 November 1950, 213 UNTS 221 (entered into force on 3 September 1953).

Convention on Cluster Munitions, opened for signature on 3 December 2008, 48 ILM 354 (entered into force on 1 August 2010).

Convention on the Elimination of All Forms of Discrimination against Women, opened for signature on 1 March 1980, 1249 UNTS 13 (entered into force on 3 September 1981).

Convention on the Prevention and Punishment of the Crime of Genocide, opened for signature on 9 December 1948, 78 UNTS 277 (entered into force on 12 January 1951).

Convention on the Rights of the Child, opened for signature on 20 November 1989, 1577 UNTS 3 (entered into force on 2 September 1990).

Convention to Suppress the Slave Trade and Slavery, opened for signature on 25 September 1926, 60 LNTS 253 (entered into force on 9 March 1923), as amended by *Protocol amending the Council of Europe Convention on Preventing and Combating Violence against women and Domestic Violence*, opened for signature on 11 May 2011, CETS No. 210 (not yet in force).

Geneva Convention relative to the Protection of Civilian Persons in Time of War, opened for signature on 12 August 1949, 75 UNTS 287 (entered into force on 21 October 1950).

Inter-American Convention on Human Rights, opened for signature on 22 November 1969, 1144 UNTS 123 (entered into force on 18 July 1978).

Inter-American Convention on the Prevention, Punishment and Eradication of Violence against Women, opened for signature on 9 June 1994, 33 ILM 1534 (entered into force on 5 March 1995).

International Covenant on Civil and Political Rights, opened for signature on 16 December 1966, 999 UNTS 171 (entered into force on 23 March 1976).

International Covenant on Economic, Social and Cultural Rights, opened for signature on 16 December 1966, 993 UNTS 3 (entered into force on 3 January 1976).

Optional Protocol to the Convention on the Rights of the Child on the Sale of Children, Child Prostitution and Child Pornography, opened for signature on 25 May 2000, 2171 UNTS 227 (entered into force on 18 January 2002).

Protocol to the African Charter on Human and Peoples' Rights on the Rights of Women in Africa, opened for signature on 13 September 2000, OAU Doc CAB/LEG/66.6 (entered into force on 25 November 2005).

Slavery Convention, opened for signature on 23 October 1953, 182 UNTS 51 (entered into force on 7 December 1953).

United Nations Convention against Transnational Organized Crime, opened for signature on 12 December 2000, 2225 UNTS 209 (entered into force on 29 September 2003).

United Nations materials

A Comprehensive Strategy to Eliminate Future Sexual Exploitation and Abuse in United Nations Peacekeeping Operations, UN Doc. A/59/710 (24 March 2005).

Committee on the Elimination of Discrimination against Women, *General Recommendation No. 19: Violence against Women*, UN Doc A/47/38 (29 January 1992).

Committee on the Rights of the Child, *Concluding Observations: Lebanon*, UN Doc. CRC/C/LBN/CO/3 (8 June 2006).

Comprehensive Review of the Whole Question of Peacekeeping Operations in all their Aspects: Letter Dated 12 July 2000 from the Permanent Representative of Namibia to the United Nations Addressed to the Secretary-General, UN Doc. A/55/138–S/2000/693 (14 July 2000).

Conflict-Related Sexual Violence: Report of the Secretary-General, UN Doc. A/66/657–S/2012/33 (13 January 2012).

Connell, R.W., *The Role of Men and Boys in Achieving Gender Equality*, UN Doc. EGM/Men-Boys-GE/2003/BP (17 October 2003).

Coomaraswamy, R., *Report of the Special Rapporteur on Violence against Women, Its Causes and Consequences*, UN Doc. E/CN.4/1997/47 (12 February 1997).

Cordell, K., 'Gender mainstreaming in peacekeeping operations – Liberia 2003–2009: Best practices report' (United Nations Mission in Liberia, September 2010).

Declaration on the Elimination of Violence against Women, UN Doc. A/RES/48/104 (20 February 1993).

Draft Model Status-of-Forces Agreement between the United Nations and Host Countries, UN Doc. A/45/594 (9 October 1990) annex.

Draft of the Arms Trade Treaty, UN Doc. A/CONF.217/CRP.1 (1 August 2012)

Ebata, M., Izzi, V., Lenton, A., Ngjela, E. and Sampson, P., 'Youth and violent conflict: Society and development in crisis?' (UNDP, 2006).

Ertürk, Y., *The Due Diligence Standard as a Tool for the Elimination of Violence against Women: Report of the Special Rapporteur on Violence against Women*, UN Doc. E/CN.4/2006/61 (20 January 2006).

General Assembly Resolution 1001 (ES-I), UN Doc. A/RES/1001 (ES-I) (7 November 1956).

General Assembly Resolution 3010 (XXVII), UN Doc. A/RES/3010(XXVII) (18 December 1972).

Human Rights Committee, *Views: Communication No. 56/1979*, UN Doc. CCPR/C/13/D/56/1979 (29 July 1981) (*Celiberti de Casariego v. Uruguay*).

———, *Views: Communication No. 52/1979*, UN Doc. CCPR/C/13/D/52/1979 (29 July 1981) (*Saldías de López v. Uruguay*).

———, *Views: Communication No. 196/1985*, UN Doc. CCPR/C/35/D/196/1985 (6 April 1989) (*Gueye v. France*).

———, *Concluding Observations: United States of America*, UN Doc. CCPR/C/79/Add.50 (3 October 1995).

———, *Concluding Observations: Israel*, UN Doc. CCPR/C/79/Add.93 (18 August 1998).

———, *Concluding Observations: Belgium*, UN Doc. CCPR/C/79/Add.99 (19 November 1998).

———, *Concluding Observations: Israel*, UN Doc. CCPR/CO/78/ISR (21 August 2003).

———, *General Comment No. 31: Nature of the General Legal Obligation Imposed on States Parties to the Covenant*, UN Doc. CCPR/C/21/Rev.1/Add.13 (26 May 2004).

———, *Concluding Observations: Belgium*, UN Doc. CCPR/CO/81/BEL (12 August 2004).

Implementation of the Recommendations of the Special Committee on Peacekeeping Operations: Report of the Secretary-General, UN Doc. A/64/573 (22 December 2009).

Implementation of the World Programme of Action for Youth to the Year 2000 and Beyond: Report of the Secretary-General, UN Doc. A/56/180 (12 July 2001).

In Larger Freedom: Towards Development, Security and Human Rights for All, UN Doc. A/59/2005/Add.2 (23 May 2005).

International Law Commission, *Draft Articles on the Responsibility of International Organizations*, UN Doc. A/CN.4/L.778 (30 May 2011).

Mainstreaming the Gender Perspective into All Policies and Programmes in the United Nations System: Report of the Secretary-General, UN Doc. E/1997/66 (12 June 1997).

Manjoo, R., *Report of the Special Rapporteur on Violence against Women, Its Causes and Consequences*, UN Doc. A/HRC/14/22 (19 April 2010).

Manual on Policies and Procedures concerning the Reimbursement and Control of Contingent-Owned Equipment of Troop/Police Contributors Participating in Peacekeeping Missions, UN Doc. A/C.5/63/18 (29 January 2009).

Popovic, N.,'Women, peace and security in Liberia: Supporting the implementation of Resolution 1325 in Liberia' (Background Paper, UN-INSTRAW, March 2009).

Recommended Principles and Guidelines on Human Rights and Human Trafficking: Report of the United Nations High Commissioner for Human Rights, UN Doc. E/2002/68/Add.1 (20 May 2002).

Report of the Fourth World Conference on Women, UN Doc. A/Conf. 177/20 (17 October 1995).

Report of the Group of Legal Experts on Making the Standards Contained in the Secretary-General's Bulletin Binding on Contingent Members and Standardizing the Norms of Conduct So That They Are Applicable to All Categories of Peacekeeping Personnel, UN Doc. A/61/645 (18 December 2006).

Report of the Panel on United Nations Peace Operations, UN Doc. A/55/305–S/2000/809 (21 August 2000).

Report of the Secretary-General: Conflict-Related Sexual Violence, Women, Peace and Security, UN Doc. A/66/657*–S/2012/33* (13 January 2012).

Report of the Secretary-General: Conflict-Related Sexual Violence, Women, Peace and Security, UN Doc. S/PV.6722 (23 February 2012).

Report of the Secretary-General: Sexual Violence in Conflict, UN Doc. A/67/792–S/2013/149 (14 March 2013).

Report of the Secretary-General: Women's Participation in Peacebuilding, UN Doc. A/65/354–S/2010/446 (7 September 2010).

Report of the Secretary-General on Women and Peace and Security, UN Doc. S/2011/598* (29 September 2011).

Report of the Secretary-General on Women and Peace and Security, UN Doc. S/2012/732 (2 October 2012).

Report of the Secretary-General on Women, Peace and Security, UN Doc. S/2010/498 (28 September 2010).

Report of the Special Committee on Peacekeeping Operations, UN Doc. A/64/19 (22 February–19 March 2010).

Report of the Special Rapporteur on the Promotion and Protection of Human Rights and Fundamental Freedoms while Countering Terrorism, UN Doc. A/64/211 (3 August 2009).

Rothkegel, S., Engelhardt-Wendt, E., Hennig, R., Papy, J., Poluda, J., Weyermann, B. and Wonani, C., 'Evaluation of UNHCR's efforts to prevent and respond to sexual and gender-based violence in situations of forced displacement' (UNHCR, 2008).

Secretary-General's Bulletin: Special Measures for the Protection from Sexual Exploitation and Sexual Abuse, UN Doc. ST/SGB/2003/13 (9 October 2003).

Security Council Resolution 50, UN Doc. S/RES/50–S/801 (29 May 1948).

Security Council Resolution 798, UN Doc. S/RES/798 (18 December 1992).
Security Council Resolution 1261, UN Doc. S/RES/1261 (25 August 1999).
Security Council Resolution 1265, UN Doc. S/RES/1265 (17 September 1999).
Security Council Resolution 1296, UN Doc. S/RES/1296 (19 April 2000).
Security Council Resolution 1314, UN Doc. S/RES/1314 (11 August 2000).
Security Council Resolution 1325, UN Doc. S/RES/1325 (31 October 2000).
Security Council Resolution 1379, UN Doc. S/RES/1379 (20 November 2001).
Security Council Resolution 1460, UN Doc. S/RES/1460 (30 January 2003).
Security Council Resolution 1539, UN Doc. S/RES1539 (22 April 2004).
Security Council Resolution 1612, UN Doc. S/RES/1612 (26 July 2005).
Security Council Resolution 1645, UN Doc. S/RES/1645 (20 December 2005).
Security Council Resolution 1674, UN Doc. S/RES/1674 (28 April 2006).
Security Council Resolution 1738, UN Doc S/RES/1738 (23 December 2006).
Security Council Resolution 1820, UN Doc. S/RES/1820 (19 June 2008).
Security Council Resolution 1882, UN Doc. S/RES/1882 (4 August 2009).
Security Council Resolution 1888, UN Doc. S/RES/1888 (30 September 2009).
Security Council Resolution 1889, UN Doc. S/RES/1889 (5 October 2009).
Security Council Resolution 1894, UN Doc. S/RES/1894 (11 November 2009).
Security Council Resolution 1960, UN Doc. S/RES/1960 (16 December 2010).
Security Council Resolution 1998, UN Doc. S/RES/1998 (12 July 2011).
Security Council Resolution 2068, UN Doc. S/RES/2068 (19 September 2012).
Security Council Resolution 2106, UN Doc. S/RES/2106 (24 June 2013).
Security Council Resolution 2122, UN Doc. S/RES/2122 (18 October 2013).
Sørensen, B., 'Women and post-conflict reconstruction: Issues and sources' (WSP Occasional Paper No. 3, United Nations Research Institute for Social Development, 1998).
Spanish Resolution, adopted by the 12th Assembly of the League of Nations, 24 September 1931.
Statement by the President of the Security Council, UN Doc. S/PRST/2004/40 (28 October 2004).
———, UN Doc. S/PRST/2005/52 (27 October 2005).
———, UN Doc. S/PRST/2007/5 (7 March 2007).
———, UN Doc. S/PRST/2007/40 (24 October 2007).
———, UN Doc. UN Doc. S/PRST/2010/22 (26 October 2010).
System-Wide Action Plan for the Implementation of Security Council Resolution 1325 (2000), UN Doc. S/2005/636 (10 October 2005) annex.
United Nations Action against Sexual Violence in Conflict, 'Strategic framework 2011–2012' (UN Action, January 2011).
———, 'Second consolidated annual progress report on activities implemented through the UN Action against Sexual Violence in Conflict multi donor trust fund' (UNDP, 31 May 2011).
———, 'Analytical & conceptual framing of conflict-related sexual violence: Summary' (UN Action, June 2011).
United Nations Commission on Human Rights, *Contemporary Forms of Slavery: Systematic Rape, Sexual Slavery and Slave-Like Practices during Armed Conflict: Update on the Final Report Submitted by Ms Gay J. McDougall*, UN Doc. E/CN.4/Sub.2/2000/21 (6 June 2000).
United Nations Department of Peacekeeping Operations, 'Mainstreaming a gender perspective in multidimensional peace operations' (DPKO, July 2000).

———, 'Ten year impact study of implementation of UN Security Council Resolution 1325 (2000) on women, peace and security in peacekeeping' (DPKO, 2010).

United Nations Department of Peacekeeping Operations and United Nations Department of Field Support, 'DPKO/DFS guidelines: Integrating a gender perspective into the work of the United Nations military in peacekeeping operations' (DPKO and DFS, March 2010).

———, *A New Partnership Agenda: Charting a New Horizon for UN Peacekeeping* (DPKO and DFS, July 2009).

———, 'Ten-year impact study on implementation of UN Security Council Resolution 1325 (2000) on women, peace and security in peacekeeping' (DPKO and DFS, 2010).

United Nations Department of Peacekeeping Operations and United Nations Department of Public Information, *Background Note: UN Peacekeeping*, UN Doc. DPI/2429/Rev.15 (June 2012).

United Nations Department of Peacekeeping Operations and United Nations Office of Military Affairs, 'Statistical report on female military and police personnel in UN peace operations prepared for the 10th anniversary of the SCR1325' (DPKO and OMA, 2010).

United Nations Development Fund for Women, 'Getting it right, doing it right: Gender and disarmament, demobilization and reintegration' (UNIFEM, October 2004).

United Nations Development Programme, 'Eight point agenda for women's empowerment and gender equality in crisis prevention and recovery' (UNDP, 2010).

———, 'The price of peace: Financing for gender equality in post-conflict reconstruction' (Synthesis Report, UNDP, October 2010).

United Nations Development Programme and United Nations Development Fund for Women, 'Policy briefing paper: Gender sensitive police reform in post conflict societies' (UNDP and UNIFEM, October 2007).

United Nations General Assembly, *Improvement of the Status of Women in the United Nations System*, UN Doc. A/Res/59/164 (10 February 2005).

United Nations High Commissioner for Refugees, 'Sexual violence against refugees: Guidelines on prevention and response' (UNHCR, March 1995).

———, 'Prevention and response to sexual and gender-based violence in refugee situations' (Inter-Agency Lessons Learned Conference Proceedings, Geneva, 27–29 March 2001).

———, 'Sexual and gender-based violence against refugees, returnees and internally displaced persons: Guidelines for prevention and response' (UNHCR, May 2003).

———, 'UNHCR handbook for the protection of women and girls' (UNHCR, January 2008).

———, 'Working with men and boy survivors of sexual and gender-based violence in forced displacement' (Need to Know Guidance No. 4, UNHCR, 2012).

United Nations High Commissioner for Refugees and Save the Children UK, 'Sexual violence and exploitation: The experience of refugee children in Guinea, Liberia and Sierra Leone' (UNHCR and Save the Children UK, February 2002).

United Nations High Commissioner for Refugees Executive Committee, *Note on Certain Aspects of Sexual Violence against Refugee Women*, UN Doc. A/AC.96/822/Corr.1 (19 October 1993).

United Nations Peacebuilding Commission, 'Declaration of the High-level Ministerial Event on Women's economic empowerment for peacebuilding', UN Doc. PBC/7/OC/3 (26 September 2013).

United Nations Population Fund, 'Nigeria Adolescents population: Selected socio-demographic variables' (UNFPA Nigeria, 2006).

United Nations Security Council, *Women, Disarmament, Non-Proliferation and Arms Control*, UN Doc. A/RES/65/69 (13 January 2011).

———, *Agenda: Women, Peace and Security – Sexual Violence in Conflict*, UN Doc. S/PV.6984 (24 June 2013).

Others

'2008–2009 UN System-wide action plan for the implementation of Resolution 1325 (2000) on women, peace and security: DPKO', *Inter-Agency Network on Women and Gender Equality*, http://www.un.org/womenwatch/ianwge/taskforces/wps/implementation_review_20082009.html (last accessed October 2013).

'About UN Action', *Stop Rape Now: UN Action against Sexual Violence in Conflict*, http://www.stoprapenow.org/about (last accessed October 2013).

'About', *Virtual Knowledge Centre to End Violence against Women and Girls*, http://www.endvawnow.org/en/about (last accessed October 2013).

'Actor and advocate Charlize Theron named UN messenger of peace', *UN News Centre* (14 November 2008), http://www.un.org/apps/news/story.asp?NewsID=28951 (last accessed October 2013).

'Commitment to gender equality', *United Nations Department of Field Support, Logistics Support Division* (2008), https://www.lsd.unlb.org/Shared%20Documents/womenatlsd.aspx (last accessed October 2013).

'Convention on the Rights of the Child', *United Nations Treaty Collection*, http://treaties.un.org/pages/viewdetails.aspx?src=treaty&mtdsg_no=iv-11&chapter=4&lang=en (last accessed October 2013).

'Country-specific configurations', *United Nations Peacebuilding Commission*, http://www.un.org/en/peacebuilding/countryconfig.shtml (last accessed October 2013).

'CROP', *Pacific Islands Forum Secretariat*, http://www.forumsec.org/pages.cfm/about-us/crop/ (last accessed October 2013).

'DRC: Sexual violence prevention and re-integration funding "falls through cracks"', *IRIN Humanitarian News and Analysis* (4 November 2009), http://www.irinnews.org/Report/86865/DRC-Sexual-violence-prevention-and-re-integration-funding-falls-through-cracks (last accessed October 2013).

'Fiji Women's Forum: Amplifying the voices of 49% of the population', *International Women's Development Agency* (31 May 2012), http://www.iwda.org.au/2012/05/31/fiji-womens-forum-amplifying-the-voices-of-49-percent (last accessed October 2013).

'Gender', *United Nations Office for Disarmament Affairs*, http://www.un.org/disarmament/HomePage/gender/gender.shtml (last accessed October 2013).

'Gender: Women UN peacekeepers – More needed', *IRIN Humanitarian News and Analysis* (20 May 2010), http://www.irinnews.org/Report/89194/GENDER-Women-UN-peacekeepers-more-needed (last accessed October 2013).

'How peacekeeping works', *BBC News* (17 April 2007), http://news.bbc.co.uk/2/hi/6524867.stm (last accessed October 2013).

'Human trafficking FAQs: Who are the victims and culprits of human trafficking?', *United Nations Office on Drugs and Crime* (2013), http://www.unodc.org/unodc/en/human-trafficking/faqs.html (last accessed October 2013).

'India to send all-women peacekeeper force to Liberia', *DNA* (15 September 2006), http://www.dnaindia.com/india/report_india-to-send-all-women-peacekeeper-force-to-liberia_1053109 (last accessed October 2013).

'National Action Plans', *PeaceWomen*, http://www.peacewomen.org/pages/about-1325/national-action-plans-naps (last accessed October 2013).

'National implementation', *PeaceWomen*, http://www.peacewomen.org/naps (last accessed February 2013).

'Overview of statistics', *United Nations Conduct and Discipline Unit* (2010), http://cdu.unlb.org/Statistics/OverviewofStatistics.aspx (last accessed October 2013).

'Post-conflict and post-disaster responses: Mission – About us', *United Nations Educational, Scientific and Cultural Organization*, http://www.unesco.org/new/en/unesco/themes/pcpd/mission (last accessed October 2013).

'Post-conflict development', *International Rescue Committee*, http://www.rescue.org/our-work/post-conflict-development (last accessed October 2013).

'Post-conflict recovery & fragile states', *Innovations for Poverty Action*, http://poverty-action.org/postconflict (last accessed October 2013).

'Promoting women's roles in peace and security', *North Atlantic Treaty Organization*, http://www.nato.int/cps/en/natolive/91057.htm (last accessed October 2013).

'Resolutions Adopted by the International Congress of Women at The Hague, 1 May, 1915', reproduced in J. Addams, E.G. Balch and A. Hamilton, *Women at the Hague: The International Congress of Women and Its Results* (New York: Humanity Books, first published on 1916, 2003 ed.) appendix 3.

'Shocking facts: Scale and impact of the arms trade', *Amnesty International* (27 June 2012), http://www.amnesty.org.au/armstrade/comments/29065 (last accessed October 2013).

'Tonga: First women-led community radio consultation', *Pacific Media Centre: Te Amokura* (6 April 2011), http://www.pmc.aut.ac.nz/pacific-media-watch/2011-04-06/tonga-first-women-led-community-radio-consultation (last accessed October 2013).

'UN follow-up with member states (sexual exploitation and abuse)', *United Nations Conduct and Discipline Unit* (27 September 2013), http://cdu.unlb.org/Statistics/UNFollowupwithMemberStatesSexualExploitationandAbuse.aspx (last accessed October 2013).

'UNHCR age, gender and diversity policy', *UNHCR: The UN Refugee Agency* (1 June 2011), http://www.unhcr.org/4e7757449.html (last accessed October 2013).

'UNSCR 1960 and the need for focus on full implementation of UNSCR 1325: Open letter to member states of the Security Council re: Res 1960', *The Global Network of Women Peacebuilders* (7 January 2011), http://www.gnwp.org/unscr-1960-and-the-need-for-focus-on-full-implementation-of-unscr-1325 (last accessed October 2013).

'Women and peace and security: Side events and activities linked to the 2012 open debate of the Security Council', *PeaceWomen*, http://www.peacewomen.org/news_article.php?id=345&type=event (last accessed October 2013).

Aker, D. and Freeman, J., 'For real global security, put women in their place – At the negotiating table', *The Christian Science Monitor* (3 December 2010), http://www.csmonitor.com/Commentary/Opinion/2010/1203/For-real-global-security-put-women-in-their-place-at-the-negotiating-table (last accessed October 2013).

Al-Ali, N., 'Embedded feminism – Women's rights as justification for war', *Gunda Werner Institute*, http://www.gwi-boell.de/web/un-resolutions-embedded-feminism-nadje-al-ali-2811.html (last accessed October 2013).

AusAID, 'Solomon Islands transitional country strategy 2006 to mid-2007' (Australian Government, March 2006).

Basu, S., 'Permanent Security Council members and resolutions on women, peace and security', *e-International Relations* (31 October 2012), http://www.e-ir.info/2012/10/31/permanent-security-council-members-and-occasional-resolutions-on-women-and-peace-and-security (last accessed October 2013).

Baumgärtner, U., 'Learning to speak a "masculine" language: Rationalization of gender equality in the United Nations peacekeeping bureaucracy' (Paper presented at the International Studies Association Annual Conference, New Orleans, 2010).

Benard, C., 'Assessing the truths and myths of women in war and peace' (Paper presented at the United States Institute of Peace Conference on Perspectives on Grassroots Peacebuilding: The Roles of Women in War and Peace, Washington DC, 14 September 1999).

Bennett, N., '"Changing gender norms is essential for peacebuilding in Congo"', *The Guardian* (UK) (20 October 2010), http://www.guardian.co.uk/world/2010/oct/20/congo-gender (last accessed October 2013).

Biketawa Declaration (31st Summit of Pacific Islands Forum Leaders, Kiribati, October 2000).

Boseley, S., 'Rwanda: A revolution in rights for women', *The Guardian* (29 May 2010), http://www.theguardian.com/world/2010/may/28/womens-rights-rwanda (last accessed October 2013).

Bougainville – New Zealand Track II Dialogue: 'Women and Land' (28–29 June 2010) http://www.pcf.org.nz/documents/Stories%20from%20Bougainville%20Participants.pdf (last accessed February 2013).

Caprioli, M., Ballif-Spanvill, B., Emmett, C., Hudson, V.M., McDermott, R. and Stearmer, S.M., 'Walking a fine line: Addressing issues of gender with WomanStats' (Paper presented at the Annual International Studies Association Conference, Chicago, 27 January 2007).

Carter, R.B., '"Stop rape now": UN agencies against sexual violence as a tactic of war', *UNICEF* (5 March 2007), http://www.unicef.org/protection/57929_38552.html (accessed October 2013).

Carvajal, D., 'Women put own stamp on mission In Liberia', *The New York Times* (23 March 2010) 12.

Colapinto, J., 'Looking good: The new boom in celebrity philanthropy', *The New Yorker* (26 March 2012) 56.

Commonwealth Secretariat, 'Youth unemployment and social harmony concerns in Solomon Islands talks', *The Commonwealth* (28 October 2006), http://secretariat.thecommonwealth.org/news/152816/152865/155792/youth_unemployment_and_social_harmony.htm (last accessed October 2013).

del Zotto, A. and Jones, A., 'Male-on-male sexual violence in wartime: Human rights' last taboo?' (Paper presented at the Annual Convention of the International Studies Association, New Orleans, 23–27 March 2002).

Dobriansky, P.J., Alattar, M., Al-Suwaij, Z., Gilly, T. and Naama, E., 'Human rights and women in Iraq: Voices of Iraqi women', *US Department of State Archive* (6 March 2003), http://2001-2009.state.gov/g/rls/rm/2003/18477.htm (last accessed October 2013).

Elliott, F. and Elkins, R., 'UN shame over sex scandal', *The Independent* (UK) (7 January 2007), http://www.humanrightsvoices.org/site/articles/?a=4009&view=print (last accessed October 2013).

Ewins, R., 'The Bougainville conflict', *Rory Ewin's Pacific Island Politics* (12 May 2002), http://speedysnail.com/pacific/bougainville.html (last accessed February 2013).

FemLINKPACIFIC (2007), http://www.femlinkpacific.org.fj (last accessed October 2013).

Ford, L., 'UN passes new resolution on women's role in peace processes', *The Guardian* (21 October 2013), http://www.theguardian.com/global-development/2013/oct/21/un-resolution-2122-women-peace-processes (last accessed October 2013).

Ford, T. and Morris, S., 'India's female peacekeepers inspire Liberian girls', *Visionews.net* (October 2010), http://www.visionews.net/india´s-female-peacekeepers-inspire-liberian-girls (last accessed October 2013).

Gettleman, J., 'Symbol of unhealed Congo: Male rape victims', *The New York Times* (5 August 2009) 1.

Guedes, A., 'Men and Boys' (Knowledge Module, United Nations Development Fund for Women and MenEngage, January 2012).

Hakena, K., 'Peace in Bougainville and the work of the Leitana Nehan Women's Development Agency', *War Resisters' International* (1 January 2001), http://wri-irg.org/nonviolence/nvse08-en.htm (last accessed February 2013).

Hendrixson, A., 'Angry young men, veiled young women: Constructing a new population threat' (Briefing No. 34, The Corner House, December 2004).

Hill, F., 'How Resolution 1325 came about and what we hoped it would achieve: A retrospective view' (Paper presented at the International Symposium on Peacekeeping in the Asia-Pacific: Gender Equality, Law and Collective Security, Melbourne Law School, 19–20 April 2012).

Human Rights Watch, 'UN: Finally, a step toward confronting rape in war' (Press Release, 18 June 2008).

icasualties.org: Iraq Coalition Casualty Count – Operation Iraqi Freedom, http://icasualties.org/Iraq/index.aspx (last accessed October 2013).

Kaufman, M., 'Sexual violence in conflict and post-conflict: Engaging men and boys' (Advocacy Brief, MenEngage and UNFPA, July 2012).

Ki-moon, Ban, 'Statement to Security Council open debate on sexual violence in conflict', *UN News Centre* (16 December 2010), http://www.un.org/apps/news/infocus/sgspeeches/search_full.asp?statID=1038 (last accessed October 2013).

Lewis, D., 'New UN "listing" mechanism aimed at combating sexual violence in armed conflict', *Program on Humanitarian Policy and Conflict Research, Harvard University* (20 December 2010), http://www.hpcrresearch.org/blog/dustinlewis/2010-12-20/new-un-listing-mechanism-aimed-combating-sexual-violence-armed-conflict (last accessed October 2013).

Ley, J., 'Chelsea's Salomon Kalou denies "handcuff" goal celebrations gesture', *The Telegraph* (29 January 2009), http://www.telegraph.co.uk/sport/football/teams/chelsea/4383376/Chelseas-Salomon-Kalou-denies-handcuff-goal-celebrations-gesture.html (last accessed October 2013).

Lutfia, I., 'Indonesia wants more female UN peacekeepers', *JakartaGlobe* (23 March 2012), http://www.thejakartaglobe.com/archive/indonesia-wants-more-female-un-peacekeepers/506456/ (last accessed October 2013).

NGO Working Group on Women, Peace and Security (2013), http://www.women-peacesecurity.org (last accessed October 2013).

Nicholas, I., 'PNG: Momis warns of independence "clock ticking" for Bougainville', *Pacific Media Centre: Te Amokura* (11 February 2011), http://www.pmc.aut.ac.nz/pacific-media-watch/2011-02-10/png-momis-warns-independence-clock-ticking-bougainville (last accessed February 2013).

Otto, D., Javate De Dios, A., Nainar, V. and Vichuta, L., 'Panel statement for the Asia-Pacific women's regional hearing on gender-based violence in conflict' (Phnom Penh, Cambodia, 10–11 October 2012).

Partnership Framework between the Solomon Islands Government and Regional Assistance Mission to the Solomon Islands (endorsed by Pacific Islands Forum Ministerial Standing Committee, 15 May 2009).

'Peacebuilding – Emerging issues: Youth, gender and the changing nature of armed conflict', *Peacebuild* (February 2008), http://www.peacebuild.ca/en/peacebuilding-resources/publications-links/peacebuilding (last accessed October 2013).

PeaceWomen, 'Feature analysis: Security Council Resolution 1820: A move to end sexual violence in conflict', *1325 PeaceWomen E-Newsletter*, No. 102 (June 2008).

PeaceWomen, http://www.peacewomen.org (last accessed October 2013).

Pray the Devil Back to Hell, http://www.praythedevilbacktohell.com (last accessed October 2013).

President George W. Bush, 'President's address to the nation', *The White House: President George W. Bush* (Archive) (10 January 2007), http://georgewbush-whitehouse.archives.gov/news/releases/2007/01/20070110-7.html (last accessed October 2013).

Sciolino, E., 'Female POW is abused, kindling debate', *The New York Times* (29 June 1992) 1.

Simić, O., 'Accountability of UN civilian police involved in trafficking of women in Bosnia and Herzegovina', *Peace & Conflict Monitor* (November 2004), http://www.monitor.upeace.org/archive.cfm?id_article=219 (last accessed October 2013).

Soccernet Staff, 'Mourinho handed three-match ban for handcuffs gesture', *ESPN FC* (22 February 2010), http://soccernet.espn.go.com/news/story?id=745726&sec=europe&cc=5901 (last accessed October 2013).

Stop Rape Now: UN Action against Sexual Violence in Conflict, http://www.stoprape-now.org (last accessed October 2013).

Storr, W., 'The rape of men', *Observer Magazine* (17 July 2011) 36.

Stout, D., 'A nation challenged: The First Lady; Mrs Bush cites women's plight under the Taliban', *The New York Times* (18 November 2001) 4.

Sylvester, C. in interview with the University of Gothenburg, *University of Gothenburg: School of Global Studies* (2010), http://www.globalstudies.gu.se/english/research/guest-researcher-programme/christine-sylvester (last accessed October 2013).

United Kingdom Government, 'Preventing sexual violence initiative', *GOV. UK* (12 December 2012), https://www.gov.uk/government/policies/preventing-conflict-in-fragile-states--2/supporting-pages/preventing-sexual-violence-initiative (last accessed October 2013).

United Nations, 'Women in peacekeeping: The power to empower', *YouTube*, http://www.youtube.com/watch?v=vAuFQj9xBYc (last accessed October 2013).

United Nations Action against Sexual Violence in Conflict, 'Get cross! Join the Stop Rape Now Campaign', *Say No: Unite to End Violence against Women* (1 February 2010), http://saynotoviolence.org/join-say-no/get-cross-join-stop-rape-now-campaign (last accessed October 2013).

———, 'UN Action public service announcement – Stop rape now, *YouTube* (10 May 2010), http://www.youtube.com/watch?v=J9fg2oHHBaM (last accessed October 2013).

United Nations Department of Peacekeeping Operations, 'Principles of UN peacekeeping', *United Nations Peacekeeping*, http://www.un.org/en/peacekeeping/operations/principles.shtml (last accessed October 2013).

———, 'Gender statistics by mission: For the month of June 2012' (June 2012), http://www.un.org/en/peacekeeping/resources/statistics/gender.shtml (last accessed October 2013).

———, 'The "new horizon" process', *United Nations Peacekeeping*, http://www.un.org/en/peacekeeping/operations/newhorizon.shtml (last accessed October 2013).

———, 'Troop and police contributors', *United Nations Peacekeeping*, http://www.un.org/en/peacekeeping/resources/statistics/contributors.shtml (last accessed October 2013).

———, 'Peacekeeping factsheet', *United Nations Peacekeeping* (31 August 2013), http://www.un.org/en/peacekeeping/resources/statistics/factsheet.shtml (last accessed October 2013).

———, 'Women in peacekeeping', *United Nations Peacekeeping*, http://www.un.org/en/peacekeeping/issues/women/womeninpk.shtml (last accessed October 2013).

United Nations Peacekeeping, http://www.un.org/en/peacekeeping (last accessed October 2013).

United Nations Department of Public Information, 'Peace inextricably linked with equality between women and men says Security Council, in International Women's Day Statement' (Press Release No. SC/6816, United Nations, 8 March 2000).

———, 'Security Council adopts text requesting detailed information on suspected perpetrators of sexual violence during armed conflict' (Press Release No. SC/10122, United Nations, 16 December 2010).

———, 'Security Council reaffirms commitment to address widespread impact of armed conflict on children, after hearing over 60 speakers in day-long debate' (Press Release No. SC/9646, United Nations, 29 April 2009).

———, 'Understanding extent of sexual violence in conflict essential for effectively protecting women, girls, Secretary-General tells Security Council debate' (Press Release No. SC/11044, United Nations, 24 June 2013).

———, 'United Nations in global effort to increase number of female police in peacekeeping operations' (Press release No. PKO/218, WOM/1751, United Nations, 7 August 2009).

United Nations Office for the Coordination of Humanitarian Affairs, 'Discussion Paper 2: The nature, scope and motivation for sexual violence against men and boys in armed conflict' (Paper presented at the UN OCHA Research Meeting on the Use of Sexual Violence in Armed Conflict: Identifying Gaps in Research to Inform More Effective Interventions, 26 June 2008).

United States Institute for Peace, 'Post-conflict recovery', *Glossary of Terms for Conflict Management and Peacebuilding*, http://glossary.usip.org/resource/post-conflict-recovery (last accessed October 2013).

Vandenberg, M.E. and Peratis, K., 'Hopes betrayed: Trafficking of women and girls to post-conflict Bosnia and Herzegovina for forced prostitution', *Human Rights Watch* (November 2002), http://www.hrw.org/reports/2002/bosnia (last accessed October 2013).

Various Authors, *Proposed Framework for Phase 2: RAMSI Assistance Mission Agreement between Solomon Islands Government and RAMSI*, Draft Paper (March 2009), p. 95 (on file with author).

Vasek, L. and Nicholson, B., 'Judicial enquiry, apology for defence force sex abuse cases', *The Australian* (26 November 2012), http://www.theaustralian.com.au/national-affairs/defence/judicial-inquiry-apology-for-australian-defence-force-sex-abuse-cases/story-e6frg8yo-1226524035737 (last accessed October 2013).

'Vois Blong Mere', *Peace Portal* (2013), http://www.voisblongmere.org.sb (last accessed October 2013).

Wallström, M., 'A glimmer of hope for the women in Congo', *Huffington Post Blog* (30 May 2012), http://www.huffingtonpost.com/margot-wallstrom/a-glimmer-of-hope-for-the_b_1555962.html (last accessed October 2013).

Wheeler, J., 'Take it like a man', *Washington Times* (20 May 2004), http://www.washingtontimes.com/news/2004/may/20/20040520-083647-9853r/?page=all (last accessed October 2013).

Wilson, C., 'Women leaders key to post-conflict development on Bougainville', *London Progressive Journal* (12 November 2011), http://londonprogressivejournal.com/article/view/894 (last accessed February 2013).

Windhoek Declaration (Windhoek, Namibia, 31 May 2000), reproduced in 'Appendix 1', *International Peacekeeping*, Vol. 8, No. 2 (2001) 115.

Young Women's International League for Peace and Freedom Australia, 'YWILPF Australia submission – Australian Draft National Action Plan on: Women, Peace and Security' (YWILPF Australia, 2011).

Zakharova, N., 'Women and peace and security: Guidelines for national implementation' (UN Women, 2012).

Zwartz, B., 'Push to make church inquiry global', *The Age* (Australia) (18 December 2012) 2.

Index